# Rhetoric in the Middle Ages

## A History of Rhetorical Theory
## from Saint Augustine to the Renaissance

# Rhetoric
# in the
# Middle Ages

## A History of
## Rhetorical Theory
## from Saint Augustine
## to the Renaissance

## James J. Murphy

University of California Press
Berkeley · Los Angeles · London

University of California Press
Berkeley and Los Angeles, California
University of California Press, Ltd.
London, England

Copyright © 1974 by
The Regents of the University of California

First Paperback Printing 1981
ISBN: 0−520−04406−1

Library of Congress Catalog Number: 73−76102
Printed in the United States of America
Designed by Steve Reoutt

1   2   3   4   5   6   7   8   9

*For Kathleen*

*Una est enim . . . eloquentia, quascumque*
*in oras disputationis regionesue delata est.*

"Eloquence is one . . . , regardless of the
regions of discourse it is diverted into."

CICERO, *De oratore* III.V.23

# Contents

# Preface

THIS book deals with the medieval history—A.D. 426 to A.D. 1416—of the preceptive rhetorical tradition.

Ancient writers divided the teaching of discourse into three major areas: Theory, Imitation, and Practice. The *Rhetorica ad Herennium,* for instance, defined Theory as "a set of rules (*praeceptio*) that provide a definite method and system of speaking" (I.ii.3). Similar statements may be found in Isocrates and other Greek writers.

The preceptive tradition, then, involved a fundamental concept of Western civilization—that of order and plan in discourse. Both the Greek and Roman cultures produced educational programs based on the fundamental proposition that useful precepts could be adduced from observed experience and then transmitted to students. This approach reached a high level of sophistication in the Roman schools, as can be seen from the work of Quintilian, and it was transmitted by Roman education directly into the Latin culture of the medieval West.

This book, then, provides the first comparative study of the various forms in which medieval writers continued the preceptive tradition. Whether applied to preaching, verse-writing, letter-writing, or other fields, it is clear that the basic preceptive assumption continues through the period from Saint Augustine to the revival of classical learning in the Renaissance.

Yet, despite the apparently large number of authors and works treated in this book, this can be only a preliminary survey. Vast areas remain to be explored. A complete history of this subject must await further patient unraveling of manuscript relationships in scores of European libraries. Consequently this book is offered as an initial step toward our understanding of the complete context of medieval theories of communication.

# On Scholarly Debts

BERNARD of Chartres, a twelfth-century chancellor of that great cathedral, once remarked that "we are dwarfs mounted on the shoulders of giants." The modern historian of rhetoric can appreciate fully the wisdom of that remark. No beginning could even be attempted without the groundwork of nineteenth-century scholars like Charles Thurot, Ludwig Rockinger, Henry Keil, and Charles Halm, or more recent ones like Edmond Faral and Noel Denholm-Young.

Yet even more of this study is owed to the living interaction of people and institutions whose assistance over nearly two decades has helped to make this volume possible. I am grateful for research grants from the faculty research committees of Stanford University, Princeton University, and the University of California at Davis. Princeton University provided a Bicentennial Assistant Professorship for the year 1961–62 which enabled me to examine manuscripts in a number of European libraries. The American Council of Learned Societies awarded me a Fellowship for 1971–72 for further research in Europe which led to the completion of the book.

The need for this study was first suggested to me in 1954 by Robert W. Ackerman of the Department of English at Stanford University. His continuing advice led me into what was at first simply a prefatory history of medieval rhetoric so that Chaucer might be better understood, but over the intervening years it has become with his help an unfolding story of a major current in the history of human communication. There would be no book without him.

I owe a special debt of gratitude to Richard W. Hunt of the Bodleian Library in Oxford. He is the living repository of the history of medieval grammar. His unfailing encouragement and his own unerring mastery of manuscript materials gave invaluable assistance without which this study would still be years from completion.

There is no satisfactory way to acknowledge the scores of people who have over the years contributed bibliographic data or suggestions, or sent along their own (often unpublished) work as part of a common effort to put together a more complete understanding of medieval rhetoric. The generosity of the scholar was, and is, overwhelming. Some very busy scholars have read and commented on drafts of various chapters; the final judgments expressed are of course my own, but their comments and suggestions have been extremely helpful; thus I am especially grateful to Morton Bloomfield of Harvard University; Robert W. Ackerman of Stanford University; Malcolm Parkes of Keble College, Oxford; Michael Leff of Indiana University; and Harry Caplan of Cornell University.

At an early stage I was privileged to have the counsel of three major English medievalists, all now departed: Father Daniel Callus on the *disputatio,* Noel Denholm-Young on the *ars dictaminis,* and Gerald R. Owst on the *ars praedicandi.* Their straightforward explications of extremely complex matters made it easier to grasp the essentials in these fields.

Above all, we all owe the greatest debt to those scholars, usually unknown to us, who wrote down and then preserved for all those centuries the thoughts of what were for them the "modern times" of what we in our chauvinism call the "middle" ages—the makers and keepers of manuscripts, the creators of what we now fondly term "primary sources."

JAMES J. MURPHY

*Davis, California*
*July 30, 1973*

# Abbreviations

| | |
|---|---|
| *ALMA* | *Archivum Latinitatis Medii Aevi* (*Bulletin Du Cange*) |
| Baldwin, *MRP* | Charles S. Baldwin, *Medieval Rhetoric and Poetic* (New York, 1928). |
| Bolgar, *Heritage* | Robert R. Bolgar. *The Classical Heritage and Its Beneficiaries*. Cambridge, England, 1954. |
| Faral, *Les arts poétiques* | Edmond Faral, *Les arts poétiques du XIIᵉ et du XIIIᵉ siècles*. Paris, 1924. |
| Keil, *Grammatici latini* | Heinrich Keil (ed.), *Grammatici latini*. 4 vols. Leipzig, 1864. |
| Manitius, *Geschichte* | Max Manitius. *Geschichte der lateinischen Literatur des Mittelalters*. 3 vols. Munich, 1911–1931. |
| Manitius, *Bibliothekskatalogen* | Max Manitius. *Handschriften antiker Autoren in mittelalterlichen Bibliothekskatalogen*. Ed. Karl Manitius. *Zentralblatt für Bibliothekswesen*, 67 Beiheft. Leipzig, 1935. |
| Migne, *PL* | J. P. Migne (ed.). *Patrologia Latina*. |
| Murphy, *Bibliography* | James J. Murphy. *Medieval Rhetoric: A Select Bibliography*. Toronto, 1971. |
| *PBA* | *Proceedings of the British Academy* |
| *QJS* | *Quarterly Journal of Speech* |
| Rashdall, *Universities* | Hastings Rashdall. *The Universities of Europe in the Middle Ages*. Ed. F. M. Powicke and A. B. Emden. 3 vols. Oxford, 1936. |
| *SM* | *Speech Monographs* |

Thurot, "Notices et          M. Charles Thurot, "Notices et extraits de
    extraits"                    divers manuscrits latins pour servir à
                                 l'histoire des doctrines grammaticales au
                                 moyen âge," *Notices et extraits* 22 (1868),
                                 1–540; now reprinted.

# Part One

✤✤✤

# Ancient Rhetorical Theory and Its Continuations

# Chapter I

❖❖❖

# The Four Ancient Traditions

ANY study of the development of Western theories of communication must begin with the first impulses toward laying down precepts (*praecepta*) for future discourse. This preceptive movement began in ancient Greece, was transmitted to Rome and from thence to medieval Europe. No other ancient civilization but the Greek made such efforts to analyze human discourse, to distill the fruits of analysis into usable precepts, and to transmit those precepts to other men for their future use. Even though medieval European culture was pervasively a Latin culture, the enormous debt of Rome to Greece demands that our study begin in Greece with the earliest attempts to establish precepts for human discourse.[1]

The most prescriptive of these arts is that of rhetoric. By laying down specific directions, based on an analysis of current practice, rhetoric enabled the experience of skilled speakers to be transmitted to later generations in the form of direct suggestions for conduct. Although the primitive orations in Homer's *Iliad* indicate that some kind of planned oratory existed in early Greece, tradition names Corax of Syracuse (fl. 476 B.C.) as the "inventor" of the art of rhetoric. His pupil Tisias is credited with developing and spreading the art.[2] Tradition holds that the sophist Gor-

---

[1] For a concise outline of the ancient developments, see James J. Murphy (ed.), *A Synoptic History of Classical Rhetoric* (New York, 1971). For the Greek period, see George Kennedy, *The Art of Persuasion in Greece* (Princeton, 1963). For the Roman period, see George Kennedy, *The Art of Rhetoric in the Roman World* (Princeton, 1972).

[2] For brief discussions of this tradition, cf. D. A. G. Hinks, "Tisias and Corax and the Invention of Rhetoric," *Classical Quarterly* 34 (1940), 59–69; George

gias introduced it to Greece about 428 B.C. There, contributions to the new
discipline were rapidly made by Protagoras, Antiphon, Lysias, Isocrates,[3]
and by Plato, whose *Phaedrus* has been termed a virtual outline for the
*Rhetoric* of his pupil, Aristotle.[4]

Aristotle's *Rhetoric*,[5] the oldest extant textbook on the subject, is probably too well known to require more than brief summary here. Aristotle
defines rhetoric in Book One as the faculty of discovering all the available means of persuasion; he then divides means of persuasion or proof
into the artistic, or that furnished by the speaker, and the nonartistic, or
that furnished by external evidence. He names three kinds of persuasion:
*ethos,* arising from the speaker's personal qualities; *pathos,* arising from
the audience's emotions; and logical proof, depending upon argument.
The speeches themselves may be forensic (judicial), deliberative (political), or epideictic (occasional), depending upon their ends, times, and
subjects. Since rhetoric is a counterpart of dialectic, the speaker may use
*topoi* or "commonplaces," such as "pain or pleasure," to find arguments.
Book Two discusses the relation of the audience to the speaker, beginning
with the emotions that a speaker may exploit to achieve his purposes. The
enthymeme, the counterpart of the deductive dialectical syllogism, is also
discussed as an element common to all three types of speeches. According

---

A. Kennedy, "The Earliest Rhetorical Handbooks," *American Journal of Philology*
80 (1959), 169–78; and Stanley Wilcox, "The Scope of Early Rhetorical Instruction," *Harvard Studies in Classical Philology* 53 (1942), 121–55. The dura-
bility of the tradition is attested by a gloss on an eleventh-century manuscript of
Cicero's *De inventione* (Oxford Bodleian MS. Laud 49, fol. 146): Corax artem
invenit, Tisias promulgavit.

[3] Although the Isocratean tradition is in many ways distinct from that of
Aristotle, its most profound expression is found in Roman rhetoric. A convenient
summary may be found in Harry M. Hubbell, *The Influence of Isocrates on
Cicero, Dionysius, and Aristides* (New Haven, 1913).

[4] Everett Lee Hunt, "Plato and Aristotle on Rhetoric and the Rhetoricians," in
*Studies in Rhetoric and Public Speaking in Honor of James Albert Winans* (New
York, 1925). There is still no adequate single history of pre-Aristotelian rhetoric.
But cf. Kennedy, *Art of Persuasion in Greece*, and Wilhelm Kroll, "Rhetorik," in
*Paulys Real-Encyclopädie der classischen Altertumswissenschaft*, Suppl. Vol. VII
(Stuttgart, 1940), cols. 1039–58. Some suggestive remarks may be found in Richard
C. Jebb, *Attic Orators from Antiphon to Isaeus*, 2 vols. (London, 1876); J. W. H.
Atkins, *Literary Criticism in Antiquity*, 2 vols. (Oxford, 1947). For recent bibli-
ographies, cf. Maurice Platnauer (ed.), *Fifty Years of Classical Scholarship* (Ox-
ford, 1954), and Charles S. Rayment, "A Current Survey of Ancient Rhetoric,"
*Classical World* 52 (1958), 75–91.

[5] Aristotle, *Rhetoric*, trans. Lane Cooper (New York, 1932). To avoid confusion
in later chapters, Latin titles will be used throughout for works which were Latinized during the middle ages. For a discussion of Aristotle's rhetorical theory, see
the essay by Forbes I. Hill in Murphy, *Synoptic History of Classical Rhetoric*, pp.
19–76, and Kennedy, *Art of Persuasion in Greece*, pp. 82–114.

to Aristotle, all enthymemes belong to a class or *topos*, of which there are twenty-eight for true enthymemes and nine for sham enthymemes. The chief inductive form of argument is example, which may be either historical or invented. Diction and arrangement are discussed in Book Three, but delivery is virtually ignored. It is argued that good style, whose essential quality is clarity, must be appropriate to both the speaker and his cause, and that metaphor is useful because it makes comparisons quickly. The language of prose is said to be distinct from that of poetry, and each kind of rhetoric is assigned a separate style. For further treatment of diction, Aristotle refers the reader to his *Poetics*. Respecting arrangement, he states that a speech consists of only two essential parts—statement and proof.

The philosophical nature of the *Rhetoric* becomes even more evident when the reader examines Aristotle's *Topica* and *De sophisticis elenchis*, two closely related logical works.[6] Inasmuch as these works provide both a commentary on the *Rhetoric* and a key to understanding certain Roman doctrines, a close examination will be useful.[7]

The *Topica*[8] deals primarily with the dialectical syllogism, but its rhetorical application is found in its treatment of the *topoi* or commonplaces from which arguments may be derived.[9] Aristotle defines a syllogism as "a discourse in which certain things being laid down, something different from the *posita* happens from necessity through the things laid down." Although a demonstrative syllogism uses true things for its premises, a dialectical syllogism uses probabilities. For example, dialectic may use a widely accepted proverb for a premise. Moreover, dialectic shows the way to the principles of different sciences, by enabling one to discuss first principles through probabilities in the singular; conse-

---

[6] The *Rhetorica* alludes to the *Topica* no less than nine times, and the *De sophisticis elenchis* begins by noting the parallel purpose of rhetoric.

[7] The two works are important in the history of medieval intellectual life, since both were standard university texts for the study of *dialectica*. Indeed, university students beginning the study of logic were often referred to as *sophistres*. See Clara P. McMahon, *Education in Fifteenth-Century England*, Johns Hopkins University Studies in Education, No. 35 (Baltimore, 1947), pp. 60 ff.

[8] References are to *The Works of Aristotle Translated into English*, ed. W. D. Ross, Vol. I (Oxford, 1924).

[9] This doctrine of topics or *loci* became an integral part of Roman rhetoric after Cicero, the Pseudo-Cicero, and Quintilian adopted Hellenistic doctrines of invention based on the theories of Hermagoras of Temnos. Cicero's *Topica* claims to be an interpretation of Aristotle's book, but there are essential differences. See below, "The Ciceronian Tradition," pp. 8–26. Aristotle also discusses the topics in *Rhetorica* II.22–24.

quently the method of discovering these probabilities is doubly important. The *topos* (Latin *locus*) is the place from which one may draw propositions on a given subject and thus discover arguments. The predicables of these propositions are of four orders—definition, property, genus, and accident—all of which may be arranged in ten classes of categories as described by the science of logic. Each of the ten classes may supply scores of *topoi,* and thus furnish an almost limitless number of syllogisms. After a lengthy discussion of suggested *topoi,* Aristotle concludes the *Topica* with an elaborate set of instructions for conducting dialectical disputations.[10]

The following excerpts may serve to provide an idea of the general tone of the *Topica.*

"Our treatise proposes to find a line of inquiry whereby we shall be able to syllogize from probabilities that are generally accepted about every problem propounded to us, and also shall ourselves . . . avoid saying anything that shall obstruct us. . . ."

The subjects of arguments are of four orders:
1. Definition is a phrase signifying a thing's essence.
2. A property is a predicate which is proper to a thing (i.e., to it alone) and is predicated convertibly of it (e.g., it is proper of a man to learn grammar).
3. Genus is what is predicated in the category of essence of a number of things exhibiting differences in kind. ("Genus is a class of things which have specific differences.")
4. Accident is neither definition, genus, or property, and yet it either belongs to the thing or it may or may not belong to it (e.g., a man "sits"). Accident can become a temporary and relative property, but it can never be an absolute property. . . .

The classes of predicates in which these four orders are found are ten:
1. Essence (what a thing is) (e.g., "Paul is man.")
2. Quantity (predication as to quantity) ("Paul is 6 feet tall.")
3. Quality (predication as to form) ("Paul is studious.")
4. Relation (in reference to something else) ("Paul is superior.")
5. Place (place) ("Paul is in Europe.")
6. Time (on the part of time) ("Paul is here today.")
7. Position (order of parts within subject) ("Paul is kneeling.")
8. State (not a measure of subject) ("Paul is feverish.")
9. Activity (subject is principle of action) ("Paul is hitting.")
10. Passivity (subject is recipient of action) ("Paul is being hit.")

Means by which we can become supplied with arguments are four:
1. The securing of propositions.

---

[10] Historians of the medieval disputation have yet to explore fully the influence of this final section upon the methods of the disputation.

2. The power to distinguish in how many senses a particular expression is used.
3. The discovery of differences of things.
4. The investigation of likeness.

The *De sophisticis elenchis*[11] is even more technical, dealing as it does with the problem of detecting logical fallacies. Aristotle points out that, just as rhetoric allows one to detect false arguments of one kind, there must be some other kind of skill in detecting *elenchi*, or syllogisms whose conclusions do not follow necessarily from their premises. The use of these false syllogisms he terms "sophistry." An *elenchus* may be due to a fault in diction, such as an ambiguous term, a colloquialism rendered too literally, an equivocation, or an incorrect figure of speech. It may also result from a paralogism, or apparent syllogism, whenever the rules of logical thought are not followed. The detection of these sophistical arguments is useful for three reasons: first, since they arise chiefly from faults in diction, they acquaint us better with the various ways of predication; again, they contribute to inquiries by oneself, thus precluding self-deception; and finally, they enhance our fame by giving an appearance of general skill. This skill in detection is an art, and cannot be learned merely by studying examples or memorizing prepared discourses.

Aristotle's rhetorical and logical works thus display a consistently philosophical approach to the problems of communication.[12] Moreover, his logical works show an equal regard for the interconnection of rhetoric and logic, particularly in the area of *inventio*. At every point he is concerned with definition, with implication, and with the relation of one art to another. He is more concerned with the principles of art than with its technique, and to this end he keeps his discussions at a high level of abstraction. For Aristotle rhetoric is a counterpart of dialectic, operating, like dialectic in the realm of nondemonstrative or nonapodeictic proofs. It is not, as his contemporary Isocrates would have it, a branch of politics.[13]

---

[11] Ross, *Aristotle*, Vol. I.

[12] The same philosophical approach colors his analysis in the *Poetica*, especially in such matters as the relation between plot and character. Since this work of Aristotle's has little part in medieval cultural life, the parallel is cited here only as a further indication of the nature of the Aristotelian tradition. See Aristotle, *Poetics*, trans. Ingram Bywater, in Ross, *Aristotle*, Vol. XI (Oxford, 1924). Some aspects of this general tradition are considered by Friedrich Solmsen, "The Aristotelian Tradition in Ancient Rhetoric," *American Journal of Philology* 62 (1941), 35–50 and 169–90.

[13] The Pseudo-Aristotelian *Rhetorica ad Alexandrum*, produced during the Alexandrian period by an unknown author, bears further witness to the general nature of Aristotelian doctrine on the arts of discourse. It is a somewhat con-

Roman rhetoric has such a distinctively homogeneous flavor, and is so traditionally associated with the name of Cicero that it seems fair to describe the works of Cicero, Quintilian, and the author of *Rhetorica ad Herennium* as partaking of a common tradition which could properly be called "Ciceronian." With the exception of two of Cicero's later rhetorical works, the major rhetorical treatises written in Rome between approximately 100 B.C. and A.D. 95 share the inventional doctrine of *status* borrowed from Hermagoras of Temnos, and all follow the fundamental teaching of Isocrates to the effect that rhetoric is a part of political science.[14] All make efficiency—that is, the procuring of results—the main criterion of good speech. All seem to share the same highly developed, rather mechanistic theories of style (*elocutio*) based upon a Hellenistic

---

fused compendium in 38 sections of the material to be found in a rather different order in the *Rhetoric* of Aristotle. Purporting to be an explanation of rhetoric written by Aristotle for Alexander the Great, it treats three kinds of speeches, two kinds of proofs, the elements of good style, and so forth. The treatise assumes a knowledge of the *Rhetorica*, although there are such verbal similarities that medieval readers sometimes accepted the work as truly Aristotle's. Not only is the treatise less than half the length of the *Rhetoric*—74 pages in the Ross edition as compared to the 198 for the *Rhetoric*—but its organization is less clear, and its treatment of each subject is sketchy. One example (6 1434[b] 1-10) may illustrate the tenor of the work:

When you wish to lengthen your speech, you must divide up your subject and in each division explain the nature of its contents and their particular and general application and state the grounds of your pleas. If we wish to make our discourse still longer, we must employ a number of words in dealing with each topic. In each division of the speech you must iterate and make your iteration brief; while at the conclusion of your speech you ought to recapitulate as a whole all that you have dealt with in detail, and treat the subject generally. In this way your speech will be of sufficient length.

It is translated by E. S. Forster in *The Works of Aristotle,* ed. Ross, Vol. XI. Authorship has been variously attributed to "a Peripatetic writer contemporary with Theophrastus" (Forster) or to Anaxamines of Lampsacos. Cf. Paul Wendland, *Anaxamines von Lampsakos* (Berlin, 1905). It survives in two medieval Latin translations, one of which was published by Martin Grabmann in *Sitzungberichte der bayerischen Akademie der Wissenschaften* 4 (1932), 1-81.

[14] For example, *De oratore* and *Orator* both display personal innovations, as will be seen below. For the Isocratean background, see Hubbell, *Influence of Isocrates*. Roman rhetoric has been studied intensively in the twentieth century. See, for instance, Martin Lowther Clarke, *Rhetoric at Rome* (London, 1953); Donald Lemen Clark, *Rhetoric in Greco-Roman Education* (New York, 1957); Brother Edilbert Parks, F.S.C., *The Roman Rhetorical Schools as a Preparation for the Courts under the Early Empire,* Johns Hopkins University Studies in Historical and Political Science, Series LXIII, No. 2 (Baltimore, 1945); Aubrey O. Gwynn, *Roman Education from Cicero to Quintilian* (Oxford, 1926); Charles S. Baldwin, *Ancient Rhetoric and Poetic* (New York, 1924). For a discussion of Ciceronian rhetoric, see the essay by Donovan J. Ochs in Murphy, *Synoptic History of Classical Rhetoric,* pp. 90-150; and Kennedy, *Art of Rhetoric in the Roman World,* pp. 103-210.

proliferation of *figurae*.[15] All are practical rather than philosophical, and thus in both detail and concept they represent a departure from the Peripatetic tradition represented most fully by Aristotle.

Any consideration of the influence exerted by this tradition must therefore begin with some note of the treatises which transmitted its doctrines to later ages.

Cicero, first of all, composed seven rhetorical treatises over a period of fifty years, but two of them, *De inventione* and *Topica,* have special significance for the middle ages. A third, *De oratore,* was to gain importance only at the end of the middle ages.

*De inventione*[16] is intended as the first section of a five-part book covering the entire subject of rhetoric.[17] Since Cicero wrote it when he was but nineteen years of age, and since it is closely parallel to the inventional portion of the nearly contemporary *Rhetorica ad Herennium,* it is evident that the book reflects the teachings of a well-established school which had developed rhetoric to a high degree of complexity.

Cicero defines rhetoric in Book One as a department of political science dealing with eloquence based on rules of art. Since oratory is a branch of political science, then, the speaker must study philosophy and possess a wide general knowledge of human actions. Oratory itself, however, deals only with special questions (*causae*), or cases involving individuals, and not with general questions (*quaestiones*) which do not involve individuals. The three types of speaking on special questions are forensic or legal, deliberative or political, and epideictic or occasional. Rhetoric has five parts: Invention (*inventio*) discovers arguments by the analysis of three (and sometimes four) issues (*constitutiones*). An issue of fact is called *coniecturalis,* an issue of definition is called *definitiva,* and an issue of the nature of an act is called *generalis* or *qualitativa.* Sometimes a fourth issue, that of competence (*translativa*), is introduced when the others fail. Topics (*loci*) are also useful for invention. Disposition (*dispositio*), the second part of rhetoric, arranges a speech into parts, the usual parts being the exordium, narration, partition, confirmation, refu-

---

[15] If the young Cicero had completed the plan begun in *De inventione,* for instance, there is no reason to believe that it would have looked much different from the *Rhetorica ad Herennium.*

[16] Text and translation in Cicero, *De inventione. De optimo genere oratorum. Topica,* trans. H. M. Hubbell, Loeb Classical Library (Cambridge, Mass., and London, 1949).

[17] Partes autem eae quas plerique dixerunt inventio, dispositio, elocutio, memoria, pronuntiatio. *De inventione* I.vii.9.

tation, digression, and peroration. The other parts of rhetoric are style (*elocutio*), memory (*memoria*), and delivery (*pronuntiatio* or *actio*), all of which Cicero promises to discuss in a later work. Book Two takes up the arguments appropriate to each issue and to each kind of speech. The basic method is analysis of issues, or *constitutiones*,[18] following the doctrine laid down by the Hellenistic school of Hermagoras of Temnos. The extremely complex treatment of issues deals with Roman law as much as with rhetoric.[19]

This brief summary may serve as a guide to the following, fuller summary of this important work, so highly regarded in the middle ages that it is referred to as *rhetorica prima* or *rhetorica vetus*.

## THE *DE INVENTIONE* OF CICERO

### BOOK ONE

I. Wisdom without eloquence does little good for states, while eloquence without wisdom often does positive harm. Therefore, if anyone neglects the study of philosophy and moral conduct, which is the highest and most honorable of pursuits, and devotes his whole energy to the practice of oratory, his civil life is nurtured into something useless to himself and harmful to his country. II. Eloquence has civilized society. III–IV. It ought to be studied to enable good men to defend the state.

V. There is a scientific system of politics which includes many departments. One of these departments—a large and important one—is eloquence based on the rules of art, which they call rhetoric (*artificiosa eloquentia quam rhetoricam vocant*); therefore we will classify oratorical ability as a part of political science. The function of eloquence seems to be to speak in a manner suited to persuade an audience; the end is to persuade by speech. The orator deals with the three fields of forensic, epideictic, and deliberative speaking. VI. Hermagoras was wrong when he said that oratory concerns itself with both general questions (*quaestiones*) which involve controversies without the introduction of specific individuals, and with special cases (*causae*) which involve definite individuals. These *quaestiones* are subjects that philosophers have been unable to solve after long deliberation, and should not engage the orator's attention.

VII. Therefore the subject matter of rhetoric seems to be that which Aristotle approved [i.e., the three types of speaking]. The parts of rhetoric are:

---

[18] The term *status* is also used by Cicero and Quintilian. Cf. Cicero, *Topica* xxv.93–95, and Quintilian, *Institutio oratoria,* trans. H. E. Butler, 4 vols., Loeb Classical Library (London, 1953), esp. III.vi ff.

[19] The intimate relation between law and rhetoric is further demonstrated by a section discussing the interpretation of documents, *De inventione* II.xl–li.

1. Invention (*inventio*), or the discovery of valid or seemingly valid arguments that render one's thoughts plausible (*excogitatio rerum verarum aut veri similium quae causam probabilem reddant*).
2. Arrangement (*dispositio*), or the distribution of arguments thus discovered in the proper order (*rerum inventarum in ordinem distributio*).
3. Expression (*elocutio*), or the fitting of the proper language to the invented matter (*idoneorum verborum ad inventionem accommodatio*).
4. Memory (*memoria*), or the firm mental grasp of matter and words (*firma animi rerum ac verborum perceptio*).
5. Delivery (*pronuntiatio*), or the control of the voice and body in a manner suitable to the dignity of the subject matter and style (*et rerum et verborum dignitate vocis et corporis moderatio*).

Since the discussion of the nature, end, and function of this art is a long task, and since we aim to describe the art and transmit its rules, we shall put off the discussion to another time. Invention is the most important of all the divisions, and is used in every kind of cause.

VIII. Every subject which contains in itself a controversy to be resolved by speech and debate involves a question about a fact or about a definition or about the nature of the act or about legal processes. This question, then, from which the whole case arises, is called the *constitutio* or "issue." There are four types of issues:

1. When the dispute is about a fact, the issue is said to be *coniecturalis,* because the plea is supported by conjectures or inferences ("Was there an act?")
2. When the dispute is about a definition, it is said to be *definitiva,* because the force of the term must be defined in words ("Was the act murder?")
3. When the nature of the act is examined, however, the issue is said to be *generalis,* because the controversy concerns the value of the act and its class or quality ("Was the murder justified?")
4. When there is a question of competence of the tribunal, the proper framing of the charge, etc., the issue is called *translativa* ("Is this the proper court to hear this case?")

One of these issues will always be applicable to every kind of case, for where none applies, there can be no controversy. [IX–X. Detailed definitions, with examples of the four *constitutiones*.]

XI. The qualitative issue seems to have two subdivisions:

1. The legal is that in which we examine the law.
2. The equitable is that in which there is a question about the nature of justice and right, or the reasonableness of reward or punishment.
   a. The absolute equitable issue is one which contains in itself the question of right and wrong done.
   b. The assumptive is that which of itself provides no basis for a counter plea but seeks some defense from extraneous circumstances.

(ɪ) *concessio* (confession and avoidance)

(ɪɪ) *remotio criminis* (shifting the charge)

(ɪɪɪ) *relatio criminis* (retort of accusation)

(ɪᴠ) *comparatio* (comparison)

XII. When the issue is determined, it is well to consider whether the case is simple or complex, and, if complex, whether it involves several questions or a comparison. In the second place, one must consider whether the dispute turns on general reasoning or on written documents. XIII. And then you must see what the question in the case is (*quaestio*), the excuse or reason (*ratio*), the point for the judge's decision (*iudicatio*), and the foundation or supporting argument (*firmamentum*). XIV. Then after all these have been discovered, the separate divisions of the whole case must be discovered. The parts of an oration are six: (1) *exordium*, (2) *narratio*, (3) *partitio*, (4) *confirmatio*, (5) *reprehensio* or *refutatio*, and (6) *conclusio*. XV. *Exordium* is a passage which brings the mind of the listener into a proper condition to receive the rest of the speech. This will be accomplished if he becomes well-disposed, attentive, and receptive. There are five kinds of cases which must be studied: (1) *honestum*, (2) *admirabile*, (3) *humile*, (4) *anceps*, (5) *obscurum*. They are: (1) An honorable case is one which wins the hearer's favor at once, without any speech of ours. (2) The difficult case is one which has alienated the sympathies of those who are about to hear it. (3) The mean one is that which the listener thinks light of and thinks unworthy of attention. (4) The ambiguous one is that in which the point for decision is doubtful. (5) The obscure case is one in which either the auditors are slow of wit or the case involves matters that are difficult to grasp. Thus *exordia* are divided into two species: *principium*, in which a direct beginning is made; and *insinuatio*, in which the approach is made unobtrusively.

XVI. Good will is secured in the direct beginning through the persons involved or through the case itself. Making the auditor sympathetic will also make him attentive. XVII. The insinuative method is to be used when the audience is hostile. XVIII. Rules for the *exordium*: the *exordium* ought to be sententious to a marked degree, and of a high seriousness, and, to put it generally, should contain everything which contributes to dignity. It should contain very little brilliance, vivacity, or finish of style, because these give rise to a suspicion of preparation and excessive ingenuity. Faults of the *exordium*: it may be too general, too common, too interchangeable, too unconnected, or too out of place.

XIX. *Narratio* is an exposition of events that have occurred or are supposed to have occurred. There are three kinds: one which contains only the case and the whole reason for the dispute; a second in which a digression is made for the purpose of attacking somebody or of making a comparison or of amusing the audience in a way not incongruous with the business in hand, or for amplification; the third kind, wholly unconnected with public issues, and recited or written solely for amusement, provides valuable training at the same time. It is subdivided into two classes:

1. One concerned with events:
   a. *fabula,* or narrative in which events are not true and have no verisimilitude;
   b. *historia,* or account of actual occurrences remote from our own age;
   c. *argumentum,* or fictitious narrative which might nevertheless have occurred.
2. One concerned with persons, in which not only events but also the conversation and mental attitudes of the persons is shown. This form of narrative should possess great vivacity, resulting from changes in fortune, contrast of characters, severity, gentleness, hope, fear, suspicion, desire, dissimulation, delusion, pity, sudden change in fortune, disaster, sudden pleasure, happy ending to the story. But these embellishments will be drawn from what will be said later about the rules of style.

XX. The narrative in a law case should be brief, clear, and plausible. It will be brief if superfluous facts and words are avoided; it will be clear if chronological order is followed. XXI. It will be plausible if it seems to embody characteristics which normally appear in real life; if the proper qualities of the characters are maintained, if reasons for their actions are plain, if they seem to have had the ability to do the deed, if it can be shown that the time was opportune, the space sufficient, and the place suitable for the events about to be narrated; if the story fits in with the nature of the actors in it, the habits of ordinary people, and the beliefs of the audience.

XXII–XXIII. *Partitio* makes the whole speech clear and perspicuous. There are two forms: one form shows the matters in which we agree with our opponent and what is left in dispute; the other shows in a methodical way the matters we intend to discuss.

XXIV–XXV. *Confirmatio* or proof is the part of the oration which by marshaling arguments lends credit, authority, and support to our case. All propositions are supported in argument by attributes of persons or of actions. We hold the following to be the attributes of persons: name, nature, manner of life, fortune, habit, feeling, interests, purposes, achievements, accidents, speeches made. XXVI–XXVIII. The attributes of actions are partly coherent with the action itself, partly considered in connection with the performance of it, partly adjunct to it, and partly consequent upon its performance. XXIX. All arguments drawn from these topics (*loci*) will have to be either probable or irrefutable. Briefly defined, an argument seems to be a device of some sort to demonstrate with probability or prove irrefutably. That is probable which usually comes to pass, or which is part of the ordinary beliefs of mankind, or which contains in itself some resemblance to these qualities. XXX. All probability used in an argument is either a sign or something credible or a point in which judgment has been given or something which affords an opportunity for comparison. These matters will be discussed in greater detail in the second book. XXXI. All argumentation is carried on by induction or by deduction. [XXXI–XLI. Rules for the use of reasoning in argument.]

XLII. *Refutatio* is that part of an oration in which arguments are used to impair, disprove, or weaken the confirmation or proof in our opponent's speech. It uses the same methods as *confirmatio*. Every argument is refuted in one of four ways: either one or more of its assumptions is not granted, or if the assumptions are granted it is denied that a conclusion follows from them, or the form of argument is shown to be fallacious, or a strong argument is met by one equally strong or stronger. [XLIII–LI. Rules for refutation.]

LII. *Peroratio* is the end and conclusion of the whole speech. It has three parts, the summing up, the *indignatio* or exciting of indignation or ill will against the opponent, and the *conquestio* or arousing of pity and sympathy. [LIII–LVI. Rules for the peroration, including sixteen methods of exciting pity in the *conquestio*.]

LIX. Praise and censure will be derived (for epideictic speaking) from the topics that are employed with respect to the attributes of persons; these have been discussed above. If one wishes to treat the subject more fully, these may be divided into mind, body, and external circumstances. A person should be praised for his use of these things, rather than for his mere possession of them.

BOOK TWO

[I–III. Reasons for collecting doctrines from many sources.] III. These two opposing sects (as we may call them) [i.e., of Isocrates and Aristotle], one busy with philosophy but devoting some attention to rhetoric as well, the other entirely devoted to the study and teaching of oratory, were fused into one group by later teachers who took into their own books from both sources what they thought was correct.

IV. The purpose of this second book is to present the arguments appropriate to each of the four issues and each of the three kinds of speeches. We shall take up forensic speeches first. IV–XVI. Forensic cases involving the issue of *coniectura;* charges, replies, and possible arguments on both sides. XVII–XVIII. Forensic cases involving the issue of *definitio.* XIX–XXXIX. Forensic cases involving the issue of *qualitas.* These are all cases of general reasoning.

XL–LI. Cases involving written documents, when some doubt arises from the nature of writing. This comes about from ambiguity, from the letter and the intent, from conflict of laws, from reasoning by analogy, from definition.

LI–LIX. The rules for deliberative and epideictic oratory. Honor and advantage are the characteristic of things to be sought, and baseness and disadvantage of things to be avoided. LIII. We shall call honorable anything that is sought wholly or partly for its own sake; it has two divisions, the simple and the complex. Everything in the first class is virtue, or a habit of mind in harmony with reason and the order of nature. Honor therefore has four parts: wisdom, justice, courage, and temperance. Their opposites will be avoided.

Cicero's interest obviously lies in forensic speaking, especially in the uses of arguments from *constitutiones,* for his organizational plan breaks down completely when he attempts in the second book to apply the *constitutiones* to deliberative and epideictic speaking. He devotes one hundred and forty sections to forensic oratory, but only nine sections to deliberative and epideictic speaking combined.[20]

The *Topica,*[21] less obviously rhetorical in nature, is important both in its own right and because of its alleged connection with Aristotle. Although the author states that he plans to explain Aristotle's *Topics,* he also includes discussions of testimony, the parts of a speech, the three kinds of oratory, and logical doctrine derived from an unidentified Hellenistic source. He defines a Topic (*locus*) as "the region of an argument" or the area in which arguments may be found, some topics being inherent in the nature of a subject and others depending largely upon authority or testimony brought in from outside the subject. In forensic speaking, Cicero points out, the three *constitutiones* explained in *De inventione* supply inherent topics for logical arguments. The frequent references to speaking problems make it clear, however, that the book is essentially a treatise on rhetorical *inventio* rather than a book on logic like Aristotle's *Topics.*[22]

## THE *TOPICA* OF CICERO

I. This book is an interpretation of Aristotle's *Topics.*

II. Every systematic treatment of argumentation has two branches, one con-

---

[20] Quintilian and the Pseudo-Cicero have the same preference; indeed, the doctrine of *status* seems inapplicable to the other two types of speaking. All the Roman rhetoricians announce that they will apply the doctrine to the three *genera,* but eventually they adopt Cicero's expedient. For a comment on this phenomenon, see D. A. G. Hinks, "Tria Genera Causarum," *Classical Quarterly* 30 (1936), 170–76.

[21] Text and translation in Cicero, *De inventione,* etc.

[22] Boethius, nevertheless, treats it in his series on the logical works of Aristotle. Boethius, *In topica Ciceronis commentariorum libri sex,* ed. J. P. Migne, *Patrologia Latina* LXIV, cols. 1040–1174.

cerned with the invention of arguments, and the other with the judgment of
their validity. Aristotle was the founder of both, in my opinion.

If we wish to track down some argument, we must know the places (*loci*)
where arguments may be found. Accordingly we may define a topic (*locus*)
as the region of an argument, and an argument as a course of reasoning which
firmly establishes a matter about which there is some doubt. Of the topics
under which arguments are included, some are intrinsic, or inherent in the
nature of the subject, and some are extrinsic, or brought in from without.
Inherent in the nature of the subject are arguments derived from the whole,
from its parts, from its meaning, and from things that are in some way closely
connected with the subject being investigated. Thus the intrinsic topics are as
follows:

      1. Definition of the whole
      2. Enumeration of parts
      3. Etymology or the meaning of words
  III. 4. Circumstances closely connected to the subject:
        a. Conjugate terms
        b. Genus
        c. Species
        d. Similarity
        e. Difference
        f. Resemblance
        g. Contraries
  IV.     h. Adjuncts or corollaries
        i. Antecedents
        j. Consequents
        k. Contradictions
        l. Cause
        m. Effect
        n. Degree or comparison

Extrinsic topics depend largely upon authority.

[V–XIX. A detailed reanalysis of the intrinsic topics, with further examples.]

XIX–XX. Extrinsic topics depend upon testimony which acquires its authority from the audience's opinion of the testifier. Testimony may be defined
as everything that is brought in from some external circumstance in order to
win conviction.

XXI. There are two possible kinds of inquiry, one into general questions
(what the Greeks call *thesis* and we call *propositum*), and one into particular
questions (what the Greeks call *hypothesis* and we call *causa*). Inquiries into
general questions are either theoretical or practical, either for knowledge or for
duty and the arousing of emotions. Theoretical questions fall into three groups:

(1) Does it exist? (2) What is it? or (3) What is its character? The first of
these is treated and answered by inference and conjecture, the second by definition, and the third by distinguishing between right and wrong. XXII. Practical
questions deal either with duty or with emotion. XXIII. Some topics are best
suited to certain questions.

XXIV. There are three kinds of speeches on particular questions: the judicial, deliberative, and epideictic or encomiastic. It will be seen from what has
gone before that certain topics apply especially to certain kinds of speeches.
But particular inquiries are built up of topics that are proper to each of them.
In judicial speaking one of three replies is possible to a person accused of a
crime: either that the crime was not committed, or that if committed it had a
different name, or that it was justified. The first is called *coniecturalis,* the
second *definitiva,* the third *iuridicalis.* Further arguments may be secured from
ambiguity, conflict, or variance between letter and intent in written documents.
XXV. The reply to the accusation may be termed *status* in Latin.

XXVI. The topics are useful in all the parts of speech; some topics are
proper to each part, of course, and some are of use to all the parts alike.

This treatise has included more than was originally intended.

The third Ciceronian work worthy of note is *De oratore,*[23] an Aristotelian dialogue generally considered to be the author's most mature
work, and the one containing his final views.[24] He alleges from the beginning that it is an attempt to distill the best from previous writers and
from his own experience. Since it is in dialogue form, with most of the
author's ideas expressed through Lucius Crassus, it is difficult to present
a systematic summary in quite the manner possible with more patently
expository works. It can be noted, however, that the general tone differs
markedly from that of *De inventione,* so that, although many of the familiar doctrines are repeated—the three *genera* of speeches, the extrinsic
and intrinsic *loci,* general versus special questions, and so forth—the whole
atmosphere is one of careful reflection on the problems of the orator.[25]

Moreover, some different ideas are broached. Crassus declares that there
are three branches of philosophy: nature, dialectic, and human action,

---

[23] Text and translation in Cicero, *De oratore,* trans. H. Rackham, 2 vols., Loeb
Classical Library (London, 1942–48). A summary is in Murphy, *Synoptic History of
Classical Rhetoric,* pp. 101–25.

[24] In it he refers to *De inventione* as a crude and unfinished essay of his youth.
*De oratore* I.iii.5.

[25] Contrast the bumptious tone of *De inventione,* whose prologue begins: saepe
et multum hoc mecum cogitavi . . . (when the author was but nineteen years of
age). *De oratore* is pleasurably readable, possessing a literary charm which helped
to make it popular among fifteenth-century humanists, as contrasted to the severely
arid textbook quality of *De inventione.*

with rhetoric concerning itself with the last. He prefers to name four parts of a speech, as Aristotle had done, rather than the six (or seven) common to other Roman treatises. In respect to style (*elocutio*), *De oratore* turns back toward the Peripatetic concepts found in Theophrastus, the disciple of Aristotle, who had named four prerequisites of good style: correct diction, lucidity, ornateness, and appropriateness. There is also a greater interest in the forms of argument, such as inference, definition, and deduction, which other Roman treatises tend to derogate in favor of the Hermagorean doctrine of *status*. Add to such instances the frequent praise of the Peripatetics, and it is apparent that in this latter work Cicero is tending more strongly toward the Aristotelian strains which help to make up the general stream of Roman theory.[26]

The remaining works of Cicero need only be mentioned. In a book called *Orator*[27] he presents a detailed discussion of prose rhythm (*numerus*), based on the theory that the human ear expects to hear an aural pattern binding words together. While admitting that it is not the same as poetic rhythm, he employs the technical terms of verse construction to describe the various forms of prose rhythm. *Brutus*[28] is a history of Roman oratory, and *De optimo genere oratorum*[29] is the preface to a translation (now lost) of Demosthenes' *On the Crown*. Cicero also wrote *De partitione oratoria*,[30] a sketchy outline of rhetorical theory for his son.

We turn next to one of the most influential books on speaking and writing ever produced in the Western world, the so-called *Rhetorica ad Herennium* of the Pseudo-Cicero.[31] This work, written within a few years of *De inventione* and possibly even from the same lecture notes or

---

[26] Roman rhetoricians generally acknowledge the existence of separate background traditions. Cf. *De inventione* II.i.6, and Quintilian, *Institutio oratoria* III.i.12–16. It is highly significant, therefore, that it is the *De inventione* and not the *De oratore* which dominates medieval rhetorical interest in Cicero.

[27] Text and translation in *Brutus*, trans. G. L. Hendrickson. *Orator*, trans. H. M. Hubbell, Loeb Classical Library (London, 1952).

[28] *Ibid.*

[29] Cicero, *De inventione*, etc.

[30] Text and translation in Cicero, *De oratore* III. *De fato. Paradoxa stoicorum. De partitione oratoria*, trans. H. Rackham, Loeb Classical Library (London, 1948).

[31] The original title is unknown, the popular title being derived from the prefatory letter to Gaius Herennius. Medieval writers refer to it as *rhetorica nova* or *rhetorica secunda*, believing Cicero's *De inventione* to be his *rhetorica vetus*. References will be to (Cicero), *Ad C. Herennium libri IV de ratione dicendi*, trans. Harry Caplan, Loeb Classical Library (London, 1954). A brief summary may be found in Murphy, *Synoptic History of Classical Rhetoric*, pp. 82–89; and see Kennedy, *Art of Rhetoric*, pp. 111–34.

textbooks as those that form the basis for Cicero's book, has been said to blend pre-Aristotelian and Peripatetic theories of *inventio* with the Hellenistic doctrine of *status*. Nevertheless, the discussion of *inventio* is essentially the same as Cicero's, a fact that may account for the widespread medieval belief that Cicero was the author.[32] The section on *memoria* is the oldest extant treatment of the subject, just as its division of *elocutio* into three levels is the oldest complete exposition. Also, because Book Four provides a full treatment of *exornationes* or "figures" of diction and thought, we may regard *ad Herennium as a complete textbook* of rhetoric.

Books One and Two parallel Cicero's *De inventione* so closely that it seems unnecessary to provide a detailed summary here. The author devotes most of this section to the doctrine of *status* in forensic speaking, the only major innovation being his division of *argumentatio* into five parts: proposition, reason, proof of the reason, embellishment, and resumé.[33] Other differences between the author and Cicero involve mere technical details of Roman law. Books Three and Four, however, present material not found in *De inventione*. After a brief discussion of *loci* for deliberative and epideictic speeches, Book Three discusses delivery under the headings of voice quality and physical movement. Memory is then divided into two parts, natural and artificial, the artificial memory consisting of what the author calls backgrounds and images. His system involves creating mental backgrounds or areas (*loci*), into which the speaker must place symbols (*images*) of the things he wishes to remember.[34]

The most influential portion of *ad Herennium,* however, is the treatment of style, which occupies all of Book Four. The author names three levels of style, the grand, the middle, and the plain,[35] giving lengthy examples of each. He states that each of these three styles should have the

---

[32] Jerome identified it with Cicero, and the belief persisted until the fifteenth century. There is no evidence that Quintilian knew the work, and indeed it apparently dropped from sight until the fourth century of the Christian era without exerting influence on later classical theory. See Caplan's Introduction, pp. vii–xviii.

[33] For the editor's discussion of this Hellenistic doctrine, see his Introduction, p. xviii, and notes on text, II.xviii.27 ff.

[34] Although interest in *memoria* extends from Greek times, this section is the oldest extant treatment. Roman interest in the subject is further demonstrated by Cicero (*De oratore* II.lxxxv.350) and Quintilian (*Institutio* XI.ii.1–51).

[35] Sunt igitur tria genera . . . Gravis est quae constat ex verborum gravium levi et ornata constructione. Mediocris est quae constat ex humiliore neque tamen ex infima et pervulgatissima verborum dignitate. Adtenuata est quae demissa est usque ad usitatissimam puri consueditudinem sermonis. *ad Herennium* IV.viii.11.

qualities of taste (*elegantia*), artistic composition (*compositio*), and distinction (*dignitas*), the last to be achieved through the judicious use of figures (*exornationes*):[36]

> Dignitas est quae reddit ornatam orationem varietate distinguens. Haec in verborum et in sententiarum exornationes dividitur. Verborum exornatio est quae ipsius sermonis insignita continetur perpolitione. Sententiarum exornatio est quae non in verbis, sed in ipsis rebus quandam habet dignitatem.[37]

Having divided the devices into the two classes, the author proceeds to define and exemplify forty-five figures of speech (*verborum exornationes*) and nineteen figures of thought (*sententiarum exornationes*), providing a total of sixty-four figures.[38]

The figures of speech are further divided into two groups, one of thirty-five figures and the second of ten. These latter ten figures of speech are not given a special name by the author, although later tradition assigned them the title of *tropi*, or "tropes." They are distinguished from other figures of speech in that the language "departs from the ordinary meaning of the words and is with a certain grace applied in another sense." [39]

Since the definitions (and often the examples) employed in *ad Herennium* play an important part in the later history of ornate language, the list of figures from Book Four[40] may serve as a useful index.[41]

The *Rhetorica ad Herennium*, then, contains a full treatment of the five

----

[36] Caplan notes that the author of *ad Herennium* does not use the term *figura* in the modern sense of "figure." Quintilian was the first to do so.

[37] *Ibid.*, IV.xiii.18.

[38] Abstruse and conflicting terminology has long complicated the study of "figures." It was common medieval practice after the eleventh century to refer to any figure as a *color* (often by analogy to the verb *coloro*), and a sometimes useful distinction between *colores grammatici* and *colores rhetoricae* was honored more in the breach than in the observance. By the fourth century more than two hundred figures were available in rhetorical treatises. But even in Cicero's lifetime, as he remarks in *De oratore* (III.lii.200), there were available: et verba et sententiae paene innumerabilis. Quintilian felt it necessary to point out that there are not really as many figures as some people claim; see his warning in *Institutio* XI.i.22–25, and his other remarks in IX.ii.19–25 on the figure *dubitatio*. For a more detailed discussion see below, Chapter Four, pp. 184–91.

[39] Ab usitata verborum potestate recedatur atque in aliam rationem cum quadam venustate oratio conferatur. *ad Herennium* IV.xxxi.42.

[40] For convenience this list employs Caplan's translation of terms. Latin terms (as used in *ad Herennium*) are placed first, then English terms in parentheses. It is indicative of the problem of terminology that many of the "English" terms are Greek in origin.

[41] For full definitions see Appendix, pp. 365–74.

Devices for Achieving *dignitas* in Style
*Rhetorica ad Herennium*, Book Four

*Figures of Speech*

1. *repetitio* (epanaphora)
2. *conversio* (antistrophe)
3. *conplexio* (interlacement)
4. *traductio* (transplacement)
5. *contentio* (antithesis)
6. *exclamatio* (apostrophe)
7. *interrogatio* (interrogation)
8. *ratiocinatio* (reasoning by question and answer)
9. *sententia* (maxim)
10. *contrarium* (reasoning by contraries)
11. *membrum* (colon)
12. *articulus* (phrase)
13. *continuatio* (period)
14. *conpar* (isocolon)
15. *similiter cadens* (homeoptoton)
16. *similiter desinens* (homeoteleuton)
17. *adnominatio* (paronomasia)
18. *subiectio* (hypophora)
19. *gradatio* (climax)
20. *definitio* (definition)
21. *transitio* (transition)
22. *correctio* (correction)
23. *occultatio* (paralipsis)
24. *disjunctum* (disjunction)
25. *coniunctio* (conjunction)
26. *adiunctio* (adjunction)
27. *conduplicatio* (reduplication)
28. *interpretatio* (synonomy)
29. *commutatio* (reciprocal change)
30. *permissio* (surrender)
31. *dubitatio* (indecision)
32. *expeditio* (elimination)
33. *dissolutum* (asyndeton)
34. *praecisio* (aposiopesis)
35. *conclusio* (conclusion)

Special Figures of Speech ("tropes")

36. *nominatio* (onomatopoeia)
37. *pronominatio* (antonomasia)
38. *denominatio* (metonymy)
39. *circumitio* (periphrasis)
40. *transgressio* (hyperbaton)
41. *superlatio* (hyperbole)
42. *intellectio* (synecdoche)
43. *abusio* (catachresis)
44. *translatio* (metaphor)
45. *permutatio* (allegory)

*Figures of Thought*

1. *distributio* (distribution)
2. *licentia* (frankness of speech)
3. *diminutio* (understatement)
4. *descriptio* (vivid description)
5. *divisio* (division)
6. *frequentatio* (accumulation)
7. *expolitio* (refining)
8. *commoratio* (dwelling on the point)
9. *contentio* (antithesis)
10. *similitudo* (comparison)
11. *exemplum* (exemplification)
12. *imago* (simile)
13. *effictio* (portrayal)
14. *notatio* (character delineation)
15. *sermocinatio* (dialogue)
16. *conformatio* (personification)
17. *significatio* (emphasis)
18. *brevitas* (conciseness)
19. *demonstratio* (ocular demonstration)

conventional parts of rhetoric. Except for some differences in the fields of *inventio,* the book fits exactly into the Roman theory represented by Cicero. It is therefore not surprising that later readers should have concluded that it was truly Cicero's.

The homogeneity of the Roman theory is further demonstrated by still another major Roman work employing the Ciceronian rhetoric—namely,

Quintilian's *Institutio oratoria*,[42] written about A.D. 92—which proposes a complete system for the education of the ideal orator, based upon both grammatical and rhetorical training. Quintilian divides the work into four parts: first, the general education of the orator (I–II.x); then rhetoric (II.x–IX); training for facility (X–XI); and finally, remarks on the Ideal Orator (XII).

The rhetorical section follows the Ciceronian tradition very closely, the doctrine of *status* furnishing the basic method of *inventio*. As is customary, forensic speaking occupies the greatest space. The section on style includes a lengthy discussion of *figurae,* in which the quibbles about technical nomenclature provide further evidence of the extent to which Roman rhetoric had accepted the concepts of *exornationes* first laid down in *ad Herennium* almost two centuries earlier.[43] Quintilian's treatment of *dispositio, actio,* and *memoria* are also typically Ciceronian.[44]

Quintilian's rhetoric, therefore, furnishes nothing new, his most significant contribution lying in the educational program prescribed for the ideal orator. In this section, he establishes a close connection between *grammatica* and *rhetorica,* a matter of some significance to the history of both subjects. In the classical period, his precepts furnished the model for Roman provincial schools, which were later attended by some of the early Fathers of the Christian Church,[45] and in the so-called "Renaissance

---

[42] Latin references are to the Loeb Classical Library edition. An English summary and concordance is furnished in Charles Little (ed.) *The Institutio oratoria of Quintilian,* 2 vols. (Nashville, Tenn., 1951). For a useful introduction, see *Institutionis oratoriae liber I,* ed. F. H. Colson (Cambridge, 1924). An outline appears in Baldwin, *Ancient Rhetoric and Poetic,* pp. 63–66, and a summary by Prentice Meador in Murphy, *Synoptic History of Classical Rhetoric,* pp. 151–76; see also Kennedy, *Art of Rhetoric,* pp. 487–514.

[43] It should be noted here that Quintilian apparently did not know the *ad Herennium.* The complex discussion of figures in Books VIII and IX demonstrates, rather, the extent to which the whole theory had permeated Roman rhetoric. Note frequent reference to Cicero in respect to stylistic matters, especially the long quotation from his *De oratore* in *Institutio* IX.i.26–45.

[44] This rhetorical portion of the *Institutio* apparently did not survive intact through the middle ages. The *textus mutilatus* available to John of Salisbury (c. 1159), for instance, had a great lacuna beginning at I.i.6 and continuing to V.xiv.12, and a portion of VIII was also missing. See Colson, *Institutionis oratoriae,* pp. lx–lxiii. Although Petrarch knew the *Institutio,* the great postclassical popularity of the book came only in the fifteenth century. During the middle ages a spurious set of declamations was ascribed to Quintilian, further complicating the tracing of his influence. See below, Chapter Three, pp. 123–30.

[45] For example, Ambrose, Jerome, Augustine, Gregory of Caesarea, Eusebius of Caesarea, John of Antioch (Chrysostom), and Basil of Caesarea. The influence of Roman education upon the medieval discourse modeled on these Fathers is surely incalculable. See Theo. Haarhoff, *Schools of Gaul* (Oxford, 1920; now reprinted).

of the Twelfth Century" his educational ideas promoted a short-lived interest in literary studies.[46] Since these ideas provide a key to the understanding of both *grammatica* and *rhetorica* in the ancient world, it may
be useful to present them in some detail here. The following summary
covers Book One in entirety, and Book Two as far as section x, at which
point a routine textbook of rhetoric begins.

Quintilian proposes that the orator's education should begin in the cra-
dle, since even the nurse's speech will provide a model for his imitation.
The child should first learn letters, then syllables, then words. Accuracy
is more important than speed at this time, because memory is almost the
only faculty which can be developed in the very young child. As soon as
he has learned to read and write easily, he should be delivered to the
*grammaticus,* or teacher of literature, who will teach him correctness and
the interpretation of the poets (*recte loquendi scientiam et poetarum enarrationem*). For the art of writing is combined with the art of speaking,
both depending upon a study of literature, and the student should read
every kind of writer, both for content and for vocabulary. The teacher
will deliver a lecture on poetry (*praelectio*), after which he will ask the
students to comment upon the verse. He will also present an oral reading
(*lectio*) from the poets and ask the students to do the same. After this,
the students should study composition by learning to paraphrase Aesop's
fables in various ways, then proceed to write aphorisms (*sententiae*),
moral essays (*chriae*), and character delineations (*ethologiae*). Throughout this training, the students should first learn by imitation and then go
on to personal invention. Delivery may be taught by an actor.

The *rhetoricus,* a second and separate teacher, can employ some of the
same methods in teaching declamation, although the spheres of the grammarian and the rhetorician should be kept separate. He should commence
with something resembling the subjects already taught under the *grammaticus,* taking up historical narration first. The study of fictitious narrative may properly be left to the grammarian, but the rhetorician should
undertake the discussion of whether a given narrative is credible. He
should also assign elementary exercises in epideictic speaking (*laudatio*
and *comparatio*), in commonplaces (*communes loci*), and in special questions (*theses*). The teacher may imitate the method of the *grammaticus*
by having students read an oration aloud for comment by the teacher.

---

[46] See especially G. Paré, A. Brunet, and P. Tremblay, *La renaissance du XII*
*siècle* (Paris, 1933), and Charles H. Haskins, *The Renaissance of the Twelfth
Century* (Cambridge, Mass., 1927; Meridian Books 59, 1957).

Readings will continue, even under the *rhetoricus,* who may also provide
full outlines of declamations[47] for the students to develop, pointing out
the proper places for emotional passages so that they may imitate him as
a model. Since these elementary exercises are merely parts of a whole, the
student who has mastered them should be brought into the study of forensic and deliberative themes.[48]

Quintilian's theory assigns definite responsibilities to each of the two
kinds of teachers, *grammaticus* and *rhetoricus,* making it plain that he
regards the fields of grammar and rhetoric as separate. It is apparent from
his remarks that even in his lifetime there was some possibility of a
blurring of boundaries between the two arts. Indeed, the second book of
the *Institutio oratoria* begins with a prophetic warning:

> Let us assign each of these professions its due limits. Let grammar (which
> turning it into a Latin word, they have called *literatura,* "literature") know
> its own boundaries, especially as it is so far advanced beyond the humility
> indicated by its name, to which humility the early grammarians restricted
> themselves. This subject, though but weak at its source, yet, having gained
> strength from the poets and historians, now flows on in a full channel; since,
> besides the art of speaking correctly, which would otherwise be far from a
> comprehensive art, it has engrossed the study of almost all the highest de-
> partments of learning. But let not rhetoric, to which the power of eloquence
> has given its name, decline its own duties, or rejoice that the task belonging
> to itself is appropriated by another; for while it neglects its duties, it is al-
> most expelled from its proper domain.[49]

Quintilian castigates rhetoricians for their unwillingness to take pains
with the small details of teaching,[50] but it is the grammarians against
whom he issues a drastic warning.

It should be noted that he provides a twofold definition of grammar:
it is first of all the science of speaking and writing correctly (*rec·e lo-*

---

[47] *Institutio* II.vi.1. See below, "Sophistic Rhetoric."

[48] *Institutio* II.x. Here begins a complete treatment of the five parts of rhetoric,
which runs to the end of Book IX. The final three books (to Book XII) discuss in
more general terms such subjects as oratorical facility and the concept of *vir bonus.*

[49] Nos suum cuique professioni modum demus. Et grammatice (quam in Latinum
transferentes litteraturam vocaverunt) fines suos norit, praesertim tantum ab hac
appellationis suae paupertate, intra quam primi illi constitere, provecta; nam tenuis
a fonte assumptis historicorum criticorumque viribus pleno iam satis alveo fluit,
cum praeter rationem recte loquendi non parum alioqui copiosam prope omnium
maximarum artium scientiam amplexa sit. *Institutio,* II.i.4. Translation by James J.
Murphy and John S. Watson, in *Quintilian on the Early Education of the Citizen-
Orator,* Library of Liberal Arts, 220 (Indianapolis, 1965), pp. 89–90.

[50] *Ibid.,* I. Pref. 4–5 and I.ix.6.

*quendi*), and then the art of interpreting the poets (*enarratio poetarum*).[51] The science of speaking or writing[52] correctly involves a consideration of what are often termed "grammatical rules" of proper word order, agreement of subject with verb, "barbarisms" and "solecisms," and the like. Quintilian characterizes these as speaking *methodicé,* or "by rule."

His concept of *enarratio poetarum* is more complex, particularly where it tends to overlap his concept of rhetoric. The *grammaticus* is enjoined to comment upon the poets by noting such features as the type of feet employed, the parts of speech in a line, and other matters easily classed under writing *methodicé*. This process begins to impinge upon the sphere of the *rhetoricus,* however, when the student is asked to compose paraphrases of works like Aesop. If the student were merely asked to transliterate from verse to verse, or verse to prose, it would be obvious that he would only be replacing words with other words. But the teacher of grammar also asks the student to compose *chriae* (moral essays) and *ethologiae* (character sketches), both of which demand some judgment concerning new material (what rhetoricians call *inventio*) and the order of parts (what the rhetoricians call *dispositio*). Thus the exercises employed in *enarratio poetarum* depart from the strictly grammatical concept of correctness, and enter a field usually reserved to the rhetorician. In Quintilian's case, of course, the provinces of the two subjects are kept distinct by his explicit directions. Consequently Quintilian serves as a guide to the classical definitions of two subjects that have often been confused. *Ars grammatica* is the twofold science of correct discourse (*recte loquendi*) and of the interpretation of poets (*enarratio poetarum*). Rhetoric, on the other hand, is the art of speaking well (*dicendi peritus*),[53] and its end (*officium*) is to accomplish things by action.[54] Quintilian maintains a separation between the two subjects by specifying that the *grammaticus* work almost entirely through *imitatio,* that is, through copying or paraphrasing models. The *rhetoricus,* on the other hand, works mainly through precepts that lay down a complete system of speech invention and presentation. Hence Quintilian distinguishes between the two by their method as well as by their ends.

---

[51] Haec igitur professio, cum brevissime in duas partes dividatur, recte loquendi scientiam et poetarum enarrationem. *Ibid.,* I.iv.2.

[52] Grammar applies to both writing and speaking; thus, he says: nam et scribendi ratio coniuncta cum loquendo est. *Ibid.,* I.iv.3.

[53] *Ibid.,* II.xv.34.

[54] Fere iudicandum est, rhetoricen in actu consistere; hoc enim, quod est officii sui, perficit. *Ibid.,* II.xviii.2.

The implication is that *grammatica* is an art whose end is understanding (*cognitione et aestimatione rerum*)[55] rather than result. This of course is especially true of the second part of grammar, *enarratio poetarum,* and it should be noted that it is into precisely this area that he warns the grammarians against extending their activities.[56]

There was not in classical or medieval times (nor is there now) any single accepted term to denote *preceptive* advice for literary production. Quintilian, after all, is concerned only with the training of the ideal orator. He draws, therefore, upon the well-developed lore of an *ars rhetorica,* which had accumulated precepts for almost seven centuries before he composed his *Institutio oratoria.* He does praise literature, "necessary for the young, a delight for the old, and the charming companion of private moments," [57] but ultimately he sees it as merely useful for educational background. He sees the same kind of usefulness in geometry, music, and philosophy. Hence he can advise the grammarian to remain within the elementary bounds of his art, and to refrain from venturing into the realm of prescriptive advice.

This would be a mere antiquarian observation were it not that Quintilian occupies a place unique in the history of the arts of discourse. As one of Rome's most influential teachers, he both reflected the prevailing practices of his century and transmitted the prevailing practice into countless provincial schools, some of which flourished after Rome itself had fallen.[58] It is probably fair to say, then, that his attitude toward nonrhetorical arts is representative of the Roman complex of rhetorical ideas which we have referred to as "the Ciceronian tradition."

Given the dominance of rhetoric in Roman education, then, Quintilian's advice to the *grammaticus* becomes more than a warning and begins to verge on the nature of an edict. It is perhaps not surprising that Roman grammarians seldom ventured into the field of prescriptive advice.[59]

---

[55] He applies these terms to arts which he calls "theoretical," although he does not give grammar as an example. *Ibid.,* II.xviii.1.

[56] Note that even when Quintilian admits the teaching of *chriae* and *ethologiae* to the province of the grammarian, he does so partly by default—because the rhetoricians will not condescend to such petty exercises. Moreover, he is at pains to point out that they are merely exercises in amplification and are therefore noninventional. *Ibid.,* I.ix.1–6.

[57] *Ibid.,* I.iv.5.

[58] Haarhoff, *Schools of Gaul,* passim. Saint Jerome refers to him, Isidore of Seville couples him with Cicero, Cassiodorus eulogizes him, and Alcuin (through Julius Victor) quotes him. See Little, *Quintilian,* II, 19 ff.

[59] It is precisely on this issue that medieval grammarians strike out into new

Since the grammarians of the thirteenth century took a rather different view of this matter, however, it might be useful at this point to describe at least briefly the major ancient works which the medieval teachers of grammar recognized as the foundations for their own work.

In Plato's *Ion* the rhapsode is made to declare his belief in a nonrational, extrahuman impetus for poetic composition. This force supplies not only the energy for composition but the very form of the discourse as well. This is not the place to argue the vexed question of the doctrine of "poetic inspiration," except to note that once such a postulate is admitted, there can be no further place for a doctrine of prescription. What cannot be learned cannot be taught.

It is perhaps significant, however, that the ancient world—so productive of *artes rhetoricae*—should have produced so very few prescriptive documents in the realm of imaginative literature. We have already noted that there was not any single denominative term which could be applied to the collection of precepts for the instruction of those interested in preparing nonoratorical discourse. There is certainly no Greek tradition of this kind. Whether due to a doctrine of inspiration or merely to a principle of identity,[60] it is true that ancient Greek poetry proceeded for the most part without accruing any residual set of principles or rules to be transmitted in formal systems.[61] Even the busy Alexandrian scholars of the second and first centuries before Christ did not produce from their critical studies anything even remotely similar to the Hellenistic rhetorical systems of the type popularized by Hermagoras of Temnos.[62]

The divergence of tradition represents a fundamental difference in method. It is one thing to say, "This line of poetry is good." It is another thing to say, "This line of poetry is good, so imitate it." But it is still another thing to make a complete preceptive system by saying, "We learn

---

areas, so that a clear understanding of this ancient principle can help us to comprehend more clearly what was attempted by writers like Geoffrey of Vinsauf and John of Garland.

[60] That is, to a recognition of a separate function and end for poetry as opposed to rhetoric.

[61] On the other hand, the *Rhetorica* of Aristotle begins with reference to what was already a considerable body of lore, and in some measure we owe the book to his efforts to correct what he saw as defects in that collection of doctrines. And the youthful Cicero is able to look back on a long prescriptive tradition: Non alienum est videre, quae dicant ei qui quaedam eius rei praecepta nobis reliquerunt. *De inventione* I.iv.5.

[62] See, for instance, John E. Sandys, *A History of Classical Scholarship* (Cambridge, 1915), pp. 105 ff. The Alexandrians produced a "canon" of poets, but not a preceptive doctrine for the composition of poetry.

from good lines of poetry that there are five rules for producing good verse, so here are the five rules to follow."

The first of these processes is usually termed "criticism," from the Greek term *kritikos* (κριτικός), meaning "able to judge." The product of the process is a judgment as to merit. The second process itself has no proper traditional name, although its product (*mimesis, imitatio*), or "imitation," is well known;[63] it should be noted that *imitatio* in this sense produces merely a recommendation for reproduction of an admired model, and does not provide for completely new invention. The third process, as we have seen, has no proper name.

Aristotle provides the major exception to the statement that the Greeks did not apply the third process to poetic composition. His *Poetica*[64] limits itself to dramatic composition (both tragic and comic, although the comic portion is lost), that is, to the direct imitation of human actions.[65] Aristotle identifies six characteristics of tragic drama: plot, character, thought, diction, spectacle, and music.[66] His whole treatment is strongly analytic in tone, leaning more toward definition and identification than toward prescriptive advice to the playwright. It is in many respects a work of "criticism." Nevertheless he does make specific recommendations, analogous to those made in his *Rhetorica* and in such logical works as *De sophisticis elenchis*.[67] The close connection of the *Poetica* to the *Rhetorica* is demonstrated in several places,[68] but especially by the direction in *Rhetorica* III that the orator should look also to the *Poetica* for further study of style.

Nevertheless, in terms of tradition-shaping influence, the *Poetica* of

---

[63] See, for instance, Erich Auerbach, *Mimesis,* trans. Willard Trask (New York, 1946).

[64] There are numerous modern translations. References here are to *Aristotle: Poetics,* trans. Gerald F. Else (Ann Arbor, Mich., 1967).

[65] "Epic composition, then, the writing of tragedy, and of comedy also; the composing of dithyrambs; and the greater part of the making of music with flute and lyre: these are all, in point of fact, taken collectively, imitative processes." *Ibid.,* p. 15. Aristotle then narrows his concern by saying that poets imitate "men in action" (p. 17).

[66] *Ibid.,* pp. 25-29.

[67] For instance, Aristotle says, "when a word is alleged to involve a contradiction, review how many senses it may have in the given sentence." *Ibid.,* p. 71.

[68] He says that even the structure of a play derives from the same general principle as that of a speech. Plot determines character, character determines thought, thought informs diction. So, in a speech, does argument determine *ethos; ethos* limits the types of enthymemes which can be useful; and all three have a bearing on suitable diction.

Aristotle was stillborn. Its period of greatest influence lies outside the limits of this study.[69]

It is to Rome, then, and to the Roman grammatical tradition that the student of the middle ages must turn, especially to two treatises which deal specifically with separate aspects of this tradition. The first is the so-called *Ars poetica* of Horace, written between 23 and 13 B.C.; the second is the *Barbarismus* of Aelius Donatus, written about A.D. 350.

The *Ars poetica*[70] of Horace consists of 476 verses giving almost random observations and advice about the writing craft. The structure is so loose that it might be proper to describe it as a collection of aphorisms. While it is apparent that some parallels exist between this treatise and those of the Ciceronian rhetorical tradition,[71] and while it is true that ancient rhetorical treatises often concern themselves with problems of narration and example,[72] the fact remains that the *Ars poetica* stands squarely in what is more properly called a grammatical tradition. Specifically, it is an extension of that part of grammar known as *enarratio poetarum*.

A brief summary of the treatise will give a clear idea of its nature.

## THE *ARS POETICA* OF HORACE

In poetry, as in painting, there must be unity and simplicity. Extremes must be avoided; avoidance of one fault must not lead to another fault. Take a subject equal to your strength. Whoever shall choose a theme within his range, neither speech will fail him nor clearness of order. The right things must be said at the right moment. License in the use of new or strange words is appropriate if done in moderation; skill in setting will make the familiar seem

---

[69] That is, in the Renaissance of the fifteenth century and after. Its medieval influence is negligible. For the medieval Latin translation made by William of Moerbeke (1278 A.D.), however, see Aristoteles, *De arte poetica Guillelmo de Moerbeke interprete,* ed. Erse Valgimigli, rev. Aetius Frenceschini and Laurentius Minio–Paluello, Aristoteles Latinus XXXIII (Bruges and Paris, 1953).

[70] Originally the proper title was probably merely *Epistle to the Pisos,* although Quintilian and writers after him refer to it as *Ars poetica.* Medieval writers often refer to it as *Poetria vetus;* Geoffrey of Vinsauf, the thirteenth-century grammarian, gave his own work the title of *Poetria nova* to mark it off as a departure from the "old poetry." References to Horace's work are to Horace, *Satires, Epistles, and Ars poetica,* trans. H. Rushton Fairclough, Loeb Classical Library (London, 1926).

[71] See, for instance, George Converse Fiske and Mary A. Grant, *Cicero's De oratore and Horace's Ars poetica,* University of Wisconsin Studies in Language and Literature, Vol. XXVII (Madison, 1929).

[72] Cf. Aristotle, *Rhetorica* II.20 and III.16; Cicero, *De inventione* I.xix; *ad Herennium* I.viii; and Quintilian, *Institutio* I.ix and IV.ii.

new. Many words that have fallen out of use will be born again, while others now in repute will fall.

Homer has shown the measure to be used in dealing with kings and wars. These types of verses—elegiac, comic, tragic—must be kept separate. Let each style keep the becoming place allotted to it.

It is not enough for poems to have beauty; they must have charm, and lead the hearer's soul where they will. In a tragedy the tones and facial expressions must fit the emotion, or the audience will laugh or fall asleep; the speech must also suit the age and rank of the speaker.

Either follow tradition or invent what is self-consistent. If you import a character, let his actions and words fit him; if you invent one, let him be consistent with himself throughout. It is often better to treat some traditional matter than to embark on entirely new ground, for it is difficult to write about general concepts in an individual way.

Beginnings should be modest, so that you will not fail in your promises. Homer always hastens to the issue, and hurries his hearer into the story's midst, as if already known, and what he fears he cannot make attractive he abandons; and so skillfully does he invent, so closely does he blend fact and fiction, that the middle is not discordant with the beginning, nor the end with the middle.

To please your hearers you must study the manners of each age, and give a befitting tone to shifting natures and their years.

Either an event is acted on the stage or the action is narrated. That which is acted is more vivid, but some things should not be acted on the stage (because of their horror).

Let no play be either shorter or longer than five acts, nor let any god intervene, nor let a fourth actor speak.

Let the chorus sustain the part and strenuous duty of an actor.

Tragedy should not mix with satire. My aim shall be poetry (*carmen*) so molded from the familiar that anybody may hope for the same success, may sweat much and yet toil in vain when attempting the same. Such is the power of order and connection, such the beauty that may crown the commonplace.

A long syllable following a short is called an *iambus*—a light foot. The spondee has taken its place in the trimeter on occasion. Handle Greek models by night and by day.

I'll play a whetstone's part, which makes steel sharp but of itself cannot cut. Though I write naught myself, I will teach the poet's office and duty; whence he draws his stores; what nurtures and fashions him; what befits him, and what not; whither the right course leads and whither the wrong.

Of good writing the source and fount is wisdom. Your matter the Socratic pages can set forth, and when matter is in hand words will not be loath to come. I would advise one who learned the imitative art to look to life and manners for a model, and draw from thence living words. At times a play marked by attractive passages (*loci*) and characters fitly sketched, though lacking in charm, though without force and art, gives the people more delight and holds them better than verses devoid of thought, and sonorous trifles.

Romans are too practical in their schooling to be great artists.

Poets aim to benefit or to amuse or to utter words at once both pleasing and helpful to life. Instruction and pleasure should be combined, for best success.

Absolute perfection is not to be expected, but a poet should be criticized for continuing to make the same mistake.

A poem is like a picture; one strikes your fancy the more, the nearer you stand; another, the farther away. A poem must be good, never mediocre, for that cannot be tolerated: a poem, whose birth and creation are for the soul's delight, if in aught it falls short of the top, falls to the bottom.

If you do write something, let it be criticized by others, then put it back in your closet for nine years. What you have not published you can destroy; the word once sent can never come back.

Often it is asked whether a praiseworthy poem is due to Nature or to art. For my own part, I do not see of what avail is either study when not enriched by Nature's vein, or native wit, if untrained; so truly does each claim the other's aid and make with it a friendly league.

It is easy for a rich poet to buy applause.

A friend will criticize your poetry honestly, lest you be laughed at later. It is dangerous to let a mad poet run abroad, for he may hurt himself or bore others.

These comments, as the summary indicates, are both generalized and personal. It is difficult to see how a reader could learn to construct a play or write a poem merely by reading the *Ars poetica*. For one thing, Horace assumes a considerable knowledge on the part of the reader; a student not already conversant with the form of tragedy, for instance, would find little concrete explanation of it in these verses. Moreover, the very structure of

the piece would be baffling to anyone attempting to learn an art which
was new to him. There is a personalized tone to certain sections which
makes the epistle uniquely charming, and by the same token tends to
remove his advice from the area of generality. Taken all in all, the *Ars
poetica* bears a striking resemblance to the kind of remarks which Quintilian expects of the *grammaticus* in his *enarratio poetarum*.[73]

Nevertheless Horace represents an extension—a further step, a projec-
tion forward—of the basic grammatical process. His comments are not
merely judgments about the merit of previously completed works (what
is usually termed "criticism"). They extend into the future. The *Ars
poetica* thus becomes a prescriptive or preceptive document. Its distillation of precepts depends upon two sources—personal experience and observation of literature. Both sources provide the author with injunctions
for those interested in future composition. Yet the book is clearly different
from the "rhetorical" works (like *De inventione*), the chief difference being that Horace is still in the mainstream of *ars grammatica*.

Equally rooted in the grammatical tradition is a second Roman work
which has major significance for the history of the arts of discourse. The
*Ars minor* and *Ars maior* of Aelius Donatus (fl. A.D. 350) profess to deal
only with the *ars recte loquendi,* but the second of these includes the so-
called *Barbarismus*, which tends to extend the control of the grammarian
over some of the *figurae* formerly handled only by the rhetoricians.

*De partibus orationis* (*Ars minor*),[74] is a simple description of the eight
parts of speech. The little treatise became so popular that the term "Do-
nat" or "Donet" became a medieval synonym for "primer" or "elementary
textbook." [75]

The *Ars grammatica* (*Ars maior*),[76] is more complex, treating not only
the eight parts of speech in greater detail, but adding in Book Three a discussion of *scemata* and *tropi*. Book Three (called *Barbarismus* from its
first word) thus represents the first recorded intrusion of *grammatica* into

---

[73] *Institutio* I.viii. A major difference, of course, is that Horace's remarks are not
limited to a single text. He intends his advice to apply in general to future compositions. For the concept of the "future poem," see below, Chapter Four, p. 135.

[74] Text in Henry Keil (ed.), *Grammatici latini,* 7 vols. (Leipzig, 1864), IV, 355–
66. It has been translated by W. J. Chase, *The Ars minor of Donatus,* University
of Wisconsin Studies in the Social Sciences and History, No. 36 (Madison, 1926).
For a brief summary, see Paul Abelson, *The Seven Liberal Arts* (New York, 1906),
pp. 36–38.

[75] Abelson calls it "the most widely read textbook on grammar throughout the
middle ages." Reginald Pecock's fourteenth-century primer of Christian religion,
for instance, is called *Donet,* meaning an introductory text.

[76] Text in Keil, *Grammatici* IV, 367–402. Book Three (*Barbarismus*) is often
circulated by itself, and may be considered a separate work.

a field heretofore appropriated by *rhetorica*. In one sense this marks a partial breakdown of ancient attempts to keep the two disciplines separate.[77] It will be remembered that in the educational scheme described by Quintilian, the student's first acquaintance with *scemata* and *tropi* comes at the hand of the *grammaticus*.[78] Yet Quintilian later devotes two books (Books Eight and Nine) to this subject, and a third (Book Ten) to facility in the use of language.[79] Cicero devotes considerable study to the same matter, as does Pseudo–Cicero in his *Rhetorica ad Herennium*. It would appear from the works of these three authors that the Roman rhetoricians take for themselves the study of *exornationes*. What, then, is the distinction between a "rhetorical" and a "grammatical" tradition in respect to *figurae*? A brief survey of the *Barbarismus* may prove helpful in evaluating its relation to the Ciceronian rhetorical tradition.

The *Barbarismus* opens with definitions of "barbarism" as a vice of a single part of speech, and "solecism" as a vice of a part of speech in context. Then Donatus points out that the barbarism in poetry is termed "metaplasm," and that the solecism, which is a fault in prose, is called a "scheme" in poetry.[80] This doctrine of the "permitted fault"[81] is further developed in the rest of the book, which deals with metaplasms, schemes, and tropes.

After brief definitions of twelve vices of diction,[82] Donatus defines "metaplasm" as a change in a word for the sake of metrical ornament.[83] Most of the devices indicated in this section depend upon the alteration

---

[77] Cf. Quintilian's warning, *Institutio* II.i.4.

[78] *Ibid.*, I.viii.16.

[79] And when Quintilian begins his treatment of rhetorical ornament (VIII.i.2), he points out that his initial discussion of language (in relation to grammar) is confined to the prevention of faults. The tangled history of the "tropes and figures" remains to be written. For a more detailed discussion of the problem see below, Chapter Four, pp. 184–91.

[80] Barbarismus est una pars orationis vitiosa in communi sermo. In poemata metaplasmus itemque in nostra loquella barbarismus, in peregrina barbarolexis dicitur . . . barbarismus fit duobus modis, pronuntiatione et scripto. . . .

Soloeocismus est vitium in contextu partium orationis contra regulam artis grammaticae factum. Inter barbarismus et soloeocismus hoc interest, quod soloeocismus discrepantes aut inconsequentes in se dictiones habet. Barbarismus autem in singulis verbis sit scriptis vel pronuntiatis. . . . soloeocismus sit duobus modis, aut per partes orationis aut per accidentia pertibus orationis. Soloeocismus in prosa oratione, in poemate schema nominatur. (Donatus, *Ars maior* III.1–2.)

[81] This ancient idea of "poetic license" is of course not unknown to the rhetoricians. Quintilian (I.viii.14) refers to it as well known.

[82] Barbarismus, soloeocismus, acyrologia, cacenphaton, pleonasmos, perissologia, macrologia, tautologia, eclipsis, tapinosis, cacosyntheton, amphibolia.

[83] Metaplasmus est transformatio quedam recti solutique sermonis in alteram speciem metri ornatusue causa.

of a letter or letters within a single word; sometimes a letter is to be
added [84] or deleted [85] or merely transposed;[86] at other times a syllable is
to be broken apart[87] or two syllables are to be merged into one.[88] Donatus
lists fourteen *metaplasmi:* prosthesis, epenthesis, paragoge, aphaeresis, syncope, apocope, ectasis, systole, diaresis, episynaliphe, synaliphe, ecthlipsis,
antithesis, metathesis. In only one type (systole) is there the addition of
another word.

The discussion of *scemata* then follows. Donatus points out that
schemes are of two kinds: figures of diction (*scemata lexeos*) and figures
of sense (*figurae sensum*). But figures of thought apply to orators, while
figures of diction pertain to grammarians.[89] There are many figures of
diction, but it is necessary to take up only seventeen of them.

Tropes are defined as expressions altered from their usual significance
for the sake of ornament.[90] Donatus, however, treats thirteen tropes, as
compared to the ten found in the *Rhetorica ad Herennium*. Moreover,
since one of his tropes has seven species, another has five, and a third has
three, it might be said that Donatus proposes almost thirty tropes.[91]

A tabular comparison of the *Barbarismus* and *Rhetorica ad Herennium*
IV.xiii ff. may serve to demonstrate the similarities and differences between the two works which in large measure shaped the doctrine of
*figurae* in the middle ages.[92]

It is apparent from such a comparison that the two sets of devices concur in the *tropi* (C), only sketchily in the *figurae verborum* (B), and not

---

[84] Prosthesis, epenthesis, paragoge.

[85] Aphaeresis, syncope, apocope. (It might be noted that, although *ad Herennium*
does not provide a separate discussion of these devices, these three and the preceding three could be included under the description of types of *adnominatio*
[paronomasia] in *ad Herennium* IV.xxi.29.)

[86] Metathesis.

[87] Diaresis.

[88] Episynaliphe.

[89] Schemata lexeos sunt et dianoeas, id est figurae verborum et sensum. Sed
schemata dianoeas ad oratores pertinent, ad grammaticos lexeos. *Ars maior* III.5.

[90] Tropus est dictio translata a propria significatione ad non propriam similitudinem ornatus necessitatisue causa. *Ibid.,* III.6. Cf. the similar definitions in *ad
Herennium* IV.xxx.42 and *Institutio* IX.i.4.

[91] J. W. H. Atkins, for instance, mistakenly credits Saint Bede with following
Isidore of Seville in expanding the standard list of ten tropes to twenty-eight. But
Bede (*De schematibus et tropis,* ed. Charles Halm, *Rhetores latini minores*
[Leipzig, 1863], pp. 611 ff.) is merely listing each of Donatus's species separately.
Cf. Atkins, *English Literary Criticism: The Medieval Phase* (New York, 1952),
p. 47.

[92] See the tabular comparison between *ad Herennium* IV and various medieval
"rhetoricians" in Edmond Faral, *Les arts poétiques du XII^e et du XIII^e siècles*
(Paris, 1924), pp. 52–54.

at all in the *figurae sententiarum* (D). The Pseudo–Cicero, like other rhetoricians, does not discuss *metaplasmi* (A). And with the larger list of tropes in Donatus, of course, the concurrence is not exact even there.[93] It thus seems fair to conclude that even in the realm of figures, there is a Roman grammatical tradition different in some ways from that represented by the Ciceronian rhetorical school.

The Roman student of rhetoric, of course, had the advantage of a curriculum which first took him through the lore of the grammarians and then later that of the rhetoricians. As a consequence he was exposed to a rather large total number of figures. But even more important, he was exposed to the whole concept of *ornatus* within the framework of a system which intended the study of the figures to be a means of sharpening the student's awareness of the niceties of language. The figures were not intended to be ends in themselves.[94] When the two sequential steps of the Roman educational process were separated and their representative textbooks were studied separately in later centuries, the distinct traditions were readily recognizable.

It is almost a contradiction in terms to use the phrase "sophistic rhetoric." For sophistry—that linguistic heresy which denies communication as an end of language—is by its very definition anti-rhetorical. Yet it is one of the paradoxes of history that the so-called "Second Sophistic" should have produced treatises perpetuating doctrines which are in the last analysis inimical to traditional concepts of rhetoric.

Historians of rhetoric commonly apply the term "Second Sophistic" to that period (approximately A.D. 50 to 400) which is characterized by exaggerated interest in oratorical declamation.[95] The practice of *declamatio,* or discourse upon a stated theme, was common in schools as early as Cicero, but the political events of the first Christian centuries made it increasingly difficult for speakers to apply their intensive schooling to public affairs. The schools, however, continued to train Romans in verbal facility, but since forensic oratory was restricted more and more to legal specialists, and deliberative oratory was forbidden by the autocratic Caesars, the

---

[93] The tropes are regarded as common to both poets and orators. Quintilian, *Institutio* I.viii.15.

[94] Quintilian, for instance, assigns them a definite place in the educational process. *Ibid.,* I.viii. 14–16 and VIII.iii.15ff.

[95] The principal tendencies of the Second Sophistic are summarized in Baldwin, *Medieval Rhetoric and Poetic* (New York, 1928), pp. 2–50. The best primary source, and the one referred to here, is probably Eunapius, *Lives of the Philosophers,* in Philostratus and Eunapius, *Lives of the Sophists,* trans. Wilmer C. Wright, Loeb Classical Library (London, 1922), pp. 319–565.

The *Barbarismus* of Donatus
Compared to the *Rhetorica ad Herennium*, Book Four,
of the Pseudo-Cicero

| *Barbarismus* | *ad Herennium* |
|---|---|
| A. *Metaplasmus* | A. (No equivalent section, but seven types of *metaplasmi* could be included under the discussion of *adnominatio (paronomasia)* in IV.xxi.29.) |
| B. *Schemata lexeos* | B. *Verborum exornationes* |
|   1. *prolepsis* | —— |
|   2. *zeugma* | —— |
|   3. *hypozeuxis* | —— |
|   4. *syllepsis* | —— |
|   5. *anadiplosis* | —— (but cf. 19, *gradatio*) |
|   6. *anaphora* | —— |
|   7. *epanalepsis* | —— |
|   8. *epizeuxis* | —— |
|   9. *paronomasia* | 17. *adnominatio* |
|   10. *schesis onamaton* | —— |
|   11. *parhomoeon* | —— (but see IV.xii.18: *O Tite, tute* . . .) |
|   12. *homoeoptoton* | 15. *similiter cadens* |
|   13. *homoeoteleuton* | 16. *similiter desinens* |
|   14. *polyptoton* | 17. *adnominatio* |
|   15. *hirmos* | —— |
|   16. *polysyndeton* | —— |
|   17. *dialyton (asyndeton)* | 33. *dissolutum* |
| C. *Tropi* | C. (*Tropi*) (Parenthetical numbers indicate order of tropes) |
|   1. *metaphora* | 44. *translatio* (9) |
|   2. *catachresis* | 43. *abusio* |
|   3. *metalepsis* | —— |
|   4. *metonymia* | 38. *denominatio* (3) |
|   5. *antonomasia* | 37. *pronominatio* (2) |
|   7. *synecdoche* | 42. *intellectio* (7) |
|   6. *epitheton* | —— |
|   8. *onomatopoeia* | 36. *nominatio* (1) |
|   9. *periphrasis* | 39. *circumitio* (4) |
|   10. *hyperbaton* | 40. *transgressio* (5) |
|     a. *hysterologia* | —— |
|     b. *anastrophe* | *perversio* |
|     c. *parenthesis* | —— |
|     d. *tmesis* | —— |
|     e. *sychisis* | —— |
|   11. *hyperbole* | 41. *superlatio* (6) |
|   12. *allegoria* | 45. *permutatio* (10) |
|     a. *ironia* | —— (*per contrarium?*) |

       b. *antiphrasis*                —— (*per contrarium*)
       c. *aenigma*                   ——
       d. *chaerentismos*           ——
       e. *paroemia*                ——
       f. *sarcasmos*              ——
       g. *astismos*               ——
   13. *homoeosis*             ——
       a. *icon*                   ——
       b. *parabole*               ——
       c. *paradigma*            ——
D. (*schemata dianoeas* excluded)    D. (Nineteen *sententiarum exornationes*)

energies of Roman speakers turned to the elaborate development of epideictic or demonstrative oratory. Schoolroom exercises became public
speeches, and the necessity of entertaining audiences placed a premium
upon methods of amplification.[96]

Perhaps nothing could better illustrate the type of speaking admired
during this period than the description Eunapius gives of a speech by
Prohaeresius (d. A.D. 367), who was a Christian sophist and holder of the
chair of rhetoric at Athens. Prohaeresius, challenged by a rival, stipulated
that shorthand reporters should take down his speech verbatim. His opponent offered him a vulgar theme, thinking to embarrass him, but Prohaeresius merely replied that he would ask the audience to withhold
applause. Eunapius goes on:

> As the speech grew more vehement and the orator soared to heights which
> the mind of man could not describe or conceive of, he passed on to the
> second part of the speech and completed the exposition of the theme. But
> then suddenly leaping in the air like one inspired, he abandoned the remain-
> ing part, left it undefended, and turned the flood of his eloquence to defend
> the contrary hypothesis. The scribes could hardly keep pace with him, the
> audience could hardly endure to keep silent, while the mighty stream of
> words flowed on. Then, turning his face toward the scribes, he said, "Ob-
> serve carefully whether I remember all the arguments that I used earlier."
> And without faltering over a single word, he began to declaim the same
> speech for the second time. . . .[97]

Eunapius reports that even his opponents were forced to applaud. What
can be learned from this passage? Granted that Eunapius may exaggerate

---

[96] For descriptions of the system used in schools, see Gwynn, *Roman Education,*
and Clark, *Rhetoric in Greco-Roman Education.* For an analysis of methods used
to suppress free speech during this period, see Chester G. Starr, *Civilization and
the Caesars: The Intellectual Revolution in the Roman Empire* (Ithaca, N.Y.,
1954).

[97] Eunapius, *Lives,* pp. 495–97.

the feats of Prohaeresius, he nevertheless supplies us with a contemporary account which glorifies the "vehement" nature of the delivery, the impassioned "flood" of eloquence, and the virtuosity of the speaker. It is significant that Eunapius does not report the subject matter, but only the speaker's treatment of it; there could be no clearer sign of the sophistic interest in the *way* a thing is said, as opposed to *what* is said.

As the exploit of Prohaeresius demonstrates, the Second Sophistic may be described as an oratorical phenomenon. It results from an abuse of traditional rhetorical training, rather than from any major change in the teaching itself. Ultimately, however, it stems from the encouragement of imagination in schoolroom exercises of declamation.

*Declamatio,* which may be defined as a school exercise in the preparation and delivery of fictitious speeches, is divided by Roman teachers into two types. The *suasoria* is an exercise in deliberative (political) oratory, and since it is regarded as the simpler form, it is placed first in the school program. The more difficult *controversia,* an exercise in forensic (judicial) oratory, is given a more advanced position.[98]

The schoolmaster would propose a "theme" (*thema, themata:* subject) for the students, perhaps even giving suggestions about handling it and sometimes providing an outline for development.[99] The student then prepared an oration which attempted to solve the problem posed by the theme, and brought it in writing to the rhetor. After correction of the text by the teacher, the student would deliver the speech aloud before his fellows in the presence of the teacher. The final step would be the *divisio,* the teacher's own comments on the oration and its delivery. This last step often included the master's own solution, as an example of how to treat the theme.[100]

---

[98] The process is described in detail by S. F. Bonner, *Roman Declamation in the Late Republic and Early Empire* (Berkeley and Los Angeles, 1949). See also Brother Edilbert Parks, *The Roman Rhetorical Schools as a Preparation for the Courts under the Early Empire,* Johns Hopkins University Studies in History and Political Science, Series LXIII, No. 2 (Baltimore, 1945); and M. L. Clarke, *Rhetoric at Rome,* pp. 90 ff.

[99] Note, for instance, Quintilian's discussions of various methods, *Institutio* II.vi.1 and II.x.5.

[100] This procedure, as Quintilian points out, is analogous to what the grammarians are to do in teaching writing. An interesting parallel occurs in directions given to Oxford university grammar masters in the early fourteenth century: Item, tenentur singulis quindenis versus dare, et literas compositas verbis decentibus non ampullosis aut sesquipedalibus, et clausulis succinctis, decoris, metaphoris manifestis, et quantum possint, sententia refertis, quos versus et quas literas debent recipientes in proximo die feriato vel ante in pergameno scribere, et inde sequenti die, cum ad scholas venerint, Magistro suo corde tenus reddere et scripturam suam offere.

The whole process thus falls into several easily identifiable steps:

1. Proposal of a theme
2. Discourse proposing a solution to the problem
3. Rhetor's solution and comments

As a classroom exercise, of course, the obvious next step would be to expand the second phase (discourse to propose a solution) by allowing two or more students to propose alternative solutions. In more abstract terms the process is then:

1. Problem
2. Proposed solutions
   a. Student A
   b. Student B
3. Master's solution[101]

The elder Seneca, Lucius Annaeus Seneca, collected a series of such declamations during the first quarter of the first Christian century. In its original state his *Oratorum et rhetorum sententiae, divisiones et colores*[102] contained ten books of *controversiae* and one of *suasoriae*, but four prefaces and several books have now been lost. Thus his treatise, which has a medieval history of its own,[103] furnishes examples of both the subjects proposed and the methods employed to handle them.

The book of *suasoriae* first presents each of the themes, then allows several declaimers to present arguments pro and con. For instance, the

---

Henry Anstey (ed.), *Monumenta academica Oxoniensis,* 2 vols. (London, 1868), II, 437–38.

[101] This of course has obvious parallels in medieval *disputatio,* in which the posing of a problem led ultimately to a master's solution (*determinatio*) after the airing of alternative solutions. See below, Chapter Three, pp. 102–106.

[102] Lucius Annaeus Seneca, *Controverses et suasories,* ed. and trans. Henri Bornecque, 2 vols. (Paris, 1902). Part of the work has been translated into English by William A. Edward in *The Suasoriae of Seneca the Elder* (Cambridge, 1927). The popular title in the middle ages was *Declamationes.* It might be noted here that the term *colores* in the original title does not refer to rhetorical figures, but denotes instead the speakers' attempts to create a certain "tone" or "coloring" in their arguments; that is, the acts of an opponent are to be construed adversely, but those of self or friend are to be interpreted in a favorable light. As pointed out earlier, the term *color* for "figure" did not become common until the eleventh century. For a discussion of these terms, see Edward, *Suasoriae,* pp. xxxiv–xxxvii.

[103] Seneca, like many another classical author, was "moralized" in the middle ages, his text being used for moral instruction. See Beryl Smalley, *English Friars and Antiquity in the Early Fourteenth Century* (Oxford, 1960), p. 180. The grammarian Fulgentius (480–550) drew allegorical interpretations of Virgil's *Aeneid* as well as of Greek mythology. In the early fourteenth century the Englishman Nicholas Trevet composed a work entitled *Declamaciones Senece reducte ad moralitatem.* A copy may be found in Paris Bibliothèque Nationale, MS. Lat. 13475, fols. 130–143^v.

first *suasoria* poses the theme: "Alexander considers whether he should sail the ocean." [104]

> ARGENTARIUS: Stop, your own world calls you back. All that the sun shines on, we have conquered. No aim is so important that for it I would endanger Alexander's safety.
>
> MARULLUS: In our quest of the seas to whom are we to give over the dry land? A world unknown is my goal, the conquered world I abandon.

After several such short arguments, the *divisio* comments that a speaker must always soothe and flatter a king, even when giving unpalatable advice—and then launches into a long amplification of this theme, so that the passage probably represents a teacher's commentary and example.

The *controversiae* were far more popular, particularly since they were an obvious preparation for a legal career, and were deemed to be more difficult. The following are examples from Seneca's first book:

> The law requires that children support their parents or be imprisoned. Two brothers disagreed. One had a son. His uncle fell on evil days, and in spite of his father's veto the boy supported him. For this reason he was disinherited, but did not protest. He was then adopted by the uncle, who inherited a fortune. The father then fell on evil days, and in spite of the uncle's veto, the young man supported him. He was disinherited.

> The law ordains that in the case of rape the woman may demand either the death of her seducer or marriage without dowry. A certain man raped two women in one night; one demanded his death, the other marriage.[105]

From these and other examples of *declamatio*, it is evident that the student was encouraged to use his imagination in supplying not only arguments but fictitious data to support those arguments. As a school exercise, there was undoubted value to the student of writing and speaking.[106] The Roman schools in the provinces—particularly in Gaul and Africa—continued this practice well into the Christian era, and thus had an undoubted influence upon the many Christian apologists and Fathers who studied or even taught in these schools. Even leaving aside the influence upon narrative technique,[107] it is possible that the structural format of the declamation—theme, alternative solutions, final solution—may well

---

[104] Edward, *Suasoriae*, pp. 39–45.

[105] Trans. M. L. Clarke, *Rhetoric at Rome*, p. 90.

[106] For an interesting reversal of an originally adverse view, see Donald Lemen Clark, "Some Values of Roman *declamatio*: The *controversiae* as a School Exercise," *Quarterly Journal of Speech* 35 (1949), 279–83.

[107] Both grammar and rhetoric teach *narratio*, of course; see above, n. 72. Nevertheless, the collections of *declamationes* (like those of Seneca and the Pseudo-Quintilian) provide a separate source of stories for imitation. Cf. J. T. Welter, *L'Exemplum dans la littérature religieuse et didactique du moyen âge* (Paris, 1927).

have played some part in determining the general mode of discourse used in the Christian Church in Scriptural exegesis, preaching, and even in philosophical inquiry.

A somewhat different tendency is revealed in the textual perpetuation of the *progymnasmata,* school exercises in narrative method. In the second century, Hermogenes' *Progymnasmata*[108] offered definitions, rules, and brief examples of fable, chria, and the like, and at the end of the fourth century Apthonius' *Progymnasmata*[109] continued the same tradition. In both treatises, the formerly wide range of rhetoric is reduced to the narrow field of *declamatio.* Emphasis is upon fixed rules and stereotyped methods, to the extent that the ancient concept of *topos* or *locus* is replaced by long lists of specific directions about things to be done. A writer or speaker wishing to describe a person, for instance, can rely on specific, detailed directions rather than upon his own inventive abilities. Hermogenes, for example, lists the following steps to be followed in praising a person:

1. Marvelous events at his birth
2. His nurture
3. His training and education
4. Nature of his soul
   a. Justice
   b. Self-control
   c. Wisdom
   d. Manliness
5. Nature of his body
   a. Beauty
   b. Stature
   c. Agility
   d. Might
6. His pursuits and deeds
7. External resources
   a. Kin and friends
   b. Possessions
   c. Household
   d. Fortune
8. How long he lived
9. The manner of his end
10. Events after his end[110]

[108] For a brief summary, see Baldwin, *Medieval Rhetoric,* pp. 23–38.
[109] Trans. Ray Nadeau, *Speech Monographs* 19 (1952), 264–85.
[110] Baldwin, *Medieval Rhetoric,* pp. 31-32. The grammarian Priscian transmitted this list of Hermogenes into the middle ages. See Priscian, *De pre-exercitamentis rhetoricis,* ed. Keil, *Grammatici,* III, 430-40.

Fitted within a broadly based rhetorical system, Hermogenes' *Progymnasmata* might be regarded as merely an extreme statement of a doctrine of commonplaces. But detached from any discussion of invention or disposition, and furnished with precisely detailed instructions as to procedures, the work becomes a set of laws rather than a collection of suggestions for invention. It is a further paradox of the Second Sophistic that a habit of unbridled imagination should have resulted in rules which forbid imagination.

In summary, then, it is important to recognize that the ancient world produced several types of documents relating to speaking or writing. The rhetorical works may be divided into two schools or traditions: the Aristotelian rhetoric, which has a philosophical and logical tone, and the "Ciceronian" rhetoric of Cicero, Pseudo–Cicero, and Quintilian, which has a pragmatic tone closely associated with Roman law. Quintilian also urges a close connection between grammar and rhetoric in his system for training the ideal orator. The Second Sophistic produced treatises dealing with *declamationes* and *progymnasmata*. The *Ars poetica* of Horace provides advice to writers of poetry, based on the grammatical tradition of *enarratio poetarum*. Donatus, although dealing only with grammar as *ars recte loquendi*, lays the groundwork for the confusion of rhetoric and grammar by including *scemata* and *tropi* in his *Ars grammatici*.[111]

All of these have in common the preceptive or prescriptive intention. Although they contemplate different species of discourse, and often lay down differing precepts even for the same species, they all subscribe to the fundamental premise that future discourse can be aided by preceptive advice. Their commonality is more important than their divergences. Thus they all bear out the saying of Cicero, that "Eloquence is one . . . regardless of the regions of discourse it is diverted into." [112] All, therefore, may truly be described as "Arts of Discourse."

---

[111] This chapter omits treatment of a number of classical works "lost" or otherwise of little influence during the middle ages. Their inclusion would not alter the conclusions reached. This category includes such works as Pseudo-Longinus, *De sublimitate,* and Dionysius of Halicarnassus, *De compositione verborum.* Others appear only fleetingly before the fifteenth-century Renaissance, as for instance Demetrius, *De elocutione.* But see Bernice Wall, *A Medieval Latin Version of Demetrius' De elocutione,* Catholic University of America Studies in Medieval and Renaissance Latin, Vol. V (Washington, D.C., 1937). Aristotle's *Poetica* has already been mentioned in this connection (see above, n. 69).

[112] Una est enim. . . . eloquentia quascumque in oras disputationis regionesue delata est. *De oratore* III.v. 23.

# Chapter II

### ✦✦✦

# Saint Augustine and the Age of Transition, A.D. 400 to 1050

THE history of the medieval arts of discourse begins in the fifth century. Although classical doctrines played a part in the two major works appearing early in the medieval period, the emphasis of Augustine and Martianus Capella was somewhat different from that of the Ciceronian tradition. That is, Augustine attempted the marriage of rhetoric and Christianity in his *De doctrina christiana,* and Martianus used his *De nuptiis Philologiae et Mercurii* to transmit the Roman concept of the liberal arts into the medieval period.

Pagan Roman rhetoric was still a viable force in the fourth century, of course, and the treatises produced in the Empire during the third and fourth centuries indicate the widespread popularity of the Ciceronian theories. Commentaries on Cicero were produced by Victorinus, Grillius, and the anonymous author of *De adtributis.*[1] Other writers composed brief abstracts or *compendia,* the most important of these being by Fortunatianus, whose *Artis rhetoricae libri III* [2] was the major source for Cassiodorus' knowledge of rhetoric, and Julius Victor, whose *Ars rhetorica*[3] was the first rhetorical work to include a section on letter-writing.

---

[1] Texts or excerpts in Charles Halm, ed., *Rhetores latini minores* (Leipzig, 1863), pp. 155–304, 596–606, and 593–595. For the complete text of Grillius, see Grillius, *Ein Beiträg zur Geschichte der Rhetorik* ed. Josef Martin (Paderborn, 1927).

[2] Halm, *Rhetores,* pp. 81–134.

[3] *Ibid.,* pp. 373–448.

Still a third group produced treatises devoted solely to *figurae*.[4] Parroting as they do the familiar Roman rhetorical doctrines, these works present nothing new. In fact, their only importance lies in their absolute acceptance of the ancient system. As one modern student has declared, their usefulness ended when the society that supported the rhetorician was shattered.[5]

Of far greater importance for the middle ages is the allegorical *De nuptiis Philologiae et Mercurii*[6] of Martianus Capella (fl. 410–427), which has been credited with introducing the seven liberal arts into the Middle Ages. Although Varro's *Disciplinarum libri novem*[7] proposed nine subjects in the complete Roman curriculum, medicine and architecture had been dropped by the fifth century, leaving seven subjects which Capella offers in the following order: grammar, dialectic, rhetoric, geometry, arithmetic, astronomy, and music.[8] The encyclopedias of Isidore and Cassiodorus confirm this general sequence in the following century, thus firmly establishing the typical pattern of trivium and quadrivium. The first three subjects deal with words, and the last four with mathematical concepts, so that together, they are regarded as a complete curriculum.[9]

The *De nuptiis* begins with two allegorical books of introduction, followed by books devoted to each of the seven arts. Grammar ("which

---

[4] *Ibid.,* pp. 1–21, 22–37, 38–62, 63–70. For these treatises in general, see A. Reuter, "Untersuchungen zu den romischen Technographen Fortunatian, Julius Victor, Capella und Sulpitius Victor," *Hermes* 28 (1893), 73–139.

[5] Martin L. Clarke, *Rhetoric at Rome* (London, 1953), p. 147.

[6] Ed. Wilhelm A. Dick, *Bibliotheca scriptorum Graecorum et Romanorum Teubneriana* (Leipzig, 1925); also, ed. Ulricus F. Kopp (Frankfurt, 1836); the section on rhetoric is printed in Halm, *Rhetores,* pp. 451–92. For a brief summary, see Charles S. Baldwin, *Medieval Rhetoric and Poetic* (New York, 1928), pp. 91–95. And see Hans Fischer, *Untersuchung über die Quellen der Rhetorik des Martianus Capella* (Breslau, 1936).

[7] Now lost. See John E. Sandys, *A History of Classical Scholarship from the Sixth Century B.C. to the End of the Middle Ages* (Cambridge, 1915), p. 178.

[8] Still useful for a rapid résumé is Paul Abelson, *Seven Liberal Arts* (New York, 1906).

[9] Grammar always comes first in medieval listings, although rhetoric sometimes precedes dialectic. The sequence of *trivium–quadrivium,* however, remains constant even when their constituent subjects change position. For comment on the significance of position changes between rhetoric and dialectic, see Richard McKeon, "Rhetoric in the Middle Ages," *Speculum* I (1926), 1–32. The use of the terms *trivium* and *quadrivium,* however, seems to date from a later period, possibly as late as Alcuin. In this connection see P. Rajna, *Studi medievali* I (1928), 4–36; and Hastings Rashdall, *Universities of Europe in the Middle Ages,* 3 vols., new edition ed. F. M. Powicke and A. B. Emden (Oxford, 1936), I, 34–35. Also see Brian P. Handley, "Wisdom and Eloquence: A New Interpretation of the *Metalogicon* of John of Salisbury," unpublished dissertation, Yale University, 1966.

teaches to read and to write") thus occupies Book Three, and dialectic Book Four. *Rhetorica* enters in Book Five:

> But while the crowd of gods terrestrial was thus disconcerted, behold a woman of loftiest stature and great assurance, with countenance of radiant splendor, made her solemn entry. Helmeted and crowned with royal majesty, she held ready for defense or attack weapons that gleamed with the flash of lightning. Beneath her armor the vesture draped Romanwise about her shoulders glittered with various light of all *figurae,* all *schemata;* and she was cinctured with precious colors for jewels. The clatter of weapons as she moved was as if thunder in the crash of a cloud aflame broke with leaping echoes. Nay, it seemed as if, like Jove, she herself could hurl the thunderbolt. For as a queen in control of all things she has shown the power to move men whither she pleased, or whence, to bow them to tears, to incite them to rage, to transform the mien and feeling as well of cities as of embattled armies and all the hosts of people.[10]

Despite this flamboyant opening, the rest of the fifth book is merely a routine compendium in the manner of Fortunatianus. Cicero supplies most of the examples for the lengthy discussion of *status,* and the section on *figurae* is taken almost verbatim from Aquila Romanus. In short, there is nothing remarkable about the compendium except its appearance in an encyclopedic guide to the whole curriculum of the seven liberal arts.[11] The contrast between the colorful picture of Lady Rhetoric and the drab theory of the compendium may be due to Martianus' inability to distinguish between the quality of the sophistic oratory he heard about him and that of the sober theory of the technicians.[12]

The *De nuptiis,* written during the first quarter of the fifth Christian

---

[10] *De nuptiis* V.425. Trans. Baldwin, *Medieval Rhetoric,* pp. 93–94.

[11] Baldwin observes that, although the *De nuptiis* as a whole had a considerable reputation in the middle ages, Book Five apparently had little separate influence. *Ibid.,* p. 95, n. 7. For the influence of Capella, see Claudio Leonardi, *I codici de Marziano Capella* (Milan, 1959–60), esp. pp. 467–84.

[12] Modern students sometimes neglect to observe the difference between the allegorical introduction to Book Five and the arid compendium which follows it. It is reasonable enough to point out, as does Sandys (*Classical Scholarship,* p. 243), that the allegorical representations of Capella find later echoes in such places as the carvings of the seven arts on the façades of Chartres (A.D. 1145). But it is rather misleading to take the introduction for the text; cf. J. W. H. Atkins, *English Literary Criticism: The Medieval Phase* (New York, 1952), p. 166, where, in a discussion of the fifteenth-century *Court of Sapience,* the writer states that the conception of rhetoric in the poem is like Capella's. The portrait of Lady Rethoryke in the *Court* may be similar to Capella's portrait, but the rhetorical doctrine found in the poem is clearly medieval; and while the "chosyn spouse" of Dame Rethoryke is Tullius, her companions are Peter of Blois, Geoffrey of Vinsauf, Richard de Pophis, and John Balbus. Cf. Anonymous, *The Court of Sapience,* ed. Robert

century, is a landmark in the history of Western culture. Its inclusion of grammar, dialectic, and rhetoric—all three dealing with discourse—is naturally a matter of some significance. But the disciplines of Martianus are still the amoral precepts of the Roman schools, without an explicit theological or even philosophical base. The pagan Roman schools presuppose some political use for rhetoric (with grammar as a preparation for the orator and logic an occasionally useful tool), but in the last analysis even the highest ideal of Quintilian (*vir bonus dicendi peritus*) is not enough for the leaders of the new Christian world taking shape in the fourth and fifth centuries. The very taint of Rome may well have been enough to bring disdain upon the things of Roman education, but Christians before the time of Martianus were already alive to problems raised by the pagan arts of discourse. Each of the three disciplines drew attack.

Arnobius, converted in his old age, tries to show his new fervor toward the end of the third century by writing a book which among other things argues that even the old grammar is no longer necessary: "Or how is the truth of a statement diminished if an error is made in number or case, in preposition, particle, or conjunction?" [13] And dialectic is viewed as a snare set to trap the believer; Hilary of Poitiers (d. 367), for instance, states that truth is impervious to "marvelous devices of perverted ingenuity" in Arian logic.[14] Another fourth-century figure, Titian, rails against literature in general and rhetoric in particular: "You have invented rhetoric for injustice and calumny. . . . you have invented poetry to sing of battles, the loves of gods, of everything which corrupts the spirit." [15]

Looking back from the vantage point of centuries of Christian acceptance of the prescriptive tradition, it is perhaps difficult to contemplate the possibility of any other development. And yet a closer look at the fourth and fifth centuries reveals a major cultural debate within the Christian community. The attacks of Arnobius, Hilary, and Titian are not isolated remarks. Rather, they illustrate one side of a general discussion forced

---

Spindler (Leipzig, 1927), vv. 1891–1932. For a further discussion of *The Court,* see James J. Murphy, "Caxton's Two Choices," *Medievalia et Humanistica* NS 3 (1972), 241–55.

[13] Arnobius, *Adversus nationes* I.59, ed. Augustus Reifferscheid. Corpus scriptorum ecclesiasticorum latinorum (*CSEL*) IV (Vienna, 1875). Arnobius makes a watchword of a phrase of Saint Paul: "The wisdom of man is foolishness before God" (I Cor. 3:19).

[14] Hilarius, *De trinitate* vii.1, ed. J. P. Migne, *Patrologia Latina* 10, col. 199.

[15] Titian, *Oratio* 1–3, quoted in Gustave Combès, *Saint Augustine et la culture classique* (Paris, 1927), p. 88.

upon the Church by the necessity of providing a Christian framework for a society imbedded in a pagan world.

A more careful examination of this debate may reveal, then, that the *De nuptiis,* however significant, is not the most important work of the period. The *De doctrina christiana* of Saint Augustine (354–430), written between A.D. 396 and 426, merits close attention both because of its later influence and because of the position it plays in the cultural ferment of its times.[16]

The importance of Saint Augustine's *De doctrina christiana* to rhetorical history has long been recognized. Charles Sears Baldwin in 1928 asserted that the book "begins rhetoric anew" after centuries of sophistry.[17] Sister Therese Sullivan in 1930 applauded it for returning to the *doctrina sana* of Cicero as a base for Christian preaching.[18] Writers of the 1950's found in the work "a Christian theory of literature" [19] or a foundation of medieval preaching theory.[20] Its influence is clearly visible, being copied or quoted by such writers as Rabanus Maurus in the ninth century, Alain de Lille in the twelfth, Humbert of Romans in the thirteenth, and Robert of Basevorn in the fourteenth.[21]

Since Augustine's attitude toward the Second Sophistic is so clearly expressed,[22] there has been some tendency to regard his work as a mere attempt to rescue rhetoric from the taint of the sophistic. Indeed, his

---

[16] Portions of the following are reprinted with permission from *Quarterly Journal of Speech (QJS).* See James J. Murphy, "Saint Augustine and the Debate about a Christian Rhetoric," *QJS* 46 (1960), 400–10.

[17] Baldwin, *Medieval Rhetoric,* p. 51.

[18] S. Aurelii Augustini, *De doctrina christiana liber quartus,* trans. Sister Therese Sullivan, Catholic University Patristic Studies, Vol. 23 (Washington, D.C., 1930), p. 8.

[19] Bernard Huppé, *Doctrine and Poetry: Augustine's Influence on Old English Poetry* (New York, 1959), p. v.

[20] Dorothea Roth, *Die mittelalterliche Predigttheorie und das Manuale Curatorum des Johann Ulrich Surgant* (Basel, 1956).

[21] Rabanus Maurus, *De clericorum institutione,* ed. J. P. Migne, *Patrologia Latina (PL)* CVII, cols. 294–420; Alain de Lille, *Summa de arte praedicatoria (PL)* CCX, cols. 110–98; Humbert of Romans, *Treatise on Preaching,* trans. Dominican Students (Westminster, Md., 1951); Robert de Basevorn, *Forma praedicandi,* in Th.-M. Charland, *Artes praedicandi,* Publications de l'Institut d'études médiévales d'Ottawa (Paris and Ottawa, 1936); now reprinted. This last work has been translated by Leopold Krul, O.S.B., in James J. Murphy, *Three Medieval Rhetorical Arts* (Berkeley and Los Angeles, 1971), pp. 114–215.

[22] E.g., *De doctrina christiana* IV.v.7 and IV.xxviii.61, *De catechizandis rudibus* 9, and *Confessions* IX.ii.4. Note also the careful discussion of the utility of pleasure in *De doctrina* IV.xxv.55–58, where pleasure is made to serve the purpose of persuasion.

firm espousal of a union between meaning and expression marks his rejection of the sophistic, as Baldwin has pointed out.

Nevertheless the attention paid to his later influence and to his rejection of the Second Sophistic may obscure Saint Augustine's role in providing an answer to a Christian dilemma of the fourth century. A brief survey of the Church's position during this period may illustrate the nature of the dilemma, and Augustine's solution of it.

The Emperor Theodosius formally abolished paganism by decree in A.D. 392, sixty-seven years after the first ecumenical council at Nicea had outlined twenty canons for the government of the Church. With the exception of lapses like that under Julian, the fourth century is marked by such gains that the converter of Saint Augustine, Ambrose of Milan (340–397), can refer to his age as Christian times, *christiana tempora*. As one twentieth-century historian has said:

> Until the peace of the Church, the hostility of the public powers had weighed heavily on the life of the Christian community. On the day when it had definitely been removed, we see the Church coming forth, as it were, from a long winter, consolidating and developing her ranks, discussing her hierarchal powers, defining the lines of her doctrines, drawing up the formulae of her faith, regulating her worship, surrounding the holy places with public marks of veneration, providing holy retreats for souls desirous of perfection, and giving to the Latin half of the Church a more faithful version of the Bible. All these fruits are the harvest of the fourth century.[23]

The century is therefore one for many decisions. During the lifetime of Augustine, for instance, the Church faced the heresies of Manichaeans, Pelagians, Donatists, and Priscillianists. But besides the problems of defining Christian doctrines in reply to heretical attacks, the Christian community faced another problem of almost equal magnitude—the problem of defining the intellectual base for a culture which would permit the Church to perform its duty of leading men to salvation. It was a matter of the greatest moment, for upon its success depended the training of future apologists to defend doctrine against heresy, the formation of future poets to carry the Word of God to the people through literature, and the very education of the people themselves.

The basic issue was whether the Church should adopt completely the contemporary culture which Rome had taken over from Greece. The fate of rhetoric, as a part of Greco-Roman culture, was involved not only in

---

[23] M. Paul Lejay, quoted in Pierre DeLabriolle, *The History and Literature of Christianity from Tertullian to Boethius* (New York, 1924), p. 231.

the debate over the larger issue but in more limited controversies about its own merits. Indeed, the contrast between *Verbum* (Word of God) and *verbum* (word of man) was stressed from the very beginnings of the Church,[24] long before the broader cultural issue was joined.

Ecclesiastical leaders of the fourth century continued the debate begun more than a century earlier when the conversion of many writers, poets, orators, and public figures had at last given the Church a corps of well-equipped apologists. From the first, some individuals reacted violently to their former pagan culture; Lactantius speaks of pagan literature as "sweets which contain poison";[25] Cyprian, who had been a teacher of rhetoric at Carthage when he was converted, renounced profane letters completely and for the rest of his life never again quoted a pagan poet, rhetorician, or orator.[26] Justin warns against undue veneration of words (i.e., literature) which are not from God.[27] Clement of Alexandria notes that this revulsion against the old order was not limited to the intellectual classes: "The common herd fear Greek philosophy just as children fear goblins." [28]

Tertullian directs an attack against Greek philosophy and other pagan writings. "Where is there any likeness between the Christian and philosophers?" he asks in his defense of pure faith, and terms philosophers "patriarchs of heresy." In a famous passage in his *De praescriptione haereticorum,* he outlines the problem as many of his contemporaries saw it:

> What indeed has Athens to do with Jerusalem? What concord is there between the Academy and the Church? What between heretics and Christians? [29]

---

[24] Saint Paul, for instance, said: "And my speech and my preaching was not in the persuasive words of human wisdom, but in the showing of the Spirit and the Power" (I Cor. 2:3-4). (Here and later, the Douay-Rheims translation has been used for Biblical passages.) Virtually every early Christian writer stresses the difference between *sapientia huius saeculi* and *sapientia spiritualis.* John of Antioch, for instance, declares in his sermon *On the Heroes of the Faith*: "But the Cross wrought persuasion by means of unlearned men; yea, it persuaded even the whole world."

[25] Lactantius, *Divinae institutiones*, CSEL XIX, 400.4.

[26] Gustave Bardy, "L'Église et l'enseignement pendant les trois premiers siècles," *Revue des sciences religieuses,* XII (1932), 1-28. The awful magnitude of this renunciation may easily be overlooked by a modern reader who does not recall the pervasiveness of teaching through *imitatio* in Roman schools.

[27] *Ibid.*

[28] Labriolle, *History of Christianity*, p. 17.

[29] For a survey of Tertullian's views on these related subjects, see Gerard L. Ellspermann, *The Attitude of the Early Christian Latin Writers Toward Pagan Literature and Learning,* Catholic University of America Patristic Studies, Vol. 82 (Washington, D.C., 1949), pp. 23-42.

The necessity for education posed a dilemma to Tertullian, who realizes that it would be foolhardy to espouse ignorance, but who declares also that it is not licit for Christians to teach literature because it deals with false gods.

Similar remarks may be found in the writings of Justin Martyr, Clement of Alexandria, Synesius of Cyrene, and the historian Socrates. As Labriolle observes: "There emerges, therefore, the fact that we can state that during the first centuries of the Empire there is hardly a Christian writer in whose case there does not intrude or show itself more or less sincerely, more or less diplomatically, a hostility in some regard to the different forms of pagan learning." [30] Nor was this antipathy short-lived, for even while Augustine was engaged in writing the first books of *De doctrina,* the fourth Council of Carthage (398) forbade bishops to read *libros gentilium* unless necessary.

From the Christian point of view there were many reasons for such attitudes. Even if Rome had not been the Rome of persecutions with their awful memories, its literature was studded with manlike gods parading what some Christian writers saw as a virtual gallery of sins. What is the use of decrees against sin, Augustine asks, when the adulteries of even Jove are portrayed by actors, painters, writers, reciters, and singers? [31] Referring in scathing tones to the fables of the pagan gods, Minucius Felix points out that men even study how to improve on such tales, "especially in the works of the poets, who have had such fatal influence in injuring the cause of truth." He adds that Plato was wise to exclude Homer from his ideal republic, for giving the gods a place in the affairs of men, and then asks: "Why should I mention Mars and Venus caught in adultery, or Jupiter's passion for Ganymedes, hallowed in Heaven? Such stories are but precedents and sanctions for men's vices." [32] At best, secular education would divert the attention of the devout toward earthly things rather than spiritual matters. And since heretics often used logical argument to attack the doctrines of the Church, there was a responding tendency to fall back upon fideism (for example, Tertullian's *regula fidei*) and decry reasoning itself.

Another aspect of Greco-Roman culture that drew fire was the rhetori-

---

[30] Labriolle, *History of Christianity,* p. 18.
[31] Augustine, *Epistle* XCI, in *Select Letters of Saint Augustine,* trans. James H. Baxter, Loeb Classical Library (London, 1930), p. 159.
[32] Minucius Felix, *Octavius,* trans. Gerald H. Rendall, Loeb Classical Library (London, 1953), xxiv.2.7.

cal excess of the Second Sophistic. Moreover, the rhetorician Fronto had been an early opponent of the Church, Minucius Felix notes. Although attacks upon rhetoric had an ancient tradition, the Christian writer often saw in the rhetoric of his time the taint of a worldly, pagan culture which could lead men away from God. It is in this light that Gregory Nazianzen reproves Gregory of Nyssa for abandoning Christian books to take up the trade of rhetorician.[33] Augustine himself was, in a certain sense, converted from rhetoric to Christianity.[34]

"Our writers do not waste their time in polishing periods," declares Basil of Caesarea, "we prefer clarity of expression to mere euphony." And again, "The school of God does not recognize the laws of the encomium," nor does it deal in "sophistic vanities." [35]

The most extreme Christian viewpoint seems to be that rhetorical forms might be dispensed with altogether. In the middle of the third century Cyprian states, "In courts of law, in public meetings, in political discussions, a full eloquence may be the pride of vocal ambition, but in speaking of the Lord God, a pure simplicity of expression (*vocis pura sinceritas non eloquentiae*) which is convincing depends upon the substance of the argument rather than upon the forcefulness of eloquences." [36] Both Ambrose and Jerome decry rhetorical excesses in their fellow preachers, calling for adherence to Paul's advice. The Donatist Cresconius goes so far as to quote Proverbs 10:19 ("In the multitude of words there shall not want sin"). Although he drew a sharp reply from Augustine,[37] the incident may serve to illustrate the temper of the times.

This is not to say, of course, that opinion was completely aligned in one direction. A true debate took place among the leaders of the Church as official persecution faded into the background and the exigencies of ecclesiastical organization forced new decisions upon its leaders. Some of the most vehement opponents of pagan literature admitted the necessity of education, while others (like Saint Cyprian) resolutely turned their backs upon the old order.

---

[33] A. S. Pease, "The Attitude of Jerome Toward Pagan Literature," *Transactions and Proceedings of the American Philological Association,* 50 (1919), 150–67.

[34] See esp. Maurice Testard, *Saint Augustin et Cicéron,* 2 vols., Études Augustiniennes (Paris, 1958), I, 137–42.

[35] Cf. James Campbell, *The Influence of the Second Sophistic on the Style of the Sermons of Saint Basil the Great,* Catholic University of America Patristic Studies, Vol. 2 (Washington, D.C., 1922).

[36] Cyprian, *Ad Donatum* 2, quoted in Ellspermann, *Early Christian Latin Writers,* p. 51.

[37] Augustine, *Contra Cresconium grammaticum et Donatistam libri IIII (CSEL LII),* I.i.2.

Saint Basil and Saint Ambrose, for example, illustrate the mixed feelings of the Fathers of the Church as they face a cultural dilemma. Basil
recommends gathering roses among the thorns of pagan literature on
one hand, and yet warns students not to abandon themselves to their
pagan professors' ideas as they would their course to a navigator of a
ship.[38] He also feels constrained to defend the Bible even though it is
written in "a barbarian tongue." This points up still another cultural
problem for the educated ecclesiastic of the fourth century, the apparently
unliterary style of the Scriptures. Basil concludes that "although their
style is unlearned, their content is true and they are the thoughts to which
we give utterance." [39]

Ambrose also has mixed feelings. Although he emphasizes the distinction between *sapientia saeculi* and *sapientia spiritualis,* he recognizes the
need for training of preachers and condemns not rhetoric itself but its
sophistic abuses. His defense of the Scriptures is based on his approval of
their simple style in contrast with the "showy" language of philosophers
and orators. Saint Luke, he asserts, excels in *stilus historicus*. Nevertheless, he admits that rhetorical ornament may sometimes be useful and,
indeed, sometimes occurs in the Scriptures themselves.[40]

His ingenious solution to the problem of pagan philosophy, on the
other hand, was one which did not win general approval. The pagans,
Ambrose states, originally found their wisdom in Scriptures; Plato went
to Egypt to "know the deeds of Moses, the oracles of the law, the worthy
sayings of the prophets." [41] As Laistner observes, this was an attractive
way out of a dilemma—one which even attracted Augustine for a time—
but one which could not long withstand inquiry.[42] Ambrose was sufficiently impressed with Roman learning, however, that he modeled his
instruction book for priests upon Cicero's *De officiis*.[43] Hilary of Poitiers
condemns Arian verbal display, yet prays for a good style in his own ser-

---

[38] Gustave Combès, *Saint Augustin et la culture classique* (Paris, 1927), p. 97.
For a survey of Basil's reactions to pagan culture, cf. Sister Mary M. Fox, *The Life
and Times of Saint Basil the Great as Revealed in His Works,* Catholic University
of America Patristic Studies, Vol. 57 (Washington, D.C., 1939).

[39] Basil, *Epistle* CCCIX, quoted in Fox, p. 89.

[40] Ellspermann, *Early Christian Latin Writers,* pp. 120–23.

[41] *Ibid.*, p. 114. The idea was of course not original with Ambrose, having antecedents in pre-Christian Alexandrian thought. Cassiodorus repeated it for the later
middle ages.

[42] Max W. Laistner, "The Christian Attitude to Pagan Literature," *History* 20
(1935), 49–54.

[43] Ambrose, *De officiis ministrorum* (PL 16, cols. 23–184).

mons. Honor, he says, is given to the word of God by one who speaks with beauty of expression.

But Saint Jerome, contemporary and friend of Augustine, may perhaps illustrate best the inner conflict faced by many Christian leaders in the fourth century. In his famous letter of advice to the virgin Eustochium,[44] he warns:

> What communion hath light with darkness? What concord hath Christ with Belial? What has Horace to do with the Psalter, Vergil with the Gospels and Cicero with the Apostle [Paul]? . . . we ought not to drink the cup of Christ and the cup of devils at the same time.

Later in the same epistle he relates a dream which came to him after he had been wrestling with the question of whether a Christian could legitimately enjoy the Greek and Roman classics:

> Miserable man that I am! I was fasting and then I began to read Cicero; after many nights spent in watching, after many tears, which the remembrance of my faults of not so long ago drew forth from the depths of my heart, I took Plautus in my hands. If by chance, on recollecting my self, I started reading the Prophets, their unadorned style awoke in me feelings of revulsion. My eyes, blinded, no longer saw the light, and it was not on my eyes that I laid the blame, it was on heaven.
>
> While the old serpent thus misused me, a violent fever penetrated the marrow of my worn-out body toward the middle of Lent, and without any respite, in an incredible manner, it so consumed my poor members that I had scarcely any flesh on my bones. Already people were thinking of my funeral. My body felt quite frozen; a remnant of vital heat no longer palpitated save in the lukewarmness of my poor breast.
>
> Suddenly I felt myself ravished away in ecstacy and transported before the tribunal of the Judge. Such a dazzling light emanated from those present that, crouched on the ground, I dared not lift up my eyes. On being asked my profession, I replied, "I am a Christian." Whereupon He who presided, thundered: "Thou dost lie—thou are not a Christian, but a Ciceronian. Where thy treasure is, there is thy heart also."

Then Jerome relates that he swore an oath in his dream: "Lord, if it ever happens to me to possess or read profane books, I shall have denied Thee." From that moment the dreamer betook himself "to the reading of the divine books with as much passion as I had formerly given to reading the books of men." [45]

---

[44] Jerome, *Epistle XXII* (*CSEL* LIV), translated in Ellspermann, *Early Christian Latin Writers*, pp. 159–60.

[45] The translation follows that of Labriolle, *History of Christianity*, pp. 11–12.

Interpretations of this dream have been many and varied, and it is generally wise to refrain from taking too literally a work designed to point up a moral. Nevertheless, Pease points out, Jerome did refrain from using classical quotations in his works for about fifteen years following the time at which the dream is supposed to have occurred. The very fact that Jerome felt it necessary to reply to Rufinus in A.D. 402 may be another indication of the state of the times, and possibly of his contemporaries' views of his so-called oath.[46]

His basic dilemma reveals itself elsewhere. At one point he is concerned because heathen sources are used to attack the doctrine of resurrection of the body, and enjoins Christians to "lay aside the weapons of the heathens" in their replies; it is better to have a just unlearnedness than an evil wisdom.[47] In another place: "We do not wish for the field of rhetorical eloquence, nor the snares of dialecticians, nor do we seek the subtleties of Aristotle, but the very words of Scripture must be set down." [48] He refers often to his desire for a simple, clear style which will avoid pomp, and yet he was a student of the famous grammarian Donatus and in later life recommended Demosthenes and Cicero to his students as models.[49]

Jerome employs the figure of the "captive woman" at one point to illustrate his desire to take from the old what was useful for the new order. The figure occurs in Deuteronomy 21:10–13:

> If thou go to fight against thy enemies, and the Lord thy God deliver them to thy hand, and thou lead them away captives, and seest in the number of the captives a beautiful woman, and lovest her, and wilt have her to wife, thou shalt bring her into thy house: and she shall shave her hair, and pare her nails and shall put off the raiment, wherein she was taken: and shall remain in thy house, and mourn for her father and her mother one month: and after that thou shalt go unto her, and shalt sleep with her, and she shall be thy wife.[50]

---

[46] A. S. Pease, "The Attitude of Jerome Toward Pagan Literature," *Transactions of the American Philological Association* 50 (1919), 150–167. Rufinus had accused Jerome of teaching the classics and of having a monk copy Cicero.

[47] Ellspermann, *Early Christian Latin Writers*, p. 157.

[48] Jerome, *Liber contra Helvidium de perpetua virginitate Mariae,* xii, quoted in Sister M. Jamesetta Kelly, *Life and Times as Revealed in the Writings of St. Jerome Exclusive of His Letters,* Catholic University of America Patristic Studies, Vol. 52 (Washington, D.C., 1944), p. 59.

[49] Jerome, *Epistle LVIII (CSEL LIV),* quoted in Ellspermann, *Early Christian Latin Writers,* p. 147. Interestingly enough, Jerome also recommends Lysias and the Gracchi. The rest of the list (e.g., for poetry, Homer, Virgil, Menander, and Terence) is reminiscent of the typical Roman grammar school curriculum.

[50] Cf. *De doctrina* II.xl.60–xlii.63, where Augustine compares pagan learning to the gold and silver which the Israelites took away from Egypt in the Exodus.

The captive woman, of course, is secular wisdom, to be purged of its falsities and dangers. The metaphor clarifies the desire of Jerome, but does not specify what is to be sheared away and what is to be kept whole.

In the case at hand—the matter of the worth of rhetoric—his feelings are ambivalent. "Saint Jerome's attitude toward rhetoric," concludes Ellspermann, "cannot be summed up in one bald statement. In the texts considered there is indeed unfeigned favor of the rhetorical art, but there are also sentiments of mixed approval and disapproval, and even of evident disapproval." [51]

Even so, it might be argued at this point that the bulk of these Christian statements might be attributed to a reluctance to acknowledge publicly the worth of the Roman cultural heritage, while at the same time taking advantage of it. The Church Fathers were trained in Roman rhetorical schools, and many had actually taught rhetoric themselves. It might be expected that they would readily avail themselves of their training.

Nevertheless, two factors must be appreciated. The first is that the few citations offered above could be multiplied many times, the abundance of Christian comment offering clear indication that this issue was one of real concern up to and including the fourth century. [52]

A second point is that, despite the rhetorical training of the major ecclesiastical orators, the fourth century marks a high point of popularity for the simple "homily" style of preaching. Students of such preachers as Chrysostom and Basil have generally concluded that their sermons show less of the contemporary sophistic than might ordinarily be expected from men of their educational background. Coupled with the many utterances denouncing the sophistic, the comparative simplicity of the homilies might be seen as further indication of the dilemma of the times. [53] The reader's attention is directed, for example, to Chrysostom's

---

[51] Ellspermann, *Early Christian Latin Writers*, p. 167.

[52] For other discussions, see Laistner, *Christianity and Pagan Culture in the Later Roman Empire* (Ithaca, New York, 1951), pp. 49–73; Franz Maier, *Augustin und das antike Rom* (Stuttgart, 1955), esp. pp. 17–36 and 206–14; E. K. Rand, *Founders of the Middle Ages* (New York, 1957, reprint), pp. 1–134; Labriolle, *History of Christianity*, pp. 6–32, and Harald Hagendahl, *Latin Fathers and the Classics* (Goteborg, 1958).

[53] Thomas E. Ameringer, *The Stylistic Influence of the Second Sophistic on the Panegyrical Sermons of St. John Chrysostom*, Catholic University of America Patristic Studies, Vol. 6 (Washington, D.C., 1921); Sister M. Albania Burns, *St. John Chrysostom's Homilies on the Statues: A Study of Rhetorical Qualities and Form*, Patristic Studies, Vol. 22 (Washington, D.C., 1930); and Campbell, *Influence of Second Sophistic*. Sample homilies are printed in a number of anthologies, including those of Guy Lee, David Brewer, and Mabel Platz.

first homily on the Statues: the sermon has no proper beginning or end, and might satisfactorily be ended at any point without damaging the speaker's point; the use of figures is comparatively restrained, and there is virtually no repetition for emphasis.

Whatever the modern critic may decide about the intrinsic merit of the homily form of the fourth century, its very appearance in a highly sophisticated age might well argue a deliberate choice on the part of the preachers. It was an age, after all, when the same man who delivered the eulogy for the arch-sophist Prohaeresius can castigate a friend for forsaking Christian books for the rhetorician's trade.[54] It was an age in which former teachers of rhetoric—Jerome, Basil, and Augustine, among others—feel that they must decide whether their former profession deserves a place in the new order.

The resolution of this question was demanded at a critical period in the history of Western culture, for the barbarian erosion of the Roman Empire was already well under way. Alaric swept into Rome itself in 410, and Augustine's episcopal seat of Hippo was under Vandal siege as he lay on his deathbed in 430. The homogeneous Roman culture had already begun to suffer from the questionings of the new Christian element within it, and at the same time it faced annihilation from without. From the Christian point of view, it was an age of selection, a time to examine the *sapientia saeculi* to extract from a thousand-year-old heritage whatever would aid in the work of the Lord. The decisions made would influence Western culture for another thousand years.

The historian is often tempted into a feeling of inevitability about events, a feeling that since events took a certain turn they could have taken no other. But it has been noted that some of the most influential Christians were at least undecided about the role of rhetoric and indeed about Roman culture in many aspects. When it is recalled that Greco-Roman culture was largely transmitted to the early middle ages through the very narrow funnel of encyclopedists like Isidore and Cassiodorus, it might well be wondered what might have occurred if a spokesman as influential as Augustine had denied rhetoric a place in Christian culture.

It was perhaps inevitable that Augustine's opinion would have a strong influence on the future development of rhetoric—if for no other reason

---

[54] This was Gregory Nazianzen. For a revealing biography of the notorious Prohaeresius, perhaps the best single exemplar of the Second Sophistic, see Philostratus and Eunapius, *Lives of the Sophists,* trans. Wilmer C. Wright, Loeb Classical Library (London, 1922).

than his general influence in a number of fields. Moreover, the *De doctrina* provides one of the few basic statements of a Christian homiletic prior to the emergence of the highly formalized "thematic" or "university style" of sermon about the beginning of the thirteenth century.[55] In light of these factors, then, it would seem useful not only to identify Augustine's contribution to the debate but to determine his own assessment of the problems presented in it.

Augustine composed the four books of *De doctrina christiana*[56] between 396 and 426, the first three books being completed almost a quarter of a century before he decided to resume work on the volume by adding Book Four. His goal is a treatise giving the preacher both the substance and the form for sermons: "There are two things necessary to the treatment of the Scriptures: a way of discovering (*modus inveniendi*) those things which are to be understood, and a way of expressing to others (*modus proferendi*) what we have learned." [57]

The first three books deal with the *materia* of the sermons, that is, with the ways in which the words of Scripture may be understood. Book One deals with signs of realities, Book Two with words as conventional signs, and Book Three with the problem of ambiguity. Throughout the three books he is concerned with the uses of words, and points out that the preacher needs a knowledge of language to equip himself with the tools of understanding. Thus he treats both ambiguities growing out of words used literally, and ambiguities deriving from words used figuratively.

It is plain throughout that he intends the student of this subject to master the ordinary things taught in the schools. Although Augustine se-

---

[55] Yet this is an extremely complex history. To the best of this writer's knowledge, the texts of the sermons preached at the University of Paris during the academic year 1230–31 were until very recently regarded as the earliest evidence of a new sermon mode. See the Latin texts in M. M. Davy, *Les Sermons universitaires parisiens de 1230–31: contribution à l'histoire de la prédication médiévale* (Paris, 1931). The earliest printed manuals of the new style are of an even later date. Cf. Ray C. Petry, *No Uncertain Sound: Sermons that Shaped the Pulpit Tradition* (Philadelphia, 1948), pp. 4 ff., and Th.-M. Charland, *Artes praedicandi*. But see below, Chapter Six, pp. 310–26.

[56] *S. Aurelii Augustini de doctrina christiana libros quatuor,* ed. H. J. Vogels, Florilegium Patristicum, Fasc. XXIV (Bonn, 1930). For an easily available translation, see *Saint Augustine on Christian Doctrine,* trans. D. W. Robertson, Library of Liberal Arts, No. 80 (New York, 1958). The fourth book is edited with translation and commentary by Sister Therese Sullivan in the Catholic University of America Patristic Studies, Vol. 23. Unless otherwise noted, translations are from Sullivan. Charles S. Baldwin supplies a brief summary of Book Four in his *Medieval Rhetoric and Poetic,* chap. ii.

[57] *De doctrina* I.i.1, repeated at IV. i.1.

verely limits the number of things which a student might profitably learn from the profane culture, he is equally quick to point out that the young should pursue "those human institutions helpful to social intercourse in the necessary pursuits of life." [58]

But it is the fourth book which contains an outspoken plea for the use of *eloquentia* in Christian oratory, making the volume what has been called "the first manual of Christian rhetoric." His basic principle is presented in an *a fortiori* argument early in the book:

> But a man who has merely an empty flow of eloquence ought the more to be guarded against as he is the more pleasing to those in his audience in those matters which have no expedience, and, as his audience hears him speak with fluency, it judges likewise that he speaks with truth. This view, indeed, did not escape even those who considered rhetorical training necessary, for they hold that wisdom without eloquence is of small avail to a country, but that eloquence without wisdom is generally a great hindrance, and never a help. If, therefore, those who have given us the rules of oratory, in the very books in which they have treated this subject are forced through the urgency of truth to make this confession, ignorant as they are of the true, the supernal wisdom which comes down from the Father of Lights, how much more so are we, the ministers and children of this wisdom, under obligation to hold no other opinion? [59]

In an effort to combat the point of view represented by such writers as Cyprian and Cresconius, Augustine restates the point in another place:

> For since through the art of rhetoric both truth and falsehood are pleaded, who would be so bold as to say that against falsehood, truth as regards its own defenders ought to stand unarmed, so that, forsooth, those who attempt to plead false causes know from the beginning how to make their audience well-disposed, attentive, and docile . . . so that the one, moving and impelling the minds of the audience to error by the force of its oratory, now strikes them with terror, now saddens them, now enlivens them, now ardently arouses them; but the other, in the cause of truth, is sluggish and cold and falls asleep! Who is so foolish to be thus wise? [60]

Augustine takes his stand, therefore, in the great debate about the use to which the new Christian society is to put the *sapientia mundi*. He de-

---

[58] *Ibid.*, II.xxxix.58. In the same book he refers to "rules of eloquence" as desirable (II.xxxvi.54). For a detailed description of Augustine's doctrine of "Sign" see Chapter VI, pp. 287–92.

[59] *Ibid.*, IV.v.8. The reference to "wisdom without eloquence" is to the opening passage of Cicero's *De inventione*.

[60] *De doctrina* IV.2.3. The *officia* of the *exordium* of a speech in Roman rhetorical theory was to render the audience "attentive, docile, and well-disposed." Cf. *Rhetorica ad Herennium* I.iv.6, and *De inventione* I.xv.20.

clares that the art of eloquence should be put into active service, and not rejected out of hand because it is tainted with paganism. To those who might reply that rhetoric is the tool of the wicked, he responds with the Aristotelian dictum that the art can serve both truth and falsehood:

> Since, therefore, there has been placed equally at our disposal the power of eloquence, which is so efficacious in pleading either for the erroneous cause or the right, why is it not zealously acquired by the good, so as to do service for the truth? [61]

Still another concern to ecclesiastical authorities in the fourth century is the matter of examples to be used in literary education. Almost every writer from Paul to Jerome had warned of the dangers inherent in sending Christians to schools which taught through *imitatio* of Homer and Virgil. Augustine's proposal is to look at the Scriptures themselves for examples of style, and most of Book Four is taken up with an attempt to demonstrate how this be done. Indeed, Augustine postulates the existence of a new type of eloquence, "fitting for men most worthy of the highest authority and clearly inspired by God. Our authors speak with an eloquence of this kind, nor does any other kind become them." [62] Since Ciceronian rhetorical doctrine insists that three levels of style be employed, however, Augustine is careful to show that all three levels exist in the Scripture.

It should be noted also that Augustine is unwilling to relegate rhetoric to the position of a mere preliminary study. Instead he wishes to use it in the active service of the ministry. Jerome and Ambrose are apparently somewhat willing to accord rhetoric a place in primary education, but are unsure of the extent to which it should be allowed later. Augustine insists upon the homilectic utility of the subject, whether its study follows *praecepta* or *imitatio*. [63]

---

[61] *De doctrina* IV.iii.3. He expresses the same idea elsewhere: *De doctrina* II.xxvi. 54, and *Contra Cresconium* I.i.2.

[62] *De doctrina* IV.vi.9. Sections xviii through xxvi of Book Four provide numerous examples, especially from Saint Paul. It is interesting to note that when St. Bede wishes to provide examples of the tropes and schemes of the Latin grammarian Donatus, he is able to produce 122 Scriptural passages to illustrate them. Bede, *Liber de schematibus et tropis,* in Halm, *Rhetores,* pp. 607-18.

[63] Roman rhetorical training followed three major methods: the teaching of rules (*praecepta*), the imitation of models (*imitatio*), and free composition on a theme (*declamatio*). Augustine in Book Four seems to favor *imitatio* as a method of acquiring eloquence (cf. IV.iii.4-5), but it must be noted that earlier he recommends study of *praecepta* (II.xxxix.58). For a comment on Augustine's possible larger uneasiness later about his recommendation, cf. Laistner, "The Christian Attitude to Pagan Literature," *History,* 20 (1935), 51.

Moreover, it will be recalled, he begins the *De doctrina* with the state-ment that the *modus inveniendi,* or means of discovery, is distinct from the *modus proferendi,* or means of expression. The structure of the whole work therefore becomes an argument for the necessity of studying the means of expression with the same care given to the study of the Scrip-tures themselves. The disproportionate amount of space accorded each of the two subjects is due to the fact that he is in a sense creating the first, while merely arguing for the use of the second. It is for this reason that he begins Book Four with the statement that he does not intend to sup-ply the rules of rhetoric which can be found elsewhere. Book Four is in-tended as a *ratio eloquentiae Christianae.*

It would therefore seem to be misleading to imply, as do some students, that Augustine intends the fourth book of *De doctrina* as a mere rejection of the Second Sophistic. Certainly his attitude toward the "empty elo-quence" of the sophistic is clear enough, but it is shared, after all, by every one of his Christian contemporaries and thus needs little proof.

Instead it might be more nearly accurate to say that Augustine sees the dangers of an opposite rhetorical heresy. The sin of the sophist is that he denies the necessity of subject matter and believes that *forma* alone is desirable. An opposite vice, one to which historians of rhetoric have never given a name, depends upon the belief that the man possessed of truth will *ipso facto* be able to communicate the truth to others.[64] It depends upon *materia* alone. Its chief proponent in ancient times was the young Plato, and it would seem fair to label it the "Platonic rhetorical heresy" just as we apply the term "sophistry" to its opposite theory. This is not to say that the ecclesiastical writers of the fourth century looked to the *Gorgias* and *Protagoras*[65] for a theory of communication, but rather that their reactions to the pagan culture of Rome led many of them to take up a somewhat similar attitude toward the rhetoric which is a part of that culture. Augustine apparently recognized a danger in this aspect of the cultural debate of his times, and used the *De doctrina* to urge a union of both matter and form in Christian preaching.

Only if one views the book as part of the great debate of the fourth century, therefore, does its historical importance emerge clearly. The reader is struck by the author's insistence upon the folly of abandoning

---

[64] John of Salisbury in the twelfth century is found fighting the same battle. See his attack on the "Cornificians" in *Metalogicon* I.7.

[65] These two Platonic dialogues include attacks on rhetoric itself—a view con-siderably different from that of the *Phaedrus,* which has been called a virtual out-line for Aristotle's *Rhetoric.*

a useful tool to the enemy, for this is a book written, not for enemies, but for other Christians. It can only be his own fellows in the Church whom he describes as "dull and cold" (*lenti frigidique*) when they try to speak as if the mere utterance of God's word would by itself move the minds of men. Augustine appreciates the role of God's grace in preaching, but he warns that the preacher must do his work well, too.[66]

Thus the *De doctrina* is doubly important. First of all, it rebuts those who would deprive the Church of a useful tool in the work of winning souls, and thereby establishes a clearly prescriptive tradition for the Christian community. And second, it lays down certain principles of discourse which are important in their own right.[67] Augustine's ideas are of such complexity, and his general tone so significant, that a concise summary of the work might be altogether misleading; for this reason it may be useful at this point to provide a close analysis of the fourth book.

As can be seen from even a cursory examination of Book Four, Augus-

---

[66] *De doctrina* IV.xv and IV.xxx. For an analysis of an earlier treatment of the same problem, see Jean Danielou, *Origen*, trans. Walter Mitchell (New York, 1955), pp. 102 ff. It should not be surprising to find Augustine impatient with his fellow Christians for a lack of willingness to take up their tools, especially after his own lifelong argument against a whole galaxy of heresies. As one profound student of Augustine has put it, "We cannot too strongly insist on the importance of this climate of controversy, and on the effects it had on the bearings of his influence." Henri Marrou, *Saint Augustine and His Influence Through the Ages,* trans. Patrick Hepburn-Scott (New York and London, 1957), p. 52.

[67] Augustine may have composed another rhetorical work which, however, is of little influence. Halm, *Rhetores,* pp. 138–51, prints a brief compendium which may be the one Augustine began as part of an encyclopedic work based on Varro's *Disciplina*; the attribution is doubtful, and the original may be lost.

Considerable study has gone into Augustine's rhetorical theories as found in *De doctrina christiana* and in scattered references in such other works as *De catechizandis rudibus, De magistro, De ordine,* and *Confessiones.* In addition to the items already cited, see: Baldwin, *Medieval Rhetoric,* Chap. II; Clarke, *Rhetoric at Rome,* pp. 152 ff.; James Burnett Eskridge, *The Influence of Cicero upon Augustine in the Development of His Oratorical Theory for the Training of the Ecclesiastical Orator* (Chicago, 1912); Roy J. DeFerrari, "Saint Augustine's Method of Composing and Delivering Sermons," *American Journal of Philology* 43 (1922), 97–123, 193–211; F. Jansen, "St. Augustin et la rhétorique," *Nouvelle revue théologique* (1930), 280–97; Henri Marrou, *Saint Augustin et la fin de la culture antique* (Paris, 1938); Marie Comeau, *La rhétorique de Saint Augustin d'après le Tractatus in Joannem* (Paris, 1930); N. Jubany, "San Agustin y la formacion oratorica cristiana: Estudio comparado del libro IV *De doctrina christiana* y del *De catechizandis rudibus,*" *Analecta sacra Terraconensia* 15 (1942), 9–22; W. H. Semple, "Augustinus Rhetor: A Study, from the *Confessions,* of St. Augustine's Secular Career in Education," *Journal of Ecclesiastical History* I (1950), 135–50; José Oroz, "El 'De doctrina christiana' o la retórica cristiana," *Estudios clasicos* 3 (1956), 452–59; Jesús G. Jiménez, "La Retórica de San Agustin y su patrimonio clásico," *La Ciudad de Dios* 178 (1955), 11–32. For an older but still valuable appraisal of the relation between Augustine's theory and his preaching, see Edwin C. Dargan, *A History of Preaching,* 2 vols. (New York, 1905; now reprinted), I, 103 ff.

tine recommends Cicero as the preceptor of the Christian orator. But he makes the recommendation with the positive ideal of spiritual conversion in mind. Hence it is not enough to seek to move men's minds, merely for the sake of power; instead, the power to move (*flectere*) is to be used to lead men to Truth (*verum*).[68] The ultimate end of discourse for the Christian must be different from that of the pagan Cicero.

In another important aspect, the matter of *imitatio*, Augustine strikes out into new ground. Whereas the traditional Roman curriculum proposes imitation for the beginning student, and a gradual increase in his inventive powers throughout his schooling, Augustine suggests that even mature men may identify the precepts of discourse by reading and hearing good examples of discourse.[69] This is an easily misinterpreted argument.[70] Augustine's intention is that certain principles of linguistic conduct should be understood; in light of the several passages discussed earlier, it is difficult to believe that he has any intention other than to plead for Christian understanding of and use of the human faculties. It is plain to him that nonartistic discourse may cripple the Christian effort —why else concern himself with his lax fellows, those he terms *lenti frigidique?* So he urges them to learn the *modus proferendi,* the "means of expression." His only divergence from the Ciceronian tradition is that he proposes an additional means of learning. In other words, he sees a place for formal preceptive training, and a place as well for a self-training process based upon the examination of models and samples. It must be remembered, in respect to this second mode, that the end result of its employment is similar to that gained from formal teaching: a knowledge of precepts. Thus he talks about "learning eloquence," and goes on to explain that education and practice will be of little avail to one who does not have a natural talent for eloquence.[71] This, of course, is a reference to the Isocratean trilogy of talent, education, and practice which is a keystone of Ciceronian tradition. Augustine points out quite rightly that eloquent men are eloquent because they possess eloquence, not because they consciously apply rules while they are speaking. The rules are to be found

---

[68] See, for example, IV.v.7: "So that he may be of benefit to his hearers."

[69] IV.iii.4-5.

[70] It may be somewhat extreme to say, for instance, that it is a break with tradition, a proposal for eloquence without rhetoric, as does Marrou in *Saint Augustin,* p. 516. It might be described more accurately as a proposal for adapting old rhetorical practice to a new situation. In assessing his intentions, moreover, it might be remembered that he had not taught rhetoric for forty years (after 386), and it is perhaps only fair to imagine that a scholar of 72 had long since learned to despise rules.

[71] IV.iii.4-5: ". . . learn eloquence by reading and hearing."

in what they say, however, because these precepts inhere in whatever is well spoken or well written.[72]

There is little in this which would disturb Cicero or Quintilian. Indeed, the difference is rather one of emphasis, because Roman rhetoric encourages the observation of good models at all levels of age and experience. What Augustine suggests, then, is an expansion of critical appreciation as a means of learning. He, like Cicero and Quintilian, is undisturbed by the realization that precepts learned in this manner may be unconscious. In all his ruminations on the several styles found in Scripture, for instance, he does not propose that the Christian should necessarily speak like Paul, or like Ambrose and Cyprian; instead he urges that the styles themselves be learned, using these examples as a sort of inductive collection of data. Hence he reminds the reader:

> And in these two [Ambrose and Cyprian] whom from among all writers I chose to quote, and in many writings of other ecclesiastical authors who say good things and say them well, that is, as the matter demands, acutely, ornately, or ardently, these three styles may be found. And students may learn them by assiduous reading, or hearing, accompanied by practice.[73]

Viewed in this light Augustine's *De doctrina* IV, with its plea for a gifted, broadly trained Christian maker of discourse, might well take its place with some other great pleas—with the *Phaedrus* of Plato, admonishing the rhetor to know men's souls; with the *Rhetoric* of Aristotle, demanding philosophical and psychological breadth in the speaker; with the *De oratore* of the mature Cicero, calling for a liberal education in the civil speaker; and, too, with the twelfth and final book of Quintilian's *Institutio oratoria,* pleading cautiously for the *vir bonus dicendi peritus* as a civil savior of a decaying society. There is a tragic commonality among all these, in that each demands perhaps more than is usually found in a single man, and surely more than is usually found at large among great numbers of men. And each is followed in time by a Dark Age: Plato and Aristotle, by the Alexandrians; Cicero, by the Principate; Quintilian, by the depths of the Second Sophistic. Augustine, finishing the *De doctrina christiana* at the age of seventy-two, finds barbarians assaulting Africa, and he dies four years later with the Vandals at the very walls of his episcopal seat of Hippo.

It was therefore left to other, later men, without the rich personal heritage of Augustine's own familiarity with Roman education, to carry on

---

[72] *Ibid.* "They fulfilled them [the precepts] because they were eloquent; they did not apply them to make themselves eloquent."

[73] IV.xxi.50.

the tradition he espoused. It is not surprising that in some ways this continuation developed in ways different from what he would have preferred, even though his name was used as a seal of approval. Although
the broad message of Augustine was powerfully influential, some of his
grand concepts of artistic fullness failed to make an impression in later
ages.

The fifth century thus began the history of the medieval arts of discourse by presenting two alternative methods of teaching, both, however,
founded on the preceptive principle. Once the major choice is made—of
accepting the preceptive principle—there remains only the question of
method: the compendia of Martianus or the *doctrina sana* of Augustine? [74]

The encyclopedic tradition was continued in the following century by
Flavius Cassiodorus Senator (480–575), who abandoned public life at the
age of sixty to devote the remaining years of his long life to promoting
monastic studies. Shortly after his retirement he completed a massive
work, *Institutiones divinarum et saecularium litterarum,*[75] designed to
give his monks a complete guide to divine and secular studies. Apparently
because of the dual nature of the work, its two parts were often copied
separately and may be said to be responsible for two separate streams of
influence. The second part, dealing with the liberal arts, influenced such
writers as Isidore, Alcuin, and Rabanus Maurus.[76] Cassiodorus turns to

---

[74] Implicit in this dichotomy, of course, is the medieval controversy of *ars versus
auctores.*

[75] *Cassiodori senatoris institutiones divinarum et saecularium litterarum,* ed.
R. A. B. Mynors (Oxford, 1937; now reprinted). Text also in Migne, *PL* LXX,
cols. 1150–1213. The section on rhetoric (II.ii.1–16) is edited by Halm, *Rhetores,*
pp. 493–504. A translation of the whole work is found in Cassiodorus Senator, *An
Introduction to Divine and Human Readings,* trans. Leslie W. Jones, Columbia
University Records of Civilization, Vol. XL (New York, 1946). Cassiodorus also
wrote a Biblical commentary notable for its analysis of the tropes and figures in
the Scriptural text: *In psalterium expositio,* Migne, *PL* LXX, cols. 9–1054. The
medieval influence of this work remains to be studied.

[76] For a discussion of its influence, see Migne, *PL,* pp. 47–58. The *Institutiones*
are mentioned in library catalogues throughout the middle ages. About the year
1405, Thomas Merke, one-time Bishop of Carlisle, cited Cassiodorus as one of his
sources in *De moderno dictamine* (British Museum MS. Royal 12 B xvii, fol. 19).
The *Variae,* the epistles of Cassiodorus, also contributed to his influence; a popular
medieval description of the kinds of writing runs as follows: Dictaminum . . .
tria sunt genera a veteribus diffinita, prosaicum, ut Cassiodori, metricum, ut Virgilii,
et rithmicum, ut Primatis. The definition is that of Thomas of Capua, quoted by
Ch. Thurot, "Notices et extraits de divers manuscrits pour servir à l'histoire des
doctrines grammaticales au moyen âge," *Notices et extraits* 22 (1868), 418. Both
Isidore of Seville and Rabanus Maurus borrow heavily from the *Institutiones.* The
*Variae* are edited by Theo. Mommsen, *Monumenta Germaniae historica, auctorum
antiquissimorum* XII (Berlin, 1894), pp. 3–385.

Donatus for most of his grammatical material. Fortunatianus is the admitted source of his rhetorical doctrine, although he also refers to Victorinus and uses Cicero for some examples. Boethius, Aristotle, and Victorinus furnish the bulk of the dialectical theory, with some debts as well to Martianus.

The first half of the work is devoted to "divine letters," those things necessary for the monks to know in their religious capacities—descriptions of various parts of the Bible, cautions in reading Scripture, notes on various Fathers, and so forth, set forth in thirty-three chapters (corresponding to the age of Christ). Toward the end of the first part, however, Cassiodorus includes a chapter entitled *De schematibus ac disciplinibus,* which outlines the rationale for the second part:

> We have decided that you ought to be cautioned about this matter too: since we can understand much in sacred literature as well as in the most learned interpreters through figures of speech, much through definitions, much through the art of grammar, much through the art of rhetoric, much through dialectics, much through the science of arithmetic, much through music, much through the science of geometry, much through astronomy, it is not unprofitable in the book which follows to touch briefly upon the elements of instruction laid down by secular teachers, that is, upon the arts and sciences, together with their divisions, in order that those who have acquired knowledge of this sort may have a brief review and those who perhaps have been unable to read widely may learn something from the compendious discussion. Beyond any doubt knowledge of these matters, as it seemed to our Fathers, is useful and not to be avoided, since one finds this knowledge diffused everywhere in sacred literature, as it were in the origin of universal and perfect wisdom. When these matters have been restored to sacred literature and taught in connection with it, our capacity for understanding will be helped in every way.[77]

Here, then, is the first Christian encyclopedist[78] setting the tone for himself, for Isidore, for Rabanus Maurus, and for a host of others after them. He employs the methodology of Martianus, but with the *ratio* of Augustine.

At the beginning of the second part he refers to the "seven pillars of wisdom" in relation to the seven liberal arts which constitute the matter for the second half of the work, and points out that in Exodus the Lord told Moses, "Thou shalt make seven lamps, and shalt set them to give

---

[77] *Institutiones* I.xxi.1, trans. Jones, p. 127.

[78] There does not yet exist an adequate history of the encyclopedic movement during the middle ages. For some suggestive remarks in this direction, see Michel de Bonard, "Encyclopédies médiévales sur la connaissance de la nature et du monde au moyen âge," *Revue des questions historiques* 112 (1930), 258–304.

light against it." [79] Moreover, Cassiodorus states, the number seven in the days of a week is being repeated over and over as time goes on, even to the end of the world. So even if there had been doubts earlier about cutting Varro's nine *disciplinae* down to seven,[80] there were to be none after Cassiodorus.

He speaks of grammar as the source and foundation of liberal studies (*origo et fundamentum liberalium litterarum*), but his treatment is very short, and he refers the reader to Donatus for further information.[81] Rhetoric, which he defines as the science of speaking well on civil questions,[82] receives a more elaborate treatment, including several diagrams to explain the relationships of such things as *constitutio qualitatis*. But it is still a brief and highly definitional discussion which does little more than identify the five parts of rhetoric, and then gives its entire attention to matters of *inventio*. There is no treatment of disposition, style, memory, or delivery. His only references to memory and delivery refer the monk to the third book of Fortunatianus, and he concludes with an injunction to practice oral delivery by reading the divine law aloud and chanting the psalms.[83]

Dialectic, a study which "separates the true from the false," [84] occupies twice the space of the chapter on rhetoric. Cassiodorus begins with distinctions between speculative and practical philosophy and then goes on to discuss Porphyry, Aristotle, the forms of syllogisms, and finally *loci* or commonplaces. He notes that topics furnish arguments alike to poets, orators, dialecticians ("philosophers"), and lawyers, but that when they deal with general questions they pertain to the dialecticians alone. At this point he tells his reader that the "threshhold of the sciences" is at hand,

---

[79] *Institutiones* I. Praef. 1. The citations are from Proverbs 9:1 and Exodus 25:37, respectively.

[80] Capella had dropped two of Varro's nine—medicine and architecture. Isidore includes a section on medicine (*Etymologia* IV) and a brief discussion of architecture (*Etymologia* XIX.vii–xix), but both these subjects fall, for Isidore, under the category of professional subjects and are not made a part of the preparatory arts.

[81] *Institutiones* II.i.1–3. His definition is: Grammatica vero est peritia pulchre loquendi ex poetis illustribus auctoribusque collecta. In the Mynors edition the section occupies only 76 printed lines. In some manuscripts, incidentally, there is also reference to a book on grammar compiled by Cassiodorus himself. Cf. Jones, p. 148, n. 25.

[82] *Ibid.*, II.ii.1: Bene dicendi scientia in civilibus quaestionibus. Earlier (II. Praef. 1) Cassiodorus warns the reader that the second half of his book is jammed with material: Sunt enim etymologiis densa et definitionum plena tractatibus.

[83] *Ibid.*, II.ii.16.

[84] *Ibid.*, II. Praef. 4: Vera sequestrat a falsis. There is no further definition.

and he launches into a treatment of the four theoretical sciences dealing with number: arithmetic, music, geometry, and astronomy.

Taken all in all, then, the sections which Cassiodorus devotes to the three arts of discourse form only a very small part of the whole work. In turn, the treatment of each one is sketchy and highly schematized. Modern students sometimes tend to overlook the extremely limited amount of classical lore contained in such encyclopedic expositions. Cassiodorus' brevity is explained partly by the fact that he wrote the book as an introduction to the studies which he expected his monks to pursue in his well-equipped library at Vivarium.[85] In any case, the early Christian encyclopedists provided only a very narrow funnel for the transmission of the ancient doctrines into the middle ages.

Still another series of works in the sixth century was to have a profound influence upon the later history of rhetoric. It will be recalled that among the works of Cicero is the *Topica,* ostensibly modeled upon the *Topica* of Aristotle but in fact developed as a discussion of rhetorical *loci* useful in argument. Cicero's work is clearly not intended as a work on logic. In attempting the stupendous task of rendering into Latin the whole of Plato and Aristotle in order to show their essential agreement, the enormously influential Anicius Manlius Severinus Boethius (c. 480–524) translated a number of Aristotle's logical works.[86] In addition, he wrote a commentary on the *Topica* of Cicero.[87]

---

[85] At the end of the section on dialectic (II.iii.18), for instance, he points out that he has for the convenience of the monks gathered into one codex the translations of Victorinus, Boethius, Apuleius of Madaura, and Cicero. In another place (II.iii.20) he states that he prefers the monks to have his own book at once rather than wait to secure a copy of Capella.

[86] Namely, *De interpretatione, Prior analytica, Posterior analytica, De sophisticis elenchis,* and *Topica.* All are in Migne, *PL,* Vol. 64. In addition see Boethius, *In Periermenias,* ed. C. Meiser (Leipzig, 1880). For a list of extant manuscripts of his Aristotelian works, see George Lacombe, *Aristoteles Latinus,* 2 vols. (Bruges and Paris, 1953), II, 1306–07, 1357, etc. A general discussion of his influence may be found in Howard Rollin Patch, *The Tradition of Boethius* (Oxford, 1935). For more specific remarks about his linguistic and logical influence, see Friedrich Solmsen, "Boethius and the History of the Organon," *AJP* 65 (1944), 67–74; Martin Grabmann, *Die Geschichte der scholastischen Methode,* 2 vols. (Freiburg im Bresgau, 1909–1911), I, 148–77; Grabmann refers to Boethius as "der letzte Römer der erste Scholastiker." See also Friedrich Ueberweg, *Grundriss der Geschichte der Philosophie* (Berlin, 1928), pp. 135–38; Maurice de Wulf, *The History of Medieval Philosophy,* trans. E. C. Messenger, 6th edition (London, 1952), I, 111–19; Hastings Rashdall, *Universities of Europe in the Middle Ages,* 3 vols., new edition, ed. F. M. Powicke and A. B. Emden (Oxford, 1936), I, 35–38, 350, 361, 440–41; III, 153, 480–82. As the numerous medieval citations of Boethius demonstrate, he ranked as an authority comparable to Aristotle and Augustine.

[87] *In topica ciceronis commentariorum libri sex,* Migne, PL 64, cols. 1039–1174. John of Salisbury refers to his commentary in *Metalogicon* II.3.

Boethius included a discussion of Cicero and Themistius in his own treatise on the topics or *loci*. This latter work, which bears the title *De differentiis topicis*, was known throughout the middle ages as *Topica Boetii*.[88] It was enormously popular; surviving today in 170 manuscripts, it appears in medieval library catalogues and university statutes throughout Europe.[89] Boethius' translations of the Aristotelian *Organon* were for centuries the staple texts for the so-called "old logic," being supplanted only by the new translations of the thirteenth century. As a consequence the *Topica Boetii* came to play an important role in the dissemination of logico-rhetorical lore.

The work is divided into four books. The first book begins with the statement that logic (*ratio disserendi*) is divided into two parts: one, for criticism and judging, is called analysis; the second, however, is for discovery (*inveniendi*), and its means are called "topics" or "loci." [90] Boethius points out at once that both Aristotle and Cicero have written on the subject. After defining such terms as proposition, question, and conclusion, he goes on to define a topic or locus as "the seat of an argument," that is, a place from which an argument may be drawn.[91] He says that there are four human activities in which topics may be used—*in dialectico, oratore, philosopho*, and *sophista*—and two kinds of arguments—probable and necessary. He does, however, stress the fundamental premise which underlies both Aristotle's and Cicero's treatment of the *loci*: namely, that

---

[88] *De differentiis topicis libri quatuor,* in Migne, *PL* 64, cols. 1173–1216.

[89] In 1431, for instance, Book Four is named in an Oxford University statute as one of the books to satisfy the reading requirement for rhetoric. See James J. Murphy, "The Earliest Teaching of Rhetoric at Oxford," *Speech Monographs* 27 (1960), 345–47. It is mentioned at Paris in 1215 (Rashdall, *Universities* I, 441 n. 3), and again at Oxford in 1268 and 1409 (*ibid.*, 153). William of Shyrewood cites it in his *Introductiones in logicam* (Martin Grabmann, "Ungedruckte lateinischen Kommentäre zur Aristotelischen Topic aus dem 13 Jahrhundert," *Mittelalter Geistleben,* 3 vols. [Munich, 1926–56], III, 142–57). The first three books of the *Topica Boetii* held a place in the logical curriculum throughout the middle ages, either with or without the fourth book.

[90] Omnis ratio disserendi, quam logicen Peripatetici veteres appelavere, in duas distribuitur partes, unam inveniendi, alter judicandi. Migne, *PL* 64, col. 1173.

[91] *Ibid.,* col. 1174: Propositio est oratio verum falsumve significans, ut si quis dicat coelum esse volubile, haec et enuntiatio et proloquium nuncupatur. Quaestio est in dubitationem ambiguitatemque adducta propositio, ut si quis quaeret an coelum sit volubile. Conclusio est argumentis approbata propositionis, ut si quis coelum ab aliis rebus probet esse volubile. . . . Locus autem sedes est argumenti, vel id unde ad propositam questionem conveniens trahitur argumentum.

the topics are merely means to discover (*invenire*) ideas for use in discourse, and are not to be taken simply as verbatim models.[92]

In Book Three Boethius notes that Themistius, a fourth-century teacher in Constantinople, had also written on the topics, and he proceeds to compare Themistius' treatment with that of Cicero.[93] Although he outlines their differences, often in tabular form, in general he sees a substantial similarity between them.

Book Four of the *Topica Boetii* is the most important. It begins with a statement that rhetoric and dialectic are both similar and dissimilar. The major difference, according to Boethius, is that dialectic deals with *thesis* —"question without circumstances"—while rhetoric deals with *hypothesis* —"question attended by many circumstances."[94] This is of course the principle by which Cicero distinguishes rhetoric from "philosophy" in his *De inventione,*[95] except that Boethius applies the distinction to logic alone and not to the whole of philosophy. It is an interesting narrowing of emphasis.

To Boethius, author of the *Philosophiae consolatio,* the term "philosophy" can no longer have the rather generalized and fuzzy connotation it had for Cicero. But more important, Boethius seems to realize that it is no longer a question of distinguishing rhetoric from philosophy, but of distinguishing the various arts of discourse from each other. He defines "logic" as *ratio disserendi,* a term which could on the face of things be applied equally to grammar, to dialectic, or to rhetoric. Boethius appears to be a logician seeking, almost uneasily, a place for rhetoric in a dialectically oriented world. The whole tone of Book Four is that of a teacher whose students must learn something of an adjacent subject without making an intensive study of it. Therefore he *accounts for* rhetoric—explains its nature, illustrates its parts, defines its major terms—but gives few details of the rhetorical doctrine itself. Thus the fourth book of *Topica Boetiis* becomes part commentary, part criticism, part exposition.

---

[92] Boethius says, for instance, that their purpose is to point the way to a multitude of arguments: Topicorum intentio est verisimilium argumentorum copiam demonstrare. *Ibid.,* col. 1182. Both Aristotle (*Rhetorica* II) and Cicero (*Topica*) make the same point.

[93] Themistius (c. 310–?390) was a prominent Eastern teacher best known for his paraphrases of Aristotle. There is no reason to believe that Boethius was familiar with Aristotle's *Rhetorica.*

[94] Dialectica facultas igitur thesim tantum considerat. Thesis vero est sine circumstantiis quaestio. Rhetorica vero hypothesibus, id est de quaestionibus circumstantiarum multitudine inclusis, tractat et disserit. Migne, *PL* 64, col. 1205.

[95] *De inventione* I. . . . For Boethius the circumstances are included under the following headings: quis, quid, ubi, quando, cur, quomodo, et quibus adminiculis.

This general tone might be illustrated further by the other differences which he sees between rhetoric and dialectic:

1. Dialectic proceeds by interrogation and response; rhetoric has uninterrupted discourse.
2. Dialectic employs perfect syllogisms; rhetoric is satisfied with brief enthymemes.
3. Dialectic seeks to dislodge an adversary; rhetoric tries to move a judge or judges.

The difference between thesis and hypothesis he identifies as a difference in matter; that between interrogation and uninterrupted discourse, as a difference in practice; that between syllogism and enthymeme, as another difference in practice; and, finally, the difference in objects, as a difference in ends.

Boethius follows this section with a statement that it is really rather difficult to decide what is proper to the *ars rhetorica*.[96] After stating that he does not intend to follow the ancient traditions of treatment, he declares it his plan to discuss rhetoric under ten categories: its genus, species, material, parts, instruments, parts of instruments, work and duty of authors, end, questions, and topics. But the bulk of what follows is devoted to the doctrine of *constitutiones* or *status*, with only brief definitions of the three *genera*, the five parts of rhetoric, and the Ciceronian six parts of a speech (which Boethius calls "instruments").[97] There is no discussion of style, memory, or delivery. The work ends with the observation that rhetoric can sometimes employ dialectical *loci* because it can apply the general to the specific case; dialectic, on the other hand, is "prior" to circumstance and operates in a generic way and so cannot benefit as easily from the use of circumstances. This is true, he says, because although the genus can be identified through species, knowledge of genus does not necessarily lead to the species.[98] Finally he recommends to the reader his own commentary on Cicero's *Topica*.

---

[96] Quanta enim sibimet ars rhetorica cognatione jungatur, non facile considerari potest, vixque est etiam ut auditu animadverti queat, nedum sit facile repertu. Migne, *PL* 64, col. 1207. This passage is also the beginning of an abbreviated version of the rhetorical section of Book Four, printed separately by Migne as *Speculatione de rhetorica cognatione*, (PL 64, cols. 1217-22). This little treatise apparently had a separate medieval history of its own, surviving today in at least three manuscripts, including Oxford Merton College MS. 309, fols. 118–121, where it is untitled and listed as anonymous. For other manuscripts, see *Aristoteles Latinus*, Nos. 472 and 1897.

[97] Of the ten columns in Migne devoted to the rhetorical compendium (cols. 1207–16), the section on *status* occupies seven columns: 1209–15.

[98] *Ibid.*, col. 1216.

THE AGE OF TRANSITION

Clearly, then, Boethius is concerned with rhetoric only as it impinges upon the field of dialectic. It is equally clear that his total concern with rhetoric as an art is with its function of *inventio*. Viewed against the framework of Boethius' other Aristotelian interests, it is a perfectly understandable position. In terms of later intellectual developments, however, it was to have a markedly negative effect on rhetorical studies in European universities, where the "old logic" was taught to young students as a preliminary discipline.

An Eastern contemporary of Boethius, the grammarian Priscian (fl. c. 510), composed four books for his students at Constantinople which were to have a wide popularity throughout medieval Europe. Just as Donatus became a hallmark for elementary grammatical education, so Priscian became synonymous with advanced instruction. His most popular work is his *Institutiones grammaticae*,[99] which survives in more than one thousand manuscripts. Priscian's own introduction provides a clear idea of its contents:

> The first book contains material concerning the voice and its aspects; concerning letters (alphabet): what is a letter, with respect to its kinds and species, and their singular forces.
>
> The second book concerns the syllable: what it is, how many letters it consists of, how many classes there are, and the characteristics of a singular syllable; concerning diction: what it is, how it differs from the syllable; concerning speeches: what is a speech, how many its parts and the appropriateness of each; concerning nouns (names): what is a noun, what its characteristics, how many are the species of particular nouns, how many titles, additions, and how many the additions.
>
> The third book concerns comparatives and superlatives and their different extremities: from their position and for what reason they are formed; concerning diminutives (parts): how many their species, from what declension of nouns, and in what manner they are formed.
>
> The fourth book concerns denominatives, verbals, participles, and adverbs: how many their kinds and in what way they come into being.
>
> The fifth book concerns the kinds of distinctions of single terminations; concerning numbers; concerning figures and their structures; concerning cases.
>
> The sixth book concerns the nominative case through single endings of all nouns, as much in speaking as in arranging them for speaking through

---

[99] Text in Henry Keil (ed.), *Grammatici latini* (Leipzig, 1853–80), II and III, 1–377. The first sixteen books, treating syntax, are known in medieval lists as his *ars maior;* Books XVII and XVIII, called *De constructionibus,* are often known as his *ars minor.*

order; concerning the original nature of the last as well as the penult syllables.

The seventh book concerns certain cases, the singular as well as the plural.

The eighth, verb and its characteristics.

The ninth, the general rules of all conjugations.

The tenth, the preterite (past absolute).

The eleventh, the participle.

The twelfth and thirteenth, pronouns.

The fourteenth, prepositions.

The fifteenth, adverbs and interjections.

The sixteenth, conjunctions.

The seventeenth and eighteenth, constructions.

Priscian wrote three other works which display an interest that immediately marks him off from his predecessor Donatus. There is a short collection of examples, *De metris fabularum Terentii,* which employs excerpts from classical Greek and Roman writers to illustrate various meters,[100] but of even greater interest is his *De praeexercitamentis rhetoricis,* which is nothing more than a translation into Latin of part of Hermogenes' *Progymnasmata.*[101] Finally, we have his protracted *Partitiones duodecim versuum Aeneides principalium,* a close grammatical analysis of the first twelve lines of Virgil's epic.[102] Priscian also wrote on numbers, weights, and measures, besides composing a treatise on accent.

Priscian is by no means the originator of the cult of Virgil, but it is apparent that his various works contributed to the esteem in which that poet was held by later generations. Moreover, by translating Hermogenes into Latin he made the *declamatio* of the Second Sophistic available to those who had no Greek; by writing on Terence and Plautus he continued the ancient literary tradition of the *grammaticus;* by using Virgil, Terence, Plautus, and others as examples he transmitted bits of classical verse directly into the middle ages; and by his approbation he helped crown Virgil the king of Roman poets.[103]

In the century following Priscian appeared the last major encyclopedic

---

[100] *Ibid.,* II, 418–29.

[101] *Ibid.,* III, 430–40; also in Halm, *Rhetores,* 551–60.

[102] *Ibid.,* III, 459–515. This is perhaps the most revealing work of all, since it demonstrates the extremely detailed manner in which the grammarian handled the texts used in teaching. Each word is literally taken apart, its case, number, or gender justified, and its relation to other words carefully explained. Priscian's discussion of the 74 words requires 56 printed pages in the Keil edition.

[103] See Domenico P. Comparetti, *Virgilio nel medio evo,* 2 vols., new edition by Giorgio Pasquali (Florence, 1937).

work of the Patristic period, the *Origines* of Bishop Isidore of Seville (c. 570–636).[104] The *Origines* supplies a whole system of education, containing both Christian and secular material. Cassiodorus had split the divine and secular studies into separate disciplines, with the aim of employing the secular to aid the divine. Isidore took the further step of attempting to lay out a whole range of studies in which the seven so-called "liberal arts" would *precede* divine studies. Thus the first three books comprise a curriculum which might be considered useful for all the clergy, whereas the remaining seventeen add miscellaneous information more useful to certain professions. If this is a correct interpretation of his plan, the use of grammar, rhetoric, and dialectic—the *trivium,* or "three ways to learning"—at the beginning of the series is a foreshadowing of the plan which was to become the standard in medieval universities. The Roman educational system had stressed grammar and rhetoric in the preparatory curriculum, but naturally had not intended them as avenues to theology, so that Isidore's program is a definite departure from the pagan system.[105]

Isidore's treatment of the arts of discourse is no more original than that of Martianus or Cassiodorus; if anything, it is even more terse and laconic. But, like them, he is squarely in the Ciceronian rhetorical tradition. Probably his chief divergence from the Boethian point of view is his suggestion that there are more similarities between grammar and rhetoric than between logic and rhetoric: "Rhetoric is allied (*coniuncta*) to grammar," he says in one place,[106] while in another place he borrows from Cassiodorus the saying of Varro that rhetoric is like an open hand, and dialectic like a closed fist.[107] Thus he brings grammar and rhetoric together, and (like Cassiodorus) separates rhetoric explicitly from dialectic.

---

[104] Isidorus, *Etymologiarum sive originum libri XX,* ed. W. M. Lindsay, 2 vols. (Oxford, 1911; now reprinted). The text of the section on rhetoric is printed by Halm, *Rhetores,* pp. 505–22; there are brief summaries of this section in Baldwin, *Medieval Rhetoric and Poetic,* pp. 95–98, and in Ernest Brehaut, *An Encyclopedist of the Dark Ages: Isidore of Seville,* Columbia University Studies in History, Economics, and Public Law, Vol. XLVIII (New York, 1912), pp. 105–13. But the most recent important study is that of Jacques Fontaine, *Isidore de Séville et la culture classique dans l'Espagne wisigothique,* 2 vols. (Paris, 1959).

[105] Brehaut notes that the term "theology" is not actually used until the time of Abelard, although the structure of the curriculum seems clear. "It is evident that we have here, in embryo, as it were, the organization of the medieval university; law and medicine have only to be freed from their subordination to theology, and the medieval university in its complete form appears." Brehaut, *Isidore,* p. 88.

[106] *Etymologia,* II.i.2.

[107] *Ibid.,* II.xxiii.1—*Institutiones* II.iii.2.

Isidore's etymological habit soon won for the *Origines* the popular title of *Etymologia,* and medieval writers use either name in referring to the work. He begins the *Etymologia* with a single paragraph distinguishing between "art"—that which deals with the possible—and "discipline" or "science"—that which deals with truth.[108] Then he continues:

> There are seven disciplines of the liberal arts. First there is grammar, that is, the knowledge (*peritia*) of speaking. Second there is rhetoric, which on account of its luster and wealth of eloquence is deemed most useful and necessary in civil questions. The third discipline I call logic, or dialectic, which in the most exacting controversies distinguishes the true from the false.[109]

Following this he names four others: arithmetic, music, geometry, and astronomy.

He defines grammar as "the science of correctness in speaking, which is both the origin and the foundation of the liberal arts." [110] The material which follows is taken largely from Donatus, with some debts to Cassiodorus, and includes a brief section *De schematibus* (I.xxxvi) and another *De tropis* (I.xxxvii) derived from Donatus. He concludes Book One with a rapid discussion of historiography as a type of narrative composition.

Isidore's treatment of rhetoric is very brief, and indeed blends almost imperceptibly into his discussion of dialectic in the same second book. Cassiodorus is a major source, supplying in some cases verbatim excerpts.[111] Isidore pays very little attention to *inventio* as a separate part, except to note the three traditional types of causes, and the traditional concept of *status.* In respect to *dispositio,* however, he departs from the Ciceronian doctrines: "There are four parts of a discourse in the art of rhetoric: exordium, narration, argument, and conclusion." [112] This list

---

[108] For an early but useful survey of this rather tangled question, see J. Mariétan, *Problem de la classification des sciences d'Aristote à St. Thomas* (Paris, 1901); Fontaine, *Isidore,* does not comment on this passage.

[109] *Etymologia,* I.ii.1.

[110] Grammatica est scientia recte loquendi et origo et fundamentum liberalium litterarum. *Ibid.,* I.v.1. Cf. the broader, more classical definition of Rabanus Maurus, *De institutione clericorum,* ed. Aloysius Knopfler (Munich, 1899), III.18.

[111] For instance, the section on the difference between dialectic and rhetoric (the closed-fist analogy) is from Cassiodorus, as is the etymological definition of rhetoric itself (*Etymologia* II.i.1 — *Institutiones* II.ii.1). For a rather general discussion of sources for the rhetorical compendium, see Fontaine, *Isidore,* 187–337.

[112] Partes orationis in Rhetorica arte quattuor sunt, exordium, narratio, argumentatio, conclusio. *Etymologia* II.vii.1. This is the same number of parts as Aristotle named in *Rhetorica,* but Isidore names another set: introduction, statement, proof, epilogue. Fontaine, *Isidore* (I, 249–54) believes that Isidore's plan is derived,

omits two parts usually found in the Ciceronian theory: division and refutation. Isidore also includes the syllogism under rhetorical argumentation, although he points out that it is more useful for the dialectician; he declares that syllogisms may be either inductive or "ratiocinative." This latter category has two types: the enthymeme, an "imperfect syllogism," and the epicheireme, which is described as leading to a conclusion through a more remote set of syllogisms.[113] He uses Cicero to support this part of his exposition, although earlier he uses Virgil's *Aeneid* to illustrate the types of causes.

At this point Isidore inserts a paragraph on law, followed by brief paragraphs on *sententiae, catesceva et anasceva, prosopopoeia, ethopopoeia,* and the difference between general and special questions. Then (II.xvi.1) he begins a discussion of style, which runs to the end of the section of rhetoric. The major part is devoted to figures of words and thoughts derived from Donatus, although there are occasional references and examples from various rhetorical sources like *Rhetorica ad Herennium* and Quintilian. While Virgil and Cicero are the major exemplars, there are also illustrations taken from Scripture. Isidore's treatment of *figurae* nevertheless is somewhat diffuse and is not clearly organized.[114] There is no mention of the other two traditional parts of rhetoric—memory and delivery.

His exposition of dialectic follows the plan and thought of Cassiodorus very closely: definition, relation to rhetoric, logic as a branch of philosophy, comments on Porphyry, Aristotle, and Victorinus, and finally the syllogism with its topics. Isidore does add a final paragraph on "opposition" which is not in Cassiodorus.[115]

After these discussions of the arts of discourse, he turns to the four numerical disciplines of what was later to be termed the *quadrivium:* arithmetic, geometry, music, astronomy. Then he takes up medicine, law, time, Holy Scripture, and other subjects.[116]

---

through Sulpicius Victor, from Cicero's *Partitiones oratoriae.* But the matter, like several others in Isidore's theory of communication, is difficult to determine. For a discussion of "Ambiguité et timidité d'Isidore rheteur," cf. Fontaine, I, 332–34 and 316–19.

[113] Sequitur epichirema, descendens de ratiocinatione latior et executior rhetoricis syllogismis, latitudine distans et productione sermonis a dialecticis syllogismis, propter quod rhetoribus datur. *Etymologia* II.ix.16.

[114] See Fontaine, *Isidore,* I, 295–319.

[115] *Ibid.,* II, 593–645. For a comment on the significance of the addition, see especially II, 640–44.

[116] Some modern students feel that Isidore's paragraph on law, which he includes in the section on rhetoric (II.x.1–6), may have influenced the medieval coupling of

The *Etymologia* of Isidore of Seville, then, provides some exposition, however brief, of the ancient arts of grammar, rhetoric, and dialectic, set within the now-familiar pattern of the "seven liberal arts." The medieval reader could learn from Isidore the rudiments of the grammar of Donatus, together with the lore of *figurae,* which he would find included both under grammar and under rhetoric. In the sections on rhetoric and dialectic he would find coupled the names of Cicero and Aristotle, at least in respect to the *loci* or "topics" useful to both rhetoric and grammar. If the reader knew the *De inventione* of Cicero, however, he might wonder at the four-part division of a speech in Isidore's theory, and if he knew the *Rhetorica ad Herennium* he might wonder even further at the mélange of figures in Isidore. The reader would find no mention of memory or of oral delivery, and if he turned to Cassiodorus or Boethius to check this detail, he would find the absence confirmed by their works.

But the *Etymologia* is for two reasons a landmark in the transition from ancient to medieval thought in respect to the arts of discourse. First of all, it preserves a body of ancient lore. It is matched in this respect by the *Institutiones* of Cassiodorus and the *De nuptiis* of Martianus, but it was far more popular in the middle ages than either of these works, and might therefore be said to have exerted a greater and more widespread influence.[117] Second, it preserves the ancient theories in a work which makes the seven liberal arts the preliminaries to further studies in both profane and divine subjects. This is not true even of Cassiodorus, and it certainly cannot be said of Martianus or Boethius.

Nevertheless the work displays by its contradictions and confusions the sorry state of learning in Spain during the lifetime of Isidore. Like other encyclopedists he was trying merely to salvage what he could from the ancient heritage. The Dark Ages had begun, and the Mediterranean world soon ceased to be the intellectual center of Europe. It is not surprising, then, that the next treatise of interest should come from an English rather than a continental hand.

If the *Liber de schematibus et tropis*[118] of Saint Bede (673–735) is re-

---

law and rhetoric in the universities. But Cicero's own *De inventione* is so strongly legalistic in tone (and his *De legibus* so well known) that Isidore's influence in this connection must have been negligible. Moreover, *Etymologia* V.A. is devoted wholly to law, with virtually no reference to rhetoric.

[117] For a brief remark about the influence of Isidore, see Fontaine, *Isidore,* II, 885–88.

[118] Text in Halm, *Rhetores,* pp. 607–18. See J. P. Elder, "Did Remigius of Auxerre Comment on Bede's *De schematibus et de tropis?*" *Medieval Studies* 9

garded as a rhetorical work, it is the first written in England and the first ever written by an Englishman.[119] Bede defines and exemplifies 17 *schemata* and a total of 28 *tropi,* using 122 Scriptural passages for his examples. At first glance this would seem to be a typical collection of rhetorical figures of the type made familiar by Aquila Romanus and Rutilius Lupus in the third century.[120] But a closer inspection reveals that Bede's schemes and tropes come directly from Donatus, *Barbarismus* (i.e., *Ars maior* III). In no case is any figure given a definition that would distinguish it from that of Donatus, even in those very few cases in which Bede does not present a verbatim repetition of Donatus' definition. It is scarcely necessary, therefore, to suppose that Bede drew on the rhetoricians in compiling the list. The *De schematibus* is apparently intended as a work on grammar.

This view is strengthened by an examination of another major work of Bede, his *De arte metrica.*[121] This is a work in twenty-five short sections dealing entirely with the language or linguistic forms of poetic expression. There is no treatment of invention, and virtually no discussion of arrangement of parts of a poem. A good idea of the work's general nature may be gained from the fact that of the twenty-five sections, nine are devoted to specific types of meters, seven to syllables, and two to metaplasms.[122]

The next to last section, however, points the way to what was becoming an increasingly important part of Latin poetics—the theory of *rithmus.*

---

(1947), 141–50. A translation is now available: Gussie H. Tanenhaus, "Bede's *De schematibus et tropis:* A Translation," *QJS* 48 (1962), 237–53. Miss Tanenhaus points out that Bede copies his definition of *zeugma* from Cassiodorus and is close to Isidore on *epanaphora* but that the general Donatic inspiration of Bede's terminology is otherwise quite clear.

[119] Atkins, for instance, cannot decide its proper sphere, terming it variously "metrical," "literary," and "rhetorical." J. W. H. Atkins, *English Literary Criticism: The Medieval Phase* (New York, 1943), pp. 47 ff.

[120] Cf. Halm, *Rhetores,* pp. 22–37 and 38–47.

[121] Text in Keil, *Grammatici,* VII, 227–60. Considerable interest has been shown recently in this work. For a survey of Bede's career and writings, see M. L. W. Laistner, *The Intellectual Heritage of the Early Middle Ages* (Ithaca, N.Y., 1957), pp. 93–149. On the *De arte metrica,* see Robert Palmer, "Bede as a Textbook Writer: A Study of His *De arte metrica,*" *Speculum* 34 (1959), 573–84; Robert Davies, "Bede's Early Reading," *Speculum* 8 (1933), 179–95; and Bronislas Gladysz, "Eléments classiques et post-classiques de l'oeuvre de Bède *De arte metrica,*" *Eos* 34 (1933), 319–43.

[122] Synalipha, episynalipha, diaresis. *De arte metrica* xiii–xiv. Donatus defines these three as types of metaplasm: transformatio quedam recti solutique sermonis in alteram speciem metri ornatusve causa. *Ars maior* III; text in Keil, *Grammatici,* V, 367–402.

Since this passage represents the earliest postclassical statement in this tradition, it is worth noting briefly:

> It appears that rhythmus is similar to metric, for it is a composition with modulation of words, without metrical measure, but arranged by the number of syllables to please the ears, as are the songs of vernacular poets. And thus rhythmus can be without meter, although meter cannot be without rhythm; which is why it is said, metrum is measure with modulation, rhythmus is modulation without measure.[123]

This is an early manifestation of a tendency which during the middle ages saw the creation of a whole separate grammatical discipline to deal with *rithmus*. Indeed, the typical medieval statement about the kinds of writing was that it was divided into three types: *prosaicum, metricum, rithmicum*. This medieval invention was put to use chiefly in composing hymns and in writing formal letters which employed the highly stylized form of prose which came to be called the *cursus*.[124] And, of course, *rithmus* found its earliest expression, as Bede indicates, in the composition of Latin poetry of the eighth century, a characteristic it was to retain until the thirteenth.[125]

Bede's section on *rithmus,* nevertheless, is the only part of the work which can fairly be termed a major innovation over his predecessors. Bede is an able synthesizer, bringing together a number of grammatical authors to provide his material, but he is after all still a synthesizer.[126]

It is apparent both from their structure and from Bede's own words that the two works, *De schematibus* and *De arte metrica,* are to be viewed as complementary to each other. At the end of *De arte metrica* he announces his intention of publishing a sequel: "te solerter instruerem, cui etiam de figuris vel modis locutionum, quae a Grecis schemata vel tropi

---

[123] Videtur autem rhythmus metris esse consimilis, quae est verborum modulata compositio, non metrica ratione, sed numero syllabarum ad iudicium aurium examinata, ut sunt carmina vulgarium poetarum. Et quidem rhythmus per se sine metro esse potest, metrum vero sine rhythmo esse non potest, quod liquidius ita definitur: metrum est ratio cum modulatione, rhythmus modulatio sine ratione. *De arte metrica* xxiv. Keil, *Grammatici,* VII, 258.

[124] See the texts printed by Giovanni Mari (ed.), *Il trattati medievali di ritmica latina* (Milan, 1899). For a convenient summary of the doctrine of *cursus,* see Noel Denholm-Young, "The Cursus in England," in *Collected Papers on Medieval Subjects* (Oxford, 1946), pp. 26–55.

[125] See, in connection with Bede, Charles Sears Baldwin, *Medieval Rhetoric and Poetic* (New York, 1928), pp. 107–12; Gladysz, "Eléments classiques," pp. 342–43.

[126] Cf. Palmer, "Bede as Textbook Writer," where Bede's collation of sources for his section *de littera* is carefully analyzed. It is apparent also that Bede expects the reader to be familiar with the grammatical lore, for there is no prologue or other explanation.

dicuntur, parvum subicere libellum non incongruum duxi." [127] In other
words, Bede seems to feel that a discussion of schemes and tropes would
follow rather naturally from what he has already done. A glance at the
structure of De arte metrica, in comparison to the structure of Donatus'
Ars maior III, may reveal what he had in mind.

| De arte metrica of Bede | | Ars maior III of Donatus | |
|---|---|---|---|
| capitulum | | | |
| i | letters | I | vices of diction: letters and sylla- |
| ii–viii | syllables | | bles (including doctrine of per- |
| xiii–xiv | metaplasms: synalipha, | | mitted fault) |
| | episynalipha, diaresis | II | metaplasms |
| xv–xvi | poetic license | | |
| ix, x, xii, xvii–xxiii | various meters | III | schemes |
| xxiv | rithmus | IV | tropes |
| xxv | three types of poetry | | |

Thus it is clear that Bede's De arte metrica represents a distillation of
the standard grammatical lore on that particular subject, abstracted from
its usual surroundings in an ars grammatica and broken into two separate parts.

As for the significance of the two works of Bede, three items might be
noted. First of all, the appearance of the works at this period demonstrates
the presence of a viable grammatical tradition in Anglo-Saxon England,
which is further evidenced by such later authors as Aelfric and Byhrtferth.[128] There is no evidence of a rhetorical tradition. Second, Bede's use
of Scriptural passages as examples in his De schematibus continues a
practice encouraged by Augustine and taken up in part by Isidore, who
mixes classical and Scriptural examples in his treatment of figures.[129]
Third, and perhaps the most important in view of the later history of the

---

[127] De arte metrica xxv.

[128] There is of course no native English rhetorical treatise before the Conquest,
and the prevalence of the Donatist tradition is evidenced not only by such obvious
items as Aelfric's Grammar but also by the inclusion of the Donatist schemae in the
Anglo-Saxon Manual (A.D. 1011) of Byhrtferth. See James J. Murphy, "The
Rhetorical Lore of the Boceras in Byhrtferth's Manual," in Philological Essays:
Studies in Old and Middle English Language and Literature in Honour of Herbert Dean Meritt, ed. James L. Rosier (The Hague, 1970), pp. 111–24. Byhrtferth
in fact refers to Bede in this connection: swa us heræfter gelustfullað to amearkianne
on þissum æfterfyligendum wexbredum, þe se arwurða Beda gesette.

[129] Augustine, as we have seen, devotes a large portion of the fourth book of
his De doctrina christiana to the task of demonstrating that Scriptures contain
adequate examples of all three styles described by ancient rhetoricians.

arts of discourse, Bede tends to regard *metricum* as a separate subject worthy of separate study. Here is one of the seeds of the medieval attitude toward discourse.

It is of course easy to apply hindsight to history, and to see in some past event the germinal forces which lead to still other events. But in the case of ancient grammar, which attempted to enclose under one discipline virtually every possible manifestation of language, it was inevitable that fragmentation should take place. Bede's two treatises represent just such a fragmentation. By taking *metricum* out of the *corpus grammaticae* he is following in the footsteps of Horace (and Aristotle before him, for that matter), and by separating the schemes and tropes from the parent body of grammar, he is furthering their separate study by isolating them from the *ars recte loquendi*. It is but one step from Bede to Marbodus (d. 1125), whose *De ornamentis verborum*[130] created the medieval habit of writing separate handbooks on tropes and figures.

If Bede cannot be termed the first English rhetorician, perhaps the palm could be given to Alcuin (c. 735–804), author of *Disputatio de rhetorica et de virtutibus*,[131] composed about A.D. 794 at the request of the Emperor Charlemagne. The dialogue between Alcuin and Charles is thoroughly Ciceronian. Invention is based upon *De inventione,* and the other four parts of rhetoric are taken from the doctrines of *De oratore* and *Orator* as Alcuin received them through the compendium of Julius Victor.[132] The book purports to be a discussion between Charles and Albinus Magister (Alcuin) in which the king-student asks questions of his teacher. Charles seems to press for the basic definitions of terms in each area, so that it is necessary for the master Alcuin to list the components of a law case, for instance, before showing how the doctrine of *status* can be used. Most of Charles's questions deal with politico-legal aspects of rhetoric, enabling Alcuin to cover the usual material of a compendium by describing the three issues, the three types of speaking, and the like.

Toward the end of the dialogue, however, Charles asks Alcuin to describe the four virtues which are the foundation of all others:

> Nevertheless, O master, before I can permit you to throw down your pen, you should explain to me the names and purposes of these four virtues

---

130 Marbodus, *De ornamentis verborum,* ed. Migne, *PL* 171, cols. 1687–92.

131 Text in Halm, *Rhetores,* pp. 523–50. Text and translation in *The Rhetoric of Alcuin and Charlemagne,* ed. and trans. Wilbur S. Howell (Princeton, 1941), pp. 66–155. References will be to the Howell translation.

132 For a detailed discussion of Alcuin's sources, see *ibid.,* pp. 22–33.

which you have called the roots of other virtues. A while ago we agreed that it is necessary for a speaker to have regular practice in speaking [*sermonis studium*]. Now if we ought to have practice of this kind, what subject is better than that of the superiority of the virtues, each one of which has the power to confer the greatest possible benefit upon our writing and reading? [133]

In reply, Alcuin identifies the virtues as prudence, justice, courage, and temperance. One modern student believes that this inclusion of virtues in a rhetorical treatise marks a departure from previous practice,[134] but a closer inspection of Charles's question reveals that this was not Alcuin's intention. First of all, Cicero's *De inventione* II.53 proposes the same four traditional virtues. Moreover, the enormously influential *De officiis* of Cicero does the same.[135] Further, it should be noted that Charlemagne proposes *sermonis studium*, or practice in speaking, by talking about virtue, rather than the establishment of virtue as the common topic of speech. The whole tone of the *Dialogue*, moreover, is political and secular, since Charlemagne asks about rhetoric only that he may better conduct his daily business, and even Alcuin observes at the end that the virtues have intruded into a secular discussion.

Alcuin may have been the first Englishman to write on rhetoric, but he spent the final twenty-two years of his life in France and wrote his *Dialogus* for a Frankish king. His sojourn on the Continent is perhaps indicative of the great intellectual movement of his time. The learning that had been driven out of Europe by the barbarians was returning from its insular retreat. Alcuin's students were Continental Europeans, and his ultimate influence was Continental. Only after several centuries—especially after the foundation of the great French schools at Chartres and Paris—was England to reap direct benefit again from the tradition begun at Canterbury and York and then transplanted to the court of Charles. In one sense, Alcuin took from England to the Continent a culture which only returned three hundred years later in the person of John of Salisbury.

In terms of the later history of the arts of discourse, however, Alcuin's

---

133 *Ibid.*, p. 145.

134 "What interests us chiefly at this juncture is that Alcuin introduces the subject of moral philosophy as that with which rhetorical method ought above all to be conversant, the Virtues being, as it were, the speaker's main theme, not a mere device applicable to rhetorical themes in general. This emphasis is clear, strong, and unmistakable. Here we see that classical rhetoric is being viewed in terms of its potential relation to the science of theology and the art of preaching." *Ibid.*, p. 64.

135 Cicero, *De officiis*, Loeb Classical Library (London, 1921).

treatise is stillborn. Its influence is negligible, except perhaps in terms of
the immediate successors of Alcuin.[136] Even so, men like Walafrid Strabo
and Rabanus Maurus were more likely to have imbibed their appreciation
of matters rhetorical from the lips of their master himself, rather than
from a treatise like the *Dialogus*. The dialogue of Charlemagne and
Alcuin, charming as it may be in a literary sense, provides no rhetorical
doctrine not found more easily in Cicero himself or in one of his late
classical disciples.

Rabanus Maurus (776–856), Alcuin's pupil, holds a far more significant
place in the history of medieval rhetoric. In his *De institutione clericorum*
(A.D. 819)[137] Rabanus describes various priestly duties in connection with
the Mass, public and private prayers, and the sacraments. When he turns
to the subject of speaking, in his third book, his whole approach is based
upon the function of the priest as a divinely appointed preacher, and he
chooses his doctrines from several sources instead of adopting the Ciceronian system whole, as Augustine had done. Nor does he, like Cassiodorus
or Isidore, insert into his book a verbatim transcript of a rhetorical compendium. Instead, he offers advice to the preacher gleaned sometimes
from Augustine, sometimes from Cicero, and sometimes from *dialectica*
or even from personal experience.

The importance of this selective method can hardly be overemphasized,
for the assimilation of classical rhetoric into Christian methodology is
here almost complete. The work of Rabanus is a significant milestone in
the history of preaching because he is the first of many medieval writers

---

[136] Howell lists a total of 26 extant manuscripts, 13 from the ninth century,
seven from the tenth, three undated, and only three definitely dated later than
A.D. 1000. The work is virtually unknown to medieval library cataloguers, and it
was first edited in 1529. Howell, *Alcuin*, pp. 8–10.

[137] Text in *Rabani Mauri de institutione clericorum libri tres,* ed. Aloysius
Knoepfler, Veroffentlichungen aus dem Kirchenhistorischen Seminar Munchen, No.
5 (Munich, 1901). Text also in Migne, *PL* 107, cols. 294–420. References will be to
the Knoepfler edition. Rabanus, known as *primus praeceptor Germanie* because of
his teaching, had enormous influence. He was a pupil of Alcuin at Tours, and numbered among his own students Walafrid Strabo, compiler of the *Glossa Ordinaria,*
or Biblical gloss, which became a medieval standard. For this work, see the text in
Migne, *PL* 113–14. Rabanus' own method of finding significances in Biblical and
other literary texts — a practice based in part on his reading of Augustine — had incalculable effect on the litero-linguistic habits of the middle ages. See Beryl Smalley,
*The Bible in the Middle Ages* (Oxford, 1954). For studies of Rabanus himself, cf.
Dietrich Turnau, *Rabanus Maurus der praeceptor Germanie* (Munich, 1899), and
J. Hablitzel, "Hrabanus Maurus: ein Beitrag zur Geschichte der mittelalterlichen
Exegese," *Biblische Studien* 11 (1906), 3 ff.

Rabanus is also the author of an encyclopedic work, *De universo,* which, however, does not include any discussion of language. For the text, see Migne, *PL* 111,
cols. 9–614.

to make a pragmatic choice of only those ideas which are useful to him without swallowing the whole system which gave birth to the ideas. Rabanus is freer from awe of classical learning than Isidore or Cassiodorus, and freer from external restraints than Augustine. His approach is also different from that of Alcuin, who did no more than interpret for Charles what Cicero had thought rhetoric could do to assist the man interested in public affairs.

Book Three[138] of the *De institutione clericorum* consists of thirty-nine *capitula* or sections. Rabanus begins with a paraphrase of the prologue to Gregory's *Regula pastoralis,*[139] and then explains that he is gathering a great many writings together, for the sake of brevity, to instruct those who must instruct others. Those who would take up holy orders must have "fullness of science, rectitude of life, and perfection of learning" which will assist them to employ "eloquence in preaching of sermons and discretion in teaching of dogma."[140] His argument here is that since it is a moot point whether a good life or a learned skill is of more use to the clergy, it behooves the *futurus populi rector* to have both. Following a summary of Augustine's *De doctrina christiana,*[141] he takes up the matter of understanding Scripture, and then devotes three sections (XVIII–XX) to the arts of grammar, rhetoric, and dialectic.

He names grammar (after Isidore) the "first of the liberal arts," and defines it as "the science of interpreting the poets and historians, and the science of speaking and writing correctly."[142] It is perhaps significant that Rabanus uses the term *interpretandi poetas* rather than the ancient

---

[138] The Prologue describes the contents of the whole work: Primus de ecclesiasticis ordinibus et de veste sacerdotali continet; secundus autem liber continet de officio canonicarum horarum et de jejunis et festivitatibus variis, de lectionibus et cantu ecclesiastico, de fide catholica et contrario de variis heresibus. Tertius vero liber edocet, quomodo omnia, quae in divinis libris scripta sunt, investiganda atque discenda sunt, necnon et ea quae in gentilium studiis et artibus ecclesiastico viro scrutati utilia sunt. *De institutione clericorum,* Prologus.

[139] Except for this passage and a lengthy quotation in III.37, Rabanus makes little explicit use of Gregory, although of course his whole treatise is of the same type as the *Regula pastoralis.*

[140] Scientiae plenitudinem et vitae rectitudinem . . . elegantiam in prolatione sermonem, discretionem in exhibitione dogmatum. *Ibid.,* III.1.

[141] In the first 17 sections of Book Three there are no less than 50 direct quotations from the *De doctrina.* They constitute perhaps 70 or 80 percent of the total text of this part of the book. In some cases—as in Cap. 11, for instance—the section consists entirely of a verbatim copy of Augustine's text.

[142] Grammatica est scientia interpretandi poetas atque historicos et recte scribendi loquendique. *De institutione clericorum* III.18. Isidore's definition, it will be recalled, limits grammar to syntax, and Cassiodorus refers to the poets only as sources of examples. For a comment on this broader definition, see Henry O. Taylor, *The Medieval Mind,* 2 vols. (Cambridge, Mass., 1959), I, 222–23.

*enarratio poetarum,* for he seems much interested in finding "meanings"
beneath the surface of things. He is, therefore, not merely repeating
Quintilian or Donatus in his definition of grammar, but is laying the way
open to the use of grammar as a tool in plumbing the depths of Scripture.
He seems to be seeking "signification" rather than understanding. This
tendency is further demonstrated in the same section when he quotes
Augustine (*De doctrina* I.iii.29) on the existence of tropes and figures in
Scripture. And he concludes the very brief mention of grammar—it is
little more than a set of definitions—by pointing out the use of even
the pagan poets: *ad nostrum dogma convertimus.*

His definition of rhetoric is that of Cassiodorus—"the science of speaking well in civil matters." But he points out that while this is a definition
from the secular world, it is equally relevant for ecclesiastical discipline,
for every orator and preacher can learn from the art of rhetoric. Nor
should anyone be blamed who studies the art at a proper age (*in congrua
aetate*) and who uses its precepts in speaking and preaching. Then
Rabanus quotes at length from Augustine's defense of eloquence in *De
doctrina* IV.2–3, and concludes the section by promising to say more
about rhetoric later in the book.

Dialectic is introduced with a definition from Alcuin's *De dialectica:*
"Dialectic is the discipline of rational inquiry, definition, and discourse,
and indeed of distinguishing truth from falsity." [143] This for Rabanus
is the "discipline of disciplines (*disciplina disciplinarum*) which teaches
(how) to teach." And it is particularly useful for the clergy in combating
the "sly subtlety of heretics." [144] But then he continues not by discussing
dialectical lore, but by quoting a long passage from Augustine again on
the necessity of knowing how to combat heresies effectively.[145]

Rabanus' treatment of the other four arts—arithmetic, music, geometry,
and astronomy—is derived mainly from Cassiodorus and occasionally from
Isidore, but even here there is reference to Augustine. Rabanus quotes
from his *De civitate dei* in the section on arithmetic (Cap. 22) and from
*De doctrina christiana* in the sections on arithmetic and music (Cap. 24).

Each of the seven discussions of the liberal arts is very brief, amounting

---

[143] Dialectica est disciplina rationalis quaerendi, definiendi et disserendi, etiam
et vero a falsis discernendi. *De institutione clericorum*, III.20.

[144] Quapropter oportet clericos hanc artem nobilissimam scire, eiusque iura in
assiduis meditationibus habere, ut subtilem haereticorium versutiam hac possint
dinoscere, eorumque dicta venefica veris syllogismorum conclusionibus confutare.
*Ibid.,* III.20.

[145] *De doctrina christiana* II.xxxi and xxxii.

to no more than a definition and justification. Astronomy, for instance, is seen as useful for religious argument because of its grandeur; geometry is useful in building tabernacles; and music of course trains singers for the church services. Among other things, arithmetic can help the cleric understand *mysticos numeros in divinis libris facilius*. As encyclopedic chapters on the seven liberal arts, these sections are almost useless because of their brevity and generality. But that is not their purpose; instead, they are inserted to call the attention of the clergy to those matters needful for their study.[146] In a general sense Rabanus shares the concern of Cassiodorus and Isidore, but unlike them he does not attempt to purvey the lore itself. He is content to point to the seven liberal arts, to justify them, and to turn his immediate attention to more pressing concerns.

At this point he returns to the subject of rhetoric in relation to preaching, devoting to it almost all the remaining sections of the work (Caps. 27–39). Again it is the text of Augustine's *De doctrina* which appears most frequently, with one long passage from Gregory in section 37.[147] Thus the final portions of the *De institutione clericorum* seem at first glance to be an almost random jumble of miscellaneous rhetorical advice culled from Augustine: the three levels of style, the resolving of obscurity, the three *officia* of a speaker (to instruct, delight, move), and so forth. But it is clear that Rabanus literally skipped through the fourth book of the *De doctrina* as he composed his own work, for his sections and the quoted passages follow sequentially the order of the earlier book. Rabanus concludes the treatise with a quotation from the next-to-last chapter of Augustine, to the effect that the preacher should pray God to place a good speech in his mouth.[148]

The *De institutione clericorum* of Rabanus Maurus holds a very significant position in the transition from the ancient to the medieval attitude toward the arts of discourse. Perhaps the most important reason for his significance, however, is his utter pragmatism—his constant willingness

---

[146] In the next section (26), for instance, he again insists on the utility of the seven liberal arts and quotes Augustine's analogy of "spoiling the Egyptians," from *ibid.*, II.xl.

[147] In addition to the fifty quotations already noted, there are another twenty-eight from Augustine in sections 21–39. The long quotation from Gregory in section 37, incidentally, proves to be devoted entirely to suggestions for types of "admonitions" to be used in preaching, such as admonishing the arrogant, the stubborn, and so forth. Thus Gregory is used in this passage only to suggest subject matter, and not to provide ideas on rhetorical form.

[148] Ut deus sermonem bonum det in os eius. *De institutione clericorum* II.39. The passage is from Esther 14:13.

to bend the existent disciplines around to the new urgencies of the Christian community. Everything, for Rabanus, can be used. *Ad nostrum dogma convertimus!* But in relation to the arts of discourse this produces some interesting results. Augustine, after all, had labored to salvage the very concept of the prescriptive tradition, especially as represented by Ciceronian rhetoric. The encyclopedists had labored to transmit a whole body of lore, abstracted and shrunken to be sure, but nevertheless whole and entire as far as they could make it; Martianus, Cassiodorus, and Isidore have little interest in altering the shape of the doctrine itself. But Rabanus is willing to change whatever he needs, and to select—and reject —on the basis of what the new ecclesiastical orator requires. This frank pragmatism thus marks the end of a transitional period which began with Augustine and Martianus.[149] One important reason is that Rabanus

---

[149] Between Rabanus' work, completed in 819, and the first truly medieval treatises of the eleventh century, there are few works of interest to the history of the arts of discourse. For some remarks on various minor authors, see Heinrich Fichtenau, "Rhetorische Elemente in der ottonish-salischen Herrscherurkunde," *Mitteilungen des Instituts für Osterreichische Geschichtsforschung* 68 (1960), 39–62. For an excellent résumé of how early medieval teachers utilized rhetorical and grammatical theory in teaching literature, see Berthe Marie Marti, "Literary Criticism in the Medieval Commentaries on Lucan," *Transactions of the American Philological Society* 72 (1941), 245–54.

Notker Labeo's compendium of Ciceronian rhetoric (c. 1022) is the only significant work of that type during this period. For a reconstruction of the lost work, see Paul Piper, *Die Schriften Notkers und seiner Schule* (Freiburg im Bresgau, 1882), pp. 645–84. For brief general accounts see Manitius, *Geschichte* II, 716–17, and Otto Dieter, "The Rhetoric of Notker Labeo," in *Papers in Rhetoric,* ed. Donald C. Bryant (St. Louis, 1940), pp. 27–33. (Full citation to Manitius is given in Abbreviations.)

Anselm of Besate's *Retorimachia* (or *De materia artis*) (c. 1050), is a dialogue or "disputation" in the form of a letter to his nephew Rutiland replying to the nephew's apparent misunderstanding of rhetoric. Anselm outlines a complete rhetoric. Having studied in Italy, he derives materials from both the Ciceronian and Aristotelian traditions. For a brief outline, see Manitius, *Geschichte* II, 708–15. For text, see *Gunzo epistola ad Augienses und Anselm von Besate Rhetorimachia,* ed. Karl Manitius, *Monumenta Germaniae Historica,* Vol. II (Weimar, 1958), 95–183.

A fair number of grammatical works based on Priscian and Donatus appear during this period, especially in the form of commentaries. For notices of major items, see Manitius, *Geschichte* I, 315–23, 323–39, 452–56, 456–58, 461–68, 468–69, 476–78, 490–93, 504–19; II, 664–72, 673–75, 675–82, 682–94, and 699–706. See also Julian of Toledo, *Ars grammatica, poetica, et rhetorica,* ed. F. de Lorenzano (Rome, 1797); an excerpt is in Keil, *Grammatica* V, 317–24; and cf. Manitius, *Geschichte* I, 129–33, and Charles H. Beeson, "The *Ars Grammatica* of Julian of Toledo," *Miscellanea Fr. Ehrle I* (Rome, 1924).

Arab rhetoric flourished during this period, but its history is as yet unwritten. Al-Farabi (d. A.D. 950) was a native of Baghdad who wrote a commentary on the *Rhetorica* of Aristotle and also composed a short encyclopedic work Latinized as *De scientiis.* For some general information about the tendencies of medieval Arab

replaces Cicero with Augustine as his rhetorical master. Although he does not usually acknowledge his source—another medieval habit—there are long sections in his third book which consist entirely of Augustine's words, not his own. His reliance goes far beyond mere quotation, though, because he willingly puts himself in the position of a mere prologue-writer who is composing a type of literary frame for excerpts from *De doctrina christiana*. That is to say, he does not quote Augustine to present the ideas themselves. This is *auctoritas patrum* carried forward, not only in relation to ideas, but in the form of expression itself.

This change in attitude may be slight and difficult to detect, but here in embryo is the basic postulate of the medieval arts of discourse: that the past should serve the particular needs of the present.[150] For, as the history of medieval rhetoric and grammar reveal with special clarity, all the significant original works on discourse which appear in Europe after Rabanus Maurus are merely highly selective adaptations of the old bodies of doctrine. The classical texts continue to be copied, but new treatises tend to appropriate for their purposes only those parts of the old lore which are of use to the one art. Thus it is that the medieval arts of discourse have a diverse rather than a unified history. The writers of letters select certain rhetorical doctrines, the preachers of sermons still others, and even the grammarians compound the original confusion of Donatus by broadening their studies not only into *figurae* but into *inventio* and *dispositio* as well. Since the needs are varied, the results are varied. As one modern scholar has said in relation to rhetoric, "in terms of a single subject matter—such as style, literature, discourse—it has no history during the middle ages."[151]

Consequently a study of the medieval arts of discourse must take up each distinct stream or form separately, before arriving at any general conclusions about the prescriptive tradition as a whole.

The following chapters, then, take up each of the four main streams of medieval theory, following roughly the chronological order in which they appear in Western Europe as separate entities. First in time is the survival of the ancient traditions, because they are almost continuous. In the eleventh century appears the new epistolary art, the *ars dictaminis*,

---

rhetoric and a translation of one relevant text, see Gustave E. von Grunebaum (ed. and trans.), *A Tenth-Century Document of Arab Literary Theory and Criticism: The Sections on Poetry of al-Bāqillāni's I' jāz-al-Qu'ān* (Chicago, 1950).

[150] By contrast, the main concern of early Renaissance theorists is to understand the classics, not to adapt them and change them.

[151] McKeon, "Rhetoric" (see n. 9 above).

with its adaptation of Ciceronian rhetoric to the problem of letter-writing. The twelfth century is the watershed between the old grammar of Donatus and Priscian, on one hand, and the new fourfold *ars grammatica* with its concern not only for syntax but also for the distinctions between *prosaicum, metricum,* and *rithmicum.* The *ars praedicandi,* the complex theory of the thematic sermon, appears early in the thirteenth century. By the end of the fourteenth century it is possible to detect all these medieval traditions running side by side in Europe.

It is equally easy to determine with some precision the events in the fifteenth century which led to a reversal of this truly "medieval" phase. The most important single factor in this dramatic change was probably the rediscovery of the complete text of Quintilian by Poggio Bracciolini in 1416, and the subsequent preceptive revolution caused by the impact of the *Institutio oratoria* on education. The renewed popularity of Cicero's long-neglected *De oratore* is another hallmark of this fifteenth-century reorientation. This is the subject of the final section.

# Chapter III

❖ ❖ ❖

# Survival of the Classical Traditions

THE most important single fact to be kept in mind during a study of the medieval theory of discourse is that most of the ancient documents dealing with the preceptive tradition continued to be studied and used throughout the middle ages. There were, to be sure, variations in the popularity of the classical treatises, and in a sense these variations are an index to the intellectual currents of the period. Nevertheless, the salient point is their survival. With the single very important exception of Quintilian's *Institutio oratoria,* elements of Aristotelian, Ciceronian, sophistic, and grammatical traditions of the ancient world found some kind of public recognition up to at least the fifteenth century.

The very antiquity of these works gave added weight to their own inherent or natural authority, so that the *auctoritas antiquitatis*—the "authority of antiquity"—had for the medieval mind a special value. Thus the ancient preceptors subsisted, albeit unequally, alongside the medieval theorists. Usually "Tullius" (Marcus Tullius Cicero) was portrayed as the ultimate master of the theory of discourse, even by authors who probably never read his rhetorical treatises; the towering authority of Aristotle held similar place in the writings of Brunetto Latini, the teacher of Dante. Yet it would be unrealistic to assume that the classical works received unqualified acceptance, or even unqualified respect, in comparison to treatises produced during the middle ages. Rather, it might be more accurate to say that the ancient *artes* are to be seen competing for the attention of the medieval writer and speaker—competing, that is, against the lure of the "modern" and specialized works which sprang up in various fields after about 1050—but competing with the advantage of *antiquitas*.

Any balanced assessment of the arts of discourse in the middle ages, then, must include an observation of the direct use which medieval man made of this heritage from the ancient world. For this reason it is worthwhile investigating at least briefly the actual use made of classical treatises themselves, quite apart from any influence they may have exerted on works composed by medieval writers.

The direct influence of Aristotle's *Rhetorica* is difficult to assess, but there are clear indications that the inventional portions of the *Organon* —*De sophisticis elenchis* and *Topica*—proved both popular and influential during the middle ages. Aristotle's *Ars poetica* was virtually ignored.[1]

The *Rhetorica* first reached the Latin West in the form of thirteenth-century translations from Arabic commentators. It then was rendered *en toto* by William of Moerbeke as part of the massive translation project initiated by Thomas Aquinas. William's translation, which proved to be the most popular, was completed about 1270. Commentaries on the work were composed by at least three writers, the most important of them being Aegidius Romanus, bishop of Bourges and a major figure in the development of scholastic thought at Paris in the late thirteenth century.

At first glance, therefore, it would seem probable that the surge of interest in Aristotle's works, which is so characteristic of the thirteenth century, would have established the *Rhetorica* as a dominant force in the Western theory of discourse. Instead, it is Cicero's rhetoric which dominates medieval theory despite the generally "scholastic" environment of the period. The reasons for this phenomenon seem to lie in the medieval use of Aristotle's books.

The fate of the *Rhetorica* in the late classical and early medieval periods

---

[1] For a useful guide to the medieval history of Aristotle's works, see George Lacombe, *Aristoteles Latinus,* Corpus Philosophorum Medii Aevi, 2 vols. (I, Rome, 1939; II, Cambridge, 1955). This work (hereafter referred to as *Arist. Lat.*) contains brief summaries of all known medieval Latin translations of Aristotelian works, together wtih descriptions of extant manuscripts and specimens of texts. Also, see Lorenzo Minio–Palluello, *Aristoteles Latinus: Codices, Supplementa Altera* (Bruges, 1962). For an older but still useful survey, see Aimable Jourdain, *Recherches critiques sur l'âge et l'origin des traductions latines d'Aristote et sur des commentaires Grecs ou Arabes employés par les docteurs scolastiques* (new edition by C. Jourdain, Paris, 1843; reprinted New York, 1960). For some additional remarks in respect to translations, see J. T. Muckle, "Greek Works Translated Directly into Latin," *Medieval Studies* 4 (1942), 35–42, and 4 (1943), 102–14; and Charles H. Haskins, *The Renaissance of the Twelfth Century* (Cambridge, Mass., 1927; reprinted New York, 1957), pp. 287–302.

is obscure. Boethius, for instance, assumes that it is Cicero's rhetoric which should be the standard in assessing the relation of dialectic and rhetoric;[2] this position is all the more significant because Boethius regarded himself as a serious student of Aristotle. Encyclopedists like Isidore and Cassiodorus ignore Aristotle's rhetorical theories, and the later compend-writers like Alcuin, Notker Labeo, and Anselm of Besate seem to be unaware of the book's existence.

Apparently it remained for Arab commentators to reintroduce the work into the main stream of Western life. Hermannus Allemanus about 1240 prepared a Latin translation of an Arabic gloss which he credited to al-Farabi, a ninth-century scholar.[3] Al-Farabi's commentary on the *Rhetorica* of Aristotle proceeds from the basically Aristotelian premise that all the arts of discourse should be considered together, as aspects or branches of the same *ars sermocinalis*. Arabic theory of the eighth through eleventh centuries, for instance, conceived of both poetics and rhetoric as different means by which men communicate with one another. Arabic efforts to work out a literary theory for interpretation of the Koran—analogous to the Christian desire for systematic exegesis of the Bible—eventually produced a series of stylistically oriented treatises which were not of themselves influential in the West.[4] But the movement began on a broad front, and it was the earlier rather than the later Arabic works which interested the European scholars.

Al-Farabi himself was the author of two encyclopedic works which found their way into the studies of Western scholars interested in the classification of sciences and arts. For instance, the *De divisione philosophiae* of Dominicus Gundissalinus, archdeacon of Toledo, who flourished c. 1125–1150, is based in part on the *De scientiis* and the *De ortu scientiarum* of al-Farabi.[5] In the *De scientiis* al-Farabi declares that there are five

---

[2] See especially Boethius, *In topica Ciceronis commentariorum*, ed. Migne, *PL* 64, cols. 1039–1174, as compared to his explication of Aristotle: *Interpretatio topicorum Aristotelis*, *PL* 44, cols. 910–1008.

[3] See Jourdain, *Traductions*, pp. 139–41; Lacombe, *Arist. Lat.* I, 102–13. Lacombe believes that the text was actually a paraphrase by another Arab scholar, Averroës, which includes a gloss by al-Farabi. For text, see *Declaratio compendiosa per viam divisione Alfarabi super libros rethoricorum Aristotilis* (Venice, 1481). A very brief excerpt may be found in Lacombe, *Arist. Lat.* I, 211–12.

[4] For a general discussion of Arab efforts in this vein, and a sample text, see Gustave von Grunebaum, *A Tenth-Century Document of Arab Literary Theory and Criticism: The Sections on Poetry of al-Baqillâni's I'jâz al-Qu'ân* (Chicago, 1950).

[5] Dominicus Gundissalinus, *De divisione philosophiae*, ed. Ludwig Baur in *Beiträge zur Geschichte der Philosophie des Mittelalters* 4 (1906), 164–316. For

"elements" of *logica*, that science by which knowledge can be verified: *demonstrativa*, which gives certitude; *tentativa*, which deals in doubtful conclusions; *sophistica*, which leads to error; *rhetorica*, which creates understanding approaching certitude; and *poetica*, which employs imagination because it (imagination) works more in man than does science or thought.[6] Al-Farabi goes on to declare that in addition to grammar and logic there is still another science dealing with language: *kalam*, or the science of eloquence; it is interesting to note that Gundissalinus records this *scientia eloquendi* in the table of contents of his Latin translation, but actually omits it from his text. The practical consequence of this omission, of course, is that the readers of Gundissalinus would have seen *rhetorica* treated only as a part of *logica*, or the science of verifying knowledge.[7]

Hermannus begins his translation of al-Farabi's commentary on the *Rhetorica* with a statement that both *rhetorica* and *poetica* ought to be considered as adjuncts to logic. "So they form a complement to the business of logic, following the intention of Aristotle. That these two may be books of logic, no one doubts who has examined the books of famous Arabs such as al-Farabi, Avicenna, Averroës, and others as well." [8] Hermannus notes that Cicero makes rhetoric a branch of civil science, and that Horace relates poetry to grammar; it is clear that Hermannus regards their views as mistaken, although he concedes that Cicero and Horace may be useful in understanding Aristotle.[9] Here is a clear indication that Hermannus regards the Aristotelian and Ciceronian traditions as separate, at least in their basic orientations to other sciences.

As for the *Rhetorica* itself, it received two translations into Latin from Greek, both during the thirteenth century. The first of these, sometimes

more general information about the Arabic influences, see K. Djorr, *Bibliographie d'Al-Farabi* (Paris, 1946); and Robert Hammond, *The Philosophy of Alfarabi and Its Influence on Medieval Thought* (New York, 1947).

[6] Two of these five elements may be of general interest here: rhetorica, pro sensu similibus movere animam auditoris . . . et generet in eo cognitionem proximam certitudinis; . . . poetica, imaginatio autem quoniam plus operatur in homine quam scientia vel cogitatio. Domingo Gundisalvo, *De scientiis*, ed. P. Manuel Alonso (Madrid–Granada, 1954), pp. 72–76.

[7] Vincent of Beauvais uses this portion of the *De scientiis* in his *Speculum doctrinale* III.2–3.

[8] . . . ut sic habeant complementum logici negocii secundum Aristotelis intentionem. Quod autem hi duo libri logicales sint, nemo dubitat qui libros perspexerit arabum famosum, Alfarabi videlicet et Avicenne et Avenrosdi et quorundam aliorum. Lacombe, *Arist. Lat.* I, 211.

[9] Neque excusabilis sunt, ut fortassis alicui videbitur, propter marcii tulii rethoricam et oratii poetriam. . . . verumptamen dictorum virorum scripta non minimum utilia sunt ad opera presentia intelligendum. *Ibid.*

termed *translatio vetus* to distinguish it from the later version by William of Moerbeke, was completed sometime before 1250, possibly by Bartholomew of Messina.[10] It survives in only three manuscripts, and apparently was never used in the schools. The opening of Book One may give some idea of its tone:

> Rethorica est convertibilis dialetice: utreque enim de quibusdam huiusmodi sunt, que communia quodam modo omnium est cognoscere et nullius scientie determinate. Ideo et omnes secundum aliquem modum participant utramque. Omnes enim usque aliquid et perscrutari et percipere sermonem et respondere et accusare argumentantur. Horum quidem igitur plurium hii quidem vane agunt, hii vero per consuetudinem ab habitu.[11]

Little is known of the reasons for the comparative obscurity of this translation, although it must have suffered from its anonymity in comparison to that of Moerbeke. Or it may have shared some of the prejudices created by the poor reputation of Hermannus' translation of "al-Farabi"; Roger Bacon, for instance, declared this work to be so badly done that it was impossible to understand it.[12] Or it may simply have suffered from the geographical handicap of composition away from the northern European center of Aristotelian studies.

Whatever the factors affecting the popularity of the *translatio vetus,* it would seem that the *translatio Guillelmi* (by William of Moerbeke, a student of Thomas Aquinas) had every advantage to ensure acceptance. Composed about 1270[13] at the height of Parisian interest in Aristotelian writings, it appeared to be in the mainstream of scholastic endeavors to make all the works of "the Philosopher" available to the Western world. Says a chronicle for the year 1273: "William of Brabant, of the Order of Preachers, translated all the books of Aristotle from Greek into Latin, word for word [*verbum ex verbo*], which translation scholars are now using in schools, at the instance of Thomas Aquinas." [14] The powerful

---

[10] For a brief history of the medieval translations, cf. *ibid.,* pp. 177–79. For the attribution of Bartholomew, see Leonard Spengel, *Aristotelis ars rhetorica accedit vetusta translatio latina* (Leipzig, 1867), I, 177.

[11] MS. Paris Bibliothèque Nationale Latine 16673, fol. 1, printed in Lacombe, *Arist. Lat.* I, 167.

[12] . . . male translatus est, nec potest sciri, nec adhuc in usi vulgi est, quia nuper venit ad Latinos et cum defectu translationis et squalore. Jourdain, *Traductions,* p. 143. In all fairness to Hermannus, however, it might be noted that his Arab sources tended to omit difficult passages.

[13] Henry of Hervordia reported in 1271 that Moerbeke's translations were in use in the schools. *Ibid.,* p. 68.

[14] Ap. Lindenborg, *Scriptores rerum germanicarum septentrionalium* (ed. Fabricius, 1706), p. 206, quoted in *ibid.,* p. 67.

sponsorship of Aquinas, together with the general interest in the rapidly emerging *corpus* of Aristotle's works, may help to account for the ubiquity of the Moerbeke translation of the *Rhetorica*. It is extant today in ninety-six manuscripts.[15] It is plain, therefore, that it supplanted any earlier translation, whether from the Arabic or the Greek. There is no reason to believe that Moerbeke even consulted previous renditions; in any case his independent version so completely dominated schools and libraries that for all practical purposes it may be regarded as the typical medieval Latin version.

Moerbeke's translation begins with the following passage:

> Rethorica assecutiva dialecticae est; ambae enim de talibus quibusdam sunt, quae communiter quodammodo omnium est cognoscere, et nullis scientiae determinatae propter quod est omnes modo quodam participant ambabus. Omnes enim usque ad aliquid et exquirere et sustinere sermonem, et defendere et accusare conantur. Multorum quidem igitur hi quidem fortuito haec agunt, hi autem propter consuetudinem ab habitu.

It ends:

> Finis autem locutionis congruit inconiunctus, quatenus epilogus, sed non oratio sit: dixi, audistis, habete, iudicate. Explicit rhetorica Aristotelis translata a Graeco in Latinum.[16]

Thus the Moerbeke translation is essentially a rather literal, word-by-word rendition. This was of course the medieval method, and if it did not always create an artistically perfect literary production, it did at least provide a coherent text which was adequate for purposes of study.

Tracing the actual use of the book is a rather complex task. At Paris itself, medieval university statutes make no mention of any rhetorical works as required reading. In 1215, in fact, rhetoric is cited as one of the subjects allowed for "cursory" lectures—that is, lectures delivered outside the regular schedule—but it is not specified as an ordinary part of the curriculum.[17] Statutes over the next century and a half also omit rhetoric as a requirement. The so-called "reform" at Paris in 1366, significantly, set up three main areas of study, beginning with a Bachelor of Arts pro-

---

[15] For an index to the manuscripts, see Lacombe, *Arist. Lat.*, II, 1348.

[16] The text is printed by Spengel, *Aristoteles*, I, 178–342. Lacombe also prints the opening of Book One in *Arist. Lat.* I, 167–68, from Paris Bibliothèque Nationale MS. Lat. 7695, fol. 1. Reference will be to the Spengel edition; a new critical edition of the medieval Latin text is contemplated in the Aristoteles Latinus series.

[17] . . . non legant in festivis diebus nisi philosophos et rhetoricas et quadrivalia et barbarismum et ethicam si placet, et quartum topicorum. Hastings Rashdall, *Universities of Europe in the Middle Ages*, 3 vols., new edition ed. F. M. Powicke and A. B. Emden (Oxford, 1936), I, 440.

gram which took the student directly from grammar into logic and thence to psychology.[18] Again rhetoric is omitted. The use of Aristotle's *Rhetorica* at German universities, where the curriculum was usually modeled on that of Paris, might reflect Parisian custom; it should be noted, however, that these instances are either undated or from the late fifteenth century.[19]

At Oxford there is no mention of the book in university statutes until 1431, when it is prescribed along with two Ciceronian works, and with Ovid and Virgil, as one of the alternative readings in rhetoric. The mixture of traditions represented in this statute probably indicates that Aristotle's *Rhetorica* had not been systematically studied in that university before the statute.[20] Cambridge records fail to give evidence of the book's use.[21]

It is not surprising that Italian schools ignore this book. The long rhetorical tradition at places like Pavia, Ravenna, and Bologna was based on a solid Ciceronianism. The most characteristic Italian contribution to medieval theories of discourse—the *ars dictaminis*—draws heavily upon Ciceronian concepts of *dispositio* and *elocutio*.[22] Italian universities did not

---

[18] *Ibid.,* I, 444.

[19] The Leipzig date, for instance, is 1499. *Ibid.,* I, 447, n. 5. One manuscript containing the Moerbeke translation (Vatican MS. Palat. Lat. 1589) was produced at Heidelberg between 1423 and 1428. *Arist. Lat.* II, 1198. At Vienna, on the other hand, students were enjoined in 1389 to read unum librum in Rethorica, but no particular book was named. Rashdall, *Universities* II, 243, n. 1.

[20] For a discussion of this statute in relation to rhetoric, see James J. Murphy, "The Earliest Teaching of Rhetoric at Oxford," *Speech Monographs* 27 (1960), 345–47. Oriel College, Oxford, possessed some kind of Aristotelian rhetorical work in 1375, although it may have been no more than *sententiae* culled from the book; for a discussion of the Oriel catalogue entry, see Murphy, "Rhetoric in Fourteenth-Century Oxford," *Medium Aevum* 34 (1965), 1–20.

[21] It might be noted, however, that a number of early Cambridge records were destroyed by fire in 1381. The first extant record of official university action in respect to rhetoric seems to be the creation, in 1506, of a post of lecturer on poetry and oratory. See James B. Mullinger, *A History of the University of Cambridge* (London, 1888), and Rashdall, *Universities* III, 274–324. While the records of medieval university curricula are of course fragmentary and should be evaluated with some care, the pattern in respect to rhetoric is nevertheless quite clear. It is a pattern of omission. The omissions occur, moreover, in statutes or other documents which are highly detailed in respect to other subjects such as grammar or dialectic. A Paris statute of 1255, for example, prescribes by name twenty-two books which a master was required to lecture upon. *Ibid.,* I.442–43. The omission of rhetoric from such a list could hardly be termed accidental.

[22] A number of texts of the *ars dictaminis* are printed by Ludwig Rockinger, *Briefsteller und Formelbücher des eilften bis vierzehnten Jahrhunderts,* Quellen und Erörterungen zur bayerischen und deutschen Geschichte, vol. IX (Munich, 1863–64; reprinted New York, 1960).

share the intense interest in Aristotelian philosophy which might have served as a backdrop to a renewed concentration on his rhetorical concepts.[23] Brunetto Latini, the thirteenth-century Italian encyclopedist and teacher, does indeed call on the authority of "the Philosopher" to advertise to the reader his treatment of rhetoric, but his rhetoric nevertheless is exclusively Cicero's.[24] In any case there is little reason to believe that Aristotle's rhetoric played any significant role in Italy prior to the fifteenth century.

There seems to be little or no trace of the book in such medieval derivatives of ancient rhetorical theory as *ars dictaminis, ars praedicandi,* and those parts of *ars grammatica* which deal with poetic composition.[25] Most important, Aristotle did not have a general medieval reputation as a writer on the theory of discourse; on the other hand, "Tullius" was acknowledged everywhere in Europe as the master of writing and speaking, even by those (like Chaucer or John Gower) who probably had no occasion to read his works.[26]

---

[23] Some of the differences between the Italian and northern universities are discussed in Rashdall, *Universities* I, 101 ff. and 248 ff. And see the brief statement by Paul O. Kristeller, *Die italienischen Universitäten der Renaissance,* Schriften und Vorträge des Petrarca-Instituts, I; kdn:n.d.

[24] Latini composed an encyclopedic work in three volumes. The third book deals with "Politic," which includes rhetoric. Cf. Latini, *Li livres dou Trésor,* ed. Francis J. Carmody (Berkeley and Los Angeles, 1948), III; Latini, *Il Tesoro,* ed. P. Chabaille (Bologna, 1883), IV. Cicero is the exemplar in both versions. Neither Dante nor Boccaccio rely on Aristotle's *Rhetorica* in their discussions of poetry, although Petrarch seems to refer to it in his *Invective contra medicum, liber tertius* (ed. G. Martelloti et al. in Francesco Petrarca, *Prose,* La letteratura Italiana, storia e testi, Vol. 7 (Milan and Naples, n.d.), p. 658. For remarks on the origin of Latini's rhetorical doctrines, see James East, "Book Three of Brunetto Latini's *Tresor*: An English Translation and Assessment of its Contribution to Rhetorical Theory," unpublished Ph.D. thesis, Stanford University, 1960; for a summary, see *Dissertation Abstracts* 21 (1960), 990–91. First written in French about 1260 as the *Trésor,* the work was translated into Italian as *Il Tesoro* by a friend, Bono Giambono in 1266, and into Spanish as well; see Charles Faulhaber, *Latin Rhetorical Theory in Thirteenth and Fourteenth Century Castile* (Berkeley and Los Angeles, 1972), p. 2.

[25] See below, Chapters Four, Five, and Six.

[26] Chaucer, for instance, in the Franklin's Prologue, verses 719–22, makes Cicero a synonym for rhetoric:

> I lerned never rethoryk certayn;
> Thing that I spake, it moot be bare and pleyn.
> I sleep never on the mount of Pernaso,
> Ne lerned Marcus Tullius Cithero.

Quotations here and below are from *The Works of Geoffrey Chaucer,* ed. F. N. Robinson, 2d ed. (Boston, 1957).

Yet the fact remains that Aristotle's *Rhetorica* survives in nearly one hundred medieval manuscripts—22 from the thirteenth century, 57 from the fourteenth century, and 17 from the fifteenth. Why, then, does the book play so insignificant a role in the medieval development of the theory of discourse?

The answer to this question lies in the very movement which led to the Moerbeke translation. Aquinas, of course, was first and foremost a theologian. The dominant spirit of mid-thirteenth-century University of Paris was philosophical, interested in recovering the totality of Aristotle's works so they could be put to work in understanding a Christian universe. Completing a reliable set of translations was of course only a first step. The real task lay in mastering the various works, determining first their relation to each other, and then their relation to Scriptural Revelation and other foundations of Christian belief.

It is tempting to speculate that the subject of *dialectica* in some way absorbed or took over the Aristotelian rhetoric.[27] Certainly the renewed popularity of the *Organon* should have had some effect on the fate of any work dealing with *verbum,* or "word." Both rhetoric and dialectic, of course, propose a theory of *loci* or "commonplaces" as an aid to invention of ideas,[28] and it might be supposed that this natural affinity would have led easily to a medieval linking of Aristotelian logic and Aristotelian rhetoric.[29]

Actually, however, it is more probable that Aristotle's *Rhetorica* came to be known instead as a valuable adjunct to the studies of ethics and political science. Some hint of this possibility is contained in a brief treatise written in the last quarter of the thirteenth century by Aegidius Romanus, a Parisian scholar who later became archbishop of Bourges. Aegidius had a distinguished career; after six years as a teacher at the University of Paris he was elected General of the Order of Saint Augus-

---

[27] "At the fall of Rome the Trivium was dominated by *rhetorica;* in the Carolingian period, by *grammatica;* in the high middle ages, by *dialectica.*" Charles S. Baldwin, *Medieval Rhetoric and Poetic* (New York, 1928), p. 151. Also, see Richard McKeon, "Rhetoric in the Middle Ages," *Speculum* 17 (1942), 1–32.

[28] Boethius, for instance, recognized this connection between the two arts. As a consequence the fourth book of his own work on the *Topica* is found among books of "rhetoric" at Paris in 1255 and Oxford in 1431. The conceptual relationships in this area are discussed in part by William M. A. Grimaldi, S.J., "The Aristotelian Topics," *Traditio* 14 (1958), 1–16. Also, see Martin L. Clarke, *Rhetoric at Rome* (London, 1953).

[29] Cf. McKeon, "Rhetoric."

tine in 1292, and bishop of Bourges in 1295. Before his death in 1316 he composed a large number of works, mostly commentaries, dealing with Aristotle.[30]

The very title—*De differentia rhetoricae, ethicae, et politicae*[31]—suggests at once the existence of a question as to the true position of rhetoric. While Aegidius concludes that rhetoric is apparently closer to dialectic than to politics and ethics—which are *scientiae speciales* dealing with human actions—he does concede that rhetoric could also be conceived of as operating in a realm somewhere between moral science and the rational sciences.[32] Moreover, he points out, while rhetoric does not in itself deal with "moral actions" of human beings, there is actually some involvement in moral actions whenever rhetoric is applied to real life. In this sense rhetoric is indirectly involved with those actions which are the proper subjects of politics and ethics, although rhetoric is not itself a direct part of politics. This conclusion represents a rejection of the Ciceronian tradition that rhetoric is a mere branch of political science.[33] It is equally an acknowledgment of the Aristotelian determination that rhetoric is in some way related to dialectic, and Aegidius quotes the opening sentence of the Moerbeke translation of the *Rhetorica: Rethorica est assecutiva dyalectica.* In any case Aegidius opens the possibility of a liaison between rhetoric and the "moral sciences."

The full-blown commentary written by Aegidius on the *Rhetorica* of Aristotle also points to this development. Composed toward the end of the thirteenth century (1280?), the commentary is a running exposition of Aristotle's work which presents, in turn, each sentence of the Moer-

---

[30] For brief biographical details and a list of Aegidius' works, sea Palémon Glorieux, *Repertoire des maîtres en théologie de Paris au XIIIe siècle*, 2 vols., Etudes de philosophie médiévale, XVII (Paris, 1934), I, 140–48. His career spans the whole development of Scholastic thought at Paris, and despite a condemnation late in life for doctrinal divergences, he might well be taken as a typical example of the "scholastic" scholar working in the heart of the Aristotelian revival. In addition to his voluminous writings, he is known to have taken part in at least six *quodlibet* (open) disputations, one of which takes up the question, "Whether speech is in man by nature." *Ibid.*, I, 141.

[31] Ed. Gerardo Bruni, "The *De differentia rhetoricae, ethicae et politicae* of Aegidius Romanus," *New Scholasticism* 6 (1932), 1–18. Bruni believes this treatise was written about 1282, before Aegidius' commentary on the *Rhetorica* of Aristotle; it may have come afterwards, however, because in it Aegidius refers to que in libro Rethoricorum scripsi.

[32] nam rethorica videtur quasi media inter scientias morales et rationales. *Ibid.*, p. 6.

[33] Cf. *De inventione* I.5. Aegidius acknowledges the existence of the Ciceronian position, but points out that Cicero thus makes it very difficult to distinguish between politics and rhetoric.

beke translation and then the remarks of the author. Thus the famous opening sentence of the *Rhetorica* is followed by a long dissertation on the relation between dialectic and rhetoric.[34] But there is little more to the work than an attempt to elucidate Aristotle's meaning. In fact, the author states this intention at the outset: "While I have assumed the burden of expositor in this case, I do not wish what I say to be ascribed to me, for I present only the sense of what I believe Aristotle means." [35] Certainly the work adds very little to Aristotle's text, the main effort being a mere explication. There is very little comparison of Aristotle to other authors in the same field (for instance, Cicero is seldom mentioned). Aegidius seldom if ever disagrees with Aristotle.

The nature of the commentary is especially significant in that it also allows for rather lengthy treatment of the second book on the passions which form the material for pathetic proof. On the single statement *que circa passiones nunc dicendum,* Aegidius provides a commentary almost twice as long as that used to discuss the relation between rhetoric and dialectic in the opening portion of Book One. He defines *passio,* states the number of passions, including their opposites, and makes some remarks about their use in speaking. His usual method here is to employ *divisio,* breaking up the statement into its elements; sometimes even single words become the subject.[36] So it is not any new insights of Aegidius that recommend the second book to the student, but rather the painstaking detail of the treatment. If there had been some medieval interest in considering Aristotle's *Rhetorica* as an adjunct to the study of ethics or politics, this commentary on the second book might have helped to increase that in-

---

[34] See James J. Murphy, "The Scholastic Condemnation of Rhetoric in the Commentary of Giles of Rome on the *Rhetoric* of Aristotle," in *Arts libéraux et philosophie au moyen âge,* Actes du quatrième congrès international de philosophie médiévale (Montreal and Paris, 1969), 833–41; also Reginald J. O'Donnell, "The Commentary of Giles of Rome on the *Rhetoric* of Aristotle," in *Essays in Medieval History Presented to Bertie Wilkinson,* eds. Thayron A. Sandquist and Michael R. Powicke (Toronto, 1969), pp. 139–56. Text is *Rhetorica Aristotelis cum fundatissimi arcium et theologie doctoris Egedi de Roma luculentissimis commentarii* (Venice, 1515). Cf. Brother S. Robert, F.S.C., "Rhetoric and Dialectic According to the First Latin Commentary on the Rhetoric of Aristotle," *New Scholasticism* 31 (1957), 484–98.

[35] Ubi quod onus expositoris assumpsi, nolo mihi ascripsi quod proferam, sed talem promulgabo sententiam, qualem credam Aristotelem intendisse. *Commentarii,* fol. 1ra.

[36] For instance, Aegidius sees six elements in the statement "quietat enim alterius ira maior" (fol. 55rb). A careful study of this section might well provide an illuminating view of the standard medieval scholastic viewpoint in respect to the use of emotion as rhetorical proof.

terest. Certainly the fame and importance of its author would have added weight to any such tendencies.

An examination of manuscript groupings tends to reinforce the judgment that the *Rhetorica* did indeed become allied with ethics and political science rather than with dialectic or with the theory of discourse.

The book is extant in 96 manuscripts. In 17 cases it appears alone, with no other works bound into the same volume.[37] In the remaining 79 instances, however, a striking pattern emerges. Perhaps this pattern is best shown by a brief summary of the major groupings:

| | |
|---|---:|
| Total number of manuscripts | 96 |
| Manuscripts containing *Rhetorica* alone | 17 |
| Manuscripts also containing other works | 79 |
| Number containing either *Ethica* or *Politica,* or both, of Aristotle | 69 |
| Number with both *Ethica* and *Politica* | 50 |
| Number with *Magna moralia*[38] | 33 |
| Number with *Economica*[39] | 26 |
| Number with *De bona fortuna*[40] | 16 |
| Number with dialectical works | 0 |
| Number with other rhetorical works[41] | 0 |

The nature of this pattern is further illustrated by two of the manuscripts, which describe their collections as *libri morales* in one case and *testus moralis philosophus* in the other.[42] And of the 232 known medieval Latin versions of the *Ethica,* some 54—almost one-quarter of the total—appear bound in with a copy of Aristotle's *Rhetorica.* The ratio is even higher in the case of the *Politica,* for 61 of the 103 extant medieval copies are bound in with the *Rhetorica.*

---

[37] The following analysis is based on manuscript catalogue descriptions in Lacombe, *Arist. Lat.* Numbers used are those assigned to manuscripts by Lacombe. Titles follow medieval usage, even in those cases (e.g., *Magna moralia*) in which Aristotle's authorship is doubted.

[38] Translated by Bartholomew of Messina (c. 1258–66), and possibly a second time in the same century. See *ibid.,* I, 71–72.

[39] In all but three cases where the *Economica* appears with the *Rhetorica,* it is bound in with both the *Ethica* and *Politica.* As the *incipit* indicates, it was a natural inclusion: Yconomica et politica differunt. . . . For a brief description of the translation and later recension, see *ibid.,* I, 75–77.

[40] This collection of excerpts from *Ethica* VIII received two translations into Latin. *Ibid.,* I, 72–73.

[41] Two manuscripts include copies of Aristotle's *Poetica* in Latin, and eight others have a translation of the Averroist abstract of the *Poetica.* Other items include *Metaphysica* (8 copies), *Problematica* (5), and the commentary of Aegidius (3). In one case (MS. 11) the same volume contains both the Moerbeke translation of the *Rhetorica* and the *translatio vetus* of Hermannus, as well as the *Politica.*

[42] MSS. 693 and 1783.

The omissions are equally striking. Assuming that manuscript groupings are at least partly functional—that is, that medieval volumes were put
together to satisfy the needs of readers—then it might be expected that a
strong interest in the rhetoric–dialectic relation would have shown up in
at least some of the manuscript groupings listed above.[43] The discussion
of *loci* in Book One, for instance, might well have led to a parallel study
of Aristotle's *Topica* or *De sophisticis elenchis,* where similar ideas are
treated. The same might be said about rhetorical works. This obviously
does not occur in the existing manuscripts. The complete absence of such
manuscript pairings adds conclusive weight to the judgment that Aristotle's *Rhetorica* became for the middle ages not a rhetorical [44] or dialectical work, but a treatise useful in the study of moral philosophy.[45]

---

[43] Instead, the apparatus of medieval scholarship tends to confirm the belief that
the *Rhetorica* was habitually regarded as one of a certain set of corollary books.
Note, for example, the following aids to the medieval student: London, Gray's
Inn MS. 2, fols. 177$^r$–212$^r$: Tabula ethicorum, politicorum et rethoricorum; Paris,
Bibliothèque Nationale MS. Lat. 16090, fols. 55$^v$–57$^r$: Initia capitulorum rhetoricae,
ethicae, politicae, economicae, poetriae (i.e., of Averroës). Both of these date from
the fourteenth century. A third, Paris Bibliothèque Nationale MS. Lat. 16147 (dated
at Paris, 1271), fols. 247$^r$–261$^v$, contains a work entitled Index alphabeticus in
ethicam, politicam et rethoricam.

[44] In this connection, then, it may be significant that although the Pseudo-Aristotelian *Rhetorica ad Alexandrum* received at least two separate medieval translations into Latin, it was apparently not popular. It survives today in only three
medieval manuscripts. For one medieval Latin text, see Martin Grabmann, "Eine
lateinische Ubersetzung der pseudo-aristotelische Rhetorica ad Alexandrum aus
dem 13. Jahrhundert," *Sitzungberichte der bayerischen Akademie der Wissenschaften*
4 (1932), 1–81. Also see the remarks in L. Dittmeyer, "Neue Beiträge zur die
lateinische Ubersetzung der pseudoaristotelische Rhetorica ad Alexandrum aus
dem 13. Jahrhundert," *Bayerische Blatter für das Gymnasialschulwesen* 69 (1933),
157–65, and 70 (1934), 166–72. The version edited by Grabmann (the so-called
*translatio vaticana*) is dated by him as about 1295, although Dittmeyer would assign it to the reign of King Manfred of Sicily (d. 1266). University of Illinois MS.
6, fols. 38$^r$–48$^r$, contains a second version (*translatio americana*) which is as yet
unedited. (Another copy is in Vatican MS. Lat. 2995, fols. 175$^r$–195$^r$.) This writer
is indebted to materials compiled by Roy J. DeFerrari and Martin R. P. McGuire;
a critical edition of the *Rhetorica ad Alexandrum* is contemplated in the Aristoteles
Latinus series. For an English translation of the original Greek text, see *Rhetorica
ad Alexandrum,* trans. E. S. Forster, in *The Works of Aristotle Translated into
English,* ed. W. D. Ross, 13 vols. (Oxford, 1924–1960), Vol. XI.

[45] This, then, may account for a phenomenon long noted by cultural historians:
the appearance of *sententiae* from the book in works of writers who apparently
have little interest in the study of rhetoric itself. Thus Jean de Hesdin, writing a
letter to his patron, Philip d'Alençon, about 1365, cites *Primo Rhetorice,* Cap. 22;
actually, the quotation may be from the *Politica.* Beryl Smalley, "Jean de Hesdin
O. Hosp. S. Ioh.," *Recherches de Théologie ancienne et médiévale,* 28 (1961), 323.
And after a survey of citations from the *Rhetorica* by English writers, Hultzen
concludes that the work was used in medieval England primarily as a source of
quotations on matters not connected with rhetoric. Lee Sisson Hultzen, "Aristotle's
Rhetoric in England to 1600," unpublished dissertation, Cornell University, 1932.

The methodological influence of two other Aristotelian works, however, deserves some consideration. These works are the *Topica* and the *De sophisticis elenchis*. In the sense that the medieval *disputatio* represents a distinct and well-planned type of discourse, it deserves attention as another possible influence upon medieval habits of writing and speaking. The *disputatio* may well be one of the most important formal influences in European higher education between about 1150 and 1400. Apparently every medieval university student underwent some form of the disputation process, either as an integral part of his classroom work, or as a form of examination. A university teacher of theology, by definition, was a master at disputation. As Peter Cantor, a twelfth-century teacher at Paris, expressed it, "A teaching master has three duties: to lecture, to preach, and to dispute." [46]

A *disputatio* might be defined roughly as a formal discussion of a subject by two or more people, who take opposite or differing sides. The exact format of the encounter might differ from time to time, but the basic process involved the statement of a question, then the offering of a proposition in reply to the question, followed by objections to the proposition. Finally a determination (*determinatio*) of the correct or approved answer would be presented.[47]

The organizational structure of the medieval disputation is quite clear:

---

[46] Petrus Cantor, *Verbum abbreviatum,* ed. Migne, *PL* 205, col. 25. For a treatment of the historical development of the general disputation mode, see Martin Grabmann, *Die Geschichte der scholastischen Methode,* 2 vols. (Freiburg im Breisgau, 1909–11), esp. II.17 ff. For an excellent summary of the typical disputation process, however, see A. G. Little and F. Pelster, *Oxford Theology and Theologians, A.D. 1282–1302* (Oxford, 1934), 29–56 and 246–48; another survey may be found in Glorieux, *Repertoire des maîtres,* I.15–35; also Pierre Mandonnet, *Siger de Brabant* (Louvain, 1911). Recent scholarship has brought into print the disputation reports of a number of individual masters; these "transcripts" usually bear the mark of editing after the fact, and must be reviewed critically insofar as actual content is concerned. It is nevertheless true that they probably represent the *form* of the disputation process, which would be more easily remembered than the precise language of the actual encounter. See the collections by Glorieux, *La Littérature quodlibetique de 1260 à 1320* 2 vols., Bibliothèque Thomiste, V and XXI (Paris, 1925–35). For other studies, see Douglas Ehninger and Bromley Smith, "The Terrafilial Disputes at Oxford," *QJS* 36 (1950), 333–39; Strickland Gibson, "The Order of Disputations," *Bodleian Quarterly Record* 6 (1930), 107–12; Angelo Pellegrini, "Renaissance and Medieval Antecedents of Debate," *QJS* 28 (1942), 14–18; Bromley Smith, "Extracurricular Disputations," *QJS* 34 (1948), 473–76; and Murphy, *Bibliography,* V1–V15.

[47] The scholastic emphasis upon thesis, counterthesis, and listing of arguments must have had its effect on all kinds of discourse. It would be difficult to name a more pervasive influence with so little study given to its effects. Even Boccaccio cannot defend poetry (*Genealogia deorum gentilium* XIV–XV) without sounding like a *sophister generalis,* or student in dialectic.

1. Question
2. Proposition in answer
3. Objections to proposition
4. Determination by master
5. Answers to objections (optional)

In the classroom situation this methodology could be used for interpretation of texts, testing of hypotheses, or examination of students' knowledge. It had the great advantage of focusing attention upon a proposition and upon the "proofs" for that proposition, while allowing maximum flexibility for the consideration of differing opinions. Consequently it was an intellectual tool of great value.

Outside the classroom the methodology was translated directly into a pattern for writing. Note the pattern of Thomas Aquinas (1225?-1274), the famous Dominican scholastic theologian at Paris, in his *Summa Theologica* (Part One, Question XIII):

> "Whether a name can be given to God?"
>     Objection 1
>     Objection 2
>     Objection 3
> "On the contrary, . . . I answer that. . . ."
>     Reply to Objection 1
>     Reply to Objection 2
>     Reply to Objection 3

All that Aquinas does in this written form is to omit the explicit statement of a proposition in answer to the question; but this is only a minor change, since the objections are clearly negative and imply the existence of the proposition anyway. His *determinatio* is a tightly reasoned paragraph.[48] The "Scholastic method" of Aquinas in his *Summa Theologica* is simply the classroom *disputatio* adapted to writing. It is still the same process.

---

[48] "*On the contrary,* It is written (Exod. xv.3): *The Lord is a man of war, Almighty is His name. I answer that,* Since, according to the Philosopher, words are signs of ideas, and ideas the similitudes of things, it is evident that words function in the signification of things through the conception of the intellect. It follows therefore that we can give a name to anything in as far as we can understand it. Now it was shown above that in this life we cannot see the essence of God, but we know God from creatures as their cause, and also by way of excellence and remotion. In this way therefore He can be named by us from creatures, yet not so that the name which signifies Him expresses the divine essence in itself in the way that the name *man* expresses the essence of man in himself, since it signifies the definition which manifests his essence. For the idea expressed by the name is the definition." *Basic Writings of Saint Thomas Aquinas,* ed. Anton C. Pegis, 2 vols. (New York, 1936), I, 113.

Although this process bears a superficial resemblance to that of the Roman school exercise known as *declamatio*—with thesis, reply, and solution (*divisio*) by the master—the origins of the medieval disputation lie in the twelfth-century interest in dialectic rather than in a survival of Roman influence. Interestingly enough, the popularity of the Scholastic disputation begins at exactly the point when the new Latin translations of Aristotle's logical works made available to the Western world the two ancient dialectical treatises most closely connected to Greek rhetorical theory, Aristotle's *Topica* and *De sophisticis elenchis*. The so-called "father of the Scholastic method," Anselm of Canterbury (1033–1109), refers in his treatise on grammar to *exercitatio disputandi,* but the main academic use of the *disputatio* seems not to have begun until several decades after his death.[49]

One of the catalytic agents in the twelfth-century resurgence of dialectic was surely the translation in 1128 by Jacob of Venice of the four Aristotelian works which went to make up the "New Logic": *Analytica priora, Analytica posteriora, Topica,* and *De sophisticis elenchis*.[50] The New Logic was to have a decisive influence on disputation technique. Within a few years, for instance, John of Salisbury felt justified in devoting a considerable portion of Book Three of his *Metalogicon* (1159) to a praise of the *Topica*; he was particularly concerned to point out the usefulness of the book in disputation. "Without this book," he says, "one disputes not by art, but by chance."[51] His further description of its virtues may provide an index to the reasons for its widespread adoption as a beginning university text in dialectic:

---

[49] Grabmann, *Geschichte,* II, 17 ff. It is of course true that the germ or root of the classroom disputation—*disputatio in scolis*—may be seen in ancient times. Roman declamation, after all, merely represented a final form of a pedagogical technique found earlier in Protagoras, Isocrates, Plato, and (presumably) in the lost dialogues of Aristotle. The systematic separation of *disputatio* from *lectio,* however, is largely due to developments in the twelfth century. The lecturer (or "reader") of a text of Scripture, for instance, would identify the various possible interpretations and then name the one he preferred. The simple though gradual step of formalizing this three-part process (reading–interpretation–decision) resulted ultimately in a separate operation known as the *disputatio.* See esp. Glorieux, *Repertoire des maîtres* I.15 ff., and Murphy, "Two Medieval Textbooks in Debate," *Journal of the American Forensic Association* I (1964), 1–6.

[50] The "Old Logic" included Aristotle's *Predicamenta* (or *Categorias*) and *Periermenias* (or *De interpretatione*). These appeared in the translation of Boethius, and were often linked with the Boethian version of Porphyry's *Isagoge.* The complete *Organon* then, dates from the second quarter of the twelfth century. Cf. Lacombe, *Arist. Lat.* I, 43–49.

[51] *The Metalogicon of John of Salisbury: A Twelfth-Century Defense of the Verbal and Logical Arts of the Trivium,* trans. Daniel D. McGarry (Berkeley and Los Angeles, 1955), III.10, p. 190.

Since dialectic is carried on between two persons, this book teaches the matched contestants whom it trains and provides with reasons and topics, to handle their proper weapons and engage in verbal, rather than physical conflict. It instills into its disciples such astute skill that one may clearly see that it is the principal source of the rules of all eloquence, for which it serves as a sort of primary fountainhead. It is undoubtedly true, as Cicero and Quintilian acknowledge, that this work has not merely been helpful to rhetoricians, but has also, for both them and writers on the arts, even served as the initial starting point for the study of rhetoric, which subsequently expanded and acquired its own particular rules.[52]

A little later John points out, in relation to the *De sophisticis elenchis,* that a systematic study of sophistry is useful to avoid the snares of pretended wisdom. He adds, "I would be reluctant to say that any other study could be more beneficial to the young."

By the end of the twelfth century both the *Topica* and *De sophisticis* had become the standard texts for the beginning student in dialectic. The records are fragmentary, and early university practices must often be reconstructed from chance allusion and an occasional surviving statute, but the pattern in respect to *dialectica* is clear enough. The entering student began with grammar and moved thence to dialectic. (Apparently he did not undergo a course of rhetoric at all, so that the popular conception of a regular *trivium* at the university level is largely a myth.) The earliest extant record of a regular "curriculum," as we would use the term, dates from 1215 at the University of Paris. Priscian serves for grammar, and for dialectic the student is required to read Porphyry's *Isagoge* in addition to the entire Old Logic and New Logic. Subsequent provisions in 1255 and 1366 confirmed this general pattern, which was imitated by Oxford and Cambridge in England, and by universities generally throughout medieval Europe.[53]

The contents of the two books were particularly useful to the student being prepared for the disputation.[54] One of the avowed purposes of *De*

---

[52] *Ibid.,* pp. 190–91. It is significant that John of Salisbury does not discuss *declamatio* in this connection, for he had access to Quintilian's treatment (*Inst.* II.vi).

[53] In addition to the reports of statutes published by Rashdall, *Universities,* cf. Lynn Thorndike, *University Records and Life in the Middle Ages* (New York, 1944), pp. 27–30, 52–56, 64–66. Chaucer's Clerk of Oxford, for instance ("That unto logyk hadde longe ygo"), is chided by the Host for being silent on the pilgrimage to Canterbury (Clerk's Prologue, verses 4–5):

> This day ne herde I of youre tonge a word.
> I trowe ye studie aboute som sophyme.

[54] It is difficult to see how any of the standard rhetorical works would have served the same special purpose for the medieval student. Quotations from these two books are from the translation of W. A. Pickard–Cambridge in *The Works of*

*sophisticis,* after all, is "to speak of arguments used in competitions and contests" (ii.165$^b$). It had been designed to enable an instructor to "conduct an examination (not only) dialectically but with a show of knowledge" (xxxiv.183$^b$). Aristotle summarized the whole book as a treatment of sources for detecting fallacies, and noted, "We have shown, moreover, how to question or arrange the questioning as a whole" (xxxiv.183$^b$).

The *Topica* is even closer in spirit to the matters of invention and delivery usually associated with rhetoric. The Preamble states: "Our treatise proposes to find a line of inquiry whereby we shall be able to reason from opinions that are generally accepted about every problem propounded to us, and also shall ourselves, when standing up to an argument, avoid saying anything that will obstruct us" (I.i.100$^a$). It is Book Eight of the *Topica,* however, which seems most applicable to the problems faced by the medieval disputant. This final book is nothing less than a full set of rules for conducting a disputation. Practical advice about argumentation is mixed with hints about the psychology of opponents (VIII.xiv.163$^b$–166$^b$). Like the *De sophisticis,* it is studded with references to "hearers," to "the audience," and to the "respondent."

The prevalence of these two books in medieval university programs, therefore, might well be taken as the chief form of direct influence which the ancient Aristotelian tradition exerted on the theory of discourse between about 1150 and 1400.[55]

Cicero is the unquestioned *magister eloquentiae* for the middle ages. Indeed, beginning with Horace and Quintilian, Cicero's reputation was

*Aristotle,* ed. W. D. Ross (Oxford [1949–56]), Vol. 1 (1955). It is worth noting also that John of Salisbury, as we have just seen, calls the *Topica* "the initial starting point for the study of rhetoric." Why study two separate arts, he implies, when dialectic leads into rhetoric anyway?

[55] The *Poetica* seems to have attracted very little attention before the Renaissance. See Bernard Weinberg, *A History of Literary Criticism in the Italian Renaissance,* 2 vols. (Chicago, 1961), I, 349–61, for a discussion of the emergence of Aristotle's *Poetica* at the end of the middle ages. For the text of the medieval Latin translation, see *Aristoteles de arte poetica Guillelmo de Moerbeke interprete,* ed. Erse Valgimigli, reviserunt praefatione indicibusque instruxerunt Aelius Franceschini and Laurentius Minio–Palluello, *Aris. Lat.* XXXIII (Bruges and Paris, 1953). Also see E. Franceschini, "La Poetica di Aritotele nel sec. XIII," *Atti del Reale Instituto Veneto di Scienze, Lettere e Arti* 94 (1935), 523–48; and William F. Boggess, "Aristotle's *Poetics* in the Fourteenth Century," *Studies in Philology* 57 (1970), 278–94.

maintained in a continuous tradition of superiority through the Principate, the Empire, the Patristic Age, the middle ages, the Renaissance, and the Age of Enlightment, and suffered a check only in comparatively recent times.

Saint Augustine's *De doctrina christiana,* the first truly medieval treatise on the communicative arts, is based on Augustine's professional experience as a teacher of Ciceronian rhetoric in the public schools of his day.[56] All the early encyclopedists—Cassiodorus, Isidore, Capella—assume that Cicero is the prime exemplar. Boethius does the same. Alcuin draws on the rhetoric of Cicero for doctrines of kingly behavior to recommend to Charlemagne,[57] and the abstracts of Notker Labeo and Anselm of Besate in the tenth and eleventh centuries indicate a continuation of the same interest.[58] Thierry of Chartres—one of the teachers of John of Salisbury, and the author of the massive *Heptateuchon,* or survey of all seven liberal arts—composed in the twelfth century what is probably the first medieval commentary on the *De inventione.*[59] Although Hugh of St. Victor, a contemporary of Thierry, is unwilling to do more than cite Cicero as a Latinizer of rhetoric, he does quote directly from *De inventione* to show the benefits of eloquence.[60]

Indeed, there is hardly a major medieval writer who does not mention Cicero whenever there is occasion to speak of discourse. From Thomas Aquinas to Petrarch and Boccaccio, Cicero is praised and quoted both for his eloquence and his philosophy;[61] Dante places Cicero in the first circle

---

[56] James J. Murphy, "Saint Augustine and the Debate about a Christian Rhetoric," ⟵ *QJS* 46 (1960), 400–10; and James B. Eskridge, *The Influence of Cicero upon Augustine in the Development of His Oratorical Theory for the Training of the Ecclesiastical Orator* (Menasha, Wis., 1912).

[57] Alcuin, *The Rhetoric of Alcuin and Charlemagne,* ed. and trans. Wilbur S. Howell (Princeton, N.J., 1941); see also Luitpold Wallach, *Alcuin and Charlemagne* (Ithaca, N.Y., 1959), chap. 1 (pp. 29–96): "The *Via Regia* of Charlemagne: The *Rhetoric* of Alcuin as a Treatise on Kingship."

[58] See Otto Dieter, "The Rhetoric of Notker Labeo," in *Papers in Rhetoric,* ed. Donald C. Bryant (St. Louis, Mo., 1940), pp. 27–33. For Anselm of Besate, cf. Manitius, *Geschichte,* II, 708–15.

[59] Still unedited.

[60] *The Didascalicon of Hugh of St. Victor,* trans. Jerome Taylor (New York, 1961). "Rhetoric was written in Greek by Aristotle and Gorgias and Hermagoras, and brought into Latin by Tully, Quintilian, and Titian." III.iii, p. 86. Hugh quotes Cicero's *De inventione* I.iv.5 in praise of eloquence, for "by it life is made safe, by it fit, by it noble, and by it pleasurable." II.xx, p. 75.

[61] Edward R. Rand, *Cicero in the Courtroom of St. Thomas Aquinas* (Milwaukee, Wis., 1946); for brief treatment of the Italian interest, for example, see R. R. Bolgar, *The Classical Heritage and Its Beneficiaries* (Cambridge, 1954), pp. 249–68 and 329–30. An English monk, Ingulfus (d. 1109) says that he studied both *De inventione* and *ad Herennium*; see *Chronicle of Croyland Abbey,* ed.

of the unbaptized, along with Seneca. Undoubtedly the popularity of his *De officiis* and *Tusculanae disputationes* contributed to the general esteem in which he was held,[62] but it is plain that Cicero is regarded as the standard of eloquence. Cicero's reputation is indirectly attested to by Boncompagno, early in the thirteenth century; wishing to propose to the world that he had written the ultimate rhetoric, he could think of no higher praise for himself than to call his book *Rhetorica novissima,* that is, a book even newer than the *Rhetorica nova* of Cicero.[63] The Englishman John Whetmanstede, prior of Gloucester College in Oxford and abbot of St. Alban's, praises an Italian rhetor near Siena by calling him "another Cicero." [64] The authors of letter-writing manuals and preaching manuals also call upon the authority of "Tullius" to add luster to their own works.[65] Even the fourteenth-century Nominalist William of Occam is called upon (albeit in a Florentine's dream) to praise *Marcus, romanae gloria linguae.*[66] Such instances could be multiplied indefinitely, but the point is perhaps clear that Cicero was so assumptively, so overwhelmingly, so pervasively regarded as prime *auctor* that on this ground alone we could conclude that his works must have had enormous circulation and use.

The history of medieval Ciceronianism remains to be written,[67] and

---

W. G. Birch (Wisbech, 1883), p. 128. Honorius of Regensburg (1090-c. 1156) makes Cicero the exemplar for rhetoric in his *De animae exsilio et patria* (Migne, *PL* CLXXII, cols. 1241–46); quoted in Eva M. Sanford, "Honorius, Presbyter and Scholasticus," *Speculum* 23 (1948), 397–425.

[62] Medieval teachers recognized the ethical concepts common to these two works and to the *De inventione.* The combination made Cicero an extremely useful *auctor.* See H. Baron, "Cicero and Roman Civic Spirit in the Middle Ages and Early Renaissance," *Bulletin of the John Rylands Library* 22 (1938), 72–97; Philippe Delhaye, "L'enseignement de la Philosophie Morale au XIIe siècle," *Medieval Studies* 11 (1949), 77–99; Bolgar, *Heritage,* pp. 121 and 197–98. For a warning comment in respect to Cicero's medieval "moral philosophy," however, cf. Ernst Curtius, *European Literature and the Latin Middle Ages* (New York, 1953), 522–37.

[63] Buoncompagno, *Rhetorica novissima,* ed. A. Gaudenzi, Bibliotheca juridica medii aevi II (Bologna, 1892).

[64] Ernst Kantorowicz, "An 'Autobiography' of Guido Faba," *Medieval and Renaissance Studies* 1 (1941), 253–80.

[65] For instance, *Precepta prosaici dictaminis secundum Tullium,* ed. Franz-Joseph Schmale (Bonn, 1950). The Englishman Robert of Basevorn, writing his *Forma praedicandi* in 1322, concludes a discussion of *colores* by reminding the reader that the complete treatment may be found in "ultimo libro Rhetoricae secundae Tullii." Robert of Basevorn, *Forma praedicandi,* ed. Th.-M. Charland in *Artes praedicandi* (Paris and Ottowa, 1936), Cap. 50.

[66] Francesco Landini (1325–97), quoted in Eduard Norden, *Die antike Kunstprosa,* 2 vols. (Leipzig, 1898), II.744.

[67] The few works in this field are rather generalized, and usually devote only a small portion to Cicero's place in medieval history. A glance at the prevalance of

yet from the scattered indications already available a fairly clear pattern can be seen to emerge. A summary of this pattern would run as follows:

The most frequently used Ciceronian books before the fifteenth century were his youthful *De inventione* (known as *rhetorica vetus,* or "old rhetoric") and the Pseudo–Ciceronian *Rhetorica ad Herennium* (called *rhetorica nova* or "new rhetoric" to distinguish it from the *De inventione*). Both books were universally regarded as Cicero's until Erasmus questioned the authorship of the *ad Herennium.* The *Topica* was known chiefly through the version of Boethius. Cicero's remaining rhetorical works were neglected during the middle ages, but copies of his *Epistolae* were much used, although the authors of *artes dictaminis* (the letter-writing manuals) do not usually propose them as models.

The net result of this pattern was that Cicero's theories were known to the middle ages primarily through the highly schematized rhetorical treatises of his youthful period. The humane catholicity of his *De oratore* became a major influence only in the fifteenth century. Both library catalogues and quotations by other writers demonstrate the dominance of the *rhetorica vetus* and *rhetorica nova.* Nothing could demonstrate this dominance more clearly than the number of times these two books appear in medieval library catalogues. Bolgar, in a study based on the catalogue entries collected by Manitius, cites the number of appearances by century, as the table shows.[68]

| Work | | | Number per Century | | | |
|---|---|---|---|---|---|---|
| | IX | X | XI | XII | XIII | XIV |
| *ad Herennium* | I | – | 6 | 13 | 4 | 5 |
| *De rhetorica* | 6 | 2 | 9 | | | |
| (*De inventione*) | | | | 32 | 35 | 35 |
| *De oratore* | 3 | – | I | 3 | 3 | 2 |

Insofar as rhetoric was a curricular subject in the medieval universities, it was probably the rhetoric of Cicero. There is abundant evidence from the pre-university period to indicate the widespread use of these works; indeed, John of Salisbury is often quoted by modern students to typify

---

index entries for Cicero in any literary or cultural study, however, will demonstrate at once the ubiquity and importance of his influence throughout the middle ages. See Th. Zielinski, *Cicero im Wandel der Jahrhunderte* (Leipzig, 1912); John C. Rolfe, *Cicero and His Influence* (Boston, 1923); Albert C. Clark, *Ciceronianism in English Literature and the Classics* (Oxford, 1912).

[68] Bolgar, *Heritage,* p. 396. This chart is derived from items listed in Max Manitius, *Handschriften antiken Autoren in mittelalterlichen Bibliothekskatalogen,* ed. Karl Manitius, in *Zentralblatt für Bibliothekswesen,* Supplement 67 (Leipzig, 1935).

the whole of medieval attitudes toward discourse.[69] But for the period after about 1150 most of the evidence is indirect and depends upon inference. For instance, the numerous Ciceronian citations in the works of Thomas Aquinas probably represent some interest in rhetoric at Paris in the second half of the thirteenth century; we have already noted that holiday lecturing on "rhetoric" (but including only grammar and Boethius' *Topica* IV) was permitted in the statutes of 1215 at Paris. In 1342 the library of the Sorbonne contained twenty-four of Cicero's works, including rhetorical treatises.[70] An unspecified book of Cicero appears in the account of a meeting held in Oxford about 1200.[71]

But this is the north. Italian universities have a distinctly different attitude toward the *trivium*. The words of Rashdall summarize one such important difference:

> But while the Italian universities never rivalled the scholastic fame of Paris, rhetoric, mathematics, and astrology flourished more vigorously in the Italian universities than in the north. In the former subject the text-books at Bologna were the *De inventione* of Cicero and the treatise *ad Herennium* then attributed to the same writer, or the compendium of it compiled by the Friar Guidotto of Bologna.[72]

All the indirect indications available to us make it plausible to say that the Ciceronian tradition remained vital in Italy throughout the middle

---

[69] It might be pointed out here that the availability of evidence for twelfth-century France—and also the popularity of the idea of a "twelfth-century Renaissance"—has sometimes led uncritical students to assume that what was true of Chartres must *ipso facto* have been true of the middle ages as a whole. Note, for instance, Frederick Harrison, *Medieval Man and His Notions* (London, 1947), pp. 8–9: "Rhetoric was studied chiefly in Cicero's well-known treatise, a copy of which, with a companion book, the commentary, was found in nearly every medieval library in this country [i.e., England]." The survival of architectural evidence has been another pitfall, as Sandys indicates (*Scholarship,* p. 672): "In this connexion it is interesting to point out that it was between 1134 and 1150, at a time when the influence of Bernard was still strong in Chartres, when his immediate pupils were actually teaching in its famous school, and while his brother Theodoric was successively 'master of the school' and 'chancellor,' that the right-hand door-way of the West Front of the cathedral was adorned with figures of the Seven Arts, each of them associated with an ancient personage, Grammar with Priscian, Dialectic with Aristotle, Rhetoric with Cicero. . . ." It might be well, then, to temper with caution any general conclusions drawn from Clerval, Paré, or Haskins for the general history of Cicero after about 1150. The very term "Renaissance," after all, implies that something low had risen and presumably, also, that it afterwards fell again.
[70] Bolgar, *Heritage,* p. 261.
[71] Rashdall, *Universities* III, 32n.
[72] *Ibid.,* I, 248.

ages, even though in the northern universities it was not a major factor
in the educational program. Perhaps it would be accurate to say that in
the north Cicero survived largely by reputation and in physical presence
—that is, in seldom-consulted books resting on library shelves and in
grammatical teaching—while south of the Alps Cicero exercised a direct
influence through constant use. The very emergence of the *ars dictaminis*
in Italy—based immediately and obviously upon Ciceronian doctrine—
would be proof enough of eleventh-century regard for the Roman preceptor, even without the parallel use of his rhetorical doctrines in legal
training. Brunetto Latini and Boncompagno, the major thirteenth-century redactors of Cicero, are, after all, both Italians. It is interesting to
contrast fourteenth-century Paris with Bologna: the "reform" of 1366 excluded rhetoric at Paris, but the year 1321 saw the *re*establishment of a
chair of formal rhetoric at Bologna.[73] Petrarch's Ciceronianism, too, marks
a current of interest in fourteenth-century Italy that was to flow north in
the following century and was not to reach England until the middle of
the sixteenth century.

The exacting spirit which made Paris the center of scholasticism (and
could make Aristotle's *Rhetorica* into a book of ethics) was a spirit which
distrusted the shifting, problematical influence of the basic Ciceronian
belief that the human artist of discourse can so shape and sway his audience that they are affected only by purely human factors. The scholastic
mind seeks *lex,* or at least *regulum*. If the term "humanism" has any
meaning at all, on the other hand, its meaning probably lies in the basic
belief that human artistry is in some way superior to *regula*. In this sense
the Italian approach to Cicero in the middle ages may be termed more
"humanistic" than that of the northerners.

In ancient Greece the concept of *logos* included both the *thing thought*
and the *expression of thought.* Aristotle's synthesis in this direction was
to identify each element formally, but the Romans generally chose to
emphasize the "expression" aspect. During the middle ages, after about
1150, the difference tended to be geographical: at Paris and Oxford, the
expressional aspects of dialectic (as in *Topica* VIII, for instance) were
used only to test validity; at Bologna and Ravenna the expressional theories of Cicero were actually used to promote a viable theory of discourse.
John of Salisbury's *Metalogicon* thus marks a watershed. On one hand

---

[73] In the same year the students petitioned for the appointment of a professor
of poetry, who was duly selected. Cf. Bolgar, *Heritage,* pp. 249 and 255.

he admires and praises the Quintilianistic educational regime of his preceptor, Bernard; on the other hand, quite unconsciously, he opens the way for the new wave of dialectic exactitude which enabled the *disputatio* to replace *oratio* as a central feature of the educational process. One modern critic is only partly right when he declares that "between the world of John of Salisbury and the world of Petrarch there is an intellectual kinship." [74]

Even the teaching of law in Italy demonstrates the ubiquity of Ciceronian influence. Certainly the *De inventione* and the *first* half of the *ad Herennium* would be eminently adaptable to legal studies, designed as they are for the actual study of forensic oratory. Isidore of Seville recognized this relation (*Etymologia* XX.x.1) by including a paragraph about law in his treatment of rhetoric, although the fifth book of Isidore's work treats law with hardly any mention of rhetoric. Alcuin's *Dialogus* with Charlemagne shows a keen awareness of legal lore in the Ciceronian tradition. The anonymous *Rhetorica ecclesiastica* (c. 1160–80) demonstrates the longevity of influence of the *Dialogus,* for the author quotes Alcuin along with Isidore, Gratian, and numerous decretals. The intention of the author is to utilize both law and rhetoric: "Intentio eius est, instruere personas in iudicio constituendas, partim secundam normam canonum, partim artificiosam doctrinam rhetorum." [75] The natural affinity between law and the Ciceronian doctrine of *status* must surely have made the *rhetorica vetus* and *rhetorica nova* extremely useful instruments for the Bolognese masters.[76]

A further indication of Cicero's popularity as *rex eloquentiae* is to be found in the fact that it is Cicero's rhetoric—and only Cicero's—which is

---

[74] Curtius, *Latin Middle Ages,* p. 77. The two men might have had much in common, but their worlds were vastly different.

[75] Quoted in A. Lang, "Rhetorische Einflusse auf die Behandlung des Prozesses in der Kanonistik des 12. Jahrhundert," in *Festschrift Eduard Eichmann,* ed. Martin Grabmann and K. Hoffman (Paderborn, 1940), p. 94. The anonymous author actually makes very little use of rhetorical doctrine, but it is at least noteworthy that he names the two studies together in his introduction, as if his audience will see the evident similarity.

[76] Although the formal study of law and rhetoric together was more a feature of the early than the later middle ages, developments in twelfth- and thirteenth-century Italy allied the two subjects in a different way through the rise of the *ars dictaminis* and later the *ars notaria.* A brief summary of this relation may be found in Louis J. Paetow, *The Arts Course at Medieval Universities, with Special Reference to Grammar and Rhetoric,* University of Illinois Studies, Vol. III (Urbana, 1910), pp. 70–91. And see Hermann Kantorowicz and W. W. Buckland eds., *Studies in the Glossators of the Roman Law: Newly Discovered Writings of the Twelfth Century* (Cambridge, 1938).

translated into vernacular tongues during the middle ages. Most of the translations date from the thirteenth century.[77]

Brunetto Latini (1220–94), Florentine notary and teacher, is responsible for a series of three works which rendered a large part of *De inventione* into French and Italian during the 1260's. The works are *Rettorica*, in Italian, probably written in or about 1260; an encyclopedic survey, *Li livres dou Trésor*, written in French about 1260; and *Il Tesoro*, an Italian translation of the *Trésor*, written by his friend Bono Giambono by 1266.[78] The bilingual nature of Latini's efforts may be explained by the fact that the first two books were composed during an exile in France. The *Rettorica* is a vernacular version of *De inventione* composed to please a rich and learned patron who shared his exile; it is not, however, a literal *verbum ex verbo* translation, but a liberal rendition of the sense of the source book.

The same might be said of the Ciceronian rhetorical doctrine which occupies a good part of Book Three of the *Trésor*.[79] In a manner reminiscent of Vincent of Beauvais, Latini divides his survey of knowledge (*philosophie*) into the three fields of *theorique, pratique,* and *logique,* but when he arrives at a discussion of *politique* in Book Three he provides a complete exposition of Ciceronian rhetoric, having virtually ignored the subject of logic.[80] The practical effect of this ultimate proportioning is that he does not follow his originally stated plan for the work. In any case the bulk of the third and final book is devoted to rhetoric (some 72 of 105 sections); the latter part of Book Three is devoted to the government of cities.

---

[77] The medieval history of vernacular translations, which remains to be written, might well provide us with interesting insights into the popularity and use of certain works. Why, for instance, should *any* work be translated into French or Italian from Latin, the language of the learned? A brief list of major medieval vernacular translations may be found in an appendix to Bolgar, *Heritage,* pp. 506–41. It would be useful, however, to have for the medieval vernaculars a bibliography of the type found in Clarissa P. Farrar and Austin P. Evans, *A Bibliography of English Translations from Medieval Sources,* Records of Civilization, Sources and Studies, No. XXXIX (New York, 1946).

[78] The relation between these three works is still somewhat obscure, but apparently the *Rettorica* was written first and then its material was incorporated with some changes into the encyclopedic *Trésor,* which was in turn rendered from French into Italian by Giambono as the *Tesoro.* For texts: *Rettorica,* ed. F. Maggini (Florence, 1915); *Li livres dou Trésor,* ed. Francis Carmody (Berkeley and Los Angeles, 1948); *ll Tesoro,* ed. P. Chabaille, 4 vols. (Bologna, 1878–83).

[79] The first half of Book Three, which deals with Latini's rhetorical doctrines, has been translated into English by James R. East; see above, n. 24.

[80] Latini gives the subject only 22 lines in I.v.

Although Latini mentions Aristotle's *livre ki est translaté en romans*,[81] it is obvious that he is referring not to the *Rhetorica* but to the *Politica*. The whole treatment, moreover, is Ciceronian, and the traditional six parts of a speech are used as an organizational pattern for the whole discussion. Latini, significantly, sees no essential contradiction between *De inventione* and the newer *ars dictaminis*, for he says that he means to write a treatise useful for both speaking and writing: "Or dist li mestres que le science de rectorique est en ii. manieres, une ki est en disant de bouche et un autre que l'on mande par letres; mais li enseignement sont commun, car il ne peut chaloir que l'on die un conte ou que on le mande par letres." [82] The Italian translation by Bono Giambono (*Il Tesoro*) is a faithful rendering of the French *Trésor*, differing mainly in that Giambono often substitutes Italian names or examples for those used by Latini in the original.

Still another Italian vernacular rendering of the thirteenth century is the *Fiore di rettorica* or *Rettorica nuovo di Tullio*, composed before 1266 by either Guidotto da Bologna or Bono Giambono.[83] This work presents a paraphrase of *ad Herennium* rather than a literal translation, indicating at least that the author was familiar enough with his original to hazard putting the ideas into his own terms without following the Ciceronian text too closely.

The same might be said about the fourth vernacular treatise, the French compendium of both *De inventione* and *ad Herennium* composed in 1282 by Jean d'Antioche de Harens. The combination of the two pieces resulted in a six-part treatise which d'Antioche called *Rettorique de Marc Tulles Cyceron*.[84] Although d'Antioche's translation is far more literal than the others of the thirteenth century, he explains in a lengthy postscript that the difference between the French and Latin languages made it necessary for him to acquire an intimate knowledge of the two Ciceronian works before undertaking the translation.

Little needs to be said about the contribution to rhetorical knowledge made by these various works. There was little, even in Latini's linking of Cicero and *ars dictaminis*. The same material was readily available in

---

[81] *Trésor* III.ii.

[82] *Ibid.*, III.iv.

[83] *Il fiore di Rettorica*, ed. V. Nannucci, Manuale della letteratura del primo secolo della lingua Italiana, Vol. II (Florence, 1858).

[84] Leopold Delisle, "Notice sur la rhétorique de Ciceron traduite par maître Jean d'Antioche," *Notices et extraits* 36 (1899), 207–67. Delisle prints excerpts from the unique MS. 590 of the Musée de Condé, for instance, "Réthorique est plus jointe a gramaire que n'est a logique. Logique est necessaire es desputeisons et es escoles, et réthorique es jugemenz et es plais" (p. 217).

the Latin originals.[85] But the significance of the translations lies in their obvious Ciceronianism, their early date, and their geographical position. It was not until the fifteenth century that Enrique de Villena translated the *ad Herennium* into Castilian (now lost), and Alfonso de Cartegena translated *De inventione*, also into Castilian (1422–32). The first English language version of Ciceronian rhetoric did not appear until Thomas Wilson's *Arte of Rhetorique* in 1530. Aristotle's *Rhetorica*, moreover, was not put into any English version until the paraphrase of Thomas Hobbes in the early seventeenth century.

Another type of activity occurred in fourteenth-century France. In 1356 the Consistoire du Gai Savoir at Toulouse promoted the composition of a joint work called *Las leys d'amours,* designed to be a comprehensive treatment of grammar, rhetoric, poetic, and metric. The Consistoire, a poetical society founded in 1323, appointed Guilhelm Molinier as chairman of a committee to draft an *ars poetria* in the vernacular. The result was a treatise in three books using precepts drawn largely from Brunetto Latini, Albertano da Brescia, Alexander of Villedieu, Priscian, and Donatus. It might be noted also that the *L'Art de dictier* (1392) of Eustache Deschamps is significant partly because it breaks away from the tradition that had made versification a part of rhetoric; Deschamps places versification under music. The previous tradition was so strong in France that some writers used the term *seconde rhétorique* to denote versification, and denoted prose by the term *première rhétorique*.[86]

Medieval culture was, of course, essentially a Latin culture. Some major

---

[85] And not only in the originals, of course, because there were *compendia* available to condense the originals and make them even more readily available in schematic form. A library catalogue at Arezzo in 1338 lists a book in rethorica sub compendia. Manitius, *Bibliothekskatalogen,* p. 34. A fifteenth-century manuscript now in the Bodleian Library, Oxford, MS. Digby 15, presents a rapid summary of *ad Herennium* in only eight small quarto pages (fols. 129–33).

The doctrine of *memoria* in *ad Herennium* III apparently had a separate medieval history. Aquinas wrote a commentary on Aristotle's treatise on memory, and in the late middle ages the section from *ad Herennium* is found circulating separately. See Frances Yates, "The Ciceronian Art of Memory," in *Medioevo e Rinascimento Studi in Onore di Bruno Nardi* (Florence, 1955), pp. 873–902, and her later book, *The Art of Memory* (London, 1966). For an older study, cf. Helga Hadju, *Das mnemotechnische Schrifttum des Mittelalters* (Vienna, 1936).

[86] For a description of the Provençal text of *Las leys d'amours* and a list of editions, see Warner Patterson, *Three Centuries of French Poetic Theory, 1328–1630,* University of Michigan Publications in Language and Literature, Vols. XIV–XV (Ann Arbor, 1935), XIV.35–39. Two prose versions and one verse version have survived. For Deschamps' work, see Eustache Deschamps, *Oeuvres complètes,* ed. Gaston Raynaud, 9 vols. (Paris, 1891), VII, 266–92. For a discussion of the *seconde rhétorique,* cf. *Recueil d'arts de seconde rhétorique,* ed. E. Langlois, Documents inédits sur l'histoire de France (Paris, 1902), pp. i–vi.

Latin philosophical works were translated into the vernacular—for instance, Nicholas Oresme rendered Aristotle's *Ethica* into French—but apparently no vernacular writer translated a logical or grammatical work during this period. Since grammar was used to teach Latin, and logic was regarded as a learned study, this omission is scarcely surprising.

Thus the translations of Cicero's works can only indicate a high regard for him.

Still another indication of this regard is to be found in the medieval commentaries on the *De inventione* and *Rhetorica ad Herennium*. In the context of medieval society, the existence of commentaries can only mean the use of a book in the schools. Unfortunately, to the best of my knowledge, not one single complete text of these commentaries has ever been printed, so that it is impossible to attempt any extensive study at this time.

The late Roman schoolmasters who taught the Ciceronian doctrines in schools of the Empire had composed a number of commentaries on the *De inventione*. (The *Rhetorica ad Herennium* was not popular before the latter half of the fourth Christian century, and so it did not receive the same kind of treatment.) Two such ancient commentaries were those of Grillius and of Victorinus; Victorinus' proved more popular, although both had some medieval use.[87]

Recent scholarship in this field has unearthed many medieval commentaries which have not yet been studied completely. One or two have been examined in detail, and John O. Ward has recently completed a massive study which includes a check list of known commentaries on *De inventione* and the *ad Herennium*.[88] Nevertheless, our present knowledge is

---

[87] For Grillius, a fourth-century writer, see Josef Martin, *Grillius, ein Beitrag zur Geschichte der Rhetorik*, Studien zur Geschichte und Kultur des Altertums, Band XIV, Heft 2, 3 (Paderborn, 1927). Martin notes that Benzo of Alba (fl. 1061) ranked Grillius (and Quintilian!) among the great writers of the middle ages. Victorinus, another fourth-century rhetorician who is mentioned by Saint Augustine (*Confessio* VII.ix), wrote his commentary before becoming a Christian, but this made little difference in his treatment. For text, see Charles Halm, *Rhetores latini minores* (Leipzig, 1863), pp. 155–304. Also, cf. J. de Ghellinck, *Le mouvement théologique du XIIe siècle* (Paris, 1914), pp. 175–77.

[88] John O. Ward, "Artificiosa eloquentia in the Middle Ages," unpublished dissertation, University of Toronto, 1972. This two-volume work of nearly 1200 typescript pages treats the *De inventione* and *ad Herennium* (and their commentaries) to the thirteenth century, as well as Quintilian's *Institutio oratoria*. I was not able to obtain a complete copy of the dissertation before this book went to press, but it clearly deserves careful study. For a study of a particular commentary, see Harry Caplan, "A Mediaeval Commentary on the *Rhetorica ad Herennium*," in Harry Caplan, *Of Eloquence: Studies in Ancient and Medieval Rhetoric* (Ithaca, N.Y., 1970), pp. 246–76.

somewhat sketchy, and so it will be useful at this point to outline briefly the kinds of things we do know from earlier work.

An early medieval commentary on the *De inventione* is that of Thierry of Chartres, composed about the middle of the twelfth century. Thierry, brother of that Bernard whom John of Salisbury called "the greatest font of learning in Gaul in recent times," was himself a prolific author. He is best known for his *Heptateuchon*,[89] a massive encyclopedia of the seven liberal arts; his primary interests are perhaps indicated by the fact that of the 595 leaves in the manuscript, 434 are devoted to the verbal subjects of the *trivium*, while only 161 are used for the four subjects of the *quadrivium*. Grammar occupies almost twice as much space as rhetoric, Donatus and Priscian being the primary sources. Rhetorical doctrine is solidly Ciceronian, with debts to *De inventione, ad Herennium,* and *Partitiones,* and also to Julianus Severus and Martianus Capella. Thierry has been noted as the first to handle the whole *Organon* of Aristotle in such an encyclopedia, but he omits the *Analytica posteriora* even though he treats the other five books, including the *Topica* and *De sophisticis elenchis.*

Although John of Salisbury terms Thierry "a very assiduous investigator of the arts," John's attitude toward him is unclear. Thierry was John's first teacher in rhetoric, but the student was later to say that he did not learn very much from the experience; indeed, John said he learned more about rhetoric later from a grammarian, Peter Helias.

Whatever John may have thought of his rhetorical knowledge, however, Thierry's allusions to Victorinus, Grillius, and the speeches of Cicero indicate that he had made a wide survey of the books available to his age. Later in the century he was praised as *orator et rhetor et artis amator grammaticae, logicae.*[90] And his commentary was sufficiently regarded to be copied a number of times, as is attested by its survival in five manuscripts.

Thierry's *Super Cicero de inventione,*[91] written as part of a general

---

[89] Still in manuscript. For summaries, cf. Manitius, *Geschichte,* III, 200–01, and A. Clerval, *Les écoles de Chartres au moyen âge* (Chartres, 1895), pp. 220–40.

[90] By the biographer of his pupil, Adalbert, who later became bishop of Mainz. *Monumenta Moguntina,* ed. P. Jaffé (Berlin, 1866), p. 708.

[91] Edited in part by W. H. D. Suringar in *Historia critica scholiastarum latinorum* (Leiden, 1834), Part I, pp. 213–252. Suringar's text is based on a fragment found in a Leiden manuscript, which bears no title for the work; his text includes the whole prologue, and the commentary on passages as far as the discussion of deliberative oratory.

Neither is there a title in London, British Museum MS. Arundel 348, a twelfth-

glossing movement at Chartres during the middle of the twelfth century, shows his concern for matters of definition, and for the relation of rhetoric to other arts. It is evident also that the prior commentaries of Victorinus and Boethius have influenced his approach to the problem of explicating the text of Cicero. His basic method is to cite Ciceronian passages, in order as they occur in the *De inventione,* and then to add his own explanation or comment; occasionally he departs into a digression suggested by a passage, but these instances are not frequent.

A passage from his introduction indicates the general tenor of the commentary:

> Circa artem rethoricam X consideranda. Scilicet quid sit genus artium. Quid sit ipsa ars. Quid sit materia. Quid sit officium. Quid sit finis. Quid partes. Quid species. Quid instrumentes. Quid sit artifex. Quare rethorica vocatur.[92]

A little later Thierry acknowledges that past authors have produced a number of different definitions of the art of rhetoric. One defines it as "the science of speaking well"; another would make it "the science of employing full and perfect eloquence in private and public causes"; still another would say that it is "the science appropriate for speaking to persuade concerning a specific cause." In any case, he says, those who wish to learn more about these different approaches may do so by reading Quintilian's *Institutio oratoria.*

Nor is it sufficient merely to produce a definition, Thierry points out.

---

century manuscript which contains the commentary on fols. 102–79ᵛ. The *incipit* is: Ut ait Petronius nos magistri in scolis soli relinqimur. References below are to this manuscript. The work survives in at least four other manuscripts: Brussels, Royal Library MS. 10057–62, fols. 2–31; Leiden University Library MS. 189, fols. 42–47; London, British Museum MS. Phillips 9672; and Munich Latin. MS. 3565, fols. 174–319.

The meager bibliography on this commentary is based on the Brussels manuscript. The first notice seems to be that of Paul Thomas, "Un commentaire du moyen âge sur la rhétorique de Cicéron" in *Mélanges Graux* (Paris, 1884), pp. 41–45; Thomas prints two short excerpts concerned with the identification of the author, and also notes that the following authors are cited by Thierry: Aristotle (Old Logic), Boethius, Cicero (*De oratore,* and Verrine and Phillipic orations), *ad Herennium,* Grillius, Horace, Juvenal, Lucan, Martianus Capella, Ovid, Persius, Petronius, Quintilian (*Institutio*), Statius, Terence, Victorinus, and Virgil.

F. Masai (*Scriptorium* 5 [1951], 117–20) proposes some corrections in the text of the excerpts printed by Thomas.

Philippe Delhaye includes a number of excerpts from the commentary in his article, "L'enseignement de la philosophie morale au XIIᵉ siècle," *Medieval Studies* II (1949), 77–99. These deal with remarks about the deliberative and demonstrative types of speaking as allied to the study of ethics through a consideration of *honestas* and *utilitas.*

[92] London, British Museum MS. Arundel 348, fol. 102ᵛ.

He notes that a number of people have been turned away from a study of rhetoric because both Plato and Aristotle seem to condemn it. Plato's attack is that rhetoric is not an art but is in man by nature; Aristotle's assault stems from his observation that although it is an art, it may be used evilly to impugn the truth and induce men to hold false rather than true opinions. Thierry calls upon the authority of Boethius to affirm Cicero's dictum that rhetoric is an art which is a major part of civil science or politics.[93]

This kind of discussion evidently reflects the kind of teaching being done at Chartres during the middle of the twelfth century. Thierry had at his disposal the major writings on rhetoric that had been produced up to his own time—Cicero, Quintilian, Grillius, Victorinus, Boethius—and he was prepared to use them in explicating what he thought to be one of the most significant of them all: Cicero's *De inventione*. His was the same spirit which produced glosses on Lucan and Ovid at Orléans and Chartres in the same century. What the teacher uses, the teacher explains.

Of these commentaries, Thierry's is the one most often remembered today because he was a prominent member of an illustrious group of teachers, and because his *Heptateuchon* gained him some renown as well. But other writers, mostly unknown, wrote commentaries throughout the middle ages which serve further to demonstrate the overwhelming medieval designation of Cicero as the assumptive *magister eloquentiae*.

One commentary even earlier than Thierry's is that of Manegold of Lautenbach (c. 1030–1103), who taught in France toward the end of the eleventh century. His commentary on *De inventione* survives in only one manuscript, but it may have had some medieval popularity, for it is quoted in another, anonymous commentary composed about 1118 to explicate both *De inventione* and *ad Herennium*.[94] Medieval library cata-

---

[93] *Ibid.*, fol. 104ᵛ.

[94] Manegold's commentary begins: Quam Greci vocant rhetoricam, latini dicut artificiosam eloquentiam. A copy survives in Cologne Cathedral MS. CXCVII (Darmst 2170), fols. 1–40ᵛ. I am indebted to Miss Mary Dickey and R. W. Hunt of the Bodleian Library, Oxford, for information about this commentary, and the citations of additional manuscripts for that of Thierry. Miss Dickey has also identified a quotation from Manegold in a twelfth-century commentary on both the *De inventione* and *ad Herennium*. This latter work's *incipit* is: In primis materia et intentio huius rethoris, scilicet Ciceronis, quarenda est. It is extant in two English manuscripts: Durham Cathedral MS. C.IV.7 and York Minster MS. XVI.M.7, fols. 1–69ᵛ.
A thirteenth-century catalogue of the library at Hammersleven lists a copy of Manegold's commentary (Manitius, *Bibliothekskatalogen*, p. 22), and the Dover library had a copy in 1389 (*ibid.*, p. 333).

logues are studded with terms that indicate the presence of rhetorical commentaries, but the authors are usually not named. The Benedictine library at Engelberg, Switzerland, for instance, records a list of books on hand about 1150, including an item *Glosse super Rhetoricam Tullii*.[95] Is this the work of Victorinus or of Grillius, or of Manegold or Thierry? Or it may be that of some writer unknown to the modern world. In all likelihood we shall never know the answers to such questions.

It is clear, however, that the practice of writing commentaries continued throughout the middle ages, although definitive statements about this whole movement must await the collection and edition of the numerous texts which have survived. Both the *rhetorica vetus* and *rhetorica nova* drew the attention of the commentators, sometimes in the same discussion. An anonymous author, whose work survives in a fifteenth-century manuscript now in Magdalen College, Oxford,[96] treats the early portions of the *ad Herennium* with frequent cross-references to the *De inventione*. In the basic matters of *inventio* and *dispositio* there is of course a good deal of correspondence between the two treatises, and the author notes

---

[95] Paul Lehmann and Paul Ruf, *Mittelalterliche Bibliothekskatalogen Deutschlands und der Schweiz,* 3 vols. (Munich, 1918–39), I.32. The difficulty of identifying particular Ciceronian works is demonstrated by the varying habits of medieval cataloguers. In the case of the Hammersleven copy of Manegold (noted above), the complete entry reads as follows: liber rhetoricorum primus qui sic incipit "Quam Greci vocant rhetoricam." Now, the usual medieval reference to the *Rhetorica* of Aristotle (which has three books) is liber Aristotilis rethoricorum or liber rethoricorum. Cicero's works are seldom listed this way. Without the *incipit*—not always given in medieval catalogues—it would be difficult to determine absolutely which book was designated. Another kind of problem is exemplified in two entries in the Durham library records. A twelfth-century book list simply gives names of authors—Seneca and Boethius, for instance—without names of books; the same list, however, identifies a copy of the Victorinus commentary on *De inventione*. By 1391, the library had grown to 508 volumes, most of them carefully recorded by name and *incipit*. When Robert de Langchester turned them over to his successor William de Appleby, Langchester had simply listed a glosa super retoricem without specifying the author or subject. Presumably it is the same commentary by Victorinus which had appeared in the twelfth-century book list, but how would we know this if we did not have another catalogue entry against which to check this rather ambiguous entry? See Surtees Society, *Catalogi veteres librorum ecclesiae cathedralis Dunelmis* (London, 1838), pp. 1–9, 10–82.

Delhaye (*Medieval Studies* 11 [1949], 97) concluded that there were not many commentaries on Cicero's rhetoric composed during the eleventh and twelfth centuries: "les commentaires de rhétorique sont rares pour l'époque que nous occupe." But he did not seem to be aware of Manegold's commentary, or that of the anonymous author of "In primis materia." Given the ambiguity of medieval catalogue entries, and our own lack of research into this problem, it would be hazardous to assume too readily that we have already identified all or most of the works of this type.

[96] Oxford, Magdalen College MS. 82, fols. 1–104ᵛ. *Incipit:* Omnium arcium doctrinam duplicem esse, secundum preceptum sententiamque Varronis.

them; he does, however, point out that the two books differ somewhat in relation to *dispositio*. When he comes to the subject of *pronuntiatio*, he explains that it is no longer possible to make the cross-references because Tullius does not handle the subject in his other book. It is obvious that he expects the reader to know the *De inventione*. The commentator then goes on to handle *memoria* and *elocutionis doctrina*, which occur in Books Three and Four of the *ad Herennium*. Unfortunately, the last leaf of the commentary, which might have contained a colophon with some hint of the author's name, has been cut out of the manuscript.

A commentary on the *ad Herennium*, which is contained in a fourteenth-century manuscript now in the Bodleian Library, originated in Italy, possibly at the Dominican convent of Santi Giovanni e Paolo in Venice.[97] After a very short prologue it launches into a direct exposition of the four books in turn. Another commentary, also in Oxford, begins its discussion of the *ad Herennium* with a reference to Quintilian:

Ut ait Quintilianus in rethoricam plures invehi solent et quidem indignissiumum si in rethoricam accusandam viribus utuntur rethorice.[98]

This reference, as it turns out, is merely an introduction to the usual prefatory discussion of the question whether rhetoric is an art. As usual, Plato's objection is noted, and the anonymous author arrives at the expected conclusion: "It is manifest to everyone that rhetoric is an art." [99] The work ends after treating only two of the four books.

Still another type of Ciceronian commentary is that which takes up both the *De inventione* and the *ad Herennium* in the same volume. An example is the anonymous twelfth-century *Glose super Rethoricam Ciceronis*,[100] which makes little distinction between the two works in the text. Nothing could better illustrate the existence of a "Ciceronian" tradition. One such extant manuscript, that in Durham Cathedral, begins with the following:

In primis materia et intentio huius rethoris, scilicet Ciceronis, quarenda est. Sed quia quidam, nescientes differentiam inter oratorem et rethorem, materiam et intentionem oratoris rethori attribuunt, videndum est prius quid

---

[97] Oxford, Bodleian Library MS. Lat. Class. d.36, fols. 1ᵛ–98. An interesting indication of readers' interests may be seen in a marginal notation to the prologue: ut ponit philosophus 4 metaphysice et octavo topicorum. Que omnia autem igitur hoc posterior indecet maiori perfectione actio intellectualis contollit. *Incipit:* Plena et perfecta locutio triplici comparatur adminiculo regulari.

[98] Oxford, Corpus Christi College MS. 250, fols. 1–17. *Incipit:* Ut ait Quintilianus . . .

[99] Rethorica igitur omnibus esse artem sit manifestum. *Ibid.,* fol. 1ʳᵇ.

[100] See above, note 94.

orator, quid rethor et que materia, et que intentio utrique attribuenda sic, ut in nullo decipiamus.

The inclusion of both works in one volume may account for an occasional medieval reference to the "six books" of Cicero's rhetoric. An entry in the library catalogue at Heiligenkreuz in 1354, for instance, lists *Rethorica nova li(ber) VI,*[101] which may actually be a combination of *De inventione* and *ad Herennium*. It will be remembered that Jean d'Antioche de Harens translated both works together to make a total of six books in one treatise.

The presence of these various commentaries thus indicates a continuing interest in and use of the rhetorical works of Cicero that belong to his youthful period. The more sophisticated *De oratore* appears only infrequently during the period up to 1400, and even in Italy where there was interest in the work toward the end of the century, humanist scholars had to content themselves with a partial and mutilated text. There seems to be no indication of a medieval commentary on the *De oratore*. The rediscovery of the complete text in 1422 was, like the rediscovery of the complete Quintilian, a catalytic boost to fifteenth-century studies; the impact of the *De oratore* was reserved, therefore, for the Renaissance, and not the middle ages.

The direct imitation of Cicero is of course another indication of his popularity. The *ad Herennium* was a major influence on the writings of Jacques de Dinant, a thirteenth-century author of four works on discourse: *Ars arengandi, Breviloquium, Expositiones breviloquii,* and a *Summa dictaminis.*[102] The *Ars arengandi* (Art of Pleading) is a virtual paraphrase of *ad Herennium,* and may have some relation to the rhetoric employed in the Italian communes. As if to dispel any doubt about his sources for the *Breviloquium,* which is a set of stylistic rules for *dictatores,* Jacques refers the reader to *Tullius libro quarto Rethorice nove.*[103] Even

---

[101] Manitius, *Bibliothekskatalogen,* p. 23.

[102] Details of these works, together with text materials, may be found in André Wilmart, "L'Ars arengandi de Jacques de Dinant, avec un Appendice sur ses ouvrages 'De dictamine,'" in *Analecta Reginensia: Extraits des manuscrits latins de la reine chrétien conservés au Vatican,* printed in *Studi e Testi* 59 (1933), 113-51.

[103] That is, in Jacques' *Expositiones breviloquii,* a commentary on his own *Breviloquium.* It was not uncommon for Italian *dictatores* to compose commentaries on their own works, especially if (like the Frenchman Dinant) they used their own works in teaching. Dinant's *Expositiones* is printed in part by Wilmart, "L'Ars arengandi," pp. 139-45.

Taken by itself, however, the reference to the fourth book of the *ad Herennium* does not necessarily indicate a knowledge of the whole work. In Dinant's case, because of his *Ars arengandi,* we may feel sure of his intimate familiarity with the Pseudo-Cicero. But the section on *exornationes* in the *ad Herennium* was so

his *Summa* has a Ciceronian connection, for it has the same *incipit* as the Pseudo-Ciceronian treatise: *Etsi negotiis familiaribus impediti*.[104] Although Jacques' works are of some importance in the history of dictamen theory, it is interesting at this point to note his heavy reliance on the "new rhetoric" of Cicero.

Thus the medieval history of Cicero's rhetoric is primarily that of his early work. His more sophisticated *De oratore* was largely neglected until it burst forth on the Italian scene in the early fifteenth century. The rediscovery of the complete text of this dialogue at Lodi in 1422 was in a sense one of the boundary markers separating the "medieval" from the "Renaissance" phases of European cultural history.

The medieval history of Quintilian's *Institutio oratoria* is similar to that of *De oratore*, with the important exception that the educational and moral precepts of Quintilian apparently had a wider effect than the actual use of the book itself. Like the *De oratore*, it had some use in the earlier middle ages—and exercised a considerable influence during the so-called "Renaissance of the Twelfth Century." Then, shortly after its period of greatest use at Chartres and Bec in the mid-1100's, it dropped almost entirely from sight until the latter half of the fourteenth century, when Italian humanists like Petrarch became interested in the fragmentary text then available. The rediscovery of the complete text by Poggio Bracciolini at St. Gall in 1416 was a major milepost in the history of Western rhetoric, education, and even literature.[105]

It is especially important that the modern student distinguish carefully

---

widely used as a separate piece—and so routinely used by grammarians as a supplement to Donatus—that mere references to it should be viewed with great caution if evidence of the whole work is sought. Edmond Faral has shown (*Les arts poétiques*, pp. 52–54) how many medieval works depended on *ad Herennium* IV for the doctrine of the *figurae*.

[104] Dinant, of course, is interested in a play on words. His opening words are: Et si negotiis familiaribus inpeditus nec non leccionibus cotidianis rethorice facultatis existam. . . . The *ad Herennium* opens with the author's address to Herennius: Et si negotiis familiaribus inpediti vix satis otium studio suppeditare possumus, et it ipsum quod datur otii libentius in philosophia consumere consuevimus. . . .

[105] The survey of these developments made by F. H. Colson in 1924 is still valuable as a comprehensive treatment of the pattern, subsequent studies having done little to alter the main outline of growing use, dominance, disappearance, and resurgence after rediscovery. F. H. Colson, *M. Fabii Quintiliani institutionis oratoriae Liber I* (Cambridge, 1924), Introduction, esp. pp. ix–lxxxix. The following account is derived from Colson unless otherwise indicated.

between various types of medieval references to Quintilian. The task of tracing this author through the middle ages is complicated by the existence of at least four forms in which medieval writers might have come upon "Quintilian,":

1. The complete text of the *Institutio*.
2. The *textus mutilatus*, or text with the "great lacunas"; two versions of this text were available.
3. Excerpts in *florilegia*.
4. Pseudo-Quintilian, *Declamationes* (also known as *De causis*).

With this in mind, then, the investigator should proceed with some caution in making sweeping judgments about individual items of evidence. When Bertrand and Arnald La Fytes arrived at Oxford in 1289, for example, and accepted the gift of certain items to help them in their academic careers, it was noted that they possessed a "Quintilian." [106] From this single word, it is extremely difficult to determine just what the brothers La Fytes actually did possess.

Actually, the number of medieval references to Quintilian is not very large, even including the proliferation of quotations and allusions in twelfth-century France. A brief résumé of the major notices may serve to present a reasonably coherent picture.

The *Institutio* did not loom large in the centuries following the death of its author.[107] For Saint Jerome (d. 420), however, Quintilian is second only to Cicero among prose writers, and his famous letter to Laeta adapts the Roman's educational ideas for the training of the young girl. Cassiodorus and Isidore both use Quintilian, although Alcuin and Rabanus Maurus do not seem to do so. Servatus Lupus of Ferrières (d. c. 866) in a passage often quoted, writes to the Pope asking him for complete copies of the *De oratore* and of the *Institutio*, noting that he already possesses the two works in incomplete form; in another letter he asks the bishop of York for a copy of Quintilian.[108]

---

[106] Ernest Savage, *Old English Libraries* (London, 1911), p. 290. It is interesting to note, incidentally, that Savage assumes that each reference to "Quintilian" means that the *Institutio* is intended by the cataloguer. This assumption hardly seems warranted, especially in light of the popularity of the declamations of the Pseudo-Quintilian.

[107] Julius Victor, a fourth-century Roman rhetorician, draws heavily on Quintilian in his *Ars rhetorica Hermagorae, Ciceronis, Quintiliani, Aquili, Marcomanni, Tatiani*. The text is in Charles Halm, *Rhetores latini minores* (Leipzig, 1863), pp. 373–448. The use of Julius Victor's work by Alcuin may account for that author's apparent reliance on Quintilian. Alcuin's list of books in the library at York (Migne, *PL* 101, cols. 843–44) does not include a copy of Quintilian.

[108] Ep. 103 and Ep. 62. For Lupus see Charles H. Beeson, *Lupus of Ferrières, Scribe and Textual Critic* (Cambridge, Mass., 1930).

After this instance, shortly past the middle of the ninth century, there is almost complete silence for a century and a half. "Neither in the tenth nor in the eleventh centuries," says Colson, "can I find any clear indication of a knowledge of Quintilian." The positive evidence for Quintilian's use up to the year 850 is meager enough, but even that trace fades out of sight until we come to the phenomenon of Chartres in the early twelfth century.

At some time prior to 1100, perhaps in the ninth century, the text of the twelve-book *Institutio oratoria* had undergone a series of contractions or elisions, with the result that for the greater part of the middle ages the complete text was not available. The resultant *textus mutilatus,* which itself took two forms, suffered from some major gaps or lacunas. Colson identifies two types of omissions:[109]

|  | *Type A* | *Type B* |
|---|---|---|
| 1. | Proem. 1 to a point not earlier than I.i.6 | 1. Same |
| 2. | V.xiv.12 to VIII.iii.64 | 2. Same |
| 3. | VIII.vi.17 to VIII.vi.67 | 3. Same |
| 4. | IX.iii.2 to X.i.107 | 4. IX.iii.2 to X.i.45* |
| 5. | XI.i.71 to XI.ii.33 | 5. Same |
| 6. | XII.x.43 (some earlier) to end | 6. Same |

* Fragment X.i.46–107 written at end of manuscript.

It is interesting to note that the pedagogical or educational portion of the work (Book I and Book II, sections i–x) remained virtually intact. It is perhaps significant that most of the losses occur in the middle sections, which presents a full-fledged textbook of rhetoric. The mutilated text nevertheless retains the section on *inventio* most clearly parallel to Cicero's *De inventione.* Two of the lacunas break into the discussion of *figurae* in the eighth and ninth books. There is little to indicate that medieval readers were aware of, or troubled by, these omissions, but by the end of the fourteenth century Gasparino da Barzizza thought it worthwhile to expend "much labor" in an attempt to supply the sense of the missing parts.[110] Certainly Poggio's discovery of the complete text seems to have ended, abruptly and completely, any further use of the *textus mutilatus.*

The *Institutio,* besides being mutilated, had also fallen prey to the medieval habit of collecting *flores*—"flowers" or choice excerpts—from

---

[109] Colson, *Quintilian,* p. lxi.
[110] See William H. Woodward, *Vittorino da Feltre and Other Humanist Educators* (Cambridge, 1921), pp. 12 ff.

useful texts. Vincent of Beauvais, for instance, probably relied on some *florilegium* for the citations in his *Speculum doctrinale*—a fact which might make an unwary reader believe that Vincent had studied the *Institutio* itself. Certainly the high moral tone of the book would lend itself readily to such culling of *sententiae*. One such collection, drawn from the opening sections on education, dates from the twelfth century and has survived in four copies. It is reasonable to expect that other excerpts circulated in the numerous *florilegia* compiled throughout the middle ages.[111]

Still another source of medieval "Quintilianism" was the Pseudo-Quintilian *Declamationes maiores* and *Declamationes minores* (also known as *De causis*), two sets of declamations which had some medieval circulation. There were two copies at Bec in the twelfth century, and one each at Durham, Glastonbury, and Canterbury in the same century. A copy is also recorded in a thirteenth-century library catalogue for Pontigny. By the end of the fourteenth century Durham may have had three copies.[112]

With these various possibilities in mind, then, it is possible to understand more easily the peculiar fate which overtook the reputation of Quintilian after his brief rise to popularity in the twelfth century. Most of the citations adduced to demonstrate his use during the middle ages may be seen to occur during a period of about eighty years, and most stem from France, particularly in connection with the schools at Chartres and Bec.

---

[111] Quintilian is among the *auctores* cited in medieval *florilegia,* or collections of "flowers" from various sources. See, for instance, Philippe Delhaye and C. H. Talbot, *Florilegium morale Oxoniense,* Analecta mediaevalia Namurcensia V–VI (Louvain, 1956), VI, pp. 5–15 and passim. As early as the tenth century, Gerbert of Rheims had linked ethical and rhetorical teaching in a passage reminiscent of Quintilian's own definition of rhetoric: . . . cum studio bene vivendi semper coniunxi studium bene dicendi. Quoted in Eduard Norden, *Die antike Kuntsprosa,* 2 vols., 5th ed. (Leipzig, 1918), p. 706. The same spirit may account for the citations from Quintilian in educational treatises as well. Cf. James A. Corbett, *The De instructione puerorum of William of Tournai, O.P.,* Texts and Studies in the History of Medieval Education, III (Notre Dame, Ind., 1955). Another study of Quintilianism is based primarily on *florilegia:* Priscilla S. Boskoff, "Quintilian in the Late Middle Ages," *Speculum* 27 (1952), 71–78.

[112] Manitius, *Bibliothekskatalogen,* pp. 131–34. Boccaccio left a copy of *De causis* in his will. Cf. Cornelia C. Coulter, "Boccaccio's Knowledge of Quintilian," *Speculum* 33 (1958), 490–96. There are modern editions of the two sets of declamations: *Declamationes minores,* ed. C. Ritter (Teubner, 1884); and *Declamationes maiores,* ed. G. Lehnert (Teubner, 1905).

It is perhaps noteworthy that Pierre d'Ailly (1350–1420) lists "Declamationes Quintiliani" among the works studied at Paris in his lifetime, but includes the declamations with the poets, not with "rhetorica" (which belongs to Tullius). Quoted in Paetow, *Arts Course,* p. 61, n. 51. (See n. 76 above.)

Wibald of Corvey (d. 1158) praises Quintilian's educational program.[113] Alexander Neckham (d. 1217), in a famous passage often quoted to characterize medieval rhetorical ideals, ranks Quintilian with Cicero; the passage occurs in a listing of the books which should be used for various studies:

> In rethorica educandus legat primum Tullii rethoricam et librum ad Herennium et Tullium de oratore et causas Quintiliani et Quintilianum de oratoris institucione.[114]

Ulrich of Bamberg (d. 1127) used some portions of Books Eight and Nine in discussing *figurae* in his *Epitomae rhetoricae,* although he concludes the section by referring the reader to the fourth book of the *ad Herennium* for more complete treatment.[115] Quintilian's reputation as a rhetorician is also attested by Nigel Wirecker, and by Alain de Lille whose *Anti-Claudianus* (III, vv.233–235) ranks him among the great rhetoricians. Guibert de Nogent and Richard de Fournivall both know him. There are some other scattered references during the same century.

But it is the schools of twelfth-century France which provide the impetus for a renewed study of Quintilian. If there is any real meaning to the term "renaissance of the twelfth century," it probably lies in the renewed interest in the very kind of careful yet broad humane study recommended by Quintilian himself. It is difficult to give an absolute answer to the question of whether Chartres popularized Quintilian or whether, on the other hand, Quintilian made Chartres possible. Certainly it is significant that the same book—the *Institutio oratoria*—should have played a major role in both the renaissance of the twelfth century and the renaissance of the fifteenth century.

Whatever the initial cause, the results are apparent. After a study of the period, up to about 1200, one modern student concludes that a veritable vogue of Quintilianism swept across France from centers in Bec and

---

[113] Lege Quintilianum de institutio oratoria, qui ab utero matris susceptum infantem limare incipit et formare in substantiam oratoris perfecti. Ep. 147 to Manegold, quoted in Colson, *Quintilian,* p. lii.

[114] Quoted in Charles H. Haskins, "A List of Textbooks from the Close of the Twelfth Century," in *Studies in the History of Medieval Science* (Cambridge, Mass., 1924), p. 374.

[115] Paul Lehmann, "Die Institutio oratoria des Quintilianus im Mittelalter," *Erforschung des Mittelalters,* 4 vols. (Leipzig, 1941–60), II (1959), 1–28; reprinted from *Philologus* 89 (1934), 349–83. Lehmann prints (pp. 21–25) excerpts from Ulrich. For Ulrich himself, cf. Manitius, *Geschichte* III, 287–89.

Chartres.[116] It is known, for instance, that Philippe de Harcourt brought a copy of the *Institutio* to Bec in 1164. Most indicative of Quintilian's position at Bec, however, is the fact that the poet-teacher Stephen of Rouen prepared an abstract of the *Institutio* in 1164 for his students in that school: the abstract is about a third of the length of the approximately ten books condensed.[117]

John of Salisbury has left us a graphic picture of his own education at Chartres under Bernard and Thierry of Chartres, William of Conches, and Richard Bishop. So graphic is the picture, indeed, that there is some danger that modern students will read all too much into the charming account as set forth in the *Metalogicon* (1159). Yet even a cursory reading of John's first book will bring to mind not only specific allusions to passages in Quintilian but his educational program as a whole. "No other medieval writer," notes Baldwin, "gave this work [of Quintilian's] more attention." [118] So much has been written about this aspect of the *Metalogicon* that it is perhaps unnecessary to do more here than indicate one or two salient points.

Quintilian, by John's own statement, was the preceptor for Chartres in the field of grammatical instruction, and John's lengthy description of the methods used at Chartres is reminiscent of the first two books of the *Institutio*. Note, for instance, the opening section of the twenty-fourth chapter of Book One:

> One who aspires to become a philosopher should therefore apply himself to reading, learning, and meditation, as well as the performance of good works, lest the Lord become angry and take away what he seems to possess. The word "reading" is equivocal. It may refer either to the activity of teaching and being taught, or to the occupation of studying written things by oneself. Consequently the former, the intercommunication between teacher and learner, may be termed (to use Quintilian's term) the "lecture" (*prelectio*); the latter, or the scrutiny by the student, the "reading" (*lectio*), simply so called. On the authority of the same Quintilian, "the teacher of grammar should, in lecturing, take care of such details as to have his students analyze verses into their parts of speech, and point out the nature of the metrical feet which are to be noted in poems. He should, moreover, indicate and condemn whatever is barbarous, incongruous, or otherwise against the rules of composition." He should not, however, be overcritical of the poets, in

---

[116] A. Mollard, "La diffusion de l'Institution oratoire au XIIe siècle," *Moyen âge* 44 (1934), 161–75, and 45 (1935), 1–9. Also, by the same author, "L'Imitation de Quintilian dans Guibert de Nogent," *Moyen âge* 44 (1934), 81–87.

[117] Cf. Colson, *Quintilian*, pp. li ff.

[118] Baldwin, *MRP*, p. 169. For a summary of the book, see *ibid.*, pp. 158–68.

whose case, because of the requirements of rhythm, so much is overlooked that the very faults are termed virtues. A departure from the rule that is excused by necessity, is often praised as a virtue, when observance of the rule would be detrimental. The grammarian should also point out metaplasms, schematisms, and oratorical tropes, as well as various other forms of expression that may be present. He should further suggest the various possible ways of saying things, and impress them on the memory of his listeners by repeated reminders.[119]

In speaking more particularly of the methods employed by his own teacher, Bernard, John points out the desirability of frequent practice:

> A further feature of Bernard's method was to have his disciples compose prose and poetry every day, and exercise their faculties in mutual conferences (*collationibus*), for nothing is more useful in introductory training than actually to accustom one's students to practice the art they are studying.[120]

It might also be noted that all of this educational process is designed to take place in a high moral atmosphere—"A man cannot be the servant of both learning and carnal vice"[121]—so that grammar is seen as one part of the general education of the human person. This is, of course, a concept to which Quintilian's *Institutio* readily lends itself.

And yet, for all the sympathy which John of Salisbury shows for the grammatical and moral teachings of Quintilian, the *Metalogicon* itself contains the seeds of the new spirit which was to drive Quintilian back to the library shelf. The *Metalogicon* thus marks a watershed in European attitudes toward the arts of discourse. On one side, represented in the first book with its Quintilianistic spirit, is the humane attitude of literary students like Bernard. On the other side, represented by the later books with their praise of dialectical argument, is the "scholastic" attitude which was to attract men like Abelard, Peter Lombard, and eventually an Aquinas.[122]

The dichotomy of attitude so implicit in the *Metalogicon* may give us a clue to the medieval fate of Quintilian's *Institutio oratoria*. The *Institutio*, after all, is really a work with three major parts. The first part, com-

---

119 *Metalogicon* I.xxiv, pp. 65–66.
120 *Ibid.*, p. 70.
121 *Ibid.*, pp. 70–71.
122 The ultimate effect, in terms of the book itself, is that the subject of rhetoric is squeezed out, and plays very little part in it. The effect in northern Europe is somewhat similar, over the next two centuries. It might be remembered again that John ignores Quintilian's discussion of rhetorical *declamatio*, in favor of the new dialectic so attractively presented in the *Topica* and *De sophisticis elenchis*.

prising Book One and the first ten sections of Book Two, is a treatise on the education of an orator. The whole middle of the book, running from Book Two up through a part of Ten, is a treatise on rhetoric. The remainder of Ten and final two books are a general set of reflections on style, the social role of the educated orator, and such matters. It is easy enough to understand what happened to each of the three sections after the middle of the twelfth century. Since the educational portion seemed to cover teaching methods which were also common to medieval grammatical practices, this part of the *Institutio* had little to recommend it as a separate work. The rhetorical works of Cicero covered in much shorter compass the material included in the middle part of Quintilian, and so they preempted the attention that might otherwise have been given to the *Institutio* for that reason. Finally, the very nature of medieval political life rendered the final two books largely irrelevant.

Given an increasing interest in matters dialectical, then, the *Institutio* simply dropped out of the mainstream of European thought about the nature of discourse. For two centuries it seems to have played no significant role. When it burst upon the world of Vittorino da Feltre and P. P. Vergerius in the fifteenth century, it found a congenial cultural climate which again enabled it to exert a great influence in the humane tradition. That humane spirit is present in the *Metalogicon,* but so is the new admiration for the dialectical control of discourse. It is rare that one book so clearly demonstrates the end of one era and the beginning of another.

It remains to note briefly the medieval survivals of the ancient grammatical and sophistic works composed in the first few Christian centuries. A more detailed discussion of grammar belongs to a later chapter, but it might be noted that the two little treatises of Aelius Donatus continued to be the primers for grammar all through the middle ages and even past that time. As I have said earlier, the term "Donet" became a synonym for "primer," or first book, in a subject. When the fourteenth-century Englishman Reginald Pecock composed a summary of the Christian religion, he gave it the title *Donet* to indicate that it covered the basic fundamentals of his subject.[123]

---

[123] Ed. Elsie V. Hitchcock. Early English Text Society, 156 (Oxford, 1921).

The *Institutio grammatica* of Priscian, although suffering from the competition of medieval works like the *Doctrinale* of Alexander of Villedieu, continued to be a major advanced work throughout the middle ages. Priscian's explication of the opening lines of the *Aeneid* was also enormously popular.[124]

The *Ars poetica* of Horace enjoyed a medieval reputation as *Poetria*, to the extent that Geoffrey of Vinsauf felt it useful to title his own thirteenth-century work *Poetria nova* to indicate that he was offering a departure from the old lore. The existence of glosses by other writers also indicates interest.[125]

The sophistic tradition is more difficult to trace. Priscian's *Preexercitamenta*, which was a collection of the *progymnasmata* of Hermogenes, appears in an eleventh-century catalogue from Amplonius, but otherwise there seems to be little trace of this book.[126]

The *Declamationes* of the Elder Seneca, on the other hand, were consistently popular, acquiring both a commentary and a "moralization" during the fourteenth century. The declamations appear in medieval reference as *declamationes* or as *liber de causis* or as *liber de controversiis*. It is interesting to note, however, that the declamations do not serve as models of discourse but rather as sources of tales or *exempla*. About the year 1300 an Englishman, Nicholas Trivet, wrote a commentary on the declamations. About twenty years later another Englishman, Robert Holcott, prepared a work which appears under the title *Liber in declamaciones Senece moralizatas*.[127]

All in all, it does not seem likely that the sophistic tradition as derived from these books had a widespread or significant influence on the medieval theory of discourse. It is of course difficult to determine the

---

[124] See below, Chapter Four. Some indication of the ubiquity of Priscian's works may be gained by a perusal of the library holdings listed in Manitius, *Bibliothekskatalogen*, pp. 305–17. Also, see R. W. Hunt, "Studies in Priscian in the Eleventh and Twelfth Centuries," *Medieval and Renaissance Studies* 1 (1941), 194–231, and 2 (1950), 1–56.

[125] For instance, Durham (saec. XII), "glosae super poetriam"; Corbie (saec. XII) "oratii expositio"; Prague (1370) "Gloza super poetriam"; Manitius, *Bibliothekskatalogen*, pp. 55–61.

[126] *Ibid.*, p. 316 and p. 309. It should be noted again, however, that the so-called "Second Sophistic" of the Roman Empire was largely due to an exaggerated use of normal curricular exercises. The devices of Hermogenes, therefore, are not inconsistent with ordinary grammatical training in composition, and might well have been incorporated into medieval literary instruction without much explicit acknowledgment of source.

[127] Beryl Smalley, *English Friars and Antiquity in the Early Fourteenth Century* (Oxford, 1961).

extent to which some sophistic practices—the progymnasmata, for instance —may have survived in the ordinary grammatical curriculum. Actually most of the oratorical excesses of the so-called Second Sophistic in the Roman Empire were merely extravagances which carried to great lengths what were in essence the staple exercises of the grammatical and rhetorical curricula of the Roman schools. In the sense that individual poets or orators may have been highly regarded for their rhetorical flourishes, the sophistic of the ancient world may have influenced medieval writers from time to time.[128] But the preceptive documents of the Second Sophistic probably had no such influence, and may be regarded as of negligible importance for the middle ages.

In summary, then, the history of the arts of discourse in the middle ages is at least in part the history of the survival of classical works. The most important ancient author in this connection is Cicero, the acknowledged *magister eloquentiae*. His influence for the middle ages stems largely from two works: his youthful *De inventione,* and the more complete *Rhetorica ad Herennium,* which it was assumed he had also written. Quintilian had a brief period of popularity in the twelfth century, but became widely influential only in the fifteenth. Aristotle's *Rhetorica* was distributed in numerous copies, but apparently as a work of "moral philosophy" rather than a book on discourse; his *Ars poetica* was almost ignored. Thus the ancient and the medieval *artes* sometimes appeared side by side during the period from Augustine to Poggio.[129]

---

[128] For instance, Sidonius Apollinaris. Baldwin, *MRP,* pp. 2–50 and 75–87, points out several instances of such influence. But the highly complex stylistic patterns recommended in medieval works on both verse and prose would also have influenced the development of the same kind of style, especially after about 1050.

[129] Occasional notice is found of the medieval survival of other ancient works. See, for example, Bernice V. Wall, *A Medieval Latin Version of Demetrius's De elocutione,* Catholic University of America Studies in Medieval and Renaissance Latin, Vol. V (Washington, D.C., 1937).

# Part Two

✦ ✦ ✦

# Medieval Rhetorical Genres

# Chapter IV

# *Ars poetriae:*
# Preceptive Grammar, or
# the Rhetoric of
# Verse-Writing

WITHIN the space of about a century—about 1175 to sometime before 1280—European teachers of grammar produced six Latin works about verse-writing which can only be called preceptive. These six works are Matthew of Vendôme's *Ars versificatoria* (c. 1175); Geoffrey of Vinsauf's *Poetria nova* (1208–13) and *Documentum de modo et arte dictandi et versificandi* (after 1213); Gervase of Melkley's *Ars versificaria* (c. 1215); John of Garland's *De arte prosayca, metrica, et rithmica* (after 1229); and Eberhard the German's *Laborintus* (after 1213, before 1280). They are preceptive in that they all deal with what one modern student has called "the future poem." [1] Each one attempts to provide advice for a writer wishing to compose verse in the future. To the extent that each work distills the precepts born of experience and observation and transmits these as injunctions for discovery, order, plan, and wording, then to that extent each of the six shares in the essence of that preceptive spirit which has always characterized rhetoric.

Yet at the same time it is clear that all the authors were teachers of

---

[1] Douglas Kelly, "The Scope of the Treatment of Composition in the Twelfth- and Thirteenth-Century Arts of Poetry," *Speculum* 41 (1966), 261–78. He makes the remark (p. 273) in reference to Vinsauf. See also Kelly, "The Theory of Composition in Medieval Narrative: Poetry and Geoffrey of Vinsauf's *Poetria Nova*," *Mediaeval Studies* 31 (1969), 117–48.

the *ars grammatica,* not the *ars rhetorica.* All looked to the production of written materials rather than the oral *oratio* which had been characteristic of ancient rhetoric.

As a consequence it is absolutely essential that a modern reader understand the nature of medieval grammar before attempting to analyze the contributions of these six works. Some have termed these authors "rhetoricians." [2] Nevertheless, the background of their art—as they understood it—can assist our own understanding of their efforts.

This chapter therefore presents a brief description of the main features of medieval grammatical thought, followed by a treatment of each author in turn, and a discussion of the semi-independent doctrines of tropes and figures which were so often associated with both grammar and rhetoric during the middle ages. In this fashion it may be possible to identify more precisely both the grammatical and the rhetorical elements in the six works.

The first thing for any modern reader to remember is that the meaning of the term "grammar" as commonly used today is severely narrowed down from the broader meaning that was familiar to ancient and medieval man. For us it merely denotes some standards of "correctness" in usage, or at most it denotes "syntax"—the study of sentence structure.[3] When we speak of an epic or a fictional narrative or lyric poetry, or such written forms as the short story or novel, we tend to use the term "literature" rather than "grammar" to describe them.

Early medieval grammarians made no such distinction. The *ars grammatica* included not only correctness in speaking or writing (*ars recte loquendi*) but also the further study of what we would today tend to call literature (*enarratio poetarum*), or the analysis and interpretation of existing literary works. This double function of grammar had ancient roots in the Roman school system, which led students first through a

---

[2] For instance, John M. Manley, "Chaucer and the Rhetoricians," *Publications of the British Academy* 12 (1926), 95–113. For a discussion of his arguments, see James J. Murphy, "A New Look at Chaucer and the Rhetoricians," *Review of English Studies* NS 15 (1964), 1–20.

[3] See, for instance, a typical modern dictionary definition of the term: "Grammar n. 1. The study of the formal features of a language. 2. These features or constructions themselves: *English grammar.* 3. A book dealing with these features. 4. Grammatical rules, esp. as criteria for evaluating speech or writing: *He knows his grammar.* 5. Knowledge or usage of the preferred or prescribed forms in speaking or writing. . . . *Random House Dictionary of the English Language, College Edition* (New York, 1968), p. 573.

series of complex exercises with the *grammaticus* before advancing them to rhetorical studies. As we saw in Chapter I, Quintilian described the process in detail in his *Institutio oratoria* (A.D. 95).[4] When first Donatus and then Priscian recorded the standard rules for the Latin language, they quite naturally included examples from what we would today call "literature," for instance, Virgil's *Aeneid*. They and their imitators also wrote books interpreting literary works; for example, Priscian's lengthy *Duodecim* analyzed the first twelve lines of the *Aeneid*.

Given the wide range of "grammatical" interests, then, it is not surprising to find that medieval writers had a deep respect for the importance of grammar as they understood that term. "Grammar," says John of Salisbury, "prepares the mind to understand everything that can be taught in words."[5]

Among the Romans, grammar prepared the way for rhetoric, while for Augustine and other Christians it prepared the way to an understanding of Scripture. But regardless of purpose, every medieval writer on the subject acknowledges that grammer is the first of subjects. Without it there can be no learning. For Isidore it is "both the origin and the foundation of the liberal arts,"[6] and Rabanus Maurus terms it "the first of the liberal arts."[7] William of Conches, at the end of his *De philosophia mundi,* declares his intention to write a work on grammar, "because grammar precedes every doctrine."[8] Even John Wycliffe, inveighing against *sermones vana curiositate theologorum,* is forced to concede that grammar, like logic, is a necessary tool for the theologian.[9] As one medieval writer puts it: "Grammar is the gateway of all other sciences, the most apt purgatrix of stammering speech, the helper of logic, the master of

---

[4] Quintilian's educational plan was spelled out in Book One and Book Two, sections 1–10. The process was already in vogue in Cicero's time, two centuries earlier.

[5] John of Salisbury, *Metalogicon,* trans. Daniel D. McGarry (Berkeley and Los Angeles, 1955), I.xxi, p. 60.

[6] Isidore of Seville, *Etymologarium sive Originum Libri XX,* ed. W. M. Lindsay (Oxford, 1911), I.v.1.

[7] Rabanus Maurus, *De institutione clericorum,* ed. Aloysius Knoepfler (Munich, 1900), III.18.

[8] Quoted in M. Charles Thurot, "Notices et extraits de divers manuscrits latins pour servir à l'histoire des doctrines grammaticales au moyen âge," *Notices et extraits* 22 (1868), 1–540 (now reprinted), p. 17.

[9] ". . . true grammar and true logic are necessary to theology and an aid to its master, especially, as Augustine says, wherever an art is able to clear up difficulties in theology which can be handled by no other science." Iohannes Wyclif, *Sermones,* ed. John Loserth, 4 vols. (London, 1887–88), I, 209.

rhetoric, the interpreter of theology, the refreshment of medicine, and the most praiseworthy foundation of all the quadrivium." [10]

Grammar is always the first-named subject in any list of the liberal arts, even though the next two—rhetoric and dialectic—sometimes change their position in the catalogues. Even if it were to be viewed simply as a mere preliminary study in the use of words, grammar would be an important part of the medieval concern for the arts of discourse. But medieval grammar eventually came to be a great deal more than a preliminary study. Ultimately it came to include a wide variety of linguistic subject matters, including not only syntax but metrics, rhythmics, modes of signification, and such "rhetorical" matters as the arrangement of parts of a discourse. Professors of grammar even appropriated for themselves the right to teach the *ars dictaminis,* the art of letter-writing, which originally sprang up to meet political needs. Why should this change have come about in such a comparatively short period of time?

The history of medieval grammar may be divided into two parts, with the twelfth century as the dividing mark.[11] Generally speaking, Priscian, Donatus, and their commentators dominate the field up to about the year 1200. After 1200 there are major developments which somewhat alter the emphasis of medieval grammar. These developments include the appearance of two new widely accepted textbooks—the *Doctrinale* of Alexander of Villedieu and the *Graecismus* of Evrard of Bethune—as well as the popularity of logically oriented treatises on the *modus significandi;* even more important, this second period sees the appearance of specialized grammatical works dealing with both *metricum* and *rithmicum.* Thus medieval grammar becomes a subject of some complexity, moving far beyond the mere concern for syntactical correctness and extending into the realms of the preceptive arts.

---

[10] Grammatica est ostiaria omnium aliarum scientiarum, linguae balbutientis expurgatrix aptissima, logicae ministra, rhetoricae magistra, theologiae interpres, medicinae refrigerium et totius quadrivii laudabile fundamentum. Quoted by Dietrich Reichling in Alexander de Villadei, *Doctrinale,* in *Monumenta germaniae paedigogica,* Band XII (Berlin, 1893), p. iii, n. 1.

[11] Thurot (n. 8 above) remains the most comprehensive treatment of medieval grammatical history. Also cf. R. H. Robins, *Ancient and Medieval Grammatical Theory in Europe* (London, 1951); Paul Abelson, *The Seven Liberal Arts* (New York, 1906); and Richard W. Hunt, "Studies in Priscian in the Eleventh and Twelfth Centuries," *Medieval and Renaissance Studies* 1 (1941), 194–231; and 2 (1950), 1–56. It might be noted that Thurot is more than a century old, Robins is extremely brief, Abelson is both old and schematic, and Hunt is rather specialized. Nevertheless, these works provide an introduction to the field, which still lacks a definitive history.

Donatus, Priscian, and their imitators, copyists, and commentators dominate grammatical instruction during the period up to A.D. 1200. The little *Ars minor* of Donatus is probably the most successful single textbook in the history of Western education. Short enough to be memorized, and yet complete enough to provide materials for essential training, this brief treatment of the eight parts of speech was literally ubiquitous in medieval Europe both before and after 1200.[12] The third part of the *Ars maior* of Donatus—the so-called *Barbarismus* (from its first word)—enjoyed an independent existence because of its treatment of figures and tropes.[13]

Priscian's works also enjoyed wide popularity throughout the middle ages, although the *Doctrinale* (1199) replaced his *Institutio grammaticae* as the standard advanced grammatical textbook after 1200.[14] Even Priscian suffered a division into parts, since the final two books (XVII and XVIII) of his *Institutio* circulated separately under the title of *Constructionum*.[15] This *Ars minor* or "little book" of Priscian also earned itself the name of *Priscianellus*. Another popular work was Priscian's detailed treatment of the first twelve lines of Virgil: *Partitiones duodecim versum Aeneides principium*. This latter work had two valuable assets for the medieval teaching of grammar: It deals with a major classical poetic exemplar, and it deals with the epic in an extremely detailed fashion consistent both with traditional teaching method and with the dialectically influenced methods of the scholastic period.

The major encyclopedists, moreover, all wrote long after the Donatus–Priscian domination in grammar had been woven firmly into the fabric of Western culture, so it is not surprising that Isidore, Cassiodorus, Ra-

---

[12] As we have seen earlier (Chapter III n. 123), Reginald Pecock, Bishop of St. Asaph, called his primer of the Christian religion (Donet.) See Pecock, *The Donet of Christian Religion*, ed. Elsie V. Hitchcock, Early English Text Society, 156 (Oxford, 1921).

[13] At Lorsch in Germany, for instance, a ninth-century catalogue lists *Donati grammatici de barbarismo et de ceteris vitiis*. Manitius, *Bibliothekskatalogen*, p. 178.

[14] *Ibid.*, pp. 307–17. The *Doctrinale*, for instance, had replaced Priscian in the statutes of 1366 at the University of Paris. See Lowrie J. Daly, *The Medieval University, 1200–1400* (New York, 1961), p. 84; and Rashdall, *Universities*, I, 443.

[15] A ninth-century catalogue of St. Gall lists Libri Prisciani de octo partibus XVI. Item eiusdem de constructione partium orationum libri II. Manitius, *Geschichte*, I, p. 305. At Fleury in the following century is found the listing: Prisianus maior cum minore de constructione. *Ibid.*, I, 310. Thereafter, numerous references all over Europe to *Priscianus minor* or *de constructione* or *Priscianellus* add testimony to the separate circulations of Books XVII and XVIII of Priscian's major work.

banus Maurus, and such later writers as Vincent of Beauvais should have followed traditional Latin grammatical forms. The middle ages retained the traditional eight "parts" of speech, the classical systems of conjugation and declension, the strong interest in syntactical rules. Indeed, granted some changes in practice due to the fact that Latin was still a living language, it is probably accurate to say that the rules for medieval Latin follow fairly closely on ancient formula. This is true both before and after 1200, and the medieval encyclopedists generally follow in this tradition.[16]

It must be remembered, however, that the history of medieval grammar before 1200 is the history of two basic subjects: syntax and *figurae*. All of Donatus' *Ars minor,* the first two parts of his *Ars maior,* and the first sixteen books of Priscian's *Institutio* are devoted to the structure of language as treated in an analysis of the eight "parts" and their relations to each other. Even the tedious detail of the *Duodecim* of Priscian does no more than examine in excruciating detail the exact role played by case, gender, and number in the first twelve lines of Virgil's epic. In this sense the *Duodecim* serves as an excellent example of how Priscian's own rules could be applied to an actual use of language. But the *Duodecim* does not teach how to compose. Even the final two books of Priscian's *Institutio,* known separately as the book on "composition," do not teach how to compose meaningful language. They merely form a treatise on the relations between units of language which are larger than single words or phrases. Composition, in the sense of a prescriptive art leading to the preparation of coherent discourse, is not usually the direct concern of *ars grammatica* proper during the early middle ages.

The separate existence of the *Barbarismus,* the third book of Donatus' *Ars maior,* also tended to create a special grammatical interest in the lore of *figurae.* It will be recalled that this little treatise discusses a total of thirty-three figures and tropes. Since there was also a separate rhetorical tradition of writing treatises devoted entirely to figures and tropes,[17] it

---

[16] Robins concludes that even the impact of the scholastic logic "left the grammatical systems of Donatus and Priscian more or less intact." Robins, *Ancient and Medieval Theory,* p. 78, n. 5.

[17] A number of third- and fourth-century treatises of this type are edited by Charles Halm, *Rhetores latini minores* (Leipzig, 1863), pp. 1–77. The practice continued throughout the middle ages. The *De ornamentis verborum* of Marbodus (c. 1050), *PL* CLXXI, cols. 1687–92) is an example. For an analysis of the use of figures by certain minor writers, see Heinrich Fichtenau, "Rhetorische Elemente in der Ottonischsalischen Herrscherurkunde," *Mitteilungen des Instituts für Österreichische Geschichtsforschung* 68 (1960), 39–62.

can be seen that the eleventh- or twelfth-century student of either grammar or rhetoric would have been exposed to the lore of the *exornationes*.

It is in the works of commentators, however, that the ultimate development of medieval grammar is most clearly foreshadowed. Two types of commentaries must be distinguished. One type discusses a literary work, while the second type discusses grammatical theory itself. Twelfth-century writers were aware of this distinction, as Hugh of St. Victor points out:

> Two separate concerns, then, are to be recognized and distinguished in every art: first, how one ought to treat of the art itself; and second, how one ought to apply the principles of that art in all other matters whatever. Two distinct things are involved here: treating *of* the art and then treating *by means of* the art. Treating of an art is, for instance, treating of grammar; but treating by means of that art is treating some matter grammatically. Note the difference between these two—treating of grammar and treating some matter grammatically. We treat of grammar when we set forth the rules given for words and the various precepts proper to this art; we treat grammatically when we speak or write according to rule. To treat of grammar, then, belongs only to certain books, like Priscian, Donatus, or Servius; but to treat grammatically belongs to all books.[18]

The type of commentary dealing with a grammatical textbook or rule book was common even in ancient times.[19] A continuous stream of such works appeared in Europe throughout the middle ages, including works by such early authors as Sedulius Scotus (fifth century), Virgilius Maro (fl. 630), Julian of Toledo (642–690), and Peter of Pisa (died by 799).[20] Two of the most famous commentators before the twelfth century were Smaragdus of St. Mihiel (fl. 819), who wrote on Donatus,[21] and Remigius of Auxerre (841–c. 908), who wrote commentaries on both Donatus and Priscian as well as works dealing with a variety of poets.[22]

Yet this pattern of commentary did not continue as an isolated phenomenon. Major questions were raised. Fundamental linguistic problems were identified. The result was a sweeping change in medieval attitudes toward grammar.

---

[18] Hugh of St. Victor, *Didascalicon*, trans. Jerome Taylor (New York, 1961), III.5.

[19] A number of such texts are printed in Keil, *Grammatici latini*.

[20] For brief accounts of these writers see Manitius, *Geschichte*, I, 119–456. Thurot, *Notices et extraits*, pp. 4–58, provides a survey of grammatical writers to the fifteenth century.

[21] Migne, *PL* 102, cols. 13–594; and Manitius, *Geschichte*, I, 461–68.

[22] Cf. Manitius, *Geschichte*, I, 504–19, and Thurot, pp. 8–11.

This change did not come about by accident. This evolution from a largely descriptive grammar to one that can fairly be called preceptive—from the classifications of Donatus to the quasi-rhetorical advice of Vinsauf—occurred largely as a result of twelfth-century re-examinations of the nature of language. It must be remembered, too, that there were three other consequences of this same inquiry: (1) the development of so-called "speculative grammar" (*grammatica speculativa*); (2) the analysis of the *ars rithmica;* and (3) the extension of grammatical study into the field of prose writing as applied to letters (*ars dictaminis*).

As early as the eleventh century, the time of Saint Anselm (d. 1109), there was penetrating discussion of the nature of grammar. D. P. Henry has pointed out the significance of Anselm's *De grammatico,* once regarded as a mere school exercise.[23] In a dialogue Anselm has a student ask whether "paronyms" denote substance or quality. In Priscian and other late Latin grammarians the term "paronym" is used to mean any kind of derivation from a *nomen;* the meaning of *nomen* is of course broader than that for the modern English "noun," since the Latin term can include adjectival or other kinds of attributes of the thing named. What Anselm is doing is raising the question of whether a term like *grammaticus*—a term applied to a human being—denotes both the nature of the human being and also a "quality" of that human being. Anselm concludes, in Henry's view, that the term *grammaticus* really means "a person possessed of the ability to be grammatical"; that is, it denotes a person who possesses *grammatica* (as a science permitting performance of the art of literacy). This science of grammar includes practice both in identifying correctness and in predicting the meanings that will result from language use. The term *usus loquendi* is applied to the first of these skills; Anselm uses the term *significatio* for the broad area of meaning-study necessary for the second. By implication, Anselm proposes that absolute predictability for meanings is a concern of logicians rather than grammarians. However, he does not go further into the question of possible limits on the grammarian's ability to predict meaning.

Within a few years, Aristotle's complete *Organon* was to be available in Latin translation in Western Europe. His two major dialectical works, *Topica* and *De sophisticis elenchis,* were translated in 1128 by Jacob of Venice. John of Salisbury, as we have noted earlier, praised these newly

---

[23] D. P. Henry, "Why *grammaticus?*" *ALMA* 28(1958), 165–80.

available treatises in his *Metalogicon* (1159).[24] Aristotle's basic distinction between absolute ("apodeictic") demonstration and other kinds of belief-creation is very close to the one voiced by Anselm, that is, the difference in the degrees of predictability of response. For Aristotle, dialectic is reasoning based on what he calls "opinion," and it is close to rhetoric because rhetoric also deals with "the common opinions of mankind." Neither dialectic nor rhetoric has a subject matter of its own. But both arts deal in the nonabsolute. Both arts deal with human variables. As we have already seen, the rhetoric-dialectic relationship was a matter of some interest to later medieval scholastic commentators like Giles of Rome.[25]

Unfortunately we do not yet know fully the extent to which dialectical concepts impinged upon the study of grammar in the twelfth century. One can only imagine the personal response of a learned grammarian of the mid-century—say, Ralph of Beauvais—when contemplating the fact that Aristotle's *De sophisticis elenchis* states that one type of dialectical refutation depends on language, with six forms: ambiguity, amphiboly, combination, division of words, accent, and form of expression. A thoughtful grammarian might well wonder how this idea fitted into his studies of language using Donatus and Priscian!

The complete answer to this question awaits more complete studies of the commentaries and other treatises of the twelfth century. We know something of the key commentators. Peter Helias was teaching at Paris in 1142 and was still alive in 1166; John of Salisbury studied rhetoric, not grammar, under Peter (a fact which is probably an index of the willingness of these various masters to study and teach all the arts of discourse). Ralph of Beauvais (c. 1125-1185) apparently carried on the same general line of study begun by Peter. There are others known by name and a single work, like Abelard of Bath; a host of *anonymi* may have penned commentaries on Donatus and Priscian during this period.

Richard W. Hunt has provided the most comprehensive statement so far of the contributions made by these scholars.[26] He notes that their pri-

---

[24] See above, Chapter III, pp. 104-05.

[25] For Giles, see above, Chapter III, pp. 98-100. Another evidence of wider concerns is an interest in the moral value of the exemplary materials used in teaching. See M.-D. Chenu, O.P., "Grammaire et Théologie aux XIIe et XIIIe siècles," *Archives d'histoire doctrinale et littéraire du moyen âge* 10(1936), 5-28.

[26] Hunt, "Studies in Priscian" (see above, n. 11). The articles include some useful sample text fragments. For Helias, also see Thurot, *Notices et extraits*, pp. 18-24.

mary mode of discourse was not the independent treatise but rather the "commentary" or *glose*. The method was to take the text of Donatus or Priscian and add to it explanatory material of their own. Naturally the original text tended to supply the basic ideas for comment, and perforce the commentary itself followed the organizational plan of the original. As Hunt remarks dryly, "The method of developing one's views in a commentary is necessarily unsystematic." Helias' major work, for instance, was his *Summa super Priscianum maior,* an explication of the first sixteen of the eighteen sections of Priscian's *Ars grammatica.* Helias's commentary was widely used, and was incorporated in part into Vincent of Beauvais' *Speculum doctrinale.* Any modern analysis of the ideas expressed in such commentaries must proceed with full awareness of the double context of each remark: each is an expression of the glossator's personal views as well as his understanding of what the original author intends. This factor complicates systematic study of this important period; moreover, it is not at all clear that we have even identified all the critical texts needed to complete our picture of twelfth-century grammatical history.

Hunt's study was undertaken, he says, because so little had been done since Thurot's book in 1868. He bases the second half of his own investigation on only three glosses from the half-century between Peter Helias and Alexander of Villedieu. He concludes that these glosses shed very little light on such questions as whether the dialectical *disputatio* was separate from other exercises in the medieval arts of discourse. On the other hand, he detects what he calls "a preoccupation with questions of logic" that seems to foreshadow the later development of the so-called speculative grammar of the *modistae.* The glossators of the early twelfth century, he remarks, suffered from the "disastrous legacy from the ancient grammarians" in their hunt for etymologies and derivations; the commentators of the second half of the century worked most fruitfully in the organization of syntax.

All of this showed very little concern for what we might call the study of "literature," that is, the *auctores* like Virgil. Yet the arts of preceptive grammar, the so-called "arts of poetry," flourished in Europe (especially in France) right at the end of this period of grammatical introspection. What seems to have happened is that the monolithic *ars grammatica* of Donatus and Priscian, even when buttressed by centuries of approving commentary, simply broke up into its constitutent parts around the year 1200. The philosophical tensions inherent within it finally proved unbearable to a great many intelligent students of language. It proved impossible to carve out a single *ars* which could accommodate sensible principles concerning every one of the questions that had been brewing since Quintilian's time: the uses of etymology, the role of tropes and figures, the nature of meaning, the criticism of literature, the creation of literature, the place of rhythmical language, the nature of "parts of speech," the question of a universal grammar, the problem of "correctness" versus "invention," the demarcation of boundaries between grammar and other arts like rhetoric and dialectic—and a host of other subordinate problems like that of the doctrine of *transsumptio*.[27]

In typically pragmatic medieval fashion a number of apparently new approaches to language appeared on the scene. Their very existence may help us to understand that the new "art of poetry" under discussion here was in the last analysis simply another example of that fragmentation. The authors of the new *artes poetriae*, after all, were grammarians themselves.

For this reason it would be wise at this point to describe briefly the various segmental forms of the medieval art of grammar. However, it is not simply a matter of evolutionary chronology, with one new form leading to another. The dispersive forces generated by twelfth-century analyses resulted in new texts which appeared over a period of a century as parallel but separate developments in syntax, rhythmics, metrics, and "speculative" grammar.[28] The thirteenth-century *ars grammatica* is a multi-faceted array of varied sub-arts radically different from the traditional *ars grammatica* of the early twelfth century.

It is therefore necessary for us, in the words of Richard Schoeck, "to rather substantively modify and expand our sense of the *ars grammatica*." [29] The wisdom of this endeavor will be apparent to the reader who

---

[27] That is, does the "transformation" (*transsumptio*) of a word into another word by a letter change also make a substantial change in the root concept? All three medieval rhetorical genres advocate its use for amplification, but implicit in its use is a profound question of *significatio*.

[28] Both the *ars dictaminis* and the *ars praedicandi*, on the other hand, show an "evolutionary" growth through a clearly identifiable set of sequential developments. The growth of these two medieval arts is described in Chapters V and VI respectively.

[29] Richard J. Schoeck comments as follows: ". . . we isolate with peril under the *ars grammatica* such treatises on style as those of Geoffrey of Vinsauf, Matthew of Vendôme, and John of Garland, unless we rather substantively modify and expand our sense of the *ars grammatica*." The remark appears as a conclusion to "On Rhetoric in Fourteenth-Century Oxford," *Mediaeval Studies* 30 (1968), 214–25.

considers the nature of the treatises produced during the grammatical revolution of the late twelfth and thirteenth centuries. He will soon see that each set of books constitutes a sort of sub-genre of its own.

There is, first of all, the traditional study of such matters as syntax and phonology; then there is the *ars rithmica,* dealing with the principles of patterning clause endings to produce certain effects; and finally there is the *grammatica speculativa,* or "speculative grammar," probing the very nature of language and its effects. Each of these sub-genres produced significant new treatises during this period. It is essential for the modern reader to keep in mind that all three of these developments were important elements in the intellectual milieu which fostered the composition of the six preceptive *artes poetriae.*

The *Doctrinale* (1199) of Alexander of Villedieu is the major traditionalist grammar text of this period.[30] This work of 2645 hexameter lines rapidly displaced Priscian as the standard advanced textbook, and was in use in some European universities as late as the seventeenth century. The book is divided into twelve sections dealing with syntax, etymology, quantity, accent, and the tropes and figures.

L. R. Lind has reconstructed Alexander's career from the data available within the author's various works. Alexander was born about 1170 in Villedieu-les-Poeles, a town in Normandy just north of Avranches. When he died, about 1250, he was canon of the church of Saint-André in Avranches. He studied in Paris in the company of two friends, a fellow townsman named Ivo and an Englishman named Adolphus. Apparently Alexander, Ivo, and Adolphus worked jointly to accumulate a mass of material dealing with a wide variety of subjects. When the trio broke up—Ivo died and Adolphus went back to England—Alexander inherited the mass of notes.

Alexander himself explains the genesis of his *Doctrinale.* In the intro-

---

Schoeck's article is a response to James J. Murphy, "Rhetoric in Fourteenth-Century Oxford," *Medium Aevum* 34 (1965), 1–20. The grammatical background of the listed authors is largely ignored by older studies like that of J. W. H. Atkins, *English Literary Criticism: the Medieval Phase* (Cambridge, 1943). The lack of a critical modern history of medieval grammar has severely hampered efforts to evaluate authors like Vinsauf.

[30] Text in *Das Doctrinale des Alexander de Villa-Dei,* ed. Dietrich Reichling, *Monumenta germaniae paedagogica* 12 (Berlin, 1893). Reichling lists some 239 extant manuscripts and 267 printed editions of the book; for Alexander's life and career see *Alexander of Villa Dei, Ecclesiale,* ed. and trans. L. R. Lind (Lawrence, Kansas, 1958), "Introduction."

duction to a rhymed glossary called the *Alphabetum maius*,[31] which now survives in only a fragment, he says that he has also written two other books, *Doctrinale* and *Ecclesiale*. He explains that he put into the *Doctrinale* matters pertaining to grammar, and devoted the *Ecclesiale* to the "computus," or church calendar.[32] In other words, what might originally have been planned as a massive encyclopedic work became instead a number of separate works dealing with comparatively narrow topics. He wrote the *Doctrinale* first (1199), then the *Ecclesiale* (1200). He was also the author of a book called *Algorismus, or De arte numerandi*; a prose treatise known as *De spaera*; a *Summarium biblicum*; and a *Computus ecclesiasticus, or Missa compoti*.[33]

This inventional background of the *Doctrinale* is extremely important, for it reveals Alexander as an author who flourished in the midst of the swirling intellectual movements of the late twelfth century.[34] There is little in any of his works to indicate that he was an innovative thinker. He was capable of attacks on his intellectual adversaries, especially those in the school of Orléans, as he shows us in the opening lines of the *Doctrinale*. But for the most part his sober eclecticism enables him to march steadily through an enormous mass of detailed grammatical lore. Alexander is, in short, the great distiller of late twelfth-century grammati-

---

[31] Alexander refers to it in his *Doctrinale*, vv. 26–27: Post Alphabetum minus haec doctrina legetor; / Inde leget maius, mea qui documenta segueter. The "Alphabetum minus" named in line 26 is now lost, though its *incipit* has survived: laicorum idioma habetur. See Lind, p. 2.

[32] Quae Doctrinali sunt scripta vel Ecclesiali,
Libro cuncta fere fuerant contenta priore.
Quae de grammatica sunt visa mihi magis apta,
In Doctrinali pro magna parte locavi;
Compotus et quidquid circa ius officiumque
Ecclesiae dixi, ponuntur in Ecclesiali.

[33] For details of these works and their relation to each other, see Lind, pp. 3–9.

[34] The remark of Lind (p. 9) is illuminating: "Alexander shows in the *Ecclesiale* an active and well-informed interest in the medieval educational curriculum, in the works of Peter of Riga, in allegorical interpretations, national history, geography, cosmology, the social history of his age, in Christian symbolism, martyrology, hagiology, the liturgy, the popes, and the creeds, and in canon law as well as in calendar computistics. His miscellaneous information is often curious. He knows well the cult of the pagan authors at Orleans. He forms an important part of the twelfth century reaction against the teaching of the Latin poets, rhetoric, and allied subjects; as Paetow shows, theology was soon to win out over the *auctores* as the chief element in the curriculum, and Alexander was to be proved right as far as the weight of influence and prestige was concerned, just as the weight of science has been greater than that of the humanities in the modern curriculum, especially in the university."

cal judgments. His success was undoubtedly due to his ability to graft the results of contemporary analysis onto the solid base of Priscian. In the year 1199 the Latin language was still basically the same as it had been in the time of Cicero, but Alexander had the talent to accommodate to it the changes that had occurred over a millenium, and to add the Christian flavor which Priscian of course lacked.

Paul Abelson has stated four reasons for the vast popularity of Alexander's *Doctrinale*:

> (1) The entire grammar was in verse. In an age when memorizing was so prominent a feature of instruction because of the scarcity of books, the versified form was certainly a boon to the teacher. This innovation was the original feature of the textbook.
>
> (2) In his treatment of the subject the author took into account the changes which the Latin language had undergone in the seven centuries since Priscian wrote his famous grammar. He incorporated in his book many words from Scriptures; also Latinized Teutonic words. It therefore was a grammar meeting the practical requirements of the living language of the day.
>
> (3) The Syntax of Priscian was no longer adequate to the requirements of an age when the logical aspects of grammar were to be emphasized rather than the literary.
>
> (4) His treatment of prosody and figures was likewise an improvement on the work of Priscian and furnished much new material.[35]

Alexander's short introduction to the *Doctrinale* (vv. 1–28) declares that the book is written for the young ("Scribere clericulis paro"). He does not mean, however, that it is written as a basic introduction to grammar for the very young—Donatus would still be the best book for that, presumably—but rather for the young student who has already mastered the rudiments of the subject. He also acknowledges the presence of a factor which Donatus and Priscian did not have to contend with in their teaching of Latin grammar, that is, the students' knowledge of a vernacular language (*laica lingua*) in addition to Latin. Alexander also makes a slighting reference to other teachers who present students with the "jests" of the poet Maximian—an oblique attack on the literary studies of the school at Orléans.

Then he names the subjects he will take up in the book, with a mention of Peter Riga in connection with syntax. Although the book falls into twelve *capitula* or chapters, some medieval manuscripts divide it

---

[35] Abelson, *Seven Liberal Arts*, p. 43. Reichling, *Monumenta*, points out that one Allesandro Gallo even translated the *Doctrinale* into Italian.

into three main parts, as follows: etymology (actually, declination and conjugation, frequently using etymology), *Cap*. I–VII; syntax, *Cap*. VIII–IX; and quantity, accent, and figures, *Cap*. X–XII.[36]

The book is literally "doctrinal." That is, it lays out concepts and rules. Its examples are all intended as illustrations of particular rules. Its enormous medieval success certainly indicates that it was regarded as an efficient coverage of the major grammatical doctrines.

As an accurate reflection of accepted Latin grammar at the end of the twelfth century, then, the *Doctrinale* deserves careful study by any serious student of medieval communication. The seemingly dry sections on such matters as the formation of verbs (*Cap*. VII, vv. 1048–1073), for instance, can provide revealing insights into the doctrines of language use that were standard during the lifetimes of men like Geoffrey of Vinsauf and John of Garland. All the writers of the *ars poetriae* urge their readers to go beyond the "ordinary" uses of language to devise new ways of expression. How can any of us gauge their efforts if we do not determine what was, for their time, the "ordinary" use of language? Alexander's *Doctrinale,* and particularly his third section, provides a statement of the accepted doctrine.

More than a third of the total book, 1095 verses out of 2645, is devoted to the three subjects of quantity (vv. 1550–2281), accent (vv. 2282–2340), and figures (vv. 2341–2645). His discussion of Latin quantity and accent are far too complex to summarize here; it is worth noting, however, that he does devote much space to these quasi-oral matters. Alexander then goes on to discuss what he calls "figures of speech" (*figurae loquelae*). He says there are three kinds: tropes, schemes, and metaplasms (though he later includes 23 more figures for which he gives no general name). Altogether he discusses 80 figures.

He first lists 16 *metaplasmi* derived from Donatus: prothesis, epenthesis, paragoge, auferesis, syncopa, apocopa, systola, ectasis or caesura, dieresis, syneresis, episynaliphe, syncrisis, antithesis, metathesis, and ecthlipsis.

His next category is *schema,* which includes 16 figures also taken from Donatus: prolempsis, zeugma, sylempsis, hypozeuxis, anadiplosis, epanalempsis, epizeuxis, anaphora, paronomoen, schesis onomaton, homoteleuton, paronomasia, polyptoton, homoptoton, polysyndeton, and dialyton or asyndeton.

---

[36] For a discussion of this medieval division, see Reichling, p. lxxi. One manuscript of the year 1305 bears the title "Tres partes Alexandri grammatici,"

His 25 *tropi* are arranged into the same thirteen categories proposed by Donatus: metaphora, metonomia, antonomasia, catechresis, metalempsis, onomatopeia, epitheton, homozeuxis (icon, paradigma, parabola), synecdoche, periphrasis, allegoria (antiphrasis, charientismos, enigma, paroemia, sarcasmos, ironia, astismos), hyperbaton (syncresis, temesis, hysterilogia, anastropha, parenthesis), and hyperbole.[37]

Alexander concludes his discussion with 23 figures to which he does not give a general title: prothesis, liptota, topographia, chronographia, hypallagium, prosopopoeia, apostrophe, conversio, ebasim, emphasis, euphonia, antitosis, antitheton, anthypophorum, anticlasis, aposiopasis, euphemismus, synepthesis, oliopomenon, homophesis, epimonen, anthropospathos, and homopathios.[38]

The medieval treatment of the tropes and figures will be discussed in more detail later in this chapter, but it is significant that even a book purporting to be a straightforward exposition of standard grammar devotes considerable space to these subjects. Clearly, any medieval student studying the *Doctrinale* would have been exposed to descriptions and examples of numerous figures and tropes. Alexander himself seldom engages in abstract speculation—his workaday style does not permit that—but it is interesting to note that one medieval glossarist of his book remarks at the end of this final section that "grammar is triplex, that is, preceptive, permissive, and prohibitive." [39] Alexander had noted (vv. 2640–41) that some of the things pointed out in his book should not be imitated —(i.e.) were intended as examples of faults—and the commentator added the more sweeping statement that grammar had to handle both positive, negative, and permitted uses of language. As we shall see in respect to the doctrine of the figures, this was to be the main thrust of the argument in support of purposeful alterations of ordinary or normal language usage to create special effects. Alexander was clearly devoted to outlining the

---

[37] Names of figures in parentheses are listed by Alexander as species of the figure whose name precedes the parenthesis. It is not uncommon, incidentally, for medieval writers to alter the order of their discussions after announcing their plans. Here Alexander lists the figures in one order (tropes, schemes, metaplasms) but actually discusses four (not three) sets of figures, and in a different order. Editorial precision is a comparatively modern habit.

[38] Five figures in this fourth list have counterparts in *Rhetorica ad Herennium* IV: antitheton, anticlasis, aposiopasis, epimonen, and synepthesis. But even so, there are some significant differences which lead to the conclusion that the *ad Herennium* cannot be considered a direct source for Alexander's list.

[39] Quia triplex est grammatica, sc. praeceptiva, permissiva et prohibitiva, ideo concludens se excusat (auctor) praeceptivam praecipisse, permissivam permisisse et prohibitivam prohibuisse. Quoted in Reichling, *Monumenta*, p. 178n.

"normal" or "standard" or "ordinary" usage for the living Latin of his day. But even Alexander included a discussion of the very usages which are by nature non-normal, non-ordinary, non-standard. The tradition for this goes back to Donatus, of course, and Alexander is squarely in the tradition of Donatus and Priscian. His inclusion of the figures and tropes, in other words, shows conclusively that such material was considered to be an integral part of the ordinary *ars grammatica*.

This same conclusion can be drawn in respect to the second most important grammatical treatise of this period, the *Graecismus* (1212) of Evrard of Bethune.[40] It was second in popularity only to the *Doctrinale*; when the *Doctrinale* was introduced into the curriculum of the University of Paris in 1366, for instance, the *Graecismus* was inserted along with it. Evrard wrote the sprawling 4440-line hexameter poem as a mere commentary on the third part of Donatus' *Ars maior,* but its fame grew so rapidly that within a few decades Evrard was named by Henri d'Andeli (in the *Battle of the Seven Arts,* 1259) as a champion of grammar equal to Alexander. The *Graecismus* takes its title from the opening word of a section on Greek terms. Evrard divided the book into 15 chapters, the first three of which treat 103 figures under three categories of "permissive, prohibitive, and preceptive." The matter-of-fact way in which Evrard handles this subject shows again that medieval grammarians routinely regarded figures and tropes as an integral part of their study.

The sections on figures and tropes cover 260 verses of the total 4440, about the same number of lines as Alexander gave them. The remainder of the book treats etymology, orthography, noun and pronoun forms, and Greek derivatives. The *Graecismus* discusses 28 metaplasms, 30 schemes, 21 tropes, and 23 "colors of rhetoric." A brief listing of these items will suffice to show how Evrard divides them.


### I. PERMISSIVA

De figuris metaplasmi. Prothesis, auferesis, syncopa, epenthesis, apocope, paragoge, systole, diastole, extasis, elipsis, synalimpha, eclipsis, aposiopasis, pleonasmos, dieresis, synderesis, temesis, synethesis, epidiasis, metathesis, anastrophe, antithesis, epibasim, metabolen, epimone, epizeuziz, hypallage, exallage.

---

[40] Text in *Eberhardi Bethuniensis Graecismus,* ed. Ioh. Wrobel. Corpus grammaticorum medii aevi, 1 (Bratislava, 1887).

De figuris scematis. Asyntheton (dialyton), polysintheton, anadiplosis (ana-
polensis), parenthesis, hendiadis, liptote, prophonesis, etymologia, synacrismos,
epidiocesis (correctio), antitheton, sindyasmos, sarcasmos, chronographia, topographia, cosmographia, catatyposis, characterismos, anthypophora, idiopasis,
allopasis, epilogus, epitrochasmos, brachylogia, climax (gradatio), teretema
(colorus rhetoricum), periphrasis, eflexegesis, tropologia (apostropha), poly-
toton.

De figuris tropi. Synecdoche, hyperbaton, hyperbole, antonomasia, onomatopeia, metonymia, proposopopeia, ethopoeia, antitheson, antifrasis, ironia,
emphatica, phantasia, somatopoeia, epitheton, evocitatio, conceptio, allegoria,
paraeigma, parabola, metaphora.

## II. PROHIBITIVA

De figuris barbarismi et soloecismio. Cacenphaton, euphonia, amphibolia,
anthropospathos, tapinosis, perissologia, macrologia, tautologia, cacosyntheton,
aleoteta, pleonasm.

## III. PRECEPTIVA
### DE PROSODIA

De coloribus rhetoricis. Repetitio, conversio, complexio, traductio, contentio,
exclamatio, ratiocinatio, sententia, articulus, consimilis cadere, agnominatio,
subiectio, gradatio, definitio, transitio, correctio, occupatio, disiunctum, adiunc-
tum, conduplicatio, commutatio, dubitatio, praecisio.

Since the ubiquitous primer of Donatus taught a number of figures,
and since both these two popular advanced grammatical texts also handled a large number of them, it can only be concluded that any medieval
student of grammar had plenty of opportunity to learn about this particular form of stylistic invention. It may or may not be important that
some figures came into the thirteenth century as "grammatical figures"
while others came as "rhetorical figures"—the distinction has never been
clear, either then or now—but it must be important to remember that
even "traditional" grammar texts like these included the subject in some
detail.

Closely allied to the "traditionalist" grammar of syntax, etymology,
and the like was another grammatical movement whose dimensions have
only begun to be clear to modern scholars. This was the application of
dialectical investigative modes to the subject matters of traditional grammar. Donatus and Priscian could quite legitimately content themselves

with the taxonomy of grammar, that is, with naming the parts of speech, distinguishing between nouns and verbs, and so forth. But it is quite a different question to ask, "What is a 'name' (*nomen*)?" or "In what way does a proper name (e.g., 'Paul') signify?"

This is the realm of what medieval writers called "speculative grammar" (*grammatica speculativa*). Its origins are visible by the beginning of the twelfth century, and it surely received a boost from the translation into Latin of Aristotle's *Organon* during the first half of that century; the movement reached its peak, however, in the latter part of the thirteenth century at the University of Paris. Most of the major writers in the field—Siger of Courtrai, Martin of Dacia, John of Dacia, Thomas of Erfurt, Boethius of Dacia, Michael of Marbais—wrote in the period from about 1275 to perhaps 1325. These writers of speculative grammars are commonly known as *modistae*.[41]

Geoffrey L. Bursill-Hall has pointed out that we do not yet have sufficient texts available to trace the movement completely.[42] Yet the main outlines can now be seen. He sees three stages. First, twelfth-century grammarians like William of Conches and his student Peter Helias endeavored to accommodate dialectical methods within traditional grammatical studies; in a sense the syntactical emphasis of traditional grammarians like Alexander of Villedieu may have been one result of this effort. Bursill-Hall notes that very little is known about the second phase, roughly the first half of the thirteenth century. The third and most active phase began, he believes, about 1250. By that time dialectic was solidly entrenched in the University of Paris, of course, and there had already been considerable study of the works of Aristotle and his Arabic commentators. About 1245 Roger Bacon wrote a *Summa gram-*

---

[41] An excellent brief account of this movement may be found in Robins, *Ancient and Medieval Theory*, pp. 77–89. For a concise review of scholarship up to 1951, see Grabmann, "Die geschichteliche Entwicklung der mittelalterlichen Sprachphilosophie und Sprachlogic. in Uberblick," in *Mélanges Joseph de Ghellinck*, 2 vols. (Gembloux, Belgium, 1951), II, 421–33. Jan Pinborg, *Die Entwicklung der Sprachtheorie im Mittelalter. Beitrage zur Geschichte der Philosophie und Theologie des Mittlalters*. Band 42, Heft 2 (Münster and Copenhagen, 1967).

[42] G. L. Bursill-Hall, *Speculative Grammars of the Middle Ages: The Doctrine of the Partes orationis of the Modistae* (The Hague and Paris, 1971), p. 32. Robert Kilwardby's commentary on Priscian, for instance, remains unedited, and yet this text was used for lectures on grammar in the faculty of arts at Paris in the thirteenth century, according to Grabmann, *Mittelalerliches Geistesleben* 1 (Munich, 1926), p. 118. Also available now is an edition of a key work: Thomas of Erfurt, *Grammatica speculativa*, ed. and trans. G. L. Bursill-Hall (London, n.d. [1972]). However, see the review by Morton Bloomfield (*Speculum* 49 (1974), 102–05) of both the edition and the earlier book by Bursill-Hall.

*matica* arguing that grammar is one, even though in particular languages, such as Latin or Greek, there may be variations which might obscure that fact. Bacon was not a grammarian but a philosopher, of course, but Bursill-Hall regards his book as an immediate precursor of the main body of modistic writings which flourished shortly thereafter. Bacon's thesis is expressed quite succinctly in another passage which has been widely quoted: "Grammar is one and the same in all languages, substantially, though it may vary, accidentally, in each of them." [43] In other words, there are at least two kinds of grammar: that dealing with the grammar of a single language, and that dealing with grammar *qua* grammar. Thus Alexander of Villedieu's *Doctrinale* is a grammar dealing with Latin as a single language, but the *modistae* went on to write about that other kind of grammar dealing with all language. They were what we would call today "linguists." It is their purposeful divergence from the Latin-centered descriptive methods of traditionalist works like the *Doctrinale* and *Graecismus* that demonstrates the essential unity of their movement, and its separate direction.

The resulting treatises, which are only now coming to light in reliable editions, deal with the philosophy of language. They assert that logic and grammar are separate, but inevitably they use the philosophical and dialectical methodology of their own times. It is as yet too early to state with precision the exact relations between this movement and the other intellectual currents of the thirteenth century, and indeed that story lies outside the scope of this study. It is to be hoped that the investigations now under way will soon illuminate this whole matter, however, because after all the movement was growing during exactly the period in which the *artes poetriae* were composed by other grammarians who took a different tack. We cannot know the *artes poetriae* completely until we know more fully the intellectual environment in which they were composed.

What kinds of questions did the *modistae* raise? Bursill-Hall has examined in detail some major investigations into one concept, that of the "parts of speech." That one topic received complex and even intricate

---

[43] Grammatica una et eadem est secundum substantiam in omnibus linguis, licet accidentaliter varietor. *Grammatica Graeca,* ed. E. Nolan (Cambridge, 1902), p. 27. This key passage is cited by John Edwin Sandys, *History of Classical Scholarship,* 3 vols. (Cambridge, 1915), I, 595; Robins, *Ancient and Medieval Theory,* p. 77; Bursill-Hall, *Speculative Grammars,* p. 38; and Siger de Courtrai, *Summa de modorum significandi,* ed. G. Wallerand, *Les Oeuvres de Siger de Courtrai: Les philosophes belges* VIII (Louvain, 1913), p. 43.

treatment.[44] An example of their concerns occurs in the *De modis significandi* of Martin of Dacia (d. 1304), a Danish scholar writing in Paris toward the end of the century.[45] Samples of his chapter headings from Book One may reveal his primary concerns:

21. De subdivisione nominis proprii
22. De modis accidentalibus nominis in communi
23. De modo significandi accidentali qui facit speciem
24. De modo significandi accidentali qui facit genus
25. De modo significandi accidentali qui facit figuram
26. De modo significandi accidentali qui facit numeram
27. De modo significandi accidentali qui facit casum
28. De modo significandi accidentali qui facit personam
29. Quomodo pronomen dividitur in modum relationis et demonstrationis.

Another Dane, John of Dacia (fl. 1280), wrote a *Summa grammatica* which is also known under the title of *Grammatica speculativa*.[46] John points out that grammar is the "idiom of philosophers," and then proceeds to use Aristotle's four causes (from *Metaphysics* I.3) to treat the modes of signification.

Perhaps this whole tendency of the *modistae* (i.e., authors concerned with "modes of signification") can be understood quickly from a modern summary of one writer's theories:

One of the most important of this class of grammarian is Siger de Courtrai (c. 1300). He begins with an account of the semantic functioning of words, a general theory of meaning, based on scholastic philosophy. To understand his grammatical method, and it is typical of the period, we must understand his semantics, which also is, in general, common ground to the Modistae as a group and itself depends on scholastic metaphysics of the time. Things, according to this scheme, possess as existents various qualities or modes of being (*modi essendi*). The mind apprehends these by the active modes of understanding (*modi intelligendi activi*), to which there correspond the passive modes of understanding (*modi intelligendi passivi*), the qualities of things as apprehended by the mind. In language the mind confers on vocal noises (*voces*) the active modes of signification (*modi significandi activi*), in

---

[44] Bursill-Hall, pp. 66–325. He includes in his Appendix E an illuminating "Glossary" of 44 terms (adverbium, figura, nomen, signum, vox, etc.) as defined by Martin of Dacia, Siger of Courtrai, and Thomas of Erfurt. Bursill-Hall also includes a useful bibliography (pp. 400–06).

[45] *Martini de dacia opera*, ed. Henricus Roos, Corpus philosophorum Danicorum medii aevi II (Hauniae, 1961), pp. 1–118.

[46] *Johannis Daci opera*, ed. Alfredus Otto, Corpus philosophorum Danicorum medii aevi (Hauniae, 1955), I, 45–220; II, 221–511. John of Dacia, incidentally, links rhetoric and logic under Avicenna's term *scientia rationalis*, and quotes al-Farabi on the importance of grammar as the *prima scientiarum*.

virtue of which they become words (*dictiones*) and parts of speech (*partes orationis*), and signify the qualities of things; these are now represented by the passive modes of signification (*modi significandi passivi*), the qualities of things as signified by words.[47]

Clearly, there is little in all this to give aid and comfort to those medieval grammarians interested in literary studies, that is, that part of *ars grammatica* concerned with "interpretation of the poets." The *modistae* concerned themselves exclusively with dialectical explications, retaining, to be sure, the nomenclature of the ancient Priscianic tradition, but driving the subject ultimately in a far different direction. This movement carried all through the middle ages, so that one of the later *modistae*, Michael of Marbais, was prominent enough to merit the caustic censure of Erasmus himself at the beginning of the Renaissance.[48]

Thus neither the traditionalist grammar of Alexander of Villedieu nor the speculative grammar of the *modistae* could be expected to give direct aid and comfort to the would-be literary artist. Both the *Graecismus* and the *Doctrinale,* of course, depend ultimately on Donatus and Priscian, and upon the whole tradition of teaching grammar as *ars recte loquendi et dicendi.* There was little in the tenth- and eleventh-century commentators to indicate a strong desire to go beyond this goal of composing language "correctly." The unique contribution of twelfth- and thirteenth-century preceptive theorists, in a way, is the realization that whenever a writer writes, he must write *in some way.* That is, he composes prose of a certain kind, or verse of a certain genre. He never composes in a vacuum. Even the examples which the grammarian uses to illustrate his rules must be drawn from special types of writing.

Thus it became increasingly difficult for some grammarians to content themselves with mere correctness. Note the contrast, for instance, between Hugh of St. Victor (d. 1154) and John of Garland, writing a century later. Hugh is solidly in the older tradition: "Grammar, simply taken, treats of words, with their origin, formation, combination, inflection, pronunciation, and all things else pertaining to utterance alone. . . . Grammar is the knowledge of how to speak without error" (*Didascalicon* II.28, 30).[49] Almost exactly a century later, the very broadness of the

---

[47] Robins, *Ancient and Medieval Theory,* pp. 81–82. For an older summary, see Thurot, *Notices et extraits,* pp. 155–56.

[48] Thurot (pp. 41–42) identifies Michael as the *Michael modista* attacked by Erasmus in his *Conflictus Thaliae et barbariei.*

[49] Hugh of St. Victor also wrote a short tract on grammar. Linking grammar to the liberal arts, he declares his primary concern for "correctness" as the pur-

title of John's major theoretical work reveals the extent to which the concept of grammar teaching had changed since the days of Hugh: *De arte prosayca metrica et rithmica.* Two manuscripts of this work, in fact, define grammar as an art devoted to coherent composition (*congrue loqui*). This is a new element.

If the mere correctness of the traditionalists was not imaginative enough, and the speculation of the dialectical analyzers was not productive enough, there was still a third branch of grammatical study in the twelfth and thirteenth centuries which did allow for some experimentation. This was in the field of *rithmus,* or *ars rithmica.*

To comprehend this development we have to remember that medieval authors considered writing to have three main forms, rather than the two (prose and poetry) we commonly name today. The medieval forms are "the prosaic," "the metrical," and "the rhythmical." The famous distinctions of Thomas of Capua, a thirteenth-century dictaminal writer, are often quoted in this connection. In his introduction to a book on letter-writing (*dictamen*), he takes pains to distinguish the three forms for the purpose of staking his claim to the "prosaic" form:

> There are three kinds of writing defined from of old, the prosaic form as in Cassiodorus, the metrical form as in Virgil, and the rhythmical form as in Primatis.[50]

He goes on to declare that prose proceeds in a continuous way without recourse to metrical rules; the metrical form involves the number of feet and sounds, with scansion; and the rhythmical form involves the number of syllables and consonance of sounds.[51]

In the late nineteenth century Giovanni Mari collected a number of texts dealing with *rithmus.* He pointed out that it was studied at Vercelli, Vienna, Paris, Lyons, Blois, Orléans, Tours, and Rheims, usually in

---

pose of the subject: Grammatica est scientia recte loquendi secundum liberalium litterarum instituta, quae in disciplinis post litteras communes inventa caeteris regula facta est et origo. Text in Jean LeClercq O.S.B., "Le *De grammatica* de Hugues de Saint-Victor," *Archives d'histoire doctrinale et littéraire du moyen âge* 14 (1945), 263–322.

[50] Dictaminum . . . tria sunt genera a veteribus diffinita, prosaicum, ut Cassiodori, metricum, ut Virgilii, et rithmicum, ut Primatis . . . *Die Ars Dictandi des Thomas von Capua,* ed. Emmy Heller (Heidelberg, 1929), p. 13.

[51] (Prosaicum) quod solutum a lege metrica longa sed congrua continuatione procedit; (metricum) quod pedum numero et vocum attenditur scansione; (rithmicum) quod sillibarum numero et vocum consonantiis est contextum. Thomas also provides a more specific definition: Rithmicum dicitur a "rima" vel rithimorum quod est diffinitio vel distinctio, quia sub certa computatione sillibarum cum finali consonantia distinguitor, sicut et diffinitur.

connection with grammar.[52] It is important to note that these studies seem to have been separate from the studies of that type of rhythmical prose called the *cursus,* which was used in its own way in the *ars dictaminis,* or art of letter-writing. (The *cursus* is discussed below, in Chapter V.) That is to say, there was separate grammatical study of the phenomenon known as *rithmus.* We do not yet know in detail the relation between this comparatively abstract investigation and the much more practical use of the *cursus* in letter-writing theory. It is well known that the particular *cursus* developed at Orléans—a center of grammatical study—had characteristics somewhat different from the *cursus* developed in the dictaminal centers of Bologna and Florence. Yet the full story remains to be told.

In any case, Mari provided the grounds for beginning such an investigation. Four of the treatises in his collection share a common definition: *Rithmus est consonans paritas sillibarum certo numero comprehensarum.*[53] These four treatises are devoted entirely to technical expositions of various forms which *rithmus* can take. It seems to be generally assumed by these writers that its two chief uses are in composing letters and in writing hymns. The discussions are usually quite technical. One writer provides the following analysis, perhaps best retained in the Latin of the text:

> Distinctio debet constare ex quator sillabis ad minus, et ex sexdecim ad plus.
> Clausula debet constare ex duabus distinctionibus ad minus ex quinque ad plus.
> Rithmus dividitur . . . alius monotongus, alius diptongus, et alius triptongus.
> Rithmorum aliie sunt transformati alii equicomi, alii orbiculati, alii serpentini.[54]

Master Sion of Vercelli repeats these divisions (except that he provides for a division as far as pentaptongus), but adds, *rithmorum alii caudati, alii non caudati.*[55] The other two writers in the group of four follow the same doctrine, with profuse examples for each category, some of the examples having alternate twelve-, thirteen-, fourteen-, or fifteen-syl-

---

[52] Giovanni Mari, *I trattati medievali di ritmica Latina,* Memorie del reale istituto lombardo di scienze e lettere 20 (Milan, 1899). Mari prints eight texts, some of which are excerpted from larger works.

[53] *Ibid.,* pp. 11, 17, 23, and 28.

[54] *Ibid.,* pp. 11–16.

[55] *Ibid.,* p. 17.

lable lines. The whole emphasis is upon the mathematical structure of lines according to mechanical limits. As is usual in medieval manuals, the space given to examples outweighs the description which the examples illustrate.[56]

Although writers like Thomas of Capua say that *rithmus* is to be used for composing hymns or letters, medieval preachers also could draw on the theory for help in sermon composition. Thomas of Todi (fl. 1380), for instance, devotes one-sixth of his *Ars sermocinandi ac etiam faciendi collationes* to the twelve kinds of rhythms he believes to be useful in preaching.[57] The first of his five rules for the use of *rithmus* is that rhythm should be formed for the delectation of the ears of the hearer, and he goes on to show with profuse examples how to do this by adroit combination of various line lengths and syllabic patterns. For Thomas, the use of complicated rhythms is a mode of *amplificatio* holding equal rank with the citation of authorities or the use of narrative *exempla*.[58]

The most complete theoretical treatment of *rithmus* is that of John of Garland in the final portion of his *De arte prosayca, metrica et rithmica*.[59] The following summary of the text printed by Mari will give some idea of his doctrine:

> *Rithmus* is a species of art like music. Music is divided into mundane, which consists of due proportion of elements; into human, which consists of the proportion and concord of human beings; and into instrumental, which consists of the concord of instruments. These species are lyrical, metrical, and rhythmical. *Rithmica* is the art which teaches the making of *rithmus*. *Rithmus* is a consonance of clause endings ordered with a certain measure but without metrical feet. Consonance, as in music, is either of the voice or of things, of *concordia discors* or *discordia concors*, or their contraries. The term "clause endings" is used to distinguish *rithmus* from lyrical composition, just as the term "certain measure" signifies that it may consist of more or fewer syllables. Also, it is said to be "without metrical feet" to distinguish it from metrical composition. The term "ordered" means that

---

[56] John of Garland's *Ars de himnis usitatis,* for instance, treats nineteen methods of hymn construction solely by providing nineteen hymns as examples (Mari, *I trattati,* pp. 60–80).

[57] Thomas of Todi, *Ars sermocinandi ac etiam faciendi collationes,* ed. June Babcock, unpublished M.A. thesis, Cornell University, 1941.

[58] The use of *rithmus* in preaching was not universally popular, however. Stephen Langton in his *Tropologia super duodecim prophetas* has this pungent comment about the practice: Sed qui in predicatione sua magis venatur ornatum et vocum concidentiam et verba similiter cadentia quam propriam voluntatem ut utilitatem subditorum: non bene clangit. Assumit enim ritmici carminis officium, et relinquit officium predicationis. Oxford Bodleian MS. Oriel 53, fols. 103ᵛ–104ʳ.

[59] Mari, *I trattati,* pp. 85–86. For the complete text, see below, n. 83.

the clauses should fall into a rhythmical pattern. *Rithmus* takes its origin
from the rhetorical color which is called *similiter desinens*. In a sense *rithmus*
proceeds like iambic meter or like spondaic. By iambus in this connection is
meant an expression whose penultimate term is shortened, for an iambus is
made from short and long. A spondeus in this sense is an expression in the
spondaic mode. [Then follows an 88-line poem as an example of the two
meters.] Colors of rhetoric are necessary in *rithmus* as in metrics, and especially the following:

1. similiter desinens or homoteleuton
2. conpar in numero sillibarum
3. annominatio
4. traductio
5. exclamatio
6. repetitio

[Then follows a 79-line hymn in four- and six-line stanzas, *De beata virgine
rithmus diversimode coloratus.* The treatise concludes with a discussion of
various rhythmical modes.]

Thomas of Capua notes that there are two general uses for rhythmical
compositions: *ad epistolare dictamen* (*et*) *Dei invocatio auxilio*—that is,
in composing either letters or hymns. We have already noted that John
of Garland includes hymn-writing as a part of the study of *rithmus,*
but there is another branch of rhythmical composition which was never
used for hymns but was devoted solely to epistolary composition—the so-
called *cursus,* or system of rhythmical clausulae.[60] Its major medieval
use begins with the twelfth-century Roman Curia, in the bulls of Pope
Gelasius II (1118–19), and spreads throughout European chanceries during succeeding centuries. Albert C. Clark identifies three species, more
often defined by example than by statement:

1. *planus,* for example,     *vincla perfregit*
2. *tardus,*                   *vincla perfregerat*
3. *velox,*                    *vincla fregeramus*[61]

---

[60] A brief summarizing study may be found in Noel Denholm-Young, "The
Cursus in England," in *Collected Papers on Medieval Subjects* (Oxford, 1946),
pp. 26–55. Two older standard treatments, both by Albert C. Clark, are *The
Cursus in Medieval and Vulgar Latin* (Oxford, 1914), and *English Prose Rhythm*
(Oxford, 1913). See also Reginald Lane Poole, *Lectures on the History of the
Papal Chancery* (Cambridge, 1915). It might be noted here that the problems
raised in the study of the *cursus* are typical of those which make difficult any
study of rhetoric in the middle ages: The *cursus* apparently gained its popularity
in Italy for some quite pragmatic political reasons, but grammarians, especially
French grammarians, also became teachers of its theory. Cf. Thurot, *Notices et
extraits,* pp. 480–83.

[61] Clark, *Cursus,* p. 10. Charles S. Baldwin *Medieval Rhetoric and Poetic* (New
York, 1928), pp. 223–37, uses the terms "cadence" and "rhythm" interchangeably in
connection with these examples. See the more complete description of Toynbee,
below, Chapter V, pp. 251–53.

The essential point of the theory is that the writer should compose his periods in such a fashion that he can control the way in which the prose accent falls; the *cursus* is therefore akin to the *prosimetricum* (or mixed form) as well as to *rithmus*. It is not necessary—as it is in verse—to count quantity, but only to count the number of syllables and determine the place of the accent. Once the concept of accent is introduced into prose, it is perhaps inevitable that some purely metrical terms should be employed to describe prose.[62] For the purposes of this study, it is sufficient to note that *rithmus* attempts to introduce into certain kinds of prose some of the compositional principles usually employed in writing verse. Little attention was paid to this problem in classical rhetoric, and medieval practice seems to have been based on the example of the Papal Curia rather than on classical precept.[63]

The *ars rithmica,* therefore, may be regarded as that branch of *ars grammatica* which treats the art of rhythmical composition in both verse and prose. Its chief medieval uses are in hymn-writing and letter-writing, with some use in preaching as well. Although modern investigators have traced the tradition of rhythmical prose far back into ancient times, the medieval emphasis upon its rules and precepts may be regarded as a significant departure from ancient practice. Its study by grammarians like Garland serves to emphasize again the basic medieval assumption that language is for the ear.

We have seen, then, that the once unitary traditional grammar of Donatus and Priscian had begun to fragment into several parallel movements as a result of probing investigations in the twelfth century. One result was an updated traditional grammar, in the *Doctrinale* of Alexander of Villedieu and the *Graecismus* of Evrard of Bethune. Meanwhile dialectical analysis led off in a different direction, which was to result in the late thirteenth-century speculative grammar of the *modistae.* In a third and parallel development, grammarians studied the nature of rhythmical language. It was in this climate of grammatical revolution that the six preceptive grammars[64] of the *ars poetriae* were composed.

---

[62] For instance, one thirteenth-century text defines the *cursus* as *matrimonium spondeorum cum dactilis,* Thurot, *Notices et extraits,* p. 481.

[63] To my knowledge it is rarely discussed by ancient writers, but see Cicero, *Orator* 212.

[64] All the major writers—Vendôme, Vinsauf, Gervase, Garland, Eberhard the German—were teachers, and all but Vinsauf discussed detailed pedagogical problems in their works. Their constant concern with syntactical matters is a further key to their primary interests. See Walter B. Sedgwick, "The Style and Vocabulary of the Latin Arts of Poetry," *Speculum* 3 (1928), 349–81.

The chronology of this preceptive movement is interesting. It begins, rather hesitantly, with Matthew of Vendôme about 1175, reaches a peak —its most "rhetorical" stage—with Gervase of Melkley and Geoffrey of Vinsauf around 1210, begins to falter with the abortive attempt at collation by John of Garland two decades later, and sputters out almost cynically shortly after mid-century with Eberhard the German. It was, in other words, a fairly short-lived movement with some visibly evolutionary features within it. Matthew in 1175 points to the novelty of his work, dedicated to "the elegant joining of words, and the expression of the characteristics and the observed quality of a thing." Eberhard eight decades or so later laments tiredly that "when the word flowers, the mind dries up."

It is a much-discussed and little-understood movement. An important event in the modern study of these authors was the publication in 1924 of key texts and their analysis by Edmond Faral.[65] A considerable bibliography has grown up since then, especially for Geoffrey of Vinsauf, and it is clearly the opinion of modern literary historians that these authors deserve careful attention as potential influences on both Latin and vernacular literatures of the middle ages.[66]

The development and decline of the movement can best be seen by

---

[65] Edmond Faral, *Les arts poétiques du XII⁰ et du XIII⁰ siècles,* Bibliothèque de l'école des hautes etudes, fasc. 238 (Paris, 1924; reprinted Paris, 1958), hereafter referred to as Faral. Faral includes biographies of authors, an analysis of doctrines found in the texts, and the Latin texts of works by Matthew, Geoffrey, and Eberhard. There are brief summaries of Gervase of Melkley and John of Garland. An important supplement to Faral's book may be found in Walter B. Sedgwick, "Notes and Emendations on Faral's *Les arts poétiques,*" *Speculum* 2 (1927), 331–43; some useful material, including a word index to Faral's collection, may also be found in the Sedgwick article cited in the previous note.

[66] Some discussion of these works may be found in John W. H. Atkins, *English Literary Criticism: The Medieval Phase* (New York: Macmillan, 1943). It might be noted, however, that Atkins assumes a wide distribution and use of these treatises in England as well as on the Continent. For a contrary view, see James J. Murphy, "A New Look at Chaucer and the Rhetoricians," *Review of English Studies* NS 15 (1964), 1–20.

See also Douglas Kelly, "The Scope of the Treatment of Composition in the Twelfth- and Thirteenth-Century Arts of Poetry," *Speculum* 41 (1966), 261–78; Baldwin, *Medieval Rhetoric,* pp. 289–96; Edmond Faral, "Le Manuscrit 511 du 'Hunterian Museum' de Glasgow," *Studi medievali* NS 9 (1936), 18–119; E. Lobel, "The Medieval Latin Poetics," *PBA* 17 (1931), 309–24; Paul Salmon, "Uber den Beitrag des grammatischen Unterrichts zur Poetik des Mittelalters," *Archiv für das Studium der Neuern Sprachen und Literaturen* 199 (1962), 65–84. There are frequent references in such major literary histories as Ernst Curtius, *European Literature and the Latin Middle Ages,* trans. Willard R. Trask, Bollingen Foundation Series, No. 36 (New York, 1953), and Franz Quadlbauer, *Die antike Theorie der genera dicendi im lateinischen Mittelalter* (Graz, Vienna, and Cologne, 1962).

an examination of each writer in turn, before any conclusions are drawn about the relation of the *artes poetriae* to either the *ars grammatica* or the *ars rhetorica*.[67] A brief summary of the work of each grammarian is presented below. The descriptions of the six works may, in fact, give a better ground for the reader's own conclusions than any remarks that might be made by this writer.

Matthew of Vendôme was a teacher who had studied under Bernard Silvester at Tours and then taught grammar himself at Orléans before departing angrily for Paris after a dispute with another teacher, Arnoulf. It was at Paris, shortly before 1175, that he composed his *Versificator's Art* (*Ars versificatoria*).[68] The book is in prose with numerous verse examples. It is divided into four main parts, with sections numbered consecutively within each part: "Ideas" (118 sections); "The Form of Words" (46 sections); "The Quality of Expression" (52 sections); and "The Execution of the Subject in Poetic Fables" (51 sections).

In his brief Prologue Matthew attacks his enemies and detractors, asserting that the book is written to provide "some sort of instruction" (*qualiscumque instructio*) in the making of verses. This may be an attack on Arnoulf, disguised under the name "Rufinus" in the Prologue.[69] It should be noted that Matthew assumes a great deal of knowledge on the part of his readers—of poetic genres, of basic grammar, of the uses of description, and so on. Thus his work may well have been intended for stu-

---

[67] Faral believes that a number of treatises concerning *figurae* constitute a second form of the *ars poetriae,* in that they were intended for use by versewriters. Vinsauf, for instance, also composed a *Summa de coloribus.* However, this is a complex subject best handled on its own merits. Accordingly a more detailed discussion of medieval attitudes toward *tropi et figurae* is reserved for a separate place later in this chapter.

[68] Text in Faral, pp. 109–93; outline on pp. 106–08; biography on pp. 1–3. A summary of the treatise may also be found in Robert R. Bolgar, *The Classical Heritage and Its Beneficiaries* (Cambridge, 1954), pp. 211–13. For a translation, see Ernest Gallo, trans., "Matthew of Vendôme: Introductory Treatise on the Art of Poetry," *Proceedings* of the American Philosophical Society, Vol. 118, No. 1 (Philadelphia, 1974). It might be remarked here that the assiduous work of Faral, even after half a century, still provides the bulk of all the reliable biographical data for these several authors. This is both a benefit and a danger, in that Faral's data must often be accepted by default in the absence of further detailed investigations.

[69] Matthew's slashing attacks in his Prologue bear a striking resemblance to similar remarks made by Anonymous of Bologna around 1135 in the prologue to *Rationes dictandi* (*The Principles of Letter-Writing*). The Bolognese author asks that "the tooth of the envious should not bite." Matthew even says Rufinus should bark less, since he cannot bite. For the 1135 prologue see James J. Murphy, ed., *Three Medieval Rhetorical Arts* (Berkeley and Los Angeles, 1971), p. 5.

dents beyond the elementary level of grammatical study. Following is a brief summary of the work.

## THE *ARS VERSIFICATORIA* OF MATTHEW OF VENDÔME

### PROLOGUE

Since many are called *versificatores,* without being truly qualified as such, this work is presented to instruct in the art. Verse is metrical discourse, proceeding through clausula, provided with embroidery through the marriage of beautiful words and flowers of sense, containing neither anything too mean nor anything useless. Neither the connecting of words, the counting of feet, nor the marking of quantities makes verse, but rather the elegant joining of words in proper expression which matches the proper and accurate epithet to the thing.

### I

Epithet attributes a certain accident to a substantive. Thus an epithet pertains either to the good, the bad, or the indifferent.

A beginning may be made in one of four ways: zeugma, ypozeusis, methonomia, sententia or proverbia.

The discourse should avoid incongruities of disposition of parts, as well as incongruities of word position (e.g., cacosyntheton).

In giving descriptions, a person other than the person described should give it. Words will be better if they proceed from the manliness of the person, the flexibility of his mind, his desire for honor, and his distaste for servitude. The properties of persons ought to be observed; for instance, age, duty or position, sex, place of birth, and other properties which Cicero calls *personae attributa.* Horace agrees, and uses these methods. [Then follow thirteen pages of examples, supplying complete descriptions of a Pope, Caesar, Ulysses, David, Marcia, Helen, Beroe.] These examples may also be applied to disparaging descriptions, but it is better to teach by good examples, because of the natural tendency to incline toward vice. Proper names of particular persons may be employed as epithets descriptive of general qualities; for example, Caesar's name may convey the idea of a certain age, condition, or some other attribute. Many epithets ought to be assigned to the description of one person, for the better description of him. Some attributes are proper to link with either men or women. Description should follow what is true or what is like the truth.

Description may be of two kinds, both suited to either praise or vituperation. The first kind is of the exterior (*superficialis*), dealing with the beauty of the body or external appearance. The second kind deals with internal (*intrinseca*) attributes of a person.

    I. Name
   II. Nature
      A. Body
      B. Spirit
      C. Others
        1. Nation (*secundum genus suae linguae*)
        2. Patria (*secundum locum originalem*)
        3. Age
        4. Kindred
        5. Sex
  III. Social relations
  IV. Fortune
   V. Deportment
  VI. Zeal
 VII. Disposition
VIII. Counsel
  IX. Calamity (*casus*)
   X. Deeds
  XI. Speech

All eleven of these attributes are just like *argumentum* in logic, since they are each *locus a nomine vel a natura.*

Next to be considered is the description of affairs, either of deeds or words. There are nine *attributae negotionis:* name or definition, cause (impulsive or reasoned), circumstances before the fact, circumstances during the fact, circumstances after the fact, opportunity for acting, quality of the act, time, and place. Just as a house is more secure that sits on many columns, so will a description be more valued that supplies many examples. It is also useful to employ zeugma, ypozeusis, and all the other schemes and tropes.

## II

There are three sources of beauty or elegance in poetry: the beauty of internal thought, the ornament of words, and the manner of speaking. [Following this statement there is a lengthy treatment of individual case endings, syllable values, comparatives and superlatives, and so forth; the section is difficult to summarize because of its detail, and is indeed purely grammatical.]

## III

The quality of expression (*sive modus dicendi*) depends upon polished words, colors of speaking, and interior intricacy. The mode of expression produces beauty more often than the substance or material does. Just as in a statue, where the material itself is not beautiful and art must be employed to produce beauty, so in a poem the material of words is not of itself beautiful

but is made so by artificial working (*artificiali appositione*). The three subjects
to be studied in this connection are schemes, tropes, and colors of rhetoric.

There are seventeen schemes, of which thirteen are useful in the exercise
of composing verses: zeugma, ypozeusis, anaphora, epynalensis, anadiplosis,
epyzeusis, paranomasia, paranomeon, scesisonomaton, omoetholeuton, polipto-
ton, polissinteton, dialiton sive assinteton.

There are thirteen tropes, of which nine are most useful in versifying: metaphora, antithetus, methonomia, sidonoche, peryfrasis, epithetum, methalemsis
sive climax, allegoria, aenigma.

There is a certain correspondence or parallelism between certain schemes
and certain tropes, as follows: contentio and antithetus, anaphora and duplicatio,
paronomasia and annominatio, epanalempsis and repetitio, scesisonomaton and
membrum orationis sive articulus, dialiton and dissolutus, polissynetheton and
conjunctum, methalempsis or climax and gradatio. Moreover, several tropes or
schemes may be found in one line of verse, as in *non parcit populis regnum
breve,* where *sententia, metaphora,* and *methonomia* may be identified.

It will be sufficient here merely to name the colors of rhetoric, since the
reader can find them treated elsewhere: repetitio, conversio, complexio, traductio, contentio, exclamatio, ratiocinatio, sententia, contrarium, membrum
orationis sive articulus, similiter cadens, similiter desinens, commixtio, annominatio, subjectio, gradatio, diffinitio, transitio, correptio, occupatio, disjunctio, conjunctum, adjunctum, conduplicatio, commutatio, dubitatio, dissolutio, praecisio, conclusio.[70]

Finally, we must point out that all three sources of beauty ought to be
present (as was said in Part II above) whenever poetry is written.

## IV

Some teachers in talking about poetic fables in school exercises think falsely
that they give an adequate commentary when they discuss only the elegant
language employed by the authors. But I feel that I have to go deeper into
the subject, and discuss the methods which the students should emulate. It is
not enough to render word for word, in order to achieve a faithful imitation
or a true interpretation of a work. Therefore I shall now discuss the subjects
treated in antiquity, and also shall discuss new subjects.

The ancients have rightly pointed out that certain words should be avoided
in verse, and that that multiplication of new genres, barbarisms, and prolixity
should be avoided.

---

[70] This list closely parallels that of the *flores verborum* of Geoffrey of Vinsauf's
*Poetria nova,* which adds five more to Matthew's 29: interrogatio, continuatio in
sententia, compar, interpretatio, and permissio. Faral provides a useful chart (pp.
52–54) listing the occurrence of figures and tropes in these various works.

Modern writers have given us directions for the proper use of personal attributes in description and for renovating old texts. There are two methods of permutation: changing the words but not the sense, and changing both the words and the sense.

The master or teacher has two primary duties: to note the vices in (student) verse, and to offer remedies for these vices. The student, on the other hand, has three duties: the admission of faults, the removal of written faults, and avoidance of future faults.

Methods of conclusion are as varied as their authors. Some methods used by the ancients are recapitulation, petition for favor, apology for the work, pleas for glory, presentation of thanks, praise of God, and abrupt ending.

Matthew of Vendôme's *Ars versificatoria,* as this summary shows, is something like Horace's *Ars poetica* in that it rather loosely organizes bits of advice to verse-makers. Matthew assumes a great deal of prior knowledge. Despite his frequent assaults on false versifiers and poor teachers, Matthew seems to be concerned primarily with students rather than with other teachers. He calls upon students to try to understand the general principles behind his examples, lest they be misled into mistaking the intentions of the authors they read.[71] It is interesting to note that Matthew customarily refers to his "hearers" (*auditores*) rather than "readers." This may mean that what we have here are published lectures, or that Matthew is merely using a convention of his time to indicate that verse is to be heard, not read.

In any case the book is clearly a grammar master's reflections on some aspects of composing verse. Horace and Ovid are his favorite exemplars. Perhaps as much as a full third of the text is composed of verse examples, some quite long; one section (I.50–56), dealing with descriptions of persons according to the "attributes" of Cicero, presents seven verse descriptions totaling 355 consecutive lines. His final section on how to correct a student's verse-writing is another indication of his pedagogical concerns.

With all its classical allusion and classroom lore, however, the *Ars versificatoria* remains a rather generalized treatment of the subject. It may tell us more about the twelfth century than it tells us about verse-writing. It tells us that twelfth-century grammar masters were interested

---

[71] Amplius auditoris intelligentia fideli memoriae studeat commendare, ut in praedictis descriptionibus per specialia nomina generalem intelligent disciplinam, ne diversum a mente scriptoris et sibi domesticum praesumat habere intellectum. I.60; Faral, p. 32.

in beginnings and endings of poems, that they toyed with ways to change words (*permutatio*), that they respected existing genres, that they taught the tropes and figures, that they looked to Cicero as well as to Horace for methods of description.

It was to be more than three decades before the next set of works appeared in this field. The next three works—those of Gervase of Melkley and Geoffrey of Vinsauf—were written within a few years of each other, from around 1208 to about 1216. The first, as far as we can tell, was the *Poetria nova* of Geoffrey, a hexameter poem written between 1208 and 1213. Then very shortly thereafter came his prose *Documentum*. Finally, after 1213 but not later than 1216, Gervase of Melkley wrote his prose *Ars versificaria*. This third treatise cites Geoffrey by name, and refers to both the *Poetria nova* and the *Documentum,* so that it seems safe to conclude that it came last. Their closeness in time, and their familiar handling of substantially common doctrines, indicates that the thirteenth century was interested in organizing more efficiently the comparatively inchoate ideas of writers like Matthew of Vendôme. These three works demonstrate the conscious existence of an "art of verse-writing" at the beginning of the century.

Gervase, in fact, notes that Matthew had developed the "art" of versifying "thoroughly," Geoffrey even more thoroughly, but Bernard Silvester the most thoroughly.[72] This third judgment may puzzle modern readers, as Bernard's *De mundo universitate,* quoted often by Gervase, is a prose-verse (*prosimetricum*) treatment of mythology rather than a book on verse-writing. But Gervase's ranking of Matthew and Geoffrey does indicate an awareness that there is indeed a separate *ars* dealing with verse-writing. Why, indeed, should Geoffrey write both a verse and a prose exposition of essentially the same materials? Again, the answer is probably that as a teacher of the art he wished to present two

---

[72] Scripserunt autem hanc artem Mattheus Vindocinensis plene, Gaufroi Vinesauf plenius, plenissime vero Bernardus Silvestris, in prosaico psitacus, in metrico philomeno. Text in *Gervais von Melkley: Ars Poetica,* ed. Hans-Jurgen Grabener, *Forschungen zur romanischen Philologie* 17 (Munster [1965]), p. 1. Biography in Faral, pp. 34–37; summary, pp. 328–30. (It might be noted that Faral [p. 37] has incorrect numbers for two Oxford manuscripts of Gervase's work; the proper citations should be Oxford Balliol College MS. 263 and Balliol College MS. 276.) Gervase apparently had very little immediate influence; his work does show up, however, as a source for Thomas Merke's *De moderno dictamine,* written at Oxford in 1405. For Merke, see James J. Murphy, "Rhetoric in Fourteenth-Century Oxford," *Medium Aevum* 34 (1965), 1–20; and Murphy, "A Fifteenth-Century Treatise on Prose Style," *Newberry Library Bulletin* 6 (1966), 205–10.

versions of his teachings.[73] Geoffrey also wrote a brief treatise on the tropes and figures as an adjunct to his main texts.

Before taking up each of the treatises, one cautionary observation must be made. Both Geoffrey and Gervase write in the fullness of developed doctrine. Yet more than thirty years had elapsed since Matthew's pioneer work. Are we to believe that during all that time no other writers took up these matters? Gervase names only Matthew and Geoffrey, and yet commentaries (on both Cicero and Priscian) flourished during this period, and we must not overlook the possibility that other authors still unknown to us made contributions utilized by Geoffrey and Gervase. Fully developed ideas seldom appear in human history without antecedents; it is such a far cry, conceptually, from Matthew to Geoffrey that we must at least keep in mind the possibility of someday discovering a good deal more about the emergence of this art. Matthew is in a sense the literary product of his teacher Bernard Silvester; but who was the Plato to Geoffrey's Aristotle? Our conclusions about this movement must always be tempered by the realization that we do not yet know precisely how it all began.

The great attention paid to Geoffrey of Vinsauf, especially by students of Chaucer, may also mislead us into thinking that this field has been well explored. Actually, very little is known of Geoffrey's career. He seems to have been an Englishman, probably studied in Paris, and may have taught in Hampton, England. He states in the preface to the *Poetria nova* that he had visited Rome. (The poem is dedicated to Pope Innocent III.) His surname (*de vino salvo*) comes from a treatise on the conservation of vines that was attributed to him. There is also a suggestion that he may have been a guest lecturer in a *studio* in Bologna. Yet the prevalence of the name *Gaufridus* in medieval records has made it very difficult to isolate true reference to Vinsauf.[74]

---

[73] The same phenomenon occurs in the *ars dictaminis,* where, for instance, the famous teacher Guido Faba wrote a total of nine books dealing with various aspects of that art, and Jacques de Dinant even wrote a commentary on one of his own books. See below, Chapter Five. This sort of thing does not occur with the *ars praedicandi,* whose treatises are designed for private reading and not for classroom use.

[74] One English "Geoffrey" (Galfridus Anglicus), sometimes confused with Vinsauf, proves to be Geoffrey of Everseley, author of a dictaminal work called *Ars epistolarium ornatus.* Noel Denholm-Young first opened the question of this Geoffrey's identify in "The Cursus in England," in *Oxford Essays in Medieval History Presented to Herbert Edward Salter* (Oxford, 1934), pp. 68–103. For a summary of the present knowledge of Geoffrey of Everseley and his work, see Charles Faulhaber, *Latin Rhetorical Theory in Thirteenth- and Fourteenth-Cen-*

On the other hand, Geoffrey of Vinsauf's *Poetria nova* is well known. It was translated three times in a recent four-year period,[75] and is mentioned in virtually every serious modern study of medieval literature. More than half a hundred articles, book chapters, and other studies have linked Geoffrey of Vinsauf and the English poet Geoffrey Chaucer since the publication in 1926 of John M. Manly's *Chaucer and the Rhetoricians*.[76] Yet for all the print lavished on the alleged influence of the book, its own origins and its place in thirteenth-century intellectual life remain virtually unexplored. Ernest Gallo has traced its debts to the *Rhetorica ad Herennium* and to Horace's *Ars poetica*,[77] but otherwise much remains to be learned about its genesis.

A brief summary may provide an idea of its contents. (The summary is based on the text in Faral, pp. 197–262.) Vinsauf's *Poetria nova* falls into seven sections: Preface (vv. 1–42), General Observations (43–86), Disposition (87–202), Amplification and Abbreviation (219–736), Ornaments of Style (737–1968), Memory and Delivery (1969–2065), and Epilogue (2066–2116).

## THE *POETRIA NOVA* OF GEOFFREY OF VINSAUF

General Observations. Just as a person building a house first plans what he is to do, so a poet must plan his poem in advance of the writing. The poet must first find things to say, either in his mind or from material things. Then he must consider the order in which he says these things, the language in which he says them, and finally the use of voice, countenance, and action.

Disposition. There are two forms of orders, the natural and the artificial. There is only one kind of natural beginning (that is, beginning at the beginning), but there are eight forms of artificial orders: beginning at the end,

---

*tury Castile,* University of California Publications in Modern Philology, Vol. 103 (Berkeley and Los Angeles, 1972), pp. 99–103. For a brief biography of Vinsauf, see Faral, pp. 15–33, as well as the introductions to the translations listed in n. 75.

[75] For three translations see Jane Baltzell Kopp, "The New Poetics," in Murphy, *Three Medieval Arts,* pp. 32–108; Margaret Nims, *Poetria Nova of Geoffrey of Vinsauf* (Toronto, 1967); and Ernest Gallo, *The Poetria Nova and Its Sources in Early Rhetorical Doctrine* (The Hague and Paris, 1971), pp. 15–29. The Gallo translation has the Latin text on facing pages.

[76] John M. Manly, *Chaucer and the Rhetoricians.* Wharton Lectures on English Poetry XVII (London, 1926); also published in *PBA* 12 (1926), 95–113. (For a rejoinder to Manly, see above, n. 66.) See also Robert O. Payne, *The Key of Remembrance: A Study of Chaucer's Poetics* (New Haven, Conn., 1963).

[77] Gallo, *Poetria nova,* pp. 133–223. Gallo's efforts to trace the influence of Quintilian, on the other hand, are less convincing.

beginning in the middle, sententia at the beginning, sententia in the middle, sententia at the end, exemplum in the beginning, exemplum in the middle, exemplum at the end.

Amplification and Abbreviation. In the beginning, art lays out the general plan; you must carry it out, either by shortening or lengthening. If you wish to amplify, you may use the following methods: interpretatio, circumlocutio, collatio, apostropha, prosopopeia, digressio, descriptio, oppositio. If you wish to abbreviate, you may use the following methods: emphasis, articulus, ablativus, prudentia dicti, sensus multarum clausus in una, and asyndeton.

Ornaments of Style. Whether short or long, let the discourse color itself inside and out, but with the proper class of colors. One kind of color is achieved by the changing of words (*transsumptio*) to make new (*homo ad rem similem, re ad hominem similem*); or the replacement of a word by a more effective word having the same metrical usefulness; or the movement of words for emphasis or clarity; opposition of sense; or the joining of all meanings in one expression or word. No matter which of these methods is used, grammatical rules must be followed. When the following are used, the sound of the voice will bring joy to the ear and will touch the mind with new delight: [translatio], permutatio, pronominatio, nominatio, denominatio ⌐ (*forma pro re, effectus pro causa, instrumentum pro utente eo, materia pro* ⌐ *re, vice contenti quae continet*), yperbolicus, intellectio, abusio, transgressio. You must be careful that the use of these colors does not make your expression obscure. Though you speak yourself, you speak among others, who must hear you. There are two other types of *florida verborum:* the first is *flores* — *verborum:* repetitio, conversio, complexio, traductio, contentio, exclamatio, interrogatio, ratiocinatio, sententia, contrarium, membrum, articulus, continuatio in sententia (in contrario and in occlusione), compar, similiter cadens, similiter desinens, subjectio, gradatio, diffinitio, transitio, correctio, occupatio, disjunctio, conjunctio, adjunctio, conduplicatio, interpretatio, commutatio, permissio, dubitatio, expeditio, dissolutio, praecisio, conclusio. There is also another group called *sententiae,* or figures of thought: distributio, licentia, diminutio, descriptio, disiunctio, frequentatio, expolitio per sermocinationem, and expolitio per exsuscitationem (*de re simplici cum ratione, de re duplici cum ratione, de re duplice sine rationibus, per contrarium, per similitudinem, per exemplum, per conclusionem*), commoratio, contentio, similitudo, exemplum, imago, effictio, notatio, sermocinatio, conformatio, significatio, brevitas, demonstratio. Other effects may be gained by conversions, that is, by changing verbs into nouns, or adjectives into nouns. Moreover, the simple style can be aided by collecting clauses or words together appositively [Faral: théorie des déterminations]. Finally, in respect to style, there are some general observations to be made: choose words appropriate to persons and circumstances; choose words appropriate to poetry. The plain style is appropriate to comedy. Only three things can be comic: spirit, things, or words. These faults should be avoided: hiatus, repetition of the same ending, overly long periods, forced metaphors. Finally, the writer should submit his work to a triple judgment of mind, ear, and usage.

Memory and Delivery. Memory is best served by repetition and rehearsal of what is new or novel; the system outlined by Tullius is too difficult. No one praises an inept recitation, so we must study this subject. There are three languages in reciting: the voice, the countenance, and movement. All should be moderate, and suited to the matter of the recitation. Everything should concur at once—the invented matter, the smooth discourse, the polished sequences, the ready memory. An inept recitation of good material is as bad as a beautiful recitation of poor material.

As we have noted earlier, Geoffrey of Vinsauf composed a prose work entitled *Documentum de modo et arte dictandi et versificandi*,[78] apparently shortly after the *Poetria nova*. In most respects this work is a repetition of the ideas found in the *Poetria nova*, though often in a different order. The *Documentum* employs a somewhat different technical vocabulary, one notable instance being the use of the terms *ornata facilitas* and *ornata difficultas* for sets of figures which appear in the *Poetria nova* without that designation. Roger P. Parr has provided a chart which shows that virtually every item in the *Documentum* appears in the *Poetria nova*.[79] Geoffrey's own summary of the *Documentum* can give a clear idea of its contents:

> In summation let us draw together those things which were treated extensively above. This has been said concerning the beginning and the transition. Concerning the beginning what has been said? How a natural beginning is made one way and an artistic beginning in eight ways. Concerning the transition, first, how it is to be continued in the beginning. For the continuation is easy if the beginning is natural. But if it is artistic it is to be continued in three ways: one way, if the beginning is taken near the middle or end, another way if the beginning is taken from a proverb, a third way, if the beginning is taken from an exemplum. Afterwards it was stated how it happens that shorter matter can be enlarged, and extensive matter made shorter: we treated fitting and sufficient theory for amplifying brevity and for abbreviating extended matter. Third, we treated how in the continuation of the matter there are two methods of expressing something well: one

---

[78] Text in Faral, pp. 265–319. Translated by Roger P. Parr as *Instruction in the Method and Art of Speaking and Versifying* (Milwaukee, Wis., 1968). Parr gives no explanation for his translation of *dictandi* as "of speaking"; Geoffrey clearly means prose-writing as opposed to verse-writing. Both of Geoffrey's works include short sections on oral delivery, of course, but both books are about writing.

[79] *Ibid.*, pp. 97–105.

method is using ornamented facility, the other method is using ornamented difficulty. We taught clearly those things to which ornamented facility and difficulty are compared, subjecting general rules to an end, by which every meaning which anyone has in mind or on his tongue can be said ornately.[80]

Geoffrey then concludes the whole work by listing three ways to handle the ending of material: from the body of the matter, from a proverb, or from an exemplum.

These two treatises of Geoffrey of Vinsauf have often been termed "rhetorical." Certainly his debts to the Ciceronian rhetorical tradition are obvious, especially in the realms of description and of the tropes and figures. Both books mention oral delivery. The Horatian interest is also visible. Geoffrey accepts the existing poetic genres as a matter of course, together with the whole doctrine of "transsumption" (*transsumptio*) or word-change which so agitated the minds of twelfth-century grammarians. Thus there are both "rhetorical" and "grammatical" elements in the two treatises. Quibbling about these terms has limited usefulness to us in our attempts to understand what Geoffrey and his fellows were about.

It might be more useful to note that Geoffrey is writing two preceptive treatises. They are preceptive in much the same way that Cicero's *De inventione* is preceptive; that is, they give specific advice for the composition of future discourse. Insofar as this preceptive element in the Western world has resided in the *ars rhetorica,* then to that extent Geoffrey is "rhetorical." But he was also a teacher of grammar, in effect borrowing from rhetoric some elements to increase the effectiveness of his advice to verse-writers. He remains to that extent "grammatical." That is why it might be best to think of this whole movement as productive of treatises of "preceptive grammar"—a hybrid term for a hybrid movement. Geoffrey is the high point of the movement, but understanding his colleagues can help us to understand him. Did they detect a relationship between grammar and rhetoric?

Geoffrey's contemporary, Gervase of Melkley, faces this issue squarely at the outset of his *Ars versificaria*. He declares that in seeking help for writers one should not despise the advice of Donatus or of Horace or of Cicero. Moreover, he adds, it is a moot point whether elegance is gained more from grammar or from rhetoric. Priscian and Cicero teach us directly, while Donatus does so indirectly by pointing out faults to be avoided. Gervase notes that three elements are involved in his own art:

---

[80] *Ibid.,* p. 95.

talent, instruction, and practice.[81] Instruction in theory is not sufficient without practice, which includes assiduous reading of authors to detect not only their errors but also their use of rhetorical topics and colors.

Faral (p. 328) has remarked with some justice that Gervase's treatise is original only in that it attempts to reorder under novel headings the concepts found also in Vinsauf and Vendôme. Nevertheless Gervase casts a very wide net indeed, acknowledging the value of rhetoricians, poets, other grammarians (especially Matthew of Vendôme and his own contemporary Geoffrey of Vinsauf), Horace, Ovid, Seneca, John of Hanville (*Architrenius*), and Bernard Silvester. He makes frequent use of a hitherto unknown poem, *Pyramis et Thisbe,* which Faral has printed (pp. 331–335).

Gervase divides his work into three parts:

Part One, "Rules Common to Discourse in General," treats identity, similitude, contrariety, elegance, and argument.

Part Two, "Special Rules for Verses," consists of fourteen short paragraphs, with examples, discussing such things as vices of the hexameter and pentameter, multisyllable locutions, hexameters beginning with dactyls, and the qualities of a versificator (such as knowledge of all kinds of literature).

Part Three, "Dictamen Prosaicum," states that *dictamen* has three kinds: metric, rhythmic, and prosaic. About half of this short section is devoted to *accentus,* Gervase having noted that it is grammar that supplies the rules by which it can be known whether a given syllable is short or long. (The technical term *cursus* is not mentioned, and Gervase's account here is very generalized; he does not, for instance, name the five parts of a letter, though he does acknowledge that *dictatores* have said much more about this subject.)

Many of the ideas found in Vinsauf appear in these sections of Gervase.[82] If it were not for the almost simultaneous composition of Geoffrey of Vinsauf's two treatises, the work of Gervase might well seem to rank along with the earlier one of Matthew of Vendôme; that is to say, Gervase's rearrangement of ideas into these categories might seem to be a mere pedantic exercise. But Gervase clearly assumes an audience similar to Geof-

---

[81] This is of course a standard Ciceronian statement, derived ultimately from Isocrates. For text of Gervase, see above, note 72.

[82] Faral (pp. 328–30) provides a loose and somewhat confusing summary. He does, however, list the figures and tropes which appear in Part One. Gervase often uses terms different from those of Geoffrey, making brief summary very difficult.

frey's—one concerned about the relation of grammar and rhetoric, and one that looked for specific advice about verse-writing. Hence Gervase states the relation of practice to theory, and suggests a way for readers of literature to study that literature by looking for specific things. Geoffrey is one step beyond Gervase in that he attempts to distill the precepts that might thus be learned; if Geoffrey is more preceptive as a consequence, Gervase is more critical. But each author can be a commentary on the other, and there is no doubt much for us to learn from a closer study of this comparatively neglected contemporary of the famous Geoffrey.

By the early thirteenth century, then, it is clear that teachers of grammar regarded themselves as capable of writing preceptively about all aspects of discourse—prose, verse, rhythmics, or mixed forms. The grammarian's broad definitions included oral language as well—the traditional province of the ancient rhetorician. His success in maintaining these claims naturally varied from place to place and from time to time, but taking the middle ages as a whole the grammarian probably won out over his traditional rival, the rhetorician, more often than he lost. It is interesting to note that the *ars rhetorica* does not become a major subject in the universities until almost the end of the middle ages, while *ars grammatica* is the first subject for every student at universities all over Europe from the twelfth century onward. At the lower school level— that is, in the pre-university or elementary schools—grammar was so obviously supreme that to this day the term "elementary school" and "grammar school" are virtually interchangeable terms. And of course even the student of logic had to learn his grammar before he could hope to begin to study philosophy.

The career and writings of John of Garland (c. 1195–1272) illustrate, perhaps better than any other single set of data, the course which medieval grammarians set for themselves. John attempted the master preceptive collation.

Born in England toward the end of the twelfth century, he tells us that he studied at Oxford under John of London about the year 1212. But he left England for Paris, and his whole professional career centered on the Continent rather than the island of his birth. It is for this reason that medieval scribes usually term him "John of Garland," after the place of his major teaching, rather than "John of England" after his birthplace. Apparently he was one of the illustrious teachers who attracted students to the *clos de Garlande* on the left bank of the Seine during the early years of the thirteenth century. This was a formative period for the University of Paris, so that John's appearance there about 1220 placed him in the forefront of the burgeoning Latin Quarter.

In 1229, however, occurred an event which marked him off from other Parisian grammarians. Count Raymond VII of Toulouse established a university in Toulouse, for which it was stipulated that two masters of grammar be appointed. John of Garland was chosen as one. He went to Toulouse for a time, but returned to Paris when it became obvious that he would not prosper at the new university under Raymond's eye. During an illustrious teaching career in Paris he composed a great variety of religious and grammatical works, including some rhythmical Latin hymns of merit. His major work, *De arte prosayca, metrica, et rithmica,* is an excellent illustration of his claims as a grammarian. First of all, he includes all three major forms of writing, bound together by common theoretical assumptions about the nature of composition. It is especially noteworthy that he includes the *ars dictaminis* under the rubric of prose-writing; grammarians eventually took over the whole province of the epistolary art, following his lead. A second feature worth noting is Garland's emphasis upon modes of amplification—perhaps the major thirteenth-century contribution to preceptive theory. Like his contemporary, Geoffrey of Vinsauf, John is even willing to posit himself as a teacher of both oral and written composition. Clearly, the medieval grammarian of Garland's caliber was not content to limit himself to the mere *ars recte loquendi.* What he attempted was the logical outcome of Geoffrey's preceptivity, applied as a natural second step to all of the forms of discourse instead of just to verse-writing. It is a *reductio ad completam.*

The very completeness of John's attempt makes it difficult to summarize briefly. We have already seen, in our discussion of the *ars rithmica,* what he had to say about that subgenre. The following is an abstract of the remaining parts of the *De arte prosayca, metrica, et rithmica.*[83]

---

[83] The first two parts (on prose and metrics) are edited by Giovanni Mari in *Romanische Forschungen* 13 (1902), pp. 885–950; the third part (on *rithmus*) is edited by Mari in *Il trattati* (see above, n. 52). The entire work has now been published under its sometime medieval title (based on the two opening words): *The Parisiana poetria of John of Garland,* ed. and trans. Traugott Lawler (New Haven, Connecticut, 1974). It is evident from the full title, however, that Garland's work, taken as a whole, cannot be described as a typical *ars poetria;* the first portions, however, do fit into the mainstream of the tradition. Admont Monastery Codex 637, used by Mari, bears the following title for the whole work: Incipit poetria magistri Johannis Anglici, de arte prosayca, metrica, et rithmica. Apparently the scribe took the title from the opening words of the treatise—a frequent medieval practice. The term *Poetria,* then, should not be taken here to be descriptive of the whole treatise.

# THE *DE ARTE PROSAYCA, METRICA, ET RITHMICA* OF JOHN OF GARLAND

This book is divided into seven parts: the doctrine of invention, the method of selecting material, disposition and ornamenting of material, parts of letters and vices in letter-writing, rhetorical ornament (amplification and abbreviation), examples of letters, metrical and rhythmical composition.

Whoever treats an art should define its terms. Prose is ornate and sententious discourse written without meter and distinguished by appropriate sequences of clausulae. [Then follow two letters as examples.] Verse is a regular ordering of feet, a foot being a certain measure of syllables and quantities.

As Horace says in *Poetria,* we ought to find material before selecting any of it, and should select before we arrange in any order. Therefore invention or finding of material is our first concern. As Tullius says in *Secunda rethorica,* invention is the devising of matter, true or probable, that would make the case convincing. There are five species of invention:

I. Ubi invenitur
   A. Persons
      1. curiales
      2. civiles
      3. rurales
   B. Examples
      1. proverbs
      2. persons
   C. Etymology
II. Quid invenitur
III. Quale invenitur
IV. Qualiter invenitur
   A. Either praise or blame
   B. Seven useful *colores*
      1. annominatio
      2. traductio
      3. repetitio
      4. gradatio
      5. interpretatio
      6. diffinitio
      7. sermocinatio
V. Ad quid invenitur: according to the final cause of the invention

Care should be taken to choose words—nouns, verbs, and adjectives—which are appropriate to their subjects, as Virgil has done. The boy (or student) should know how to transsume nouns into verbs, and adjectives into nouns, and be familiar with the method of circumlocution.

Following invention comes the selection of material. Tullius places disposition after invention, then adds style, memory, and delivery. But in poetical and epistolary writing it is useful for selection of material to follow invention. We ought to choose material for three reasons: because it is useful or profitable, offers pleasure to our minds, and offers delight or beauty to our sight. The material should be easy to write, clearly understandable, and either brief (as in letters) or prolix (as in poems). If some of the material is difficult to understand, we should pass over that which is easy and amplify that which is difficult. There are ten ways to amplify difficult material:

1. Property for the subject
2. Matter for what is made from it
3. Consequent for antecedent
4. Part for whole
5. Whole for part
6. Cause for the caused
7. Contents for the container
8. Genus for species
9. Species for genus
10. Conversion

As to the problem of memory, it is best to follow Cicero's method of providing areas in which to place the things we wish to remember. But I also propose that you make three columns within each area, corresponding to the three types of persons and the three appropriate styles. [Then follow two charts, one rectangular and one circular, in which are shown examples of proper words for the styles. The circular chart—the *rota Virgili*—is reproduced by Faral on p. 87.]

If you wish to abbreviate difficult material, you may do it by the ten methods listed above, or by changing verbs into nouns, nouns into adjectives, etc.

After invention and selection of material come the beginning and disposition. It is important that the parts of a discourse be in the mind of the writer before they are in his mouth. There are three parts to consider: beginning, progression, and end or conclusion. There are two kinds of beginnings, natural and artificial. The natural method relates things in the order in which they occur. The artificial method begins at the end or in the middle, and either with or without a proverb.

In letters, however, there must always be a certain beginning method.

There are six parts to a discourse (*oratio*) whenever we wish to persuade or dissuade. [Then follows an 81-line hexameter poem as an example.]

There are five ways to abbreviate material: emphasis, conversion of a verb to a participle, disjunction, ablative absolute, and choice of expressive words. There are five ways to amplify material: digressio, descriptio, circumlocutio, prosopopeia, and apostrophe (which includes five colors of rhetoric: exclamatio, subjectio, duplicatio, dubitatio, and interpretatio).

There are six vices of composition which must be avoided in poetry even more than in prose: the mixing of comedy and tragedy in the same part of the work; unsuitable digressions; obscure brevity; unsuitable mixing of styles; improper mixing of subjects; and the use of endings not suitable for the type of writing. For instance, recapitulation is suitable for orators or preachers; exemplum or proverb is suitable for poetry; and letters usually end with a clause beginning *ut, ne,* or *quia.*

There are three styles, according to the three states of men. Accordingly, Virgil has written three types of works for the three states: *Bucolics,* in the lowest style, for pastoral men; *Georgics,* in the middle style, for husbandmen; and *Aeneid,* in the highest style, for the most important men. [Then follows a long digression on the propriety of names and appellatives to be used in letters to dignitaries, especially in *salutationes.*]

Since narration is common to both prose and poetry, I shall discuss it here. As Tullius says, narrative is of three kinds: fable, or what is neither true nor like the truth; history, or deeds from the distant past; and argument, or fictitious events of the type found in comedy. There are three kinds of poetry: dramatic, narrative, and mixed. All the following kinds of poems are historical (except comedy, which is argumentative): epithalamium, epitaph, bucolic, georgic, and lyric poetry, epodon, hymn, invective, satire, tragedy, and elegy.

Besides the three styles named by the ancients, there are four styles used by the modern writers: the Gregorian, Tullian, Hiliarian, and Isidorian. Each follows the example of the writer named.

Both prose and poetry may be ornamented by changes in word position, especially if the change results in a better sound or a more emphatic meaning. [Following this, without any transition or explanation, Garland begins a long list of figures.]

Colors of words and thought are repetitio, complexio, traductio, contentio, exclamatio, interrogatio, ratiocinatio, sententia, contrario, membrum, articulus, compar, similiter cadens, similiter desinens, annominatio (in 13 mutations), conduplicatio, subjectio, gradatio, diffinitio, transitio, correctio, occupatio, disjunctio, conjunctio, adjunctio, interpretatio, commutatio permissio, dubitatio, expeditio, dissolutio, precisio, nominatio, prenominatio, denominatio, circuico, transgressio, superlatio, intellectio, translatio, abusio, permutatio, conclusio.

Colors of thought are distribucio, licentia, diminucio, descriptio, divisio, frequentatio, explicatio, commoratio, contentio, similitudo, exemplum, imago, effectio, notatio, sermocinatio, conformatio, significatio, demonstratio.

The eleven attributes of persons may also be used as *loci rethorici.*

[The last portion of the treatise provides a sample of a tragic poem, several model letters, some comments on letter-writing, and appropriate forms to be used in various types of official documents. The discussion of *rithmus* which concludes the *De arte* is summarized on pp. 159–60 above.]

John of Garland should be applauded for his attempt. It may well seem to the modern reader that he failed to achieve his goal of blending the various forms of discourse into a single harmonious preceptive system, but at least he recognized the diversity and strove to find the unity. In a sense he shared the concern of the *modistae* for a unifying set of principles. The *modistae* chose to go beyond Latin as a language, to the metalanguage that would explicate all human utterance. John groped for a metagenre that would identify the master precepts in human discourse. Perhaps the problem was (and is) insoluble. In any case John shows that the preceptive movement was not a static settling, but rather a developing, living inquiry into the ways of discourse.

If this last statement is true, then perhaps the cynical observations of the final writer of the movement indicates that the people engaged in it eventually recognized the difficulty of finding the grammarian's touchstone.

The *Laborintus*[84] of Eberhard the German is rather different in tone, but the poetic dicta parallel those of Vinsauf, Vendôme, and Garland to such an extent that a detailed summary seems unnecessary. Eberhard devotes 238 of his 1005 lines to complaints about the plight of schoolteachers (ll. 11–83, 835–991), another 169 lines to a list of the Seven Arts (84–253), and still another 87 lines to a list of authors for study (599–686). A total of 494 lines—about half the poem—is thus spent on pedagogical matters. The remaining half is a condensed treatment of versification and style similar to that found in Melkley and Vinsauf, concluding with three sets of verse examples.

It is interesting to note, however, that Eberhard also includes examples of nearly all the figures of diction and of thought which appear in *Rhetorica ad Herennium,* except that he uses only five tropes instead of the ten in the Pseudo-Cicero's list. He thus handles 59 altogether. Moreover,

---

[84] Text in Faral, pp. 338–77; summary pp. 336–37; biography, pp. 38–39. Eberhard the German (Evrardus Allemanus) was formerly confused with another, earlier writer, the author of the *Graecismus,* Evrard of Bethune. (To avoid this confusion the Germanic form "Eberhard" is used here to denote the author of the *Laborintus.*) The confusion was fostered by Polycarp Leyser, who edited the *Laborintus* in his *Historia poetarum et poematum medii aevi* (Magdeburg, 1721), pp. 796–854.

he names *zeugma* and *hypozeuxis* as means for preparing introductions, and presents in brief form eight ways to expand material (*de modis prolongandi materiam*): periphrasis, interpretatio, comparatio, apostropha, prosopopeia, digressio, descriptio, and oppositio. He uses the term *colores* to describe all figures except tropes.

A mere chart or table of contents cannot give a clear sense of Eberhard's attitude. His very title is a complaint: *Laborintus* is a title devised from a phrase, *Labor habens intus,* meaning "Having misery in it." He is biting in his scorn for misusers of language—"They flower who with javelins of language pervert just causes"[85]—but he is far beyond mere disgust with specific unlearned or vicious opponents. He does not rail against some "Cornificius," as John of Salisbury does in his *Metalogicon,* or against some disguised but real enemy, as does Matthew of Vendôme when he attacks "Rufinus" in his *Ars versificatoria.* Eberhard seems angry at mankind as a whole, at his own art in its totality, at life in general.

In his bitterness he is probably closer in spirit to Jonathan Swift than to his thirteenth-century contemporaries. He says of the language arts (rhetoric and grammar) that they suffocate and parch him.[86] His heart quakes within him when he frets over how to disguise things with flowers of language; but most of all, he remarks sourly that "When the word flowers, the mind dries up."[87] In a section (vv. 835–990) which Faral dryly entitles "miseries of the teacher" (*les misères du maître*), Eberhard slashes his way through a pungent arsenal of specific complaints against his superiors, against lawyers, against ignorant students who can neither count nor read, against other teachers, against teaching itself. His vocabulary is caustic; for instance, the problem with the ignorant student is to "tame" him (*cohibere*); some of his colleagues are afflicted with "pride, the disease of Lucifer" (*superbia, pestis Luciferi*); Paris is "paradise for the rich" (*Parisius est divitibus paradisus*).

Eberhard knows his craft very well—the normative doctrines are summarily laid out in the *Laborintus*—but it is a craft which wearies him. We should look beyond his personal feelings, however, to note that Eber-

---

[85] Florent qui jaculis linguae pervertere causas / justas, injustas justificare sciunt (vv. 107–08). Among those who flourish, too, are grubby dealers in bodily ills (i.e., doctors), wheedlers, scurrilous men, and the venal.

[86] Per me rethoricus flos, grammaticus labor, artis / garrulitas tumulat, evacuatur, aret (vv. 95–96).

[87] Cum verbum floret, mens aret. Cor gerit intus, / Quin linguae flores dissimulare student (vv. 247–48).

hard's *Laborintus* is the last in a set of six works that began with Matthew
of Vendôme a century earlier, and may well have reached its peak with
Geoffrey of Vinsauf.

We know virtually nothing about Eberhard's career, but he seems to
have been an experienced teacher. His is not the brash complaint of a
neophyte railing against "the system" but rather the years-weary lament
of a man who has seen too much and expects to see more of the same the
next day in the classroom.

It is precisely this element which makes him an important figure in
our attempts to understand the movement called the *ars poetriae*. He
agrees that there are some ways to teach useful precepts for the making
of verses, and some useful authors to study.[88] He grinds out the long
lists of figures and their examples. It is not a perfunctory performance,
but it does seem a grudging one. There is a deep undercurrent of bore-
dom. The careful reader of the *Laborintus* can find in it, consequently, a
penetrating analysis of the preceptive movement itself. Just as Henri
d'Andeli's *Battaille des sept arts* provides us with a fascinating glimpse of
the whole sweep of thirteenth-century attitudes toward language, so Eberhard's *Laborintus* reveals to us the ultimate decay of the preceptive impulse in medieval grammar. The preceptive movement was born in the
post-Horatian reflections of Matthew of Vendôme, was crystallized in
Gervase of Melkley and Geoffrey of Vinsauf, was abortively summarized
in John of Garland, and flickered out in the conscious disgust of Eberhard. It is an interesting phase of human history.

Before leaving the subject of medieval grammar, however, there is one
important topic which needs further exploration—the lore of figures and
tropes. These devices bear a multitude of names, such as "colors" or
"tropes" or "schemes" or "permitted faults." Faral as a matter of fact
suggests that certain short treatments of tropes and figures actually form
a second type of *ars poetriae*.[89] After noting that Geoffrey of Vinsauf,
Matthew of Vendôme, and other writers include full treatments of the
figures in their longer works, he cites four short pieces devoted to stylistic
ornament.

---

[88] Eberhard specifically declares that Aristotle has written nothing on this subject: Nullus Aristotelis codex apparet in illis (v. 55). As we have noted earlier,
Aristotle's *Poetics* was not generally known in Western Europe until Renaissance
times; however, William of Moerbeke did translate the book into Latin sometime
in the 1270's, probably at Paris.

[89] See especially pp. 48–54.

1. Vinsauf's *Summa de coloribus* contains 20 *figurae verborum*, excerpted from his longer works.[90]

2. Garland's *Exempla honestae vitae* applies the term *colores* to every one of the 43 *exornationes verborum* and 16 *exornationes sententiarum* which he lists. This is a further example of the wide application given to the term.[91]

3. Marbodus' *De ornamentis verborum* lists 30 *figurae verborum*. Vinsauf employs some of Marbodus' examples in his own *Summa de coloribus*.[92]

4. An untitled manuscript, number 115 in the Bibliothèque de St.-Omer, contains the complete system of figures listed in *ad Herennium* IV, and in the same order. This so-called "treatise of St.-Omer" has been attributed to either Pierre Riga or Garland.[93]

Each of these works may be identified with *ars poetria* through specific statements in prologues or through allusions within their texts. Examples are given in verse, and the whole intent of the authors seems to be the instruction of verse-writers.[94]

It is extremely difficult, on the other hand, to determine the intended purpose of other little treatises on *figurae* which dot medieval library catalogues. Obviously the latter part of the fourth book of the *Rhetorica ad Herennium* was easily detached from the rest of the book and seems to have had a separate circulation. The *Barbarismus* of Donatus, itself a section detached from a larger book, also provided for the study of tropes and figures. Taken together with grammar texts like the *Graecismus* and *Doctrinale,* such excerpts made available a large total of figures. It would be incorrect, however, to conclude that every short treatise on the figures was intended as an aid to the composition of poetry. The *exornationes* were regarded as useful for various kinds of oral and written composition, and so these little treatises might have been intended to serve a variety of purposes.

In some cases (as seen earlier in the *ars rithmica* also), an author will

---

[90] Text in Faral, pp. 321–27.
[91] Edited by Edwin Habel in *Romanische Forschungen* 29 (1911), 137–54.
[92] Migne, *PL* CLXXI, cols. 1687–92.
[93] Ed. Charles Fierville in *Notices et extraits* 31 (1884), 100–12.
[94] This is not true of a fifth treatise which Faral lists with the four given above. The *Colores rhetorici* of Onulf of Speyer (fl. 1050) begins with the words *artis rhetoricae,* and has no clear allusion to poetics. The colophon bearing the now-common title was added after Onulf's death, so that we do not know whether Onulf himself used the title. In any case, the treatise seems more clearly in the rhetorical tradition of Labeo and Besate. The text is edited by W. Wattenbach, in *Sitzungberichte der Königlich preussischen Akademie der Wissenschaften zu Berlin* I (1894), 361–86.

specify particular figures which seem to him to be especially useful for his subject. Sometimes an author, like Robert of Basevorn, will refer to a particular source.[95] Occasionally the author of an *ars dictaminis* will note the usefulness of *colores* without making a recommendation as to source or type.

But whatever the motivation for the notice taken of *figurae* by authors of nongrammatical works, it is apparent that most medieval writers assume their study to be an *elementary* subject. It is regarded as something that every educated medieval person would have absorbed at an early stage of his training.

Therefore no adequate appreciation of medieval stylistic practice, in either Latin or vernacular literatures, is possible without an understanding of the doctrine of *figurae*.[96]

Although ancient Greek orators like Gorgias of Leontini employed a highly organized pattern of sound formations in a conscious effort to create certain auditory effects,[97] it remained for late Hellenistic theorists to codify such patterns into systems that could be taught in schools. The young Cicero attended schools utilizing the systems, which had been brought to Rome by Hellenistic teachers. There is little doubt that he would have made the doctrine of figures a primary part of the treatment of *elocutio* if he had followed through with his announced intention to write books on all five parts of rhetoric. His anonymous contemporary,

---

[95] Robert of Basevorn, *Forma praedicandi*, Cap. L, where he notes that a preacher can find a sufficient number of figures in the fourth book of Cicero's *Rhetorica secunda* (i.e., the *Rhetorica ad Herennium*). Text in Th.-M. Charland, *Artes praedicandi* (Paris, 1936), pp. 233-323.

[96] Struck by Walter Map's two radically different styles of writing, Marbury Ogle urged in 1926 that "more attention must be paid than hitherto to the methods of rhetorical training during the middle ages and to the relation between theory and practice, if we would solve the riddle of mediaeval Latin style. The question is of course important not only for mediaeval Latin, but concerns equally the rise of prose in the vernaculars, indeed in our own English, as Croll points out (*Euphues* p. xlviii)." Ogle, "Some Aspects of Medieval Latin Style," *Speculum* 1 (1926), 189. The publication of two works of classification since 1926 have not completely solved the problem. A sketchy survey appears in Leonid Arbusow, *Colores rhetorici: Eine Auswahl rhetorischer figuren und Gemeinplatz als Hilfsmittel für akademische Übungen an mittelalterlichen Texten* (Gottingen, 1948); some of the major defects are listed in a review in *Speculum* 24 (1949), 416-18. A more ambitious treatment is that of Heinrich Lausberg, *Handbuch der literarischen Rhetorik*, 2 vols. (Munich, 1960). Although Lausberg is far more complete and offers some interesting sets of classifications, he ends his study at A.D. 600. Consequently the history of the *figurae* remains unwritten.

[97] Gorgias (c. 485-380 B.C.) popularized patterns of alliteration and parallelism, but Aristotle's *Rhetoric* treats only such major figures as metaphor and in any case does not propose a *system* of such devices.

the author of *Rhetorica ad Herennium*, actually did set forth the theory, together with a discussion of 64 figures which became a standard list for many medieval writers. The Pseudo-Cicero divided his *exornationes*—literally, "means of ornation"—into 45 "figures of diction" and 19 "figures of thought." Ten of the figures of diction he regarded as being of a special kind, and later rhetoricians like Quintilian gave them the name *tropi* or "tropes." [98]

The doctrine of figures and tropes is a hallmark of Roman rhetoric. It is evident, from Quintilian's lengthy discussion of the subject in Books VIII and IX of his *Institutio*, that he took the doctrine for granted. His only concern is for the proper definitions and proper relations of the figures. Almost two centuries after the composition of the *Rhetorica ad Herennium*, then, it is possible to see in Quintilian's writings the pervasive quality of the doctrine. The sophistic concern with style in the centuries after Quintilian did little to diminish Roman interest in the subject, so it is not surprising that late Roman rhetoricians like Aquila Romanus should have developed the doctrine to include as many as 200 figures.[99]

Meanwhile, as has been noted earlier, the grammarian Donatus in the fourth century published his own treatment of tropes and figures. Roman school practice had been for the grammarian to teach certain elementary figures in the course of basic language instruction, but Donatus enlarged this sphere of activity not only by including the tropes but by expanding the number of major tropes from 10 to 13 (or 28 if the subspecies are counted). Thus began an identifiable grammatical tradition for the figures themselves, a tradition separate from the rhetorical tradition of the type popularized in late antiquity by works like the *ad Herennium*. By the time of Isidore of Seville (570–636), it was no longer possible to draw a clear line between the "grammatical" and the "rhetorical" figures.

Isidore does not, like Donatus, attempt to isolate some figures for the use of grammar and some for the use of rhetoric. Instead, when he says anything at all about figures he merely designates the place in which they might be learned. In his chapter on rhetoric in the *Etymologia*, he directs the reader back to Donatus for the remainder of the "figures of words and thought" (Isidore treats only 32 figures in this section). Truly, as he

---

[98] Quintilian, *Institutio* VIII.vi.1: "A trope is an artistic change of word or phrase from its proper signification to another."

[99] See, for instance, the texts in Halm, *Rhetores latini minores*, pp. 1–21, 22–37, 38–47, etc. (See n. 17 above.)

points out at the beginning of his chapter on rhetoric, "grammar is joined to the art of rhetoric." [100]

Even more significantly, however, Isidore reveals a broadening view toward the *metaplasmus,* the lowly transformation of words for metrical purposes which Donatus had acknowledged virtually without comment. Isidore defines a metaplasm as a "transformation of a word on account of metrical necessity or poetic license." He uses the 14 types listed by Donatus, but he goes on to note that the metaplasm—like the "scheme" —is part way between a grammatical fault and a figure. The metaplasm is therefore, at least by implication, useful as an ornament of language.

The ultimate extension of this regard for the *metaplasmi* is seen much later in the massive *Catholicon* (1286) of John Balbus of Genoa (known also as "Januensis"). Balbus declares flatly: "There are three kinds of figures: metaplasms, allothecas [schemes], and tropes." [101] Although this may be a rather extreme statement of a principle only hinted at some seven centuries earlier, it seems to be the logical development of an idea which was already old by the time of Donatus.

The whole theory of *exornationes,* after all, rests upon a principle of deviation from a norm. In the ancient world both the grammarians and the rhetoricians put forth their own reasons for this kind of verbal deviation. With Donatus and later theorists in the grammatical tradition, a common justification lay in the beautification of language by purposeful change; by the time of Isidore of Seville, even the word-change called *metaplasmus* became useful as an artistic *licentia poetarum.* But John of Balbus goes beyond this in the *Catholicon* to include the "colors of rhetoric" under the general heading of "vices." Both Isidore and Balbus thus identify certain figures technically as vices, but immediately note their usefulness in writing despite their technical fault. It will be recalled that Evrard of Bethune, author of the *Graecismus,* specifies that the metaplasm is to be regarded as a "permissive" use of language. Another attempt at classification is seen in Alexander Neckham's *Corregationes Promethei* (c. 1190?), in which a distinction is made between outright "vices" (barbarisms and solecisms) and another category of language which Alexander calls "excusable improprieties" (metaplasms, schemes, tropes, and *allothecae*).[102]

---

[100] *Etymologia* II.xxl.

[101] Johannes Balbus de Janua, *Summa quae vocatur Catholicon* (Moguntina, 1460), Cap. CXII. The *Catholicon* went through at least seven editions before 1500.

[102] Text of the Prologue is in Paul Meyer, "Notice sur les *Corregationes Promethei* d'Alexander Neckham," *Notices et extraits* 35 (1897), 641–82. A complete

What is noteworthy in all these grammatical discussions is the medieval concern for the nature of such purposeful deviations from a norm of language usage. The most popular advanced grammatical text of the middle ages, Alexander of Villedieu's *Doctrinale,* begins a long section on figures by cautioning readers to distinguish carefully between the various species:

> Pluribus est membris distincta figura loquelae.
> Haec sunt schema, tropus, metaplasmus; rursus earum
> Quamlibet in proprias species distinguere debes.
>
> (vv. 2361–63)

Rhetoricians do not have the same concern for classification. By about 100 B.C. the Hellenistic formulations of "figures of speech and thought" had been completed by teachers working in Rome. The fourth book of the *Rhetorica ad Herennium,* as we have seen, reflects this preoccupation. By the time of Quintilian (c. A.D. 95) some 10 of the figures of speech had acquired the name of *tropus,* and it will be recalled that Donatus and others later enlarged this set of tropes to as many as 28 items. But the rhetoricians, ancient or medieval, seldom inquire into the *nature* of the figures and tropes. This omission is not surprising, considering the strength and example of the Ciceronian tradition on one hand, and the obvious utility of the figures on the other. Cicero is so universally the *magister eloquentiae* for the middle ages that the mere citation of his precepts often suffices as justification of a rhetorical doctrine; medieval grammatical writers, however, seem to work in a more analytic frame of mind, which is less prone to accept authority.[103] It is perhaps significant that there is mention of university disputations about grammar but not about rhetoric; the Ciceronian rhetorical doctrine was perhaps so well developed by late classical times that it was regarded as self-sufficient and consistent with itself. Medieval commentators on rhetoric usually deal in explanation, not in inquiry.[104] Grammar, however, is in a state of self-examina-

---

manuscript text is available in MS. Bodleian 550, fols. 1–99. This is a text deserving further study. Alexander wrote it as a showpiece to demonstrate his literary talents to a potential employer. He was apparently a contemporary of the unknown author of the English poem *The Owl and the Nightingale,* which may have had a similar purpose.

[103] A late thirteenth-century manuscript from Melk, for instance, opens in this fashion: Queritur cum sermo dividatur in congruum verum et ornatum. The work, entitled *Questiones super primum Prisciani,* is credited to a "Nicholas of Paris." See British Museum MS. Lat. Misc., fols. 34 and 1.

[104] The scholastic commentator on the *Rhetoric* of Aristotle, Aegidius Romanus, is typical in that he devotes several hundred pages to a close exposition of his subject without questioning the truth or falsity of the doctrine. See above, Chapter III, p. 99.

tion from the time of Peter Helias in the twelfth century down to Renaissance linguistic reformers like Erasmus and Laurentius Valla.

For another thing, the rhetoricians' attitude toward the figures and tropes seems to have been affected by the way in which rhetorical training was conducted in Roman schools. This attitude carried through the early middle ages as well. In Cicero's time, and as late as Quintilian, it is clear that certain figures were regarded as proper subjects only for the most elementary levels of schooling; since grammar was regarded as a subject preliminary to rhetoric, the figures taught by the grammarian were necessarily less important to the *rhetor*. The author of the *Rhetorica ad Herennium* does not even acknowledge as figures some of the locutions, which he relegates to the grammarians.[105] This tendency may have served to crystallize support for certain sets of figures and tropes as "proper" to rhetoric rather than to grammar.[106]

One visible consequence of this in the middle ages is the tendency to perpetuate as a unit the entire set of figures from the most popular ancient treatise on the subject, the fourth book of the *ad Herennium*. Edmond Faral has compiled a chart to illustrate how these 65 figures and tropes appear virtually intact in nine works connected with the *ars poetria*.[107] Even the crotchety Eberhard follows the same sequence in his *Laborintus,* when he discusses figures of thought, and he breaks with the Pseudo-Cicero only in that he omits some of them entirely. There are several examples of individual manuscript copies of the fourth book, obviously intended for separate circulation apart from the rest of the book.[108]

---

[105] *Ad Herennium* IV.xii.18, in discussing *conpositio* (artistic composition) opposes excessive alliteration even though a few pages later the author lists seven metaplasmic forms of the figure *adnominatio* (paronomasia), which grammarians took over completely in later centuries. As Caplan points out ("Cicero," *Rhetorica ad Herennium,* ed. and trans. Harry Caplan, Loeb Classical Library [Cambridge, Mass., 1954], p. 274), Fortunatianus first divided figures into "grammatical" and "rhetorical," but Donatus makes the same division for the grammarians, and the resulting confusion has never been clarified.

[106] Quintilian, for instance, does not admit the colon and comma as artistic figures, relegating them to basic forms of language (*Instituto* IX.iii.98). Saint Augustine, too, notes (*De doctrina* III.29) that even figurative language itself is of two kinds, natural and artistic. Since for Augustine the grammarian handles basic language training, this seems an implication that figurative language has at least two levels.

[107] Faral, pp. 52–54. See also Dorothy Grosser, "Studies in the Influence of *De inventione* and *Rhetorica ad Herennium,*" unpublished Ph.D. dissertation, Cornell University, 1952.

[108] For instance, a catalogue of the year 1290 at Vorau lists "Tullius de ornatu verborum. Tullius de ornatu sententiarum." Manitius, *Bibliothekskatalogen,* p. 22. This seems a clear indication of the presence of the fourth book of *ad Herennium,*

Taken to its logical conclusion, such a development should have resulted in a medieval dichotomy between "rhetorical" and "grammatical" figures. But this is not what happened. Instead, teachers of grammar like John of Garland and Geoffrey of Vinsauf took over the entire teaching of prescriptive language, that is, all types of teaching designed to show students how to write or speak. It did not matter much whether their students were to learn metrics or rhythmics or ordinary prose; the medieval definitions of grammar allowed for teaching in all these forms. Eventually the grammarians even took over instruction in the *ars dictaminis,* the art of letter-writing, which grew out of the political necessities of chanceries and royal courts.[109] Consequently it was the grammarians who became responsible for the lore of the figures, and they drew on all the known sources. Some of these sources were books of rhetoric like the *Rhetorica ad Herennium,* some were grammatical works like the *Doctrinale,* and some were encyclopedic works like Isidore of Seville's *Etymologia.* The better writers also drew on their own experience and reading. The result is a medieval mélange of terms and classifications which has so far defied modern analysis.[110]

Medieval use of the terms "color" and "color of rhetoric" provides good examples which may illustrate these amorphous relations. The term *color* is a useful one, indeed, referring as it usually does to some literary device that embellishes—literally, "gives color"—to ordinary language. Its use in this sense is a medieval innovation. In ancient times writers employed such terms as *exornationes* or *figurae* to describe the whole class of such devices. By about 1050, however, Onulf of Speyer's treatise on figures is called *Colores rhetorici.* The term *color* never did acquire a precise limitation in medieval times, however: Matthew of Vendôme lists 29 *colores*

---

separated from the rest of the work. In other cases (as in Oxford Magdalen College MS. 6, fols. 210–212), the list of figures is briefly summarized without examples.

[109] Both Garland and Melkley, for instance, include *dictamen* in their major works. The Italians made the same kind of claim for rhetoric upon occasion; Brunetto Latini (*Trésor* III.3) declares that "rhetoric is of two kinds, one which consists in speaking by mouth, and another which consists in speaking by letters; but the doctrine is common to both."

[110] One of the most profound students of medieval grammar, Charles Thurot, found it impossible to establish satisfactory guidelines for analysis of the figures. His comment is worth repeating here: "L'impossibilité d'établir une demarcation rigoureuse entre les figures propres à la grammaire et telles qui sont propres à la rhetorique, et qu'on designait sous le nom *colores rhetorici,* avait introduit dans cette théorie beaucoup confusion." Thurot, *Notices et extraits,* p. 472. (See n. 8 above.)

*rhetorici,* omitting all the schemes and tropes; Geoffrey of Vinsauf applies the term only to figures of words; Evrard of Bethune says that only 25 of the figures of words can be called *colores;* on the other hand, John of Garland, certainly one of the most prominent thirteenth-century grammarians, uses the term to apply to every one of the figures. The references by Chaucer in the second half of the fourteenth century indicate that by that period the term *color rhetorici* had become a mere petrified phrase. For Chaucer it meant "figurative language" in a general sense; presumably it denoted for him any kind of decorated language.[111]

Moreover, the grammarians of the middle ages never did succeed in solving the problem of classification raised initially by Donatus, when he attempted to divide *schemae* into those pertaining to grammar and those pertaining to rhetoric. One medieval commentator, writing in 1284, struggles for an answer by asserting that a "grammatical" *color* can be identified by the fact that it "orders to signification"; that is, it is grammatical if it assists clarity and helps the reader or hearer to *understand.*[112] This is a clear reliance on the concept of grammar as the *ars recte loquendi,* the art of correctness which makes communication possible. Consequently, the writer continues, it is "rhetorical" if it "orders to moving" the hearer or reader. He proposes exactly the same solution for the classification of tropes as well.

The difficulty with this solution is that it depends upon the intention of the writer or speaker, whereas the device of language under discussion remains exactly the same no matter what name is given to it. It is as if a man building a warehouse were to pick up a brick and call it a warehouse brick, while a workman engaged in constructing a nearby school were to object that he had actually picked up a school brick. In either case the brick is a brick, and serves its function equally well under either name. Medieval theorists do not agree on a common solution, and the matter was left generally unresolved.

It is important to realize, however, that this difficulty of classification did not offer an obstacle to medieval training in language. The primary reason that it did not do so was that the same person, the "grammarian," was very often the teacher of all the verbal arts except *dialectica.* (The major exception to this rule was Italy, where the *rhetor* like Boncompagno succeeded to the kind of fame that in France went to the grammarian

---

111 See James J. Murphy, "A New Look at Chaucer and the Rhetoricians," *Review of English Studies* NS 15 (1964), 1–20.

112 Text of the anonymous writer is printed by Thurot, pp. 470–71.

John of Garland.) It did not matter very much whether a certain trope was called "grammatical" or "rhetorical" if all the tropes and figures were handled by the same teacher in the same classroom. Even more important, the student exposed to only 50 or 60 tropes and figures, with examples, no doubt had as good an idea of their application as another student who studied perhaps 90 or 100 of the devices. The principle of deviation, in other words, is more important in medieval literary instruction than the number of exemplary figures and tropes used to teach the principle.

This is a consideration that modern students of medieval writing sometimes fail to understand. Grammatical instruction during the middle ages included a considerable treatment of the principle of ornamental deviation. Since grammar was always the first of the arts to be taught, this elementary education in the tropes and figures was always a fundamental part of the educated person's background.[113] This is exactly what Eberhard the German means in the *Laborintus* when he describes the fifth part of grammatical instruction as *Sermonis partes, schema tropumque facit* (v. 144). The ubiquity of the figures and the tropes is therefore a factor which should be kept in mind during any study of medieval uses of language.

Medieval grammar, then, may be seen as a fairly unified body of preceptive materials, taking for itself the whole province of language use in prosaic, metrical, or rhythmical forms. Nevertheless a major question remained. Implicit in the medieval grammarian's jurisdictional claim was a deep-rooted tension between language as a whole on one hand, and the particular purposive uses of language on the other. This tension is seen in virtually every treatise dealing with written language, especially in the prefatory *accessus* or introduction, which attempts to relate the individual treatises to the whole of language study.[114] (Preaching manuals have less of this quality of strain, perhaps because they are so frequently able to adduce doctrinal or Scriptural authority to justify their work.)[115] But Geoffrey of Vinsauf refers to the necessity of planning a discourse, just as a carpenter must plan a house before building it. Thomas of Capua outlines the types of writing, to show where his own treatise fits into the

---

[113] For a discussion of this factor in relation to England, see James J. Murphy, "Literary Implications of Instruction in the Verbal Arts in Fourteenth-Century England," *Leeds Studies in English* NS 1 (1967), 119–35.

[114] See *Accessus ad auctores,* ed. R. B. C. Huygens, Collection Latomus, Vol. XV (Brussels, 1954).

[115] Beginning with the Council of Nicaea in A.D. 325, of course, there were also Church ordinances specifying the role of preaching. See below, Chapter Six.

scheme of things. John of Garland defines both prose and verse and then relates *rithmus* to music. Bernard de Meung, an influential *dictator* of the Orléans tradition, takes pains to distinguish two types of *dictamen*—metrical and prosaic—but finds difficulty in showing in theoretical terms how letter-writing in prose differs from the verse-writing of Virgil and Ovid.[116] An anonymous fourteenth-century writer interested in linking *dictamen* to the logical syllogism asserts that both music and grammar are preambles (*preambula*) to metrics, rhythmics, and prose.[117]

Such introductory material, usually alleging to be expository or explanatory, often appears to be defensive and may indeed reflect a certain uneasiness with the commonly cited classifications of discourse. By the end of the fourteenth century even a professional theorist like Francisco da Buti feels unable to do more than to compile three separate sets of *reguli* for rhetoric, for grammar, and for dictamen. He describes himself as a professor of his subject: *Ego Franciscus de Buti pisanus civis grammaticae ac rectoricae profexor.* Yet what he produces is a tripartite collection, not a unified discussion.[118]

Despite the efforts of writers like Siger of Courtrai and John of Garland —each, in his own way, convinced of the fundamental unity of human discourse—the practical needs of poets, letter-writers, and preachers continued to build up specific preceptive traditions suited to the exigencies of those fields. Even within the ranks of the grammarians themselves there was simultaneous recognition of both unity and diversity. Garland and Vinsauf, after all, were both grammarians, but their answers to this implicit question stemmed from differing points of view.

The twelfth and early thirteenth centuries witnessed a lengthy debate over the matter of the "classification of the sciences."[119] A number of writers attempted to distinguish the exact relations between grammar, rhetoric, and logic. Dialecticians were especially interested in the problem, since all three members of the traditional *trivium* dealt with the use of words, and they naturally wished to define the proper sphere of each discipline in order to clarify dialectic itself. The complexities of this debate

---

[116] Leopold DeLisle, "Notice sur un *Summa dictaminis* jadis conservée à Beauvais," *Notices et extraits* 36 (1899), 171–205.

[117] Paris, Bibliothèque Nationale MS. Lat. 16252, fols. 29–32: Libellus de dictamine et dictatorio syllogismo.

[118] Oxford Bodleian MS. Lat. Misc. e.52, fols. 81–98: Reguli recthoricae. Reguli gramaticae. Tractatus epistolare.

[119] See Charles A. Baldwin, *Medieval Rhetoric and Poetic* (New York, 1928), Chapter VI, for summaries of some key works.

need not detain us here—the debate had very little to do with the actual use of preceptive doctrines—but it is important to recognize that the implicit grammatical controversy between unity and diversity did have a widespread and profound effect on the course of medieval rhetorical development. Consequently it is more important in the long run than the more obvious but less influential academic clashes of the scholastic en cyclopedists.[120]

In sum, perhaps the history of medieval grammar may be characterized by the efforts of grammarians to expand their ancient concern with the *ars recte loquendi* and with the *enarratio poetarum*. Going far beyond the province laid out by Donatus and Priscian, they laid claim to jurisdiction over all uses of language: the grammarians produced preceptive doctrine for poets, for prose-writers, and for preachers, and even (through the analysis of *significatio*) encroached upon the chosen domain of the logicians. This proved an impossible claim.[121]

Unable to achieve unanimity even among themselves, the grammarians were faced not only with the continuing presence of ancient Ciceronian rhetoric but with the burgeoning vitality of two new movements which were to become the hallmarks of medieval rhetorical development—the *ars dictaminis* and the *ars praedicandi*. Both movements were committed to diversity, that is, to the principle of adapting basic theories to the specific needs of writers or speakers. It is for this reason that Cicero, rather than Donatus or Priscian, became the dominant influence on medieval discourse and exercised a profound effect on European theory, which has lasted virtually to our own time.

---

[120] This was of course a controversy among academicians, and the debate may have resulted in keeping certain kinds of teaching out of some universities; one may judge the real effect, however, when it is noted that more than 300 manuscripts of the *ars praedicandi* have come down to us, that manuscripts representing 55 *dictamen* writers still exist, and that copies of the *artes poetriae* abound in every major European depository to this day. Evidently the opinions of the encyclopedists did little to influence the energetic production of specialized works in these fields.

[121] It might be recalled that Quintilian had warned (*Institutio* II.i.1) that grammarians should be prevented from trying to encroach upon the proper sphere of the rhetoricians.

# Chapter V

❖ ❖ ❖

# *Ars dictaminis:*
# The Art of Letter-Writing

THE *ars dictaminis* is a truly medieval invention. It marks a sharp break with ancient rhetorical practice.

The practice of sending messages over distance from one person to another, orally, appears in the very earliest records of Western civilization. By the time of Homer's *Iliad* (c. 700 B.C.), the Greeks had developed complex patterns of representation by ambassadors, envoys, and other message-carriers who transmitted their senders' ideas orally to their recipients.[1] Apparently such envoys came to have wide latitude in the way they transmitted their messages, as in Demosthenes' lifetime, when public debate in Athens sometimes revolved around the question of whether an ambassador had been accurate and faithful in carrying out his tasks.[2]

This ancient practice of oral transmission was of course supplemented on occasion by written documents. Frequently, however, the written document was merely read aloud to the addressee; apparently the desired end was accuracy of message transmission, not the replacement of oral language by the written.[3] Message transmission remained a function of oral language throughout the ancient world.

---

[1] See for instance the complex rhetorical relations implied in the herald's wand or scepter in the *Iliad*, as outlined by Frederick M. Combellack, "Speakers and Scepters in Homer," *Classical Journal* 43 (1948), 209-17.

Portions of the following have appeared as "Alberic of Monte Cassino: Father of the Medieval *Ars dictaminis*," in the *American Benedictine Review* 22 (1971), 129-46.

[2] In Demosthenes' famous speech *On the Crown* he devotes some time to a detailed account of certain ambassadors' duties in the conflict with Philip. See *Demosthenes On the Crown: A Critical Case Study of A Masterpiece of Ancient Oratory*, ed. James J. Murphy (New York, 1967), esp. sections 25-45 (pp. 65-68).

[3] *Ibid.*, sections 39, 77, etc. Demosthenes tends to treat "letters" as if they were the speeches of either witnesses in his defense or opponents of his policy.

Indeed, there was strong insistence upon language as essentially oral. Plato, for example, declares in his *Phaedrus* that writing distorts oral language. Aristotle's basic statement (*On Interpretation* I.i) is that "spoken words are symbols of mental experiences, and written words are symbols of spoken words." Roman rhetoricians like Cicero and Quintilian follow the lead of Isocrates in declaring speech to be the basis for all social order.[4] It is not surprising therefore that the ancient world produced no separate rhetorical doctrine about writing. Ancient education—and Roman schools especially—aimed at preparing a student to be adept in both writing and speaking. Eloquent letters, like eloquent speeches, were expected to be the product of broad rhetorical education. In fact, it was common to dictate (*dictare*) a letter aloud for a scribe to copy out.[5]

It was not until the fourth Christian century that a discussion of *epistola* figured in the works of a Roman rhetorician. C. Julius Victor, after presenting a summary of the Ciceronian rhetorical tradition in his *Ars rhetorica*,[6] adds three brief appendices: *de exercitatione, de sermocinatione,* and *de epistolis.* The first deals with the virtues of practice; the second, however, is more important because Victor points out at once that regular rhetorical theory does not cover the *sermo,* or informal discourse. Since Victor goes on to say that the *epistola* follows the precepts of the *sermo,* his remarks on *ratio sermocinandi* are worth noting here.

He states that the style of the *sermo* should be "elegant without ostentation," and he notes that it goes without saying that the discourse should be brief. Timely proverbs may be welcome and, where suitable, "the memory of old examples and the knowledge of new things." The *sermo* should not be delivered like an oration, especially since the usual closeness of the hearers would make a declamatory delivery "rustic and barbarous." Victor is evidently referring to conversational or semi-conversational discourse, where a boisterous laugh (*cachinnus*) or wine-caused garrulity does as much to disturb the auditor as any fault of words or syllables.

In the following section, *de epistolis,* Victor distinguishes two types of letters, official letters (*negotiales*) and familiar letters (*familiares*). An

---

[4] Quintilian's aim, for example, is to produce "a consummate ability in speaking" (*Institutio oratoria,* Preface to Book One).

[5] The precise etymology of the medieval Latin word *dictamen* has not yet been traced, but it seems fair to conclude that it is derived from the classical Latin verb *dicto, dictare* because of the connection between "dictation" and the letters which were dictated. Again, the term itself reveals a concern for the oral–written relationship.

[6] *C. Iulii Victoris ars rhetorica* in *Rhetores latini minores,* ed. Charles Halm (Leipzig, 1863; reprinted Frankfurt, 1964), pp. 371–448.

official letter includes serious argumentative matter, and may use figurative language of the type found in orations. It is more graceful than historical writing, and one may write with erudition or even polemically without losing the quality of a letter. In the familiar letter brevity and clarity both call for avoiding obscure terminology, arcane proverbs, and curious language. Such obscurity is worse in a letter than in an oration or in a conversation because, Victor points out, the absence of the writer makes it impossible for him to answer the questions of an audience. Letters that are intended to be secret may be couched in language that may be unclear to all but the recipient.[7]

Victor also remarks on the differences caused by the social status of sender and recipient. If one writes to a superior, the letter should not be jocular; if to an equal, it should not be discourteous; if to an inferior, it should not be proud. The familiar letter should fit the occasion, whether to console or to do whatever fits the situation. It is a mark of friendship to reply to a letter in one's own handwriting, or to use familiar phrases like *heus tu* as Cicero does.

As for the salutations and signatures of letters (*praefationes ac subscriptiones*), they are intended to show the discriminations between degrees of friendship and degrees of station (*pro discrimine amicitiae aut dignitatis*).[8]

What can be concluded from what Julius Victor says about letter writing? First of all, it is apparent that he is making only the most general remarks based on some random observations of his own. In other words, he does not represent a well-formulated theory. (Even a rapid survey of the rest of the *Ars rhetorica* reveals how much more at home he feels with the basic rhetorical doctrine.) His brief attempt to analyze the genre of the *epistola familiaris* is poorly, almost casually organized. He well nigh ignores the *epistola negotialis,* the type that seems to be closest to the rhetorical subjects which occupy the rest of the book. In fact, by linking it with the *sermo,* Julius Victor virtually declares a letter to be a type of "conversation"—a conclusion not very different from that of Demetrius three centuries earlier. In any case, Victor had no followers in the succeeding centuries, and almost seven centuries elapsed before a theorist again took up such questions as the nature of a letter, the effect of the absent writer, and the distinction between addresses. Meanwhile the epistolary function continued for some centuries to be regarded solely as an artistic

---

[7] *Ibid., Cap.* XXVII (p. 448).
[8] *Ibid.*

matter, perhaps beyond regulation or analysis, and for the most part it was treated like a branch of literature.

One can see traces of this concept of epistolary artistry in the Patristic period. Many of the letters of Augustine, for instance, rank as important literary or philosophical documents. Jerome's letters were also popular. But Augustine and most of his fourth-century colleagues shared a literary training on the model of Quintilian, and after the last impulses of the failing Roman Empire disappeared from Western Europe in the fifth and sixth centuries, it became difficult to find any large number of writers capable of original epistolary artistry. In Merovingian and Carolingian times, when some princes and even kings were incapable of reading or writing, it was evident that a very great change had to take place in the style of message transmission.

The letters of Cassiodorus Senator (490–586), arranged in twelve books under the title of the *Variae*,[9] illustrate the nature of this change. Brilliant minister of an illiterate king in Italy (Theodoric the Ostrogoth), Cassiodorus was interested in literature, political science, historiography, Scriptural exegesis, and rhetoric. As we have already noted, his *Institutiones divinarum et humanarum lectionum* played an important part in the encylopedic movement of the early middle ages. Cassiodorus served under three rulers before retiring to a monastery at Vivarium. (It is worth noting that his friend Boethius failed to survive the political struggles of the day, and was executed under the same Theodoric.) It was to be almost a thousand years before Europe again saw such an example of a humanistic civil servant in such complete command of his situation.

But it is the relationship of message-maker to king that interests us here. Cassiodorus includes in his *Variae* a copy of the "Formula of the Quaestorship," which he himself drew up on behalf of the king in order to describe his own duties. It is worth citing briefly at this point:

> . . . the Quaestor has to learn our inmost thoughts, that he may utter them to our subjects. . . . He has to be always ready for a sudden call, and must exercise the wonderful powers which, as Cicero has pointed out, are inherent in the art of an orator. . . . He has to speak the king's words in the king's own presence . . . with suitable embellishments.[10]

---

[9] A number of items have been translated in Cassiodorus Senator, *Letters,* trans. Thomas Hodgkin (London, 1886). The Latin texts of the *Variae* have been edited by Theo. Mommsen, *Monumenta Germaniae Historica, Auctorum Antiquissimorum* XII (Berlin, 1894), pp. 3–385.

[10] *Variae* VI.

In other words, the king must now rely on the literate servant to compose as well as to write down his message. A Julius Caesar or a Cicero was
perfectly capable of both composition and transcription, because each man
was a well-educated person. If Cicero did not choose to do the actual
writing, he could call upon his faithful secretary Tiro, who had perfected
a system of shorthand for rapid dictation. As Julius Victor points out, the
Romans considered it a mark of politeness to respond to a letter in one's
own handwriting—a remark which indicates both that dictation was common and that personal handwriting was also practiced. But for a ruler like
Theodoric or Charlemagne, the personal handwriting skill did not exist.
No doubt the practice of verbatim dictation could still have been employed, but the comparatively low educational level of the dictating person
would surely have militated against any high degree of excellence in the
resulting compositions.

The employment of a verbal minister was the obvious answer to this
problem, just as it had been for the Greeks of the sixth and fifth centuries
before Christ. Note the words of Cassiodorus ". . . the Quaestor has to
learn our inmost thoughts, that he may utter them to our subjects. . . .
He has to speak the king's words in the king's own presence."

Cassiodorus' official writings, even when formulary in nature, retain
the flavor of artistry. This is perhaps best seen in the sonorous Latin phrasing of an introductory praise of medicine which begins a *Formula comitis
archiatrorum*:

> Inter utillimas artes, quas ad sustentandam humanae fragilitatis indigentiam
> divina tribuerunt, nulla praestare videtur aliquid simile quam potest auxilia-
> trix medicina conferre. (*Variae* VI.xviii.)

It is difficult, too, to imagine Theodoric himself inventing such phrases as
that addressed to the prefect Artemidorus: "We rejoice to have our justice
flourish in you (*Gaudemus in te floruisse nostra judicia*).[11] Cassiodorus
very often begins a letter with a sententious utterance about the nature of
kingship, the causes of strife, or the like, in a manner surely not native to
his king's own style of speaking. A letter to Boethius for Theodoric, discussing music, is studded with references to Orpheus, with remarks on
Terence's two types of poetry.[12]

Cassiodorus thus represents one of the last major examples of the artistic
letter-writer in the Ciceronian mode, relying on his own literary abilities

---

[11] *Ibid.*, II.xxxiii.
[12] *Ibid.*, II.xl.

in composing messages. He does not follow rigid formulas, nor does he enunciate theoretical principles about the craft of letter-writing. Quintilian would no doubt have been pleased with him. His *Variae* were distributed widely throughout the middle ages, ranking second in popularity only to the letters of Cicero.

But the Cassiodoran solution to Europe's message-making problem suffered from the same fatal flaw which has always afflicted artistic attempts to handle the practical exigencies of life—that is, that practical problems are enormous in number while artistic genius is very rare. Even Charlemagne had no Cassiodorus, though Alcuin's schools might one day have produced one if political division had not intervened with the splitting of the empire. During the seventh, eighth, and ninth centuries the literacy of kings suffered a sharp decline at the same time that the rapid decay of education made it less and less likely that a new Cassiodorus would be found in every principality in Europe.

This is not to say that learned men, capable writers, were not to be found in Western Europe. Gregory the Great (c. 540–604) wrote such fine letters as Pope that medieval grammarians often refer to him as the model for the *stilus gregorianus*. But the great names of the so-called Dark Age are educators, exegetes, or philosophers—men like Rabanus Maurus, Walafrid Strabo, or Aelfric. Meanwhile the worlds of church and state continued to develop with increasing complexity. For instance, papal registers of letters are known to have been kept as early as A.D. 352, in the reign of Liberius. Some 850 letters of Gregory the Great are extant.[13] Even the fairly narrow Italian hegemony of Theodoric had demanded from the pen of Cassiodorus a bewildering variety of forms, decisions, rescripts, decrees, inquiries, admonitions, and miscellaneous messages. The *Variae* of Cassiodorus earned at least some of their popularity from the very fact that they covered such a multitude of cases and circumstances and were therefore useful as models to later writers facing similar problems.

The very multiplicity of ranks and orders in an emerging feudal society had the effect of increasing the number of relationships—both social and legal—which came to be reflected in writing in one way or another. One ready solution to the problem of writing about such recurring situations was to draft a *formula*—a standardized statement capable of being duplicated in various circumstances. The early medieval *formulae* usually

---

[13] An excellent survey of these developments may be found in Reginald Lane Poole, *Lectures on the History of the Papal Chancery* (Cambridge, England, 1915), pp. 29 ff.

include a blank space for inserting a name, or indicate by the term
$N(= Nomen)$ that a name is to be inserted.

A number of such formulary collections have survived. Among the most
prominent are:[14]

1. *Formulae Andegavenses:* A collection of 60 private formulas compiled at Angers; the first 57 date from the beginning of the seventh
   century, and the last three after A.D. 678.
2. *Formulae Arvernenses:* Eight private formulas, composed at Cler-
   mont in the eighth century.
3. *Formulae Marculfi:* Probably the most important collection of the
   Merovingian period, dedicated to Landri, bishop of Paris from 650 to
   656. One hundred nine formulas, 57 dealing with royal acts and 52
   with private acts. They apparently derive from the chancery of the
   mayor of the palace rather than from a royal chancery.
4. *Formulae Turonenses:* Forty-five formulas composed at Tours during the eighth and ninth centuries.
5. *Formulae Bituricenses:* Nineteen formulas of Bourges, of particular
   interest because most can be dated fairly accurately. They date from
   before 720 to sometime in the ninth century.
6. *Formulae Senonenses:* A total of 69 formulas of the eighth and ninth
   centuries from Sens, divided into two sections of different date.
7. *Formulae Pithoei:* One hundred eight formulas, a fragment of a
   larger collection composed in a region under Salic, or Frankish, law
   in the eighth century.
8. *Formulae salicae "Merkelianae":* A collection of 66 items named
   after their editor. Dates range from 750 to after 817, under four date
   groupings. The formulas of an abbey are included in this set.

To judge from the number of such collections which have survived, the
practice of using repetitive formulas for at least some correspondence must
have been widespread in the seventh, eighth, and ninth centuries in the
region roughly corresponding to modern France. As an examination of
these formulas reveals very quickly, they were documents which were
intended to establish a written record of an official act as well as to convey

---

[14] This summary is derived from A. Giry, *Manuel de diplomatique,* new ed.
(Paris, 1925), pp. 482–84. Latin texts of most of the *formulae* may be found in
Karl Zeumer, ed., *Formulae merowingici et karolini aevi.* Monumenta Germaniae
Historica, Legum V (Hanover, 1886).

a message. One of Marculf's formulas, for instance, announces the establishment of a relationship between ruler and subject:

> It is right that those who have promised us unbroken faith should be rewarded by our aid and protection. Now since our faithful subject (name) with the will of God has come to our palace with his arms and has there sworn in our hands to keep his trust and fidelity to us, therefore we decree and command by this present writing that henceforth the said (name) is to be numbered among our *antrustiones* (i.e., dependents). If anyone shall presume to slay him, let him know that he shall have to pay 600 solidi as a wergeld for him.[15]

The contractual nature of such "letters" is demonstrated by one of the formulas from Tours:

> To my great lord (name), I, (name). Since as was well known, I had not wherewith to feed and clothe myself, I came to you and told you my wish, to commend myself to you and to put myself under your protection. I have now done so, on the condition that you shall supply me with food and clothing as far as I shall merit by my services, and that as long as I live I shall perform such services for you as are becoming to a freeman, and shall never have the right to withdraw from your power and protection, but shall remain under them all the days of my life. It is agreed that if either of us shall try to break this compact he shall pay ——— solidi, and the compact shall still hold. It is also agreed that two copies of this letter shall be made and signed by us, which also has been done.[16]

Some of the formulas constitute what might be called empowering documents. The granting of immunities, for instance, involved the transmission of a letter to be held by the receiving party against the time that it might be needed to prove his rights. Such a document amounted to an "open letter" or proclamation, as seen in this example from Marculf:

> Those who from their early youth have served us or our parents are justly awarded by the gifts of our munificence. Know therefore that we have granted to that illustrious man (name), with the greatest good will, the villa called (name), in the county of (name), with all its possessions . . . and he shall hold it forever with full immunity from the entrance of any public official for the purpose of extracting the royal portion of the fines from cases arising there; to the extent finally that he shall have, hold, and possess it in full ownership, no one having the right to expect its transfer,

---

[15] Translation from Oliver Thatcher and Edgar McNeal, *A Source Book for Medieval History* (New York, 1905), pp. 342–43. Latin text, Zeumer, *Formulae,* p. 55.

[16] Thatcher, *Source Book,* pp. 343–44. Latin text, Zeumer, *Formulae,* p. 158.

and with the right of leaving it to his successors or to anyone whom he
desires, and to do with it whatever else he wishes.[17]

The great bulk of the early medieval *formulae* thus deal with contractual
or semicontractual relationships in which the preservation of a written
record was as important as the message itself. Consequently it is fair to
say that they are basically notarial in nature.

But even assuming that a finite number of repetitive situations could be
identified—immunities, agreements, homages, etc.—it seems evident that
the formulary approach suffers from the inherent defect of narrowness.
Even five hundred or a thousand *formulae* would probably not be enough
to provide for the diverse demands of even a minor principality. No doubt
many adaptations were made in the basic forms, but the necessity of fore-
casting the needs must always have imposed a certain limitation. Consequently it is not surprising to find the surviving formulas grouped into
rather predictable patterns corresponding to the major facets of early
medieval feudalism. In terms of addresses, they follow the threefold division noted by Julius Victor—superior to inferior, inferior to superior, or
equal to equal. As one might expect from their quasi-legal background,
there is a strong similarity in the wording of the various formulas.

For a number of reasons, then, the formulary approach to message
transmission simply could not take care of all exigencies in early medieval
Europe. By the year 1000 the educational level of Europe was at its lowest
level since the sixth century before Christ. Even though the Roman school
system had long survived the fall of its mother city, especially in France
and Spain, the great encyclopedists of the seventh and early eighth century
had marked the ebb tide of that great movement. North of the Alps there
was no institution that by any stretch of the imagination could be called a
university, while in Italy the embryonic *studia* at such places as Bologna
and Salerno were only beginning to take shape. Manifestly, there was little
likelihood that any large number of artistic letter-writers would appear
under these circumstances. Even the Papacy, possessed at least of continuity regardless of the variations in its actual power, maintained its correspondence through a wide variety of officials up into the eleventh century.[18]
Some new solution was obviously needed.

The birth of the *ars dictaminis* and its correlative style, called the *cursus,*
or prose rhythm, is linked to the Benedictine abbey of Monte Cassino in

---

[17] Thatcher, *Source Book,* pp. 352–53. Latin text, Zeumer, *Formulae,* pp. 52–53.
[18] See Poole, *Papal Chancery,* pp. 36–75.

central Italy. The two monks who led the movement were Alberic of Monte Cassino, who first linked rhetoric and letter-writing in a formal treatise on the new art about 1087, and his pupil John of Gaeta, who emphasized the *cursus* as papal chancellor for thirty years (1089–1118) before becoming Pope Gelasius II in 1118.

Alberic of Monte Cassino is a pivotal figure in the history of medieval rhetoric. As a teacher in the oldest continuously operating Benedictine monastery in Europe,[19] he inherited the ancient traditions of learning which went back to Benedict himself. It is not surprising then to find him quoting Cicero, Sallust, Lucan, Ovid, Terence, and of course Virgil in his own works. Because of the central location of Monte Cassino and because of its reputation, it is not surprising either that its school should have had illustrious pupils like the future Pope Gelasius II.

Alberic's major contribution to the *ars dictaminis* is his application of rhetorical principles to letter-writing. Two of his works in the area of discourse are *Dictaminum radii* (or *Flores rhetorici*), dealing primarily with rhetorical ornament, and *Breviarium de dictamine*, a work which actually takes up the matter of letter-writing.

The first of these, the *Dictaminum radii*,[20] demonstrates clearly Alberic's grammatical and rhetorical background. The exact title of the treatise is of some importance to understanding its purpose, however, since a reader can gain two quite different opinions of Alberic's purpose from the two alternate titles. If the work is simply a discussion of *colores* (figures), then it belongs in the same general category as the so-called *Colores rhetorici*[21] of a German contemporary, Onulf of Speyer (fl. 1050), or the highly selec-

---

[19] Surprisingly, however, comparatively little attention seems to have been paid to the exact nature of Alberic's contribution. Charles H. Haskins (*Studies in Medieval Culture*, Oxford, 1929, pp. 170–92) summarizes the general view that Alberic initiated a new process; this opinion is expressed again in an important survey of the *ars dictaminis* to be found in J. De Ghellinck, S.J., *L'Essor de la littérature latine au XII* siècle, 2 vols. (Brussels and Paris, 1946), I, 54–68. But the most recent study of Alberic's rhetoric (*Studi Medievali* NS 18 [1952], 121–127) concentrates merely on his use of rhythmical prose (*numerus*, or *cursus*). For a later study (and text) of his *De rithmis*, see below, n. 30. Alberic is in danger of remaining a legend without a detailed history.

[20] *Alberici Casinensis Flores rhetorici*, ed. D. M. Inguanez and H. M. Willard, Miscellanea Cassinese 14 (Montecassino, 1938). But also see the textual criticism of Harald Hagendahl, "Le manuel de rhétorique d'Albericus Casinensis," *Classica et Medievalia* 17 (1956), 63–70. Also see Alberic of Monte Cassino, *Flowers of Rhetoric* trans. Joseph M. Miller in *Readings in Medieval Rhetoric*, ed. Joseph M. Miller, Michael H. Prosser and Thomas W. Benson (Bloomington, Indiana, 1973), pp. 131–61.

[21] Onulf von Speyer, *Colores rhetorici*, ed. W. Wattenbach in *Sitzungsberichte der königlich Preusischen Akademie der Wissenschaften zu Berlin* 1 (1894), 361–86.

tive *De ornamentis verborum*[22] of the later bishop of Rennes, Marbodus (d. 1132). Onulf specifically relates his work to rhetoric (*artis rhetoricae*), and Marbodus relates his thirty figures of diction to verse-writing and gives his examples in verse. Alberic's work has been edited by D. M. Inguanez and H. W. Willard under the title *Flores rhetorici,* but Harald Hagendahl has demonstrated convincingly that the proper title should be *Dictaminum radii.* For one thing, three of the four extant manuscripts of the work use this title rather than the one chosen by Inguanez and Willard.

The title of *Dictaminum radii* increases the significance of Alberic's attention to the use of rhetoric in writing rather than in speaking. Discussing introductions early in the treatise, for instance, he refers to *scriptor* rather than to speaker (II.i.). In concluding his list of "useful" *colores* at the end of the work, he says that anyone who does not know them ought not to usurp the name of "writer" (VIII.9).[23]

Alberic's intentions in writing the *Dictaminum radii* seem to be twofold: primarily he wishes to develop further some of his earlier teachings by taking his ideas past the elementary stage (*rudimenta doctrinae*) to a higher level of development, going from words themselves to actual composition. Apparently he has lectured earlier on the subject, for he speaks of his hearers (*auditores nostros*). He has a second reason: the discomfiture of an unnamed opponent or rival (*adversarius*). His book, Alberic declares, will make his rival become "silent, dumb, admiring, and astounded." [24]

With this in mind, then, it is clear that Alberic regards this treatise as a further excursion into a subject he has already treated orally. He can therefore expect his readers to know the rudiments of the field. Actually the entire work concentrates on two related subjects—*exordia* and *colores.* The discussion of *colores* is highly selective, covering only nineteen major figures and tropes together with certain grammatical vices (*barbarismus, acyrologia,* etc.). But the emphasis upon exordial material is a new element in the history of medieval rhetoric, and foreshadows what came to be a major element in the theory of the *ars dictaminis.*

Consequently the *Dictaminum radii* can be read as an elaboration on

---

[22] Marbodus, *De ornamentis verborum,* ed. J. P. Migne, *Patrologia latina* CLXXI, cols. 1687–92.

[23] Hi sunt flores, hii utillimi dictandi colores, quos si quis notat, scriptores accedere praesumat; qui nescit, nomen non usurpet scriptoris. Amen. Inguanez and Willard, p. 59.

[24] . . . hic adversarius sileat, obmutescat, miretur, obstupeat. *Ibid.,* p. 33.

a set of ideas already known to both Alberic and his students. A brief list of the nine sections of the work may serve to illustrate its divisions:

## THE *DICTAMINUM RADII* OF ALBERIC
## OF MONTE CASSINO

I.     Prologue
II.1–5. Properties of a *proemium*
III.1–6. Divisions of an oration. Rules for *salutatio*
IV.    Vices of diction
V.1–5. Figures of diction
VI.1–6. Tropes and other figures
VII.1–9. Figures of thought
VIII.1–9. Other figures

Each of the sections is very short, the entire treatise amounting to no more than twenty-five pages in print. Any discussion of *colores,* as we have seen a number of times earlier, naturally occupies a lengthy section of any work because of the necessity of treating a multitude of definitions and examples. Hence it is not surprising to see that much of Alberic's work is taken up in this manner.

What is of even greater interest, however, are the two comparatively lengthy discussions of *proemia (exordia)* and *salutationes.* Alberic reminds his readers that the parts of a speech (*orationis totius rethorica divisio*) are four in number—*exordium, narratio, argumentatio,* and *conclusio.* (Here he follows Isidore of Seville, *Etymologia* II.7, but the division is of course essentially Ciceronian.) Later he dismisses the last three parts of a speech with a brief paragraph, devoting most of his attention to the first-named part.

Alberic cites the Ciceronian objectives of the *exordium,* that is, to render the audience "attentive, docile, and well-disposed." He does not name Cicero, but that is hardly surprising for such a famous quotation. Significantly, though, Alberic uses the term "reader" (*lectorem*) instead of "audience" (*auditores*)[25]—and declares his intention to discuss those "colors" by which the reader is swayed. His choice of Latin terms is highly significant, in light of later terminology in the dictamen manuals. He

---

[25] Attentum ergo lectorem reddere si volueris, vera, honesta, utilia pollicearis (III.1, p. 36). Earlier, Alberic has named the standard parts of a "speech" (*orationis totius rethorica divisio*), but increasingly he uses terms relating not to speeches but to letters: for instance, *persona mittentis* (III.5, p. 38). Yet sonority and other sound values are never far from his mind, as in VII.9, where he discusses the utility of sound in aiding sense, attention, and memory.

writes: *Colores autem eius dico quibus capitur benevolentia, docilitas, attentio.* This seems to be the first medieval use of a word-set which later became petrified into a formal part of a letter as *captatio benevolentiae.* (In fact, some of the manuals come to use this petrified phrase as a synonym for *exordium,* so that in the following century the first two parts of a letter are often named as *salutatio* and *captatio benevolentiae.*)

In other words, then, the *Dictaminum radii* is devoted to the beginnings of "writings" (not yet defined), and to the *colores* proper to those beginnings.

The actual nature of the 'beginnings' becomes clearer when Alberic distinguishes between *salutatio* and *exordium* (III.5–6). The discussion of the relation between *salutatio* and *exordium* is the longest single treatment of any subject in the treatise. The *salutatio* clearly comes first, and is separate from the *exordium.* This can apply to nothing else but a letter or *epistola* (although he does not use that term here), and his thinking is made abundantly clear by his statement that the first thing to consider is "the person to whom and the person from whom it is sent." He suggests that it is pertinent to consider whether they are on the same or different levels, whether they are friends or enemies, and finally what their "modes" or fortunes might be. Other considerations include the subject, the intention of the writer, and the various styles appropriate to these intentions.[26]

"After the salutation [belongs] the exordium," Alberic continues, "after the exordium the narration, which will be creditable [*honesta*] if it is brief and clear." [27] Then follows a discussion of brevity with examples from Sallust. The remainder of the treatise is a mixture of rhetorical and grammatical lore concerning the *figurae.* For instance, Alberic uses examples from both Virgil's poetry and Cicero's speeches to illustrate his *colores.*

Alberic does not attempt to provide a complete discussion of any of the subjects he undertakes. There is also a certain amount of repetition, which perhaps reinforces the notion that the whole treatise is intended to be a collection of further thoughts on a subject well-known to his readers. Alberic reminds them several times of the three considerations in salutations: "subject, person, and intention." As if to make clear their relation to letter-writing, he restates them in Section VII.1 as part of *de litterarum praecepto.*

---

[26] III.5–6, pp. 38–40.
[27] Post salutationem exordium inibis, post exordium narrationem promovebis quae sic erit honesta, si brevis fuerit et clara (III.6, p. 38).

A reconstruction of Alberic's theory of letter-writing can be adduced from the *Dictaminum radii* and what is implicit in it. First of all, Alberic clearly thinks it appropriate to employ rhetorical principles in writing as well as in speaking. This is an obvious conclusion, and one which marks no real change from classical theory. But second, and far more important, Alberic had evidently been telling his students at Monte Cassino that the Ciceronian parts of a speech could be redirected to aid in the composition of epistles or letters. Moreover, he makes a critical distinction between *salutatio* and *exordium* which was to become a hallmark of the medieval *ars dictaminis*. The fact that he virtually ignores *argumentatio* and *conclusio*, concentrating on the psychological aspects of the other two parts, is further indication of the importance he attaches to these first parts of a letter.

If it is true, as Aristotle says in *Topics* VIII, that the first step in any science is the most important one, then Alberic of Monte Cassino deserves our recognition as the father of the medieval *ars dictaminis*.

This judgment is confirmed by the second of his books, the *Breviarium de dictamine*.[28] The *Breviarium* is dedicated to two pupils, Gundfrid and Guido, and it is evident from the first two prologue sections that Alberic regards the work as a supplement or continuation of discussions which have already begun with the two students. He recommends, in fact, that they add the lore of the written book to what they have already learned from listening to his voice (*ea que iam viva voce nobis referentibus edidicistis*), and to what they have gleaned from other books he has given them to study (*ea que per diversa estis scribendo opera dispertiti vos*).

This advice is extremely important, primarily because it indicates again that Alberic's school at Monte Cassino was actively engaged in discussing the nature of letters. Indeed, it would seem to indicate that Alberic was conducting a continuing series of instruction in the matter, perhaps over a number of years. He begins Section II of the *Breviarium* by noting that the written treatise will be a better aid to memory than teaching by precepts.[29] This too implies that he has made other, earlier statements on the same subject.

---

[28] Partial text in Ludwig Rockinger, *Briefsteller und Formelbücher des eilften bis vierzehnten Jahrhunderts*. 2 vols. *Quellen und Erörterungen zur bayerischen und deutschen Geschichte*, neunter band (Munich, 1863; reprinted New York, 1961), I, 29–46. Rockinger gives the simple title *De dictamine*, but Alberic clearly indicates the proper title in his Prologue and later (e.g. p. 32). Rockinger omits a section on grammar and a section (*consideratio rithmorum*) which discusses rhythm.

[29] Breviarium autem nostrum veritate auctore vere breviarium erit, quia magis notationibus quibusdam memorie conservandis quam discipline preceptionibus constabit capiunde (p. 30).

For the modern reader, then, both the *Dictaminum radii* and the *Breviarium de dictamine* should be read as expressions of a pre-existing body of doctrine, not all of which is available to us in the pages of the two texts. We shall perhaps never know whether Alberic himself first made the critical application of rhetoric to letter-writing, or whether he simply inherited an educational tradition at Monte Cassino. But a certain amount of intelligent extrapolation will help us to understand more clearly what Alberic intends to say in the *Breviarium*.

The Prologue, for instance, contains a key phrase which by itself may seem unimportant. This is the term *prosaico dictamini opus,* marking the first appearance in an extant text of a phrase which was to become a standard description of the art of letter-writing. In other words, Alberic is saying that his book is about "dictamen," and in particular about the "prosaic" branch of dictamen. It is obvious at once from his use of the qualifying adjective that Alberic conceives of *dictamen* as having more than one branch or type. He does not indicate in the *Breviarium* what other types he recognizes, but one obvious answer to this question appears in the later *Rationes dictandi prosaice* (c. 1119–24) of Hugh of Bologna. Hugh, who praises the work of Alberic as that of *monachi viri eloquentissimi,* declares that there are two types of dictamen, "prosaic" and "metric" (*videlicet prosaicum, alterum quod vocatur metricum*). As a matter of fact, the Munich manuscript used by Rockinger for his edition actually bears a plural heading—"Concerning Dictamens" (*De dictaminis*)—instead of the singular "Concerning Dictamen" (*De dictamine*) printed by Rockinger. This minor change in a word ending may be more significant than it looks at first glance, especially when we note that the whole *Breviarium* apparently consists of three major elements:

1. A section on epistles and forms (printed by Rockinger)
2. A section on grammatical means of amplification
3. A section on *rithmus*

The middle section on amplification includes verse as well as prose examples.

There is no doubt whatever that Alberic is speaking of letter-writing in the first section, for he frequently employs the term *epistola*. In speaking of examples, too, he uses such phrases as *epistole . . . patribus in niceno concilio* (*Cap.* VI), and when he discusses beginnings he observes that "prologues of epistles" can be constructed many ways (*prologi epistolarum multipliciter fiunt*). This section also includes a brief treatment of "privileges," which he defines as a "concession of the pontiff"; he notes how the writing of privileges compares to other kinds of letters (*Cap.* VII). A number of his examples have alternate modes to illustrate how word-changes can produce variety:

| | |
|---|---|
| Maledictus conceptus qui | Maledictus conceptus qui |
| non procedit ad partum: | non procedit in pactum: |
| *id est maledicta promissio* | *id est maledicta promissio* |
| *que non procedit in fructum.* | *que non procedit in factum.* |

The second section of the *Breviarium* has not yet been edited. It is possible, however, that it may have been a pre-existing treatise inserted as a means of providing further compositional advice to the two students to whom the whole work is dedicated. This untitled section begins with the words *Miramur ultra quam.* One modern scholar, Hugh H. Davis, who has examined the two surviving manuscripts of the *Breviarium,* in Munich and in Leningrad, describes it as "a treatise on synonyms and variety of expression." [30] Davis finds strong evidence of Benedictine and Cassinese content, since it contains quotations from such contemporaries of Alberic as Alfanus and Guaiferius; both these Benedictines were associated with Monte Cassino. Moreover, Davis finds both verse and rhythmical compositions of Saint Peter Damian used as examples in this second section. The inclusion of this type of material with Alberic's discussion of letter-writing is further evidence that the new epistolary theory was still closely related to the liberal arts at Monte Cassino. The *Miramur ultra quam,* then, may have been viewed by Alberic as a natural adjunct to a treatment of "prosaic" letters in the first part.

The third section is titled "Concerning Rhythms" (*De rithmis*) in the Leningrad manuscript, and *Consideratio rithmorum* in the Munich manuscript. When Rockinger printed the first section in 1863 he did not include either the second or third sections in his published text. This third section has been printed three times since 1950; the most comprehensive text and discussion is that of Davis mentioned earlier. Davis believes that Alberic's third section was written no earlier than 1054 because it includes as one example a *rithmus* lamenting the death of Leo IX. He finds a possible debt to Bede's *De arte metrica* in Alberic's discussion of the distinction between *rithmus* and *metrum.*

But Alberic's *De rithmis* is actually only a brief series of definitions and

---

[30] Hugh H. Davis, "The *De rithmis* of Alberic of Monte Cassino: A Critical Edition," *Medieval Studies* 28 (1966), 198–227. The text is pp. 208–14.

examples for nine types of Latin *rithmus*.[31] Many of the examples are from hymns. There is no mention of letter-writing, and indeed no explicit connection in the text to the rest of the *Breviarium*. There are no prose examples. It is a piece which on its own merits should be of interest mainly to hymnologists.

Nevertheless, it accompanies an important innovative treatise on letter-writing. If nothing else it adds further confirmation to the view that Latin *rithmus* was being discussed and probably taught at the Benedictine monastery of Monte Cassino in the 1070's and 1080's. Had Alberic already concluded that rhythmical prose was appropriate for formal letters? We know from other sources that his contemporaries, for instance, John of Gaeta (later Pope Gelasius II), came out of Monte Cassino with a highly developed sense of *rithmus* which they applied to letter-writing. The prose rhythms known as *cursus* were to become a constant medieval adjunct to the theory of epistolary composition. For these reasons it is tempting to speculate that Alberic's inclusion of *De rithmis* with the section on "prosaic" dictamen is a purposeful linking of letter-writing prose and the syllabic patterning of *rithmus*. This is an issue meriting further study.

In summary, one can see in Alberic's two works almost all the elements of the fully developed *ars dictaminis:* the relation of rhetoric to letter-writing, the standardization of parts of a letter, the emphasis on salutations and introductory sections with the distinction between social levels of addressees, the recommended use of *colores,* the inclusion of model letters and official forms, and even—if my conjecture is correct—the encouragement of rhythmical prose for letter-writing.

Alberic's treatises still reflected, however, a rather broad interest in general grammatical and rhetorical concerns. It is evident that he did not wish to produce a highly schematized, rigid description of letter-writing techniques. For Alberic, letter-writing was still a largely artistic and humanistic undertaking, and it is probably fair to say that he regarded rhetoric as a useful but not dominating factor. As Haskins has so aptly phrased it, "It is clear that the new epistolography has not yet become sharply differentiated from grammar and the older rhetoric." [32] It is

---

[31] The nine types are: phaleuticus, exasillabis quaternius, octosillabus, epdasillabus, decapentacus, didecasillabus, decassillabus, pentasillabus, and endecasillabus. Davis comments (*ibid.,* p. 204) on the first name used: "The incorrect naming of the Sapphic strophe as rithmus phaleuticus (sec. 2) may derive from Bede's juxtaposition of the chapters 'de metro phalecio' (17) and 'de metro sapphico' (18) and the long separate treatment preceding these."

[32] Haskins, *Studies in Medieval Culture,* p. 173.

equally clear, nevertheless, that by the 1080's the new *ars dictaminis* did exist in central Italy. Given the rhetorical background of its origins in the school at Monte Cassino, it still remained to be seen whether the new art would continue in this humane direction or whether it would develop a technical life of its own.

The answer to this question was not long in coming. Within the next few decades after Alberic, the center of the dictaminal movement shifted to the northern Italian city of Bologna, where in rapid succession a number of influential writers blocked out the details of the *ars dictaminis,* which were to remain fairly standard for more than three hundred years. The development in Bologna was possibly an outgrowth of the studies begun at Monte Cassino, even though the Bolognese writers were generally lay teachers rather than religious.

The most significant writers and their works were:

1. Adalbertus Samaritanus, *Praecepta dictaminum* (1111–1118). Theoretical treatise with model letters.
2. Hugh of Bologna, *Rationes dictandi prosaice* (1119–24). Theoretical treatise with a few models.
3. Henricus Francigena, *Aurea gemma* (1119). A model letter collection, written in Pavia.
4. Anonymous, *Rationes dictandi* (1135). Key theoretical treatise.
5. Anonymous, *Precepta prosaici dictaminis secundum Tullium* (1138–52). Theoretical treatise.
6. Bernard of Romagna, *Introductiones prosaici dictaminis* (1145). Theoretical treatise.
7. "Master A," an untitled *ars* beginning *Ad plenam scientiam dictaminum* (also of period 1138–52). Theoretical treatise.
8. Baldwin, *Liber de dictaminibus* (c. 1147–61). Theoretical treatise.[33]

After the middle of the twelfth century the *ars dictaminis* began to appear in France, especially at Orléans, and then in Germany; Peter of

---

[33] Now edited. See *Baldwini liber dictaminum,* prodit curante Sándor Durzsa. Magistri artium, Collana di studi e testi, 3 (Bologna, 1970). There is as yet no comprehensive list of known *artes dictaminis,* as there is for preaching manuals (see below, Chapter Six). The chronology of the earliest *artes* has been studied most recently by Franz-Josef Schmale, "Die Bologneser Schule der Ars dictandi," *Deutsches Archiv für Erforschung des Mittelalters* 13 (1957), 16–34. However, a useful survey of thirty-two major authors, with brief biographies and an invaluable list of *incipits,* may be found in Noel Denholm-Young, "The *Cursus* in England," in *Collected Papers on Medieval Subjects* (Oxford, 1946), pp. 170–92; this important article first appeared in *Oxford Essays in Medieval History Presented to Herbert Edward Salter* (Oxford, 1934), pp. 68–103. There is a considerable bibliography in the field; see James J. Murphy, *Medieval Rhetoric: A Select Bibliography* (Toronto, 1971), items D1–D 95.

Blois took it from France to England in the 1180's. In the thirteenth century the *dictatores* of Florence were to rival those of Bologna. But Bologna was the home of the early writers who set the basic patterns for the new art.

The first of these writers was Adalbertus Samaritanus, whose *Praecepta dictaminum*[34] was written in Bologna between 1111 and 1118. Like Alberic of Monte Cassino, Adalbertus was a teacher, but, unlike Alberic, he was apparently not in religious orders. Actually he displays not only disagreement with but some hostility to Alberic, urging his readers to "spurn the harsh, thorny, insoluble *dictamina* of Monk Alberic."[35] Although elsewhere Adalbertus calls on his readers to be charitable in their search for knowledge, he takes the same occasion to declare that "men of our times" actually do spurn the harsh and thorny dictamen he has mentioned earlier in connection with Alberic.[36]

How does one account for this attitude? This is an extremely important question because, of all the varied types of medieval treatises dealing with discourse, it is only among the authors of *artes dictaminis* that such belligerence regularly occurs. It will be recalled that Alberic himself was concerned with an unnamed *adversarius*. (This is not the same problem encountered by John of Salisbury in *Metalogicon* [1159], since the "Cornificius" he mentions represents a class of persons who are merely mistaken about learning but are not regarded as personal enemies.)[37]

The response of a second Bolognese writer, Canon Hugh of Bologna, reveals at once the nature of the quarrel. Hugh's *Rationes dictandi prosaice* was written within a few years of Adalbertus' treatise, probably between 1119 and 1124. Early in his Prologue Hugh links Adalbertus with

---

[34] *Adalbertus Samaritanus, Praecepta dictaminum*, ed. Franz-Josef Schmale, MGH, Quellen zur Geistesgeschichte des Mittelalters III (Weimar, 1961). Schmale believes that Adalbertus, not Alberic, is the true father of the *ars dictaminis:* "The decisive impetus for these studies should be attributed to Adalbertus and not, as earlier believed, to Alberic of Montecassino" (p.v). He adds that in his view the *Breviarium* of Alberic shows the ending of an old way, not the beginning of a new. In one sense there is perhaps some merit in this judgment, in that Adalbertus first displays the professional narrowing of interest so typical of later *dictatores,* but the dictaminal impetus was already there when he and his fellows began to argue their exclusive right to it.

[35] Spernat aspera et spinosa dictamina Alberici monachi insolubilia. *Ibid.,* p. 51

[36] Verum quia ab hominibus nostrorum temporum spernuntur aspera et spinosa dictamina. . . . *Ibid.,* p. 31.

[37] Though John calls Cornificius a "foolish old man" and cites his "bloated gluttony, puffed-up pride, obscene mouth" along with other loathsome qualities, he is really attacking a whole class of ignoramuses rather than an individual. See John of Salisbury, *The Metalogicon,* trans. Daniel D. McGarry (Berkeley and Los Angeles, 1955), pp. 9–20.

those whose "destructive malice wounds, slanders, and abuses" the people who are trying to do what is right. In their attempts to introduce "rash novelty and uncultured doctrine," Hugh continues, men like Adalbertus and his colleague Aginulfus even "attack the book of a most eloquent man, monk Alberic."[38]

In other words, three major areas of conflict exist between Hugh and Adalbertus. First of all, there are the natural disagreements any two theorists will have; also, Adalbertus is not a religious, while Hugh calls himself *ecclesie canonicus et sacerdos;* finally, and perhaps most important, Hugh represents the traditional educational structure of cathedral and monastery, while Adalbertus calls himself *dictator*—a new term— and is clearly aligned with the new lay schools of the city.[39] Adalbertus regards his work as a "profession," speaking of *professionis officio* in relation to his task. Unfortunately there are very few biographical details available about Adalbertus and Hugh to assist us in clarifying this rivalry, but it is such a recurring phenomenon in the *artes dictaminis* that it is worth noting at the beginning. As Ernst Kantorowicz has so clearly shown in the case of Guido Faba (c. 1225), such rivalries continued to play a part in the whole history of the art.[40] For the professional *dictator,* of course, popularity was his livelihood. If nothing else, the knowledge of such rivalries should prepare the modern reader to discount somewhat the claims of originality and invention often made by authors of the *artes* in an effort to mask their essential agreement with a rival's doctrine. The basic doctrines of the *ars dictaminis* are clear by about 1140, later changes being largely in emphasis rather than in substance.

This visible rivalry in Bologna shortly after the beginning of the twelfth century does at least indicate the existence of a thriving study of the new art of letter-writing.

Adalbertus declares in his *Praecepta dictaminum* that his students can understand the rules of dictamen very quickly, and with great utility. Nevertheless, he says, a *dictator* must know grammar, rhetoric, and dialectic. But since everything is thus necessary to the *dictator,* Adalbertus

---

[38] Si quos vero liuor edax mordet rodit et lacerat de se in se nichil fructus respicientes quem proferre valeant, et ob hoc Aginulfi vel Alberti samaritani temeritatem et indisciplinate doctrine novitatem huic introductioni preponere vel parificare satagunt, videant quod non ratione dicunt, set faucibus invidie et acerbitatis odio accensi indecenter proteruiunt, sic enim Alberici monachi viri eloquentissimi librum viciant . . . . Rockinger, *Briefsteller,* pp. 53–54.

[39] Schmale (*Adalbertus,* pp. 6–7) in fact regards this lay–cleric opposition as a key factor in the development of the new professionalism of the *dictatores.*

[40] Ernst H. Kantorowicz, "An 'Autobiography' of Guido Faba," *Medieval and Renaissance Studies* 1 (1941), 253–80.

promises to show those things most useful to him; some things, after all, are from nature and do not need science. He then provides an etymology for the term *epistola: Epistola grecum nomen est compositivum, epi enim supra, stola missio interpretatur.* Thus there are two kinds of "legations," one by mouth and one by letter (*epistola*). Then he points out that the salutation of a letter varies according to the persons involved, there being three species of letters, just as there are three types of men (*sublimis, mediocris, exilis*). After making these distinctions, however, Adalbertus goes on to note that salutations have many more than three types. He then provides thirty-four examples of *salutationes*, followed without explanation by almost two dozen model letters.[41]

What Adalbertus has done, then, is merely to confirm some of the general observations already made by Alberic. But his scope is narrow, for he considers nothing else beyond the salutation. The *Praecepta dictaminum* itself does not advance the art very far, although by implication it tells us a good deal about the state of the art in Bologna at this time. The "profession" of *dictator* seems well established, and the lay teacher Adalbertus obviously has students of the new art. The tendency to include multiple models also appears here. The incipient dilemma of brevity versus amplitude—whether to crystallize an art into a few "precepts" or whether to discuss it in full—is here left unresolved; it is manifestly absurd for Adalbertus to tell his students on one hand that they can grasp the new science quickly, and on the other hand saying that a knowledge of the entire *trivium* is necessary.[42]

Hugh of Bologna seeks a more balanced approach in his *Rationes dictandi prosaice* (1119–24).[43] Hugh identifies himself as a canon of the Church, and in his opening dedication of the book declares that he will "collect in one work the doctrine of letter-writing drawn from many accounts." [44] As we have seen, Hugh's Prologue includes an attack on Adalbertus and Aginulfus not only for their lack of doctrine but also

[41] For some comment on these letters, see Haskins, *Studies in Medieval Culture,* pp. 175–77. Haskins notes that letters 1 and 2 show a negotiation between Bologna and Cremona concerning a lay teacher of *dictamen.*

[42] "First of all, the *dictator* needs to know grammar, rhetoric, dialectic. . . ." Primum itaque dictatorem oportet cognoscere grammaticam, rhetoricam, dialecticam. . . . Schmale, *Adalbertus,* p. 31.

[43] Latin text in Rockinger, *Briefsteller,* pp. 52–94.

[44] Ex multorum gestis in unum corpus colligerem. *Ibid.,* p. 53. But it must be noted that this type of claim is very common among medieval writers wishing to impress their readers with their breadth of background. For a study of medieval introductions, see Richard W. Hunt, "The Introductions of the *Artes* in the Twelfth Century," *Studia medievali R. J. Martin* (Oxford, 1948), pp. 85–112.

for their invidious and reckless attacks on the good monk Alberic of Monte Cassino.

Whether or not one can take seriously Hugh's claim that he has drawn his doctrine "from many accounts," it is clear that Bologna in the second decade of the twelfth century was the scene of considerable discussion of the new letter-writing art. Hugh's treatise alone would be sufficient to demonstrate this fact, for he displays a carefully structured doctrine that is clearly the product of considerable thought.

Hugh begins by distinguishing two types of *dictamen,* one prosaic and the other metrical. "Metrical is drawn from the Greek *metron,*" he points out, "which in Latin is called 'measure' (*mensura*)." He names three species of *metricum:* first is *carmen,* or that measured by feet; second is *rithmus,* or that marked by the number of syllables with vocal consonance; and finally *prosimetrum,* a mixture of prose and verse.[45] This matter of *metricum,* however, he says he will leave to others and will devote his attention to *prosaicum.*

His definition of prosaic speech is that it is "speech without accountability to metrical law" (*oratio a lege metri soluta*). He makes it clear that he means epistolary prose, moreover, linking the *dictamine Sallusti et Ciceronis* with the *epistola ut Pauli.* The first reference is no doubt to Alberic's *Dictaminum radii,* which uses both Sallust and Cicero as examples, but this is the first time that the term "dictamen" is specifically defined in such a broad sense. The second reference is presumably to Saint Paul, whose epistles to the new Christian churches play a significant role in the New Testament. (This raises an interesting point which merits attention here. Despite Hugh's mention of Saint Paul in this book, Paul's epistles are absolutely ignored by medieval theoreticians: they are not used as examples, they are not analyzed for their form, and the *dictatores* do not even pay lip service to Paul by an occasional reference to him. Since the New Testament was obviously well known during the twelfth and thirteenth centuries, it is evident either that Paul's letters were regarded as sacrosanct and beyond discussion or that medieval theoreticians did not regard them as valuable models. Given the highly pragmatic nature of most dictaminal writing, the second seems the more likely.)

---

[45] This particular type of opening definition, distinguishing prose from metrics or rhythmics, became standard in dictaminal treatises. The practice does not occur in the adjacent *ars metrica* or *ars praedicandi,* however, and it seems likely that the *dictatores* felt a constant need to justify their art by relating it to other uses of language.

Hugh then declares that there are three orders of letters, just as there are three orders of persons. This is a repetition of Alberic's division into superior, equal, and inferior.

Salutations, Hugh says, ought to be written in the third person, with the addressee's name in the dative case and the sender's in the nominative case. In order to denote the variety of persons, the writer ought to add an adjective dealing with the abilities of the addressee—one for the pope, another for a king, another for a bishop, another for an abbot or monk, another for a soldier, another for a comrade or a beloved friend—so that the one written term will be enough to make the matter clear quite quickly.[46]

This is an extremely important paragraph. For one thing, it indicates a crystallization of the burgeoning theory of salutations, here seen with six levels of addressees, from pope to friend. Hugh evidently regards the salutation of the letter as extremely important, although it is not clear whether he regards it as part of the letter proper. When he lists the parts of a letter he names only three: *exordium,* which according to Cicero prepares the mind of the auditor for what is to follow; *narratio,* which is explanation by narrative of fact or likeness to fact; and *conclusio,* which is the final part or conclusion of a speech.[47] Nevertheless, Hugh lists the *salutatio* as one of the places (*loci*) in which the goodwill of the reader can be sought, ranking it equally with the exordium and conclusion; Hugh does not believe that goodwill can be secured by a narration. From this one might well conclude that he regards a letter as having four parts instead of three, although he makes no direct statement on the matter.

Hugh turns in *Cap.* x to matters of style, supplying a long series of examples, each illustrating some particular mode of writing. He begins by saying that "two things are necessary, the *coma* and the *cola,* without which the complete orator will not be eloquent." The *coma* is necessary in letters to avoid inconcinnity or awkwardness, while the *cola* is useful for versatility. Examples of short clauses follow, with a promise of further examples in subsequent letter models (*in nostro dictamine*).

---

[46] Rockinger, *Briefsteller,* pp. 55–56. Hugh is actually discussing a method for coding the letter with immediately recognizable signals for instant comprehension by a reader. Regardless of word order, for instance, designee and sender are identifiable at once by the case endings of their names.

[47] It is interesting to note that Hugh says the conclusion is the "ending point" (*exitus*) or "determination" (*determinatio*) of the letter. The term *determinatio* is used in medieval disputations to denote the master's "resolution" or "determination" of the issue under debate, and Hugh's use of the term here may indicate some reflection of contemporary dialectical practices.

Significantly, Hugh introduces his lengthy section of examples by noting that "we have sufficiently discussed the intrinsic matters of writing." [48] For Hugh, the "intrinsic" matters seem to be the doctrine of salutations and the description of the parts of a letter. The remainder of his treatise —27 printed pages as compared to the 8 discussing "intrinsics"—is taken up with examples and model letters. Although this lengthy model section is interspersed with occasional sentences of general advice on how to frame salutations and the like, it is clear that Hugh has indeed completed his theoretical discussion in *Cap.* x. He begins the models with various types of salutations:

A papa ad imperatorem (from Pope to Emperor)
Ab imperatore ad papam (from Emperor to Pope)
Ab episcopo ad papam (from bishop to Pope)
A papa ad episcopum (from Pope to bishop)
Ab episcopo ad subditos (from bishop to his subordinates)
A subditis ad episcopum (from subordinates to their bishop)
Ad episcopum ab episcopo (to bishop from bishop)
Item ad episcopum (another to a bishop)
Ad discipulos scienciam magistrum petentes (to scholars seeking wisdom
     from a teacher)
Ad magistrum (to a teacher)
Ad patrem (to one's father)
Ad amicum (to a friend)
Ad abbatem vel monachum (to an abbot or monk)
Ad fratrem (to one's brother)
Ad militem (to a soldier)
Civitas ad civitatem (inimici or amici) (city to city, hostile or friendly).[49]

The nature of these models is worth examining, since Hugh's *Rationes dictandi* offers us the first systematic approach to the problem of supplying appropriate salutatory material for all the various levels of addressees. These are no longer merely illustrative examples, designed to increase a reader's understanding of the subject. Instead, Hugh begins to provide samples of phrases and even paragraphs that can be used verbatim in other situations. Note his models for *salutationes* under the rubric *Ad patrem*:

To venerable and beloved father, *or* to respected and faithful father, *or* to kindest parent, D his beloved son (gives) everlasting service with fidelity,

---

[48] Rockinger, *Briefsteller,* p. 60.
[49] Each of these sections (*ibid.,* pp. 61–68) includes sample salutations appropriate for the people involved. Full names are seldom used, but instead an initial letter (e.g., C episcopus) is supplied to indicate where a name might be used.

*or* whatever a very fond son to his father, *or* just as a servant is put under his lord.[50]

These models give the writer six choices of phrasing. Yet Hugh's intention is unmistakably clear; these are not suggestions for rhetorical invention, but are instead models for copying.

There is no precedent for this approach in ancient rhetorical theory.[51] There is in fact no commonly accepted term to describe the intended process. The whole emphasis of both Greek and Roman rhetorical theory was on *inventio*—the discovery of materials by the speaker or writer himself. Even the most stringent reductions of the Second Sophistic, as exemplified in the *Progymnasmata* of Apthonius or Hermogenes, really did little more than present a narrow and highly schematized system of topical *inventio,* which made the speaker's work easier but still left actual composition in his own hands.[52] Nor is this *imitatio* in Quintilian's sense, for Hugh does not propose that the writer drill himself in the artful use of these models as an aid to future *inventio.* As far as Hugh is concerned there is occasional room for discretion by the writer (*aliquam videatur facere discretionem*), but the main direction of his thinking is even more clearly indicated in *Cap.* xv, when he declares that he has discussed "modes" of writing sufficiently and will simply present model letters.[53] He then provides seventeen of them.

Obviously Hugh makes a distinction in his own mind between a *theory* of letter-writing—a somewhat discretionary art with various "modes"— and the *transcription or copying* of letter parts or of letters themselves. As we have noted, there is no accepted term for this second phenomenon. Before suggesting such a term, though, it is important to note that Hugh

---

[50] Venerabili et dilecto patri, *vel* reverendo ac diligendo patri, *vel* A genitori dulcissimo, D eius dilectus filius perennem cum fidelitate servitium, *vel* quicquid patri peramans filius, *vel* quicquid domino subditus servulus. *Ibid.,* p. 64.

[51] The typical Roman term is *excogitatio*—"thinking-out"—of ideas for invention (*ad Herennium* I.i.3). Mere copying was despised. In fact, Saint Augustine's statement in his *De doctrina christiana* that a preacher could use another man's words (because of the importance of the Gospel message) was a radical break with ancient tradition.

[52] For a discussion of these works in this connection, see James J. Murphy, ed., *A Synoptic History of Classical Rhetoric* (New York, 1972), pp. 177–80.

[53] Hugh evidently regards the model letter collection as an integral part of his discussion, which thus includes both the *ars,* or preceptive treatise, and the collection of model letters (*dictamina*). This was to be the typical form of dictaminal apparatus for centuries, furnishing what might well be called a complete rhetorical system for the would-be letter writer.

has already indicated a Latin term for the letter collection itself. It will be recalled that at the end of *Cap.* x Hugh cuts off a list of examples by promising further illustrations *in nostro dictamine*—in other words, in his later model letter collection. This seems to be an early use of a Latin term—*dictaminum* (plural, *dictamina*)—which became the standard description for a collection of such model letters. The term *dictamina* appears regularly from this time onward to describe the letters themselves, and should be carefully distinguished from the term *ars dictaminis* used to describe a theoretical manual or treatise on letter-writing.

It would seem useful to use the term *reproductio* to describe the process of transcription of the models. The closest earlier analogue to the process is that associated with the *formulae* of Merovingian and Carolingian times; there, too, verbatim transcription was intended. Nevertheless, there are important differences. For one thing, the formulas of Marculf and others were generally contractual in nature and did not easily lend themselves to routine personal correspondence, nor did they attempt to distinguish with precision the various social and legal levels of society, nor were they embedded in a theoretical framework like the *ars dictaminis*. They owe their survival to *ad hoc* collections rather than to systematic teaching. The transcriptive impulse is similar, but the rationale is vastly different.

With this in mind, then, it might be useful to list the basic five terms of the new field which were in use by Hugh's time, that is, by about 1124:

*Dictamen:* The whole of writing, coming ultimately to include prosaic, metrical, rhythmical, and mixed forms.

*Dictamen prosaicum:* In practice, the writing of letters in prose; in theory, any writing in prose.

*Ars dictaminis:* The theory of writing letters in prose; the term is also applied to a treatise or manual on the subject.

*Dictator:* A professional teacher of the *ars dictaminis*.

*Dictaminum:* A collection of models, usually complete letters.

A careful distinction between these terms is critical to an understanding of the history of the field. For one thing, library catalogues often use the term *ars dictaminis* indiscriminately to describe any type of materials relating to *dictamen*. Some are merely letter collections, while others may be theoretical treatises of a quite different character. Moreover, since many letter collections include a short prologue describing the parts of a letter, such *dictamina* are sometimes mistakenly listed by medieval librarians as *artes dictaminis*.[54]

One more detail might be noted before leaving the *Rationes dictandi* of Hugh of Bologna. While he makes a formal list of only three "parts" of a letter—*exordium, narratio, conclusio*—he treats the *salutatio* at such length that he makes it a virtual fourth "part." This question of letter parts does not seem to concern Hugh very greatly, and of course he suggests that goodwill (*benevolentia*) can be sought in various parts of a letter. In *Cap.* xii, however, he begins to use the phrase *captatio benevolentiae* to describe the function of securing goodwill. He does not describe it as a "part" of a letter, since he regards it as a rhetorical function common to several places (*loci*) in an epistle. In light of later developments, though, it is a significant terminological abstraction on Hugh's part.

The next datable production in the dictaminal field is the *Aurea gemma*[55] of Henricus Francigena, written in Pavia about 1119. This is a letter collection, indicating the growing popularity of the movement toward *reproductio*. It is interesting as a further indication of directions being taken in northern Italy at that period, but offers little material for the rhetorical history of *dictamen*.

The anonymous *Rationes dictandi* (*Principles of Letter-Writing*) (c. 1135), erroneously printed by Rockinger as Alberic's,[56] demonstrates the rapidity with which the basic doctrines of the *ars dictaminis* were crystallized in the region of Bologna. The treatment is rapid, almost schematic, and in fact the author promises at the outset to handle the doctrine summarily (*summatim perstringere*). Except for a few cases in which alternatives are noted—he gives three different definitions of *dictamen*, for instance—the author's prescriptions are precise and sure. No longer do we find the generality which marks Alberic's work; the *Rationes* is

---

[54] For one such letter collection, see Helene Wieruszowski, "A Twelfth-Century 'Ars dictaminis' in the Barberini Collection of the Vatican Library," *Traditio* 18 (1962), 382–93.

[55] A brief summary is in Haskins, *Studies in Medieval Culture*, pp. 178–80. For the relation between *Aurea gemma* and other contemporary dictaminal works, see Franz-Josef Schmale, "Die Bologneser Schule der Ars dictandi," *Deutsches Archiv für Erforschung des Mittelalters* 13 (1957), 16–34. Also see Ernst H. Kantorowicz, "Anonymi 'Aurea Gemma,'" *Medievalia et humanistica* 1 (1943), 41–57. The chronology of these early works is discussed by J. De Ghellinck, *L'Essor de la littérature latine au XII*[e] *siècle*, 2 vols. (Brussels and Paris, 1946), I, 54–68.

[56] Latin text in Rockinger, *Briefsteller*, pp. 9–28. It is the only dictaminal text so far available in English: see *The Principles of Letter-Writing* (*Rationes dictandi*) trans. James J. Murphy in *Three Medieval Rhetorical Arts*, ed. James J. Murphy (Berkeley and Los Angeles, 1971), pp. 5–25.

nakedly pragmatic. There is a minimum of prologue, and the whole tone of the treatise marks it as an elementary manual for students (*rudibus ministrare*), for use by those "who make learned the tongues of infants" (*qui linguas infancium facit disertas*).

The manual is divided into thirteen sections, the longest of which treats the *salutatio*. The matter of the salutation occupies nearly one-third of the book, again indicating the relative importance of that part of a letter. A brief list of the sections will give a quick idea of the contents.

   I. Prologue
  II. Definitions of terms
 III. Definition of "epistle"
 IV. The five parts of a letter: *salutatio, benevolentiae captatio, narratio, petitio, conclusio*
  V. *Salutatio*
 VI. *Benevolentiae captatio*
 VII. *Narratio*
VIII. *Petitio*
 IX. *Conclusio*
  X. The shortening of letters
 XI. The movement of parts
 XII. The "constitution" of letters
XIII. Variation in letters

The *Rationes dictandi* offers succinct definitions of each of the five parts of a letter. These definitions, appearing at the head of the sections, show readily the author's intentions:[57]

## II. What a written composition should be.

A written composition is a setting-forth of some matter in writing, proceeding in a suitable order. Or, a written composition is a suitable and fitting treatment of some matter, adapted to the matter itself. Or a written composition is a suitable and fitting written statement about something, either memorized or declared by speech or in writing.

Now, some written compositions are metrical, others rhythmic, others prosaic.

A metrical composition is a written presentation which is properly distinguished by prescribed measures of feet and duration.

A rhythmic composition is one which is bound together syllabically according to a fixed numerical rule.

---

[57] The translation is from Murphy, *Three Medieval Rhetorical Arts*, pp. 6–7, 16–19.

But since it is our intention to treat only prose composition, let us describe more carefully what it is and how it should be written.

A prose composition is a written presentation ignoring the measures of meter, and proceeding in a continuous and suitable order. Now, here let us describe the proper meaning of this first term, for, in Greek, *proson* is said to be "continuous." Then, we say that a written statement is "suitable" in which we treat the subject under discussion in words ordered according to the grammatical rules for prose or poetry.

Let us now examine particularly how to fashion this kind of composition, either in an approved and basic format or in accordance with circumstances.

The terms "approved and basic" (*recta et simplici*) are used at this point because the words of the writer might reach even the least educated or the most ignorant persons; for example, for this purpose I might say: "O loyal one and most beloved, I well believe that it is known to you what great trust I have in you concerning all my affairs."

By the term "accordance with circumstances" we mean a method for the more experienced writers. It is an apt accordance, a set of words ordered in a way different from ordinary syntax; it must by all means be made harmonious and clear, that is, like a flowing current.

Although we could discuss a correct arrangement of words at this point, even though that will be decided more by the ear than anyone's teaching could explain, nevertheless we have enough to do here simply to provide some form of introduction to those untrained in this art.

### III. The definition of a letter.

An epistle or letter, then, is a suitable arrangement of words set forth to express the intended meaning of its sender. Or in other words, a letter is a discourse composed of coherent yet distinct parts signifying fully the sentiments of its sender.

### IV. The parts of a letter.

There are, in fact, five parts of a letter: the Salutation, the Securing of Good-will, the Narration, the Petition, and the Conclusion.

### V. What the salutation is.

The Salutation is an expression of greeting conveying a friendly sentiment not inconsistent with the social rank of the persons involved. [With 20 examples.]

### VI. The securing of goodwill.

Now that these things have been explained, especially the varieties of salutations, let us turn to the Securing of Goodwill. The Securing of Goodwill (*benevolentiae captatio*) in a letter is a certain fit ordering of words effectively influencing the mind of the recipient.

### VII. The narration.

The Narration is the orderly account of the matter under discussion, or, even better, a presentation in such a way that the materials seem to present themselves. We should by all means run through such a Narration quickly and clearly for the advantage of the sender's cause.

Some Narrations are simple, others complex. A Narration is simple that is completed by the narration of only one matter. A Narration is complex, on the other hand, in which several matters are recounted.

Furthermore, some Narrations are written about the past, others about the present, and still others about the future. The subject of handling these various forms will be taken up later in its proper place in this book.

### VIII. The petition.

Now, that discourse is called the Petition in which we endeavor to call for something.

There are indeed nine species of Petition: supplicatory or didactic or menacing or exhortative or hortatory or admonitory or advisory or reproving or even merely direct.

### IX. The conclusion.

The Conclusion, of course, is the passage with which a letter is terminated.

It is customary for it to be used because it is offered to point out the usefulness or disadvantage possessed by the subjects treated in the letter. For example, if these topics have been treated at length and in a roundabout way in the Narration, these same things are here brought together in a small space and are thus impressed on the recipient's memory.

Sections X–XIII then deal summarily with ways to rearrange the parts of a letter to fit various circumstances. The last section, XIII, quotes from *Priscianus in constructionibus* (i.e., Priscian's *Ars grammatica* XVII–XVIII) to demonstrate the use of case and number in variations.[58] The most interesting aspect of these last four parts of the manual is that the anonymous author clearly sees the need for some flexibility in following the doctrine laid out so crisply in the earlier pages.

But this is no longer the rather humane catholicity of Alberic, nor even the frame of mind that leads Adalbertus to pay lip service to the *trivium* of

---

[58] Section XIII, "On the Variation of a Letter," actually deals with such grammatical matters rather than with major alterations in the parts of a letter.

grammar, rhetoric, and dialectic. The anonymous author of the *Rationes dictandi* concentrates on letters alone, and on the highly stylized "approved format" (*per rectam constructionem*) of the five letter parts that is now clearly an aspect of the Bolognese tradition. His only reason for discussing variation at all is that he believes letters may sometimes be composed in ways appropriate to circumstances (*per appositionem*). But the disproportionate space allotted to the five-part scheme shows that he regards that format to be the standard; indeed, "variation" is discussed entirely in terms of departures from that format.[59] The author does not explain, nor does he justify; the "approved format" is presented here as a simple fact. The matter is evidently far beyond the need for proof or justification. In only one place (*Cap*. VI) does the name of Cicero appear, and that is an apparent reference to the concept of *insinuatio* or indirect approach in the *exordium* of a speech.[60]

Some minor technical differences in the approved letter-writing format still occur in other works written in the region of Bologna, as in the anonymous *Precepta prosaici dictaminis secundum Tullium* (1138–52).[61] This author declares that there are two parts to the science, *salutatio et epistola*. He then proceeds to treat the salutation at some length, but when he turns to the parts of a letter it is evident that he intends to carry out the now-familiar pattern. His only substantial change, in fact, is to use the term *causae redditio* instead of *narratio*. He treats the *colores* briefly, and concludes with a number of model letters. Despite the use of Cicero's name in the title, the treatise is a typical Bolognese manual, and his subtle distinction in dividing the salutation from the letter proper did not find many imitators.

By about 1135, then, the basic doctrines of the *ars dictaminis* appear to well established in Bologna. The application of classical rhetorical theory to letter-writing, begun by Alberic in the 1080's, has acquired a life of its own without any further need for reference to Cicero. All after this is development, not innovation.

The most striking adaptation of classical rhetoric is seen in the five-part

---

[59] Cap. X (Rockinger, pp. 22–23), for instance, includes a discussion of *integra tamen et recte formata*.

[60] . . . videlicet ordine quo Tullius in rethoricis insinuat. *Ibid*., p. 19.

[61] Anonymous, *Die Precepta prosaici dictaminis secundum Tullium und die Konstanzer Briefsammlung*, ed. Franz-Josef Schmale (Bonn, 1950).

"approved format," which is clearly derived from an analogy to the Ciceronian six parts of an *oratio*. A comparison will reveal this very quickly:

| Ciceronian Parts of an Oration | Bolognese "Approved Format" for a Letter |
|---|---|
| *Exordium* | *Salutatio*, or formal vocative greeting to addressee |
| | *Captatio benevolentiae*, or introduction |
| *Divisio* | (Omitted as a separate part) |
| *Narratio* | *Narratio*, or narration of circumstances leading to petition |
| *Confirmatio* | *Petitio*, or presentation of requests |
| *Refutatio* | (Omitted as a separate part) |
| *Peroratio* | *Conclusio*, or final part |

It is immediately apparent that the medieval *ars dictaminis* has split the Ciceronian *exordium* into two parts and has assigned its three traditional functions—to make the audience attentive, docile, and well-disposed—to two different parts of the letter.[62] Here, the *salutatio* secures attention, and the aptly titled *captatio benevolentiae* serves the other two purposes. This is a major difference; the whole subsequent history of the *ars dictaminis* indicates that these first two parts of a letter were the most important in the eyes of dictaminal theorists.

The *narratio*, which is often defined in terms reminiscent of Cicero, receives little attention compared to that usually accorded the *salutatio* and *captatio benevolentiae*. Another striking difference from the classical *dispositio* is the comparative derogation of the argumentative portions of the discourse. The *petitio* ordinarily receives very little attention from authors of the *artes dictaminis,* many of them remarking in effect that little can be said because circumstances differ so much. Consequently there is virtually no theory of the *petitio,* and this part of the letter continues to be treated almost entirely from the viewpoint of *dispositio* rather than *confirmatio*. The same can be said about the *conclusio;* very little space is given to conclusions in most manuals, some authors even going so far as to list a mere set of "farewell" (*valete*) formulas.

The matter-of-fact tone of the anonymous *Rationes dictandi* demonstrates the triumph of these doctrines at Bologna in the 1130's. A further proof is seen in the rapid spread of these same ideas into France and then

---

[62] For example, *Rhetorica ad Herennium* I.iv.6: "Its purpose is to enable us to have hearers who are attentive, receptive, and well-disposed."

into Germany and England by the end of the century. Although little is known about the actual means of transmission of the *ars dictaminis* into the north, the *Introductiones prosaici dictaminis* (c. 1144) of Bernard of Bologna may furnish us with an example of the way that the manuals were probably carried over the Alps. Charles H. Haskins has shown that the *Introductiones* was composed in the Romagna of northern Italy, revised in the same region by the author by 1152, reached France by 1159 (probably by 1152), and was known in the Cologne region of Germany by 1167.[63] Bernard, who calls himself *dictaminum professionis minister,* follows the basic doctrines of the *Rationes dictandi.* One notable addition, however, is a section on style headed *De diversis modis dictandi,* which treats the three Ciceronian levels.

It would be tedious to discuss every letter-writing manual written in the middle ages. Indeed, no complete list of authors of *artes dictaminis* has yet been compiled. Noel Denholm-Young has listed those popular in England, and a number of individual treatises have been edited in recent years. Some authors, like the "Master A" listed by Haskins, remain mere names to us. However, a considerable number of works, especially in Italy and Germany, remain unedited at this time.[64]

Nevertheless, there is ample evidence available to reconstruct the history of the *ars dictaminis* from the time it reached full form in the anonymous *Rationes dictandi* about 1135. Its history after 1135 has three main phases, as geographical.and even national developments produced variations in emphasis: the French-English, the German, and the second Italian phases. The concern with the rhythmical prose style called the *cursus* has its origins in the second Italian phase, but since it cuts across geographical lines it is best treated separately.

French interest in dictamen centered at first in the valley of the Loire, especially in the schools at Orléans. The French *artes,* consequently, are marked by a more humanistic flavor than the Lombardic handbooks. In France the dictaminal art retains close ties to the *ars grammatica,* with its interest in literary *auctores.* Most of the major French grammarians therefore include sections on dictamen, so that any complete discussion of the French phase must include treatment of important writers like John

---

[63] Haskins, "An Italian Master Bernard," in *Essays in History Presented to Reginald Lane Poole,* ed. Henry W. C. Davis (Oxford, 1927), pp. 211–26; the article is summarized in Haskins, *Studies in Medieval Culture,* pp. 182–83.

[64] Professors Virgilio Pini and Giuseppe Vecchi, both of the University of Bologna, have indicated their intention of compiling a master list of Italian works.

of Garland and Geoffrey of Vinsauf, as well as lesser-known figures like Bernard de Meung. Orléans even developed its own form of the *cursus,* which rivaled the Curial form in later centuries.

A satisfactory history of French dictamen is not yet available. It is difficult to determine the exact date of the first Orléanistic *ars dictaminis,* except that it is probably no earlier than about 1150. In any case the imported doctrine certainly came under the humanistic influence of teachers like Arnoulf of Orléans (fl. 1175).[65] The most influential of the dictaminal writers from Orléans was Bernard de Meung, whose *Summa dictaminis* was widely circulated. The Prologue to his treatise may be compared to that of the *Rationes dictandi* to indicate the difference between the traditions of Orléans and Bologna.

> In the first place, taking up the doctrine of *dictamen* and presenting this book, we ought to know what dictamen is and what are its kinds. Dictamen is a literary account brilliant with the beauty of words and adorned with colors of thought. "Literary account" is the generic term; the rest is *differentia.*
>
> Know that there are two ornaments of *dictamen,* ornaments of words and ornaments of thoughts, considering which much is said in the art of rhetoric. There are two kinds of *dictamen,* metrical and prosaic. The metrical kind is one in which the shortening and lengthening of syllables is observed, such as the Virgilian, Ovidian, and others in this mode. The prosaic kind is where the principle of meter is not followed, such as the Ciceronian, Sallustian, Gregorian, and others writing in prose. There are many kinds of prosaic *dictamen:* decretals, precepts, privileges, homilies, epistles, and many others. Leaving aside the others, let us take up the epistle. . . .[66]

---

[65] The best single treatment of these developments may be found in De Ghellinck, *L'Essor de la littérature latine,* I, 54–68.

[66] Ad doctrinam dictaminum accedentes et dantes operam, primo loco debemus cognoscere quid sit dictamen et quid sit eius species. Dictamen est litteralis editio verborum venustate eggregia, sententiarum coloribus adornata. Litteralis editio est pro genere, cetera pro differentiis.

Sciendum est quod duo sunt ornatus dictaminis, ornatus verborum et ornatus sententiarum, de quibus plenius agitur in arte rethorica. Due sunt species dictaminis, metricum et prosaicum. Metricum in quo observatur correptio et productio sillibarum, quale est Virgilianum, Ovidianum, etc. huius modi. Prosaicum est ubi metri ratio non servatur, quale est Tullianum, Salustianum, Gregorianum et aliorum prosaice scribentium. Prosaici dictaminis multe sunt species: decretum, preceptum, privilegium, omelia, epistole et plures alie. Pretermissis aliis, agamus de epistola. . . .

Text in Leopold Delisle, "Notice sur une 'Summa dictaminis' jadis conservée à Beauvais," *Notices et extraits* 36 (1899), 171–205. For a formulary by Bernard, see L. Auvray, *Documents orléanais du XIIe et du XIIIe siècle: extraits du formulaire de Bernard de Meung* (Orléans 1892). Also see Franz-Josef Schmale, "Der Briefsteller Bernhards von Meung," *Mitteilungen des Instituts für österreichische Geschichtsforschung* 66 (1958), 1–28.

In other words, Bernard de Meung continues to recognize the whole spectrum of types of composition long after the Bolognese had turned to an exclusive concern with the letters themselves.

The definition of the term *dictamen* is also characteristic of Orléans. Whereas the *Rationes dictandi* offers three somewhat ambivalent definitions, Bernard uses language reminiscent of the definition of *elocutio* in the *Rhetorica ad Herennium*. After a discussion of the five parts of a letter, Bernard provides a lengthy treatment of the *cursus* in the Orléanistic manner.

Rockinger prints an *Ars dictandi aurelianensis* of uncertain date, but probably from the period 1200–1210.[67] This has the same definition as in Bernard de Meung, although its author goes on to say that the species of prose dictamen include *oracio, rethorica, epistole*. (The meaning of *rethorica* in this context is not clear.) Otherwise the doctrine is the familiar one of the five parts of a letter, with the *salutatio* of course receiving the lion's share of attention. The author uses the term *exordium* instead of the Bolognese *captatio benevolentiae*, perhaps because of the strong Ciceronian flavor that still attaches to Orléanistic works like this one.

The treatise does indicate, however, a commentative habit of the northern schools that is lacking in the Bolognese manuals on the subject. Ordinarily the Bolognese definitions are declarative sentences without systematic proofs or justifications, especially after the doctrine is solidifiied in the 1130's. In the anonymous *Summa dictaminis aurelianensis,* however, the separate terms of a definition are frequently dissected and explained one by one, in a manner very like that used in the commentaries on Cicero's rhetoric at Chartres and elsewhere earlier in the same century. Note the handling of the term *epistola:*

> Concerning the epistle. An epistle is defined thus: An epistle is a coherent discourse, by its parts, suitably arranged, signifying fully a state of mind. I said "coherent discourse" to the exclusion of those which are not discourses. I said "its parts" because there are five parts of *dictamen:* salutation, exordium, narration, petition, and conclusion. I said "suitably arranged" because that which is first in *dictamen* should not be middle or last, or the opposite. I said "signifying fully a state of mind" because it ought to declare the mind of him who sends it to the mind of the one to whom it is sent.[68]

---

[67] Rockinger, *Briefsteller,* pp. 103–14. If this was indeed written around 1210, the anonymous author was a contemporary of Geoffrey of Vinsauf and John of Garland.

[68] *De epistola.* Epistola sic diffinitur. Epistola est oracio congrua suis e partibus convenienter conposita affectum mentis plene significans. Oracio congrua dixi ad

The analytic method is of course analogous to methods of Scriptural exegesis popular with preachers of the same period. But in this particular dictaminal manual it surely demonstrates the academic origin of the work itself, even though there is no signature or even dedication to indicate its origin.

Some further, indirect indication of French dictaminal tendencies may be gleaned from the manual written in England about 1187 by Peter of Blois, a transplanted Frenchman. His *De arte dictandi rethorice* did not have wide circulation, and indeed survives to my knowledge in only one fourteenth-century manuscript now at Cambridge; only a few lines of the Prologue have been published.[69] He credits a "Master Bernard" with writing a book on dictamen which he uses as the base for his own treatise, and cites the teachings of Tours as well. The identity of this Bernard, evidently a Frenchman, is not further discussed, although it is tempting to equate him with Bernard Silvester, who is reputed to have written a treatise on poetical dictamen, now lost. In any case Peter of Blois was associated with John of Salisbury at Chartres, and may have been his student as well.

It is evident at once that Peter sees the *ars dictaminis* within a larger grammatical and rhetorical framework than his contemporaries in Bologna. Although he states in his Prologue that his book follows the precepts of *dictatores,* he begins his text with a reference to Victorinus' commentary on the *De inventione* of Cicero.[70] Moreover, he includes both Horace and Cicero in his discussion of the grammatical matters that precede his exposition of the five parts of a letter. His treatment of metaphor (*translatio*) includes a five-member division of that trope. Nor does

---

exclusionem earum que non sunt oraciones. Suis e partibus dixi, quia quinque sunt partes dictaminis: salutacio, exordium, narracio, peticio, et conclusio. Convenienter conposita dixi, quia quod primum est in dictamine non debet fieri medium vel ultimum, vel e converso. Affectum mentis plene significans, quia ille qui mittit illi cui mittitur animum suum debet declarare. *Ibid.,* p. 103.

[69] Cambridge University Library MS. Dd.ix.38, fols. 115-121. For the Prologue see Migne, *PL,* Vol. 207, cols. 1127-28. I am currently preparing a critical edition of the Cambridge manuscript. Though Peter's preceptive treatise did not seem to attract much attention—I know of only two references to it, both from fifteenth-century writers—the letter collection attributed to him was enormously popular, surviving in at least two hundred manuscripts. See R. W. Southern, "Peter of Blois: A Twelfth-Century Humanist?" in *Medieval Humanism and Other Studies* (Oxford, 1970), pp. 105-32.

[70] *De tribus distinctionibus Victorini super rethorica.* . . . Cambridge MS. fol. 115ra. Southern notes (*Medieval Humanism,* pp. 108-113) that Peter was a student in Bologna in the early 1150's and later may have taught grammar and rhetoric at Tours before going to stay in England in 1174.

he parrot the Italian names for types of prose writing, for he completes a section titled *De 5 varietatibus dictandi* by listing the following species: *epistola, historia, testamentum, invectiva, et expositio qua glosa dicitur.* He notes that an *epistola* is also sometimes called a "letter" (*littera*). After describing the five parts of a letter, he concludes with a brief discussion of notarial matters.

Two things are clear from Peter's treatise. For one thing, he is evidently familiar with the Bolognese tradition. For another, he sees letter-writing as only one of the five main types of prose writing. His is no nakedly schematic handbook like that of Hugh of Bologna, and we can only regard as ironic Peter's admonition to his readers to join in the literary "feasts" (*epulas*) provided by the notaries of the Roman chancery.[71] His grammatical concerns no doubt reflect the teaching of Chartres and Bec, and his treatise matches the literary tone of the dictaminal productions of Orléans as well. Another, native English writer associated with the *artes poetriae,* Gervase de Melkley, includes a section on dictamen in his *Ars versificatoria* around the year 1200. Nevertheless his is a very brief and sketchy resumé buried in what is essentially a work on verse-writing.[72] We have already noted that John of Garland makes *dictamen prosaicum* one of the seven sections in his *De arte metrica, prosaica, et rithmica* early in the thirteenth century. Geoffrey of Vinsauf, one of the most catholic of the writers of the *artes poetriae,* was possibly the author of an *ars dictaminis,* now lost.[73]

There is no record of the formal teaching of the new art at the Uni-

---

[71] . . . necnon et Romanae cancellariae notarios ad suas epulas invitamus . . . . (fol. 115[ra]). Peter also notes (fol. 118[v]) that if he had more time and space he would discuss other kinds of writing as well in greater length: scilicet historia, invectiva, expositio vel glosa, causa, doctrina, mutua collocucio. He actually does devote two columns to these six types, noting in connection with the last that good examples can be found in Cicero, Seneca, Terence, Horace, Persius, and Juvenal. This is a far cry from the naked pragmatism of Bolognese *dictatores.*

[72] Text in *Gervais von Melkey Ars poetica,* ed. Hans-Jurgen Grabener, *Forschungen zur Romanischen Philologie* 17 (Münster in Westfalen, 1968), esp. pp. 224–29. Since Gervase names Geoffrey of Vinsauf as well as earlier authors like Bernard Silvester and Matthew of Vendôme, it would seem reasonable to date his own work after Geoffrey's *Poetria nova* (c. 1210).

[73] Faral (*Les arts poétiques du XIIe et du XIIIe siècle* [Paris, 1924,] p. 22) regarded this as one of the "attributions incertaines." However, Vincenzo Licitra has edited a *Summa de arte dictandi* (c. 1188–90) attributed in the text to *Gaufredo, veneranda bononia.* Licitra is unable to decide whether this could be a work of Vinsauf. See Vincenzo Licitra, "La *Summa de arte dictandi* di Maestro Goffredo," *Studi medievali,* 3d series, no. 7 (1966), 865–913. For a critique of the edition, see Franz Josef Worstbrock, "Zu Galfrids Summa de arte dictandi," *Deutsches Archiv für Erforschung des Mittelalters* 23 (1967), 549–52.

versity of Paris, although Paetow notes that Garland's writing may indicate some active discussion of it in that city around the turn of the century. Earlier, as Alexandre Clerval has shown, a letter collection and two treatises were associated with the school at Chartres.[74] Moreover, Henri d'Andeli's *La battaille des VII arts*[75] may throw further light on the rivalry between French and Italian rhetoricians of the thirteenth century. The satire pits the "authors"—that is, "literature" or "grammar"—as exemplified in the school of Orléans, against the antiliterary forces of Parisian dialectic. D'Andeli views rhetoric as an Italian product, citing *Li Lombart dame Rectorique* (v. 224) and *chevaliers Lombars / Que Rectorique ot amenez* (vv. 68–69). For him, the dictaminal products of Orléans did not loom large, or else he recognized the ultimately Lombard origin of such works.

The first French vernacular treatment of *dictamen* occurs in a work written in the 1260's by a temporarily exiled Italian, Brunetto Latini. Latini does not present a typical manual. Instead, in his *Trésor* he outlines the general field of Ciceronian rhetoric and then applies it to letter-writing two ways. For one thing, he uses the terms *de parler* and *escrire* interchangeably. Then he prefaces his discussion of *ordre* with this statement: "Now the masters teach that the science of rhetoric has two forms, one which consists in speaking orally, and another which consists in speaking by letters; but the doctrine is common to both. . . ."[76] Later in the *Trésor* Latini notes that letters generally have five parts whereas Cicero calls for six in an oration. This presents no problem to him, for he points out that in a letter the part called *demande* (i.e., the *petitio*) includes both the *confermemens* and *deffermemens* of an oration (iii.16).

The constant grammatical concern of Gallic writers in this field is further demonstrated by the four-part *Summa* (1252) of Pons (or Sponcius) of Provence. His model letters are dedicated to the students of Orléans. A manuscript now in the British Museum (Arundel 514) contains four works of Pons which, taken together, furnish the entire equipment needed for teaching the *ars dictaminis*: (1) *Summa dictaminis magistri*

---

[74] A. Clerval, *Les Ecoles de Chartres au moyen âge* (Paris, n.d.).

[75] Text and translation in Louis J. Paetow, *Two Medieval Satires on the University of Paris: La Battaille des VII Ars of Henri d'Andeli and the Morale Scolarium of John of Garland* (Berkeley, 1914), pp. 37–60.

[76] Or dist le mestres que le science de rectorique est en ii manieres, une ki est in disant de bouche et une autre que l'on mande par letres; mais li enseignement sont commun. Brunetto Latini, *Li livres dou Tresor*, ed. Francis J. Carmody, University of California Publications in Modern Philology 22 (Berkeley, 1948), III.3.

*poncii provincialis de competenti dogmate,* including the five parts of a letter and a discussion of the *cursus* (fols. 54–64); (2) *Summa de constructione,* on prose composition (fols. 64–69); (3) *Epistolarium,* a series of model letters (fols. 69–95); and (4) *Libellus de cartis,* on drawing up formal documents (fols. 95–99). We are already familiar with the practice of attaching model letter collections to an *ars dictaminis,* and even in France it is not unusual to find cartulary instructions included as well for practical reasons. But the deliberate addition of a purely grammatical work on *constructio* is a feature of French dictamen writers which is seldom found among the Italians. The title "Construction" is taken from the popular name given to the last two books of Priscian's *Ars grammatica,* the *Priscianellus* or *Priscianus minor* (Books XVII–XVIII), more commonly known as *Liber Prisciani de constructionibus.* Pons's reasons for including the treatise on composition appear in his Prologue (fol. 64^vb):

> Because it is necessary for *dictatores* to know how to compose Latin writings both coherently and ornately—and in this consists the whole dictaminal science—in construction as well as in ornament, and since ornament was fully treated in my book on dictamen beginning *De competenti dogmate,* I, Master Pons of Provence, who wrote the book just named for the benefit of my young students, now transmit a slight though complete book concerning construction. Know therefore that construction in grammar is said to be in three modes. . . .[77]

Pons then explains that grammar names three types of constructions—acts, discourses, and arrangements of words. It is this last that concerns him—what he terms in his conclusion *compositio ex recto et obliquo.*

By contrast, the Italian *dictatores* never seem to be comfortable with the problem matter of composition, or at least with the grammatical lore

---

[77] Quoniam dictatoribus est necessarium scire componere latinitates congrue et ornate, et in hoc consistat tota scientia dictatoria, in constructione videlicet et ornatu, et de ornatu plene traditus sit in summa dictaminis *De competenti dogmate,* ego magister Sponcius provincialis, qui composui summam superius nominatam ad utilitatem meorum scolarium novellorum, trado summam de constructione levissimam et perfectam. Scias igitur quod constructio dicitur in gramatica tribus modis. . . British Museum MS. Arundel 514, fol. 64^vb. The manuscript (fols. 54^va–64^vb) was written in the south of France in the late thirteenth century. Extracts from the *Summa . . . de competenti* are printed in Charles Fierville, *Une Grammaire latine inédite du XIII^e siècle* (Paris, 1886), Appendix I, pp. 175–77; and other short excerpts appear in Charles Thurot, "Notices et extraits de divers manuscrits latins pour servir à l'histoire des doctrines grammaticales au moyen âge," *Notices et extraits* 22 (1868), 1–592; reprinted Frankfurt on the Main, 1964, p. 38.

dealing with composition. Alberic of Monte Cassino, of course, wrote in a broadly based humanistic tradition, but it may be recalled that by 1135, with the anonymous *Rationes dictandi,* purely grammatical matters were relegated to the comparative limbo of "variations" in letters. Later they nearly disappeared from Italian *artes.* The highly specialized Italian manuals tended to become self-sufficient, and ultimately tried to absorb extraneous grammatical and rhetorical lore rather than acknowledge the other fields as separate; this development is a part of Italian dictaminal history to be discussed shortly, but is worth mentioning here for an illuminating comparison. The continuing influence of *ars grammatica* in France (and consequently in England) may help to explain, also, why the rhythmical *cursus* found far less favor in the northern countries than it did among the *dictatores* in Italy, who almost deliberately cut themselves off from the standard grammatical tradition. The *De constructione* of Pons, then, may be taken as a further indication of French grammatical concern.

One additional item may be noted in Pons's treatment of the five parts of a letter. He names the second part as follows: *secunda exordium sive proverbium* (fol. 54^ra^). The term *exordium* (instead of *captatio benevolentiae*) is also found in the *Ars dictandi aurelianensis* noted earlier, which was clearly derived directly from Ciceronian rhetoric. The insertion of the term *proverbium* as a third alternative form is, however, a new element. This whole matter of the doctrine of proverbs in dictaminal treatises is as yet only partly explored, despite several studies.[78] Ancient writers like Demetrius had suggested the inclusion of *sententiae* in private letters, but of course without the rigid spatial-locational demands common in medieval letter-writing theory. Cicero and others had proposed the *exordium* of a speech as an appropriate place for sententious utterances, largely for the purpose of achieving what Aristotle called *ethos.* Nevertheless, there was not in ancient times any clear-cut doctrine on the matter, and the use of *proverbia* or other sententious matter generally remained a matter of discretion rather than precept.

The medieval theory of the literary application of proverbs may be seen in such writers as Matthew of Vendôme (*Ars versificatoria,* pp. 106 ff), Geoffrey of Vinsauf (*Poetria nova,* vv. 180–202), and Eberhard

---

[78] For example, Giuseppe Vecchi, "Il 'proverbio' nella pratica letteraria dei dettatori della scuola di Bologna," *Studi mediolatini e volgari* 2 (1954), 283–302.

the German (*Laborintus,* vv. 293–294).[79] The fourteenth-century preaching theorist John of Wales recommends the use of proverbs to introduce
a Scriptural theme. Certainly there is nothing new about the deploying
of concise aphoristic wisdom, and the practice is found in even the most
unsophisticated literatures.

What occurs in Pons, however, and in other writers from time to time
on both sides of the Alps, is the suggestion that *proverbia* have a specific function in a specific place—namely, as a part of the formal introduction in an epistle. In other words, proverbs have an exordial function.
But this is just about the extent of agreement on the matter. Although
many writers discuss the use of proverbs in letters, they differ in their
views; consequently it seems fair to say that the theory of proverbs in
the medieval *ars dictaminis* is one that was of only tangential interest to
the theorist and for that reason did not receive complete development.
The mild disagreements among the *dictatores* were not explicitly resolved
—perhaps a sign that the question was not one which in their eyes demanded resolution or, perhaps, that the matter was so obvious that it
needed little further justification.

However, a number of dictamen-centered proverb collections were compiled during the middle ages. Sometimes these are attached to an existing
*ars dictaminis,* as in the case of the 171 proverbs which appear in the
*Candelabrum* of Bene of Florence. Sometimes they appear as separate,
if related, compilations, as in the massive collection of "Simon O" (in
both Latin and English) found in a manuscript of the John Rylands
Library, or in the Latin–Italian collection of Guido Faba.[80] The very
fact that the proverbs sometimes occur in bilingual form would seem to
indicate a relation to vernacular literatures. The usual dictaminal attention to *salutationes* and *captationes benevolentiae,* of course, provided
further opportunity for writers to include some proverb examples as
integral parts of the manuals themselves. In any case the exordial position
of *proverbia* in letters was clearly established by the early thirteenth
century, and very little theoretical discussion was devoted to the subject

---

[79] For these works see above, Chapter IV, pp. 163–82. Curtius notes that Hugh
of Trimberg uses the term *proverbia* to denote "sentences." Ernst Curtius, *European
Literature and the Latin Middle Ages* (New York, 1953), p. 58n.

[80] W. A. Pantin, "A Medieval Treatise on Letter-Writing, with Examples, from
the Rylands Latin MS. 394," *Bulletin of the John Rylands Library* 13 (1929),
326–82; and Virgilio Pini, "La 'Summa de vitiis et virtutibus' di Guido Faba,"
*Quadrivium* 1 (1956), 41–152.

after that. Pons of Provence is therefore in the mainstream of the dictaminal movement when he describes the *proverbium* as an alternate form of *exordium*.

The *Summa grammaticalis* of "Master William" of Provençal,[81] dating from around 1220, makes even more explicit the grammatical background of the northern *ars dictaminis*. The work is in three parts: (1) *De declinatione* (also termed *Copia nominum*), which provides about three thousand examples of names to illustrate the four Latin declensions; (2) *De regimine,* which lays out a brief guide to the rules for cases of words used in conjunction with other words; and (3) *De dictamine,* a typical letter-writing manual. It is obvious that Master William sees the *ars dictaminis* as a part of grammatical lore, as even his title indicates. In *De dictamine* he lists six parts of a letter (adding *proverbium* to the usual five), although he mentions that the Roman style does not often use proverbs—*in literalis curialibus raro utimur proverbiis.* This would seem to be another example of a sense of distinction between an Italian and a northern usage. Except for this change from the traditional views, William's handbook is typical in its emphasis on salutations and in his provision of specific examples of phrasing for various situations (e.g., *peticio scolaris*). There are no model letters. The manual's inclusion as part of a *Summa grammaticalis,* however, indicates an attitude on the part of William that is far different from his contemporaries who were *dictatores* in Bologna and Florence.

Another northern work, perhaps of Parisian origin, bears the misleading title of *Libellus de dictamine et dictatorie sillogismo.*[82] Actually there is very little of the syllogism in it, and the rhetorical bias of the anonymous author is indicated not only by his Ciceronian references but by his use of Quintilian (sic) as an authority on the syllogism in *inventio.* The book's title no doubt reflects an attempt to give the treatise an aura of dialectical respectability, and may be compared to similar titles in the field of the *ars praedicandi.*[83] While there is little evidence to identify the author of the treatise or his date, the prologue contains the phrase

---

[81] Charles Samaran, "Une 'Summa grammaticalis' du XIII^e siècle avec gloses provençales," *Archivum Latinitatis Medii Aevi* (Bulletin du Cange) 31 (1961), 157–224.

[82] Paris, Bibliothèque Nationale MS. Lat. 16252, fols. 29^rb–38^vb, and B. N. MS. Lat. 14357, fols. 123^r–130^v.

[83] For instance, Jean de Chalons, *Ars brevis et clara faciendi sermones secundum formam syllogisticam.* See below, pp. 336–37.

*dictaminum margaritam* which also appears in Pons of Provence's prologue to a letter-collection (*dictamina*).[84] Moreover, one of the two Paris
manuscripts once belonged to the library of Saint-Victor in Paris, as did
the *dictamina* of Pons. In any case, the *Libellus . . . sillogismo,* despite
its title, maintains a strong rhetorical flavor not markedly different from
that found in Peter of Blois or Pons of Provence.

The ultimate development of the northern milieu, however, is best
seen in the *Compendium rhetorice,* written at Paris in 1332 by an unknown Cistercian. In effect, he uses the form of a dictaminal manual to
introduce a treatise dealing mostly with style (*elocutio*). The *Compendium rhetorice* survives in Bodleian MS. Lat. Misc. f. 49, formerly
at the College of Cluny, Paris. The rhetorical doctrine is solidly Ciceronian, with a number of direct quotations from the *Rhetorica ad Herennium,* but the treatment is strictly medieval. The first leaf of the manuscript, which might have contained a hint of authorship, has been lost,
and the title must be inferred from a passage which refers to *presens
compendium rhetorice* (fol. 7ʳ).[85]

The treatise is divided into three books. The first (fols. 2–12) deals
with the relation of *elocutio* to dictamen and the five parts of a letter;
the second book (fols. 12ᵛ–32ᵛ), the longest part of the work, bears the
title *Liber secundus qui est de coloribus verborum et sensiarum*; the
third book (fols. 33ʳ–47ᵛ) bears no title but deals generally with the
skills and knowledge which a *dictator* ought to possess, including a
mastery of "modes of amplification."

Evidently the lost first page contained definitions of *inventio* and *dispositio.* Then the author continues with *elocutio,* one part of which he
declares to be written discourse (*dictamen*) and another part of which
is spoken discourse (*oratio*). The definitions of style, memory, and delivery are taken almost verbatim from the *Rhetorica ad Herennium.*
Then he explains the qualities of the ideal *dictator:*

> From these qualities it is plain what a *dictator* ought to be: in inventing,
> subtle; in arranging, prudent; in remembering, skillful; in styling, distin-

---

[84] B. N. MS. Lat. 16252, fol. 29ʳᵇ: Repromissam dictaminum margaritam. Cf.
Pons of Provence: Incipiunt dictamina magistri Poncii universis scholaribus qui
decorari cupiunt epistolaris dictaminis scientia gloriosa P. Magister in dictamine
salutem et neglectis actorum fabulis ad margaritam dictaminis properare. Quoted
in Thurot, "Notices et extraits," p. 39.

[85] Apparently only one leaf is missing, since the second (?) sheet continues a
discussion of arrangement from the preceding page(s). The scale of the brief
definitions of fols. 2 ff. indicates that the opening section must have been very short.

guished; in delivering, temperate. These are inseparable, and reinforce each other mutually. Insofar as our present work is concerned, it is the same to say "to be eloquent" as to say "to write *dictamen*." As for the art that is called *dictatoria,* it is not rhetoric itself but a part of it called style, which is divided into five parts as *dictamen* is, as we said earlier. And concerning the first part, that is, the Salutation, let us say a little. . . .[86]

In other words, this author names the five traditional canons of rhetoric, but in a novel departure from tradition makes the *ars dictaminis* a part of *elocutio* or style. Among other things, this of course places the *dispositio* of a letter under style—but this is obviously not a matter of concern to the writer. He is far more concerned with discussing anything that will aid the *dictator perfectus.* He cites a larger number of authors than is usual for a dictamen manual, to begin with: Cicero (*In paradoxis* as well as *De inventione* and *Rhetorica ad Herennium*), Horace, Quintilian, Donatus, Boethius, Bede, Isidore of Seville, Evrard of Bethune (*Graecismus*), Sidonius, Gregory the Great, Pope Clement IV, and four dictaminal writers—Peter de Vinea, Richard de Pophis, Thomas of Capua, and John of Sicily. Many medieval treatises of an eclectic nature are nothing but a string of consecutive quotations or copyings of various *auctores;* the author of the *Compendium rhetorice,* on the other hand, is able to write meaningfully from what seems to be a fairly wide knowledge of his sources. In discussing composition according to Donatus, for instance, he notes that the writings of Boethius bear out what Donatus had said (fol. 8ᵛ). When he introduces the subject of *tropi,* he notes that both Bede and Isidore of Seville agree with the ancient definition of a trope (20ᵛ).[87]

Another feature unusual for a dictaminal work is the author's borrowings from doctrines of the *artes praedicandi* or preaching manuals. He does so in two ways. First of all, he says that many rhetorical precepts apply to oral as well as written composition, that both preaching (*in themathe proponenda*) and the letter (*epistole*) can benefit from using *argumentatio* learned from rhetoric (fol. 41ᵛ). His stress on letter-writing,

---

[86] Ex productis colligitur que dictator debet esse. In inveniendi subtilis, in disponendo cautus. In memorando solers. In eloquendo conspicuus. In pronunciando modestus. Que cum sint inseparabilia et ad invicem colligata. De elocutione ad presens principalius prosequitus que idem est quod dictamine et eloqui quod dictare. Unde ars ista que dictatoria nuncupatur, non est ipsa rethorica sed pars eius, elocutio nuncupata, que in quinque partes dividitur. Ut dictamine est supra. Et primo de prima parte, i.e. salutatione, pauca dicetur. . . . (fols. 1ʳ–1ᵛ)

[87] . . . autem ut Ysidorus cui ven. beda concordat, dictio translata a propria significatione ad non propriam ornatus necessitatis.

however, is seen in the same passage when he concludes that not only the parts of a letter but other kinds of composition as well depend upon such things as *loci: Ex hiis et cetera salutatio num exordium, narrationum, et aliarum parcium epistole sive alterius compositionis tota vis et natura dependet.* But it is in the cross-relation of *exemplum* and *allegoria*— both topics unusual for dictamen manuals—that the relation to preaching theory is most clearly seen. Both instances occur in Book Two, which deals mainly with tropes and figures. The figure *exemplum* is taken from *Rhetorica ad Herennium* (IV.xl.x.62), as one of the *colores sentenciarum.* The writer goes beyond the simple paraphrases of definition accorded other figures to stress the medieval distinction between *exempla* with names and *exempla* without names—undoubtedly an echo of preaching theory. The second case (*allegoria*) is clearly a borrowing from both the *ars praedicandi* (the four "senses") and the *ars grammatica* of Donatus (seven "species"):

> Allegory (*permutation*) is a trope in which one thing is shown in the word and another in the meaning. Its species are many, the most prominent of which are irony, antiphrasis, enigma, charentismos, paroemia, sarcasm, and antismos. . . . allegory differs from metaphor in that in metaphor a designation already understood is meant to apply to some novel significance. . . . in allegory the signification of the term itself is not changed; rather, some new other thing is given to be understood by it.[88]

The author continues by saying that allegory is useful for writing and speaking, even though its primary use is for understanding Scripture. He then defends the four "senses": "The allegorical, that which is to be understood or believed. The anagogical, what is to be sought. The tropological, what is to be done for good works." [89] The religious background of this section is further attested by a marginal note opposite the definition of allegory: *de Christo vel ecclesia.*

The unknown author of the *Compendium rhetorice,* then, has used the occasion of a dictaminal treatise to bring a wide range of rhetorical lore to bear on the problem of composition. The format of the *ars dictaminis* is for him only an occasion, or an excuse, for a rather free

---

[88] Allegoria (permutatio) est tropis quo aliud in verbi et aliud in sentencia demonstratur. Huius species sunt multe, equibus eminent, ut hyronia, antifrasis, enigma, carentismos, paroemia, sarcasmus, et antismos. . . . Differt allegoria a metaphora que in metaphora vocabulum dudum ad aliquid significandus inventum. . . . In allegoria vero significatio vocabuli non mutata per rem ipsius alia rea datur intelligi. (fol. 24ᵛ)

[89] Quia hystoricus docet quid sit sciendum. Allegoricus quid intelligendus vel credendus. Anagogicus quid appetendus. Tropologica quid faciendus que opera bona. (fol. 24ᵛ)

discussion. Given the comparatively humanistic framework within which northern writers treated the *ars dictaminis,* this would seem to have been a very logical development.

The same tendency appears later in England in the *De moderno dictamine* (1405) of Thomas Merke.[90] Except for the writings of Peter of Blois and the brief remarks of Gervase of Melkley, there seems to have been very little native English production of the *artes dictaminis.* A number of Italian manuals circulated in England, as Denholm-Young has shown, but by and large there was not a great deal of interest in the subject. Oxford records show, for instance, that the epistolary art was taught only by private teachers outside the university, and then not until the middle of the fourteenth century. Thomas Sampson (fl. 1380) and John de Briggis (after 1351) wrote brief manuals imitative of Italian treatises, but the case of Thomas Merke is rather different. While in residence at Queen's College, Oxford, from 1401 to 1406 during a period of political turmoil, he wrote a work which is ostensibly an *ars dictaminis* but is in reality a general treatise on prose composition. He names or quotes from a number of authors not usually cited in dictamen manuals: Alanus de Insulis, Evrard of Bethune, Gervase de Melkley, Horace, Cassiodorus, Statius, Bede, and a certain unidentified Bartholemeus. But most striking of all is his use of Geoffrey of Vinsauf's *Poetria nova,* which he quotes or names a total of 24 times. Merke's distinction between the "integral" and "accidental" parts of a letter is, again, something quite different from the routine manuals. He does not abandon the five-part structure of a letter—indeed, his treatise is organized around it—but rather he takes advantage of the various parts to expand his remarks beyond the usual range of the Italian *dictatores.* Nevertheless, Merke's treatise is an isolated phenomenon. England was generally an importer and not a producer of works in the area of *ars dictaminis.* While the *cursus* itself found some popularity in England, the theory of letterwriting did not. A number of letter collections circulated, and these *dictamina* probably supplied the needs of Englishmen interested in the matter. As one medieval writer phrased it, "The English do not love public documents."[91]

In Germany, meanwhile, the Italian tradition continued in force. Ger-

---

[90] For a discussion of Merke and a list of ten manuscripts, see James J. Murphy, "Rhetoric in Fourteenth-Century Oxford," *Medium Aevum* 34 (1965), 1–20. To this list of manuscripts may now be added two more in Trinity College Library, Dublin, Nos. 343 and 424.

[91] John of Bologna, *Summa notarie,* in Rockinger, *Briefsteller,* p. 604.

man dictaminal writings are marked by two dominant features—the slavish imitation of Italian (especially Bolognese) theory, and the proliferation of model letter collections and even formularies. Rockinger has identified twenty-two German works dealing with dictamen, all but five of which are mere collections (*Formelbücher*). There is no cross-fertilization with *ars grammatica,* as found in France, even though later manuals (e.g., that of Konrad of Zurich) pay more attention to *amplificatio* than earlier works had done. There is very little reference to Ciceronian rhetoric, as found in France. In fact, the relation of German dictamen to the *ars notaria* becomes as pronounced as it was to become in Italy itself.

The major German theorists are Ludolf of Hildesheim, *Summa dictaminum* (c. 1239), and Konrad of Zurich, *Summa de arte prosandi* (1276).[92] There is little in their treatises worthy of remark; they are frankly imitative. A brief compendium of Ludolf's *Summa* found in a Halberstadt manuscript may reveal quickly the conventional nature of German dictaminal theory:[93]

### NOTABILIA DE DICTAMINE

I. Quid sit dictamen. Dictamen est litteralis edicio venustate verborum egregiisque sententiarum coloribus adornata. Vel dictamen est sermonis in mente concepti vel necessitate negotii ordinate conpositio.

Et sciendum, quod dictamen epistola quo ad prosam synonima sunt, et unum pro altero indifferenter ponitur et accipitur.

II. De partibus dictaminis. Cuius quinque sunt partes: salutatio, benevolentie captatio, narratio, petitio, conclusio . . . et tercia persona semper loquitur ad terciam in salutatione.

III. Quid sit salutatio. Salutatio est salutis adoptatio, largo sumpta vocabulo, nam dicimus salutem quidquid videtur pertinere ad salutem illius cui scribitur, ut dilectio, vel obsequium, et similia. [Then follows a brief list of addresses on three levels: *summum, medium,* and *infimum;* then sample salutations for 33 types of persons. This section occupies five and one half of the ten pages of the chapter.]

IV. Captatio benevolentie. Captatio benevolentie multipliciter dicitur. Aliquando enim exordium, aliquando proverbium, aliquando proemium appellatur. Captatio benevolentie est oratio accomodans animum auditorus sequenti

---

[92] Texts in Rockinger, *Briefsteller,* pp. 359–400 and 417–82.
[93] Text in Rockinger, *Üeber Briefsteller und Formelbucher in Deutschland wahrend des Mittelalters* (Munich, 1861), pp. 31–41.

orationi. [Then five kinds of introductions are stated, each depending upon who is writing, and to whom; three kinds of matter are named: praise, facts, or circumstances. The paragraph ends with the notation that it is not always necessary to use an introduction.]

V. De narratione. Narratio est rerum gestarum vel prout gestarum positio. Que quandoque est simplex, quandoque duplex, quandoque multiplex. Multiplex est, quando plura narrantur ibi negotia vel distinctiones. Duplex est, quando duo ponuntur negotia. Simplex, quando tantum est ibi una distinctio. . . . Clausule quoque ac distinctiones non sunt nimis extendende, quia brevitas sine obscurite multum est laudabilis.

VI. De petitione et conclusione. Sequitur de petitione et conclusione, de quibus coniunctim dicitur, quia non multum est inter eas. Est petitio illa oratio qua aliquid petimus. Conclusio est oratio sententiam intentionis explicans.

VII. Quid sit circa finem servandum in litteris. In fine distinctionis vel in fine versus dictio trisillaba vel quatrisillaba cuius penultima sit longa semper est ponenda. [One paragraph concerning clausula.]

VIII. [The actual writing of the letter. The writer should first decide whether to write or dictate, and then should compose each of the five parts in turn. Two sample letters are given.]

German dictaminal writers paid far more attention to document collections than to theory, however. As early as the eleventh century letter collections were prominent, in continuation of the formulaic tradition of Merovingian and Carolingian times. The so-called Tegernsee Collection of letters compiled by Fromund of Tegernsee is one prominent example. But the German collections, like those of Marculf, are heavily interlarded with copy samples for official documents as well as for letters themselves. A clear idea of the material presented in a typical German *Formelbuch* may be gained from a brief summary of the contents of a Baumgartenberg treatise, written before 1302:[94]

## FORMULARIUS DE MODO PROSANDI

Pars principalis prima. Dictamen est digna verborum et artificiosa congeries cum pondere sentenciarum, nichil in se habens diminitum, nichil continens penitus ociosum. Dictamen igitur sic dicitur a dictando seu a ponendo, eo quod sit quedam literalis edicio, diversorum personarum capax, venustate verborum egregia, sentenciarum coloribus adornata. [The treatise then provides examples of lines and phrases suitable for letters.]

---

[94] Text in Rockinger, *Briefsteller,* pp. 725–838.

Pars principalis secunda. [Five parts of a letter, and 16 kinds of letters, as named by Ludolf of Hildesheim. Model letters.]

Pars principalis tertia. [More form letters.]

Pars principalis quarta. [A brief introduction to Part Five.]

Pars principalis quinta. [Four kinds of *captationes; litterae papales* (52 models); *litterae emperatorum et regum romanorum* (125 models); *litterae libertatum* (15 models); *litterae generales* (44 models).]

Pars principalis sexta. Proverbia seu regule iuris:

> Sine possessione prescripcio non prescribit.
> Nemo potest ad impossibile obligari.
> Quod omnes tangit debet ad omnibus approbari.
> Generi per speciem derogatur.
> Presumitur ignoracio ubi sciencia non probatur.

[Then follow 13 paragraphs describing citation, exception, sentence, probation, and other legal terms.]

About four-fifths of the treatise is taken up with model phrases, lines, or letters. The theoretical portion is entirely conventional and is obviously intended only as a framework for the models. A total of 237 model *captationes* are presented, for instance, in what seems to be an attempt to provide for every possible contingency. Papal letters are put first (as in all *dictamen* theory), each model being followed by a one-sentence explanation of the title bestowed upon the Pope. The same procedure is followed for the other types. A sampling of the *captationes* might give some idea of its intent (the numbers are those used by the Rockinger edition):

1. Papa provincii ad fidem suscipiendum. Lucis eterne lumine destitutus lucifer, caduca superbia procurante, celo contineri nequiens, eo quod.

2. Papa romanorum regii. . . .

7. Papa capitulo coloniensi. . . .

25. Papa mandat predicari crucem. . . .

27. Papa universis principibus ecclesie. . . .

42. Papa comitisse Flandrie. . . .

53. Imperator scribit regi Francie. . . .

89. Imperator amico sue speciali. . . .

132. Romanorum rex iudicii. . . .

180. Forma privilegii quo imperator recipit monasterium in suam specialem protectionem.

187. Forma privilegii quo imperator confirmat ecclesie antiqua privilegia, ac eciam aliquid de novo concedit.

200. Cardinalis notificat regi, quod electio sua per papam est approbata. . . .

215. Clericus episcopo suo, offerendo se paratum ad obsequium suum.

Bernold of Kaisersheim's *Summa prosaici dictaminis* (1312)[95] divides the *formulae* into five sections. The first deals with 84 salutations *ad diversos status,* the second with proverbs or *sententiae* useful in letters, and the third with models of letters "without salutations." The fourth and fifth sections transcribe a total of 45 *formae* (short paragraphs of perhaps 75 to 100 words) to be used in visitations and other clerical duties. Besides a number of forms suitable for admonitions on visitations (on silence, levity, authority, etc.), the array of models even allows the cleric to choose between two *formae viatici.* Other German manuscripts emphasize forms of privileges or judicial processes. For example, the anonymous *Summa de ordine et processu iudicii spiritualis* (before 1245) devotes nine of its ten sections to legal forms.

Taken all in all, then, it is evident that German dictamen was merely imitative of developments elsewhere in Europe. The continuing interest in legal forms and documentary formats also shows the strong notarial strain that goes back ultimately to the days of the seventh-century *formulae.*

Charles Faulhaber has shown that the *ars dictaminis* was the dominant type of rhetorical treatise in medieval Castile, though he cautions that this judgment should not necessarily be extended to all of Spain or to all of the middle ages.[96] The major works were those of Geoffrey of Everseley, *Ars epistolarium ornatus* (c. 1270); Juan Gil de Zamora,

---

[95] Text in *ibid.,* pp. 845–924.

[96] Charles Faulhaber, *Latin Rhetorical Theory in Thirteenth- and Fourteenth-Century Castile,* University of California Publications in Modern Philology, Vol. 103 (Berkeley and Los Angeles, 1972). A comparison of the two works involved has shown that the *Breve compendium artis rethorice* of Martin of Córdoba, cited in Faulhaber, is not the same as the Latin treatise of "Martin of Córdoba" cited in Caplan and Charland as a preaching manual; for details see below, Chapter Six, n. 97. I am indebted to Professor Faulhaber for this information. It is not clear at this juncture whether this is a separate Martin or whether it might be a second work by the original Martin; Caplan places his Martin in the fifteenth century, while Faulhaber's author wrote no later than the early fourteenth century.

*Dictaminis epithalamium* (c. 1275?) with model letters; and Martin de Córdoba, *Breve compendium artis rhetorice* (1300–1350). Faulhaber (p. 138) calls these treatises "the entering wedge of Italian influence in Spain during the late medieval period."

Meanwhile in Italy, the mother of the *ars dictaminis,* the tensions inherent in the Bolognese evolution of the art began to tear it apart. The two centuries following the *Rationes dictandi* of 1135 saw several developments whose causes were inherent in the approach taken by the early *dictatores*. The self-professed appropriation of mastery on the part of dictaminal writers produced in thirteenth-century Bologna and Florence a number of *magistri* who not only squabbled with each over the art but in some cases took their arguments north into France and even England. Boncompagno is the most obvious example of this phenomenon. The quasi-legal nature of dictamen itself—especially in the selection of models for copying—had always raised the question of the relation between *ars dictaminis* and legal studies. Bologna, after all, was both a center of *ars dictaminis* and a center of law. Events were to prove that this question in Italy was resolved, not on a theoretical level, but on the very practical level of the new *ars notaria* of men like Irnerius and Rolandinus Passagerius. Another fundamental question, raised (but not answered) by Adalbertus, was that of brevity versus completeness: that is, should the *dictator* attempt to provide everything needed by the letter-writer, or should he place his art within some larger linguistic framework? In France generally, as we have seen, there was a clear-cut tendency to keep the *ars dictaminis* within the comparatively humanistic framework of the *ars grammatica* or at least the *trivium*. Italian writers, on the other hand, tended to provide self-contained manuals. This Italian development had two important results. One was the appropriation to dictamen of the rhythmical *cursus* already developed by the papal chancery; the other was development of the hyper-formulaic, chartistic dictamen popularized by the *Practica* of Lawrence of Aquilegia. These developments had their roots in the early twelfth century. Although Italian dictamen came to be an important influence even on writers like Dante and Boccacio, it also contained from the beginning the seeds of its own destruction.

It is neither necessary nor possible at this time to discuss every *ars dictaminis* of Italian origin. The basic doctrines continued to be repeated, the emphasis on *salutationes* remained constant, the attachment of model letters was routinely followed, and in general the original Bolognese directions were carried out. (Boncompagno tried vainly, for instance, to reduce the parts of a letter from five to three). No doubt a great many individual *artes* remain to be edited, but in terms of overall influence the major works have long since been identified and almost all of them printed. The most influential were Guido Faba (c. 1190–c. 1240), Thomas of Capua (d. 1239), and Lawrence of Aquilegia (fl. c. 1300?). Before taking up these three major figures, however, it will be useful to examine the general trends in the field, including the association of the *cursus* with the *ars dictaminis*.

A number of other individuals have been noted. Guido Zaccagnini has edited part of the *Summa dictaminis* (before 1303) of Giovanni di Bonandrea, who taught in Bologna.[97] Kristeller has recently published the *Ars dictaminis* (c. 1327) of Giovanni del Virgilio, notary, poet, and teacher who corresponded with Dante and Mussato; even though Giovanni cites Cicero and Donatus, his treatment of his subject is schematic and narrow when compared to that of any of the French treatises.[98] Other figures, like the "John of Sicily" mentioned by Thomas Merke, must remain obscure entities until their texts have been edited for closer study. Surely there must be many others not yet noted.

A brief survey of one such Italian *ars* may illustrate the conventional nature of the continuing tradition. As in any continuing movement, of course, small variations appear with each writer. The *Brevis doctrina dictaminis* of Ventura da Pergamo,[99] written in the fourteenth century, apparently survives in only one manuscript, now in the Bodleian Library at Oxford.[100]

The *Brevis doctrina dictaminis* is divided into two parts. The first deals with the five parts of a letter, each definition being followed by an explanatory section titled *notabilia* (e.g., *notabilia circa conclusionem*). The second part deals with the vices and virtues of composition, and includes an orthographical section on the correct formation of individual

---

[97] Guido Zaccagnini, "Giovanni di Bonandrea dettatore e rimatore e altri grammatici e dottori in arti dello Studio Bolognese," *Studi e memorie per la storie dell'Universita di Bologna* 5 (1920), 145–204. Extracts from the text may be found on pp. 191–94.

[98] Paul O. Kristeller, "Un 'Ars dictaminis' de Giovanni del Virgilio," *Italia Medioevale e Umanistica* 4 (1961), 181–200.

[99] Oxford Bodleian MS. Canon. Ital. 157, fols. 64–71$^r$. I am currently preparing a critical edition of this text.

[100] The author is apparently not the Dominican preacher of the same name. See Berthold Altaner, *Venturino von Bergamo O.P., 1304-46: eine Biographie* (Breslau, 1911), esp. pp. 20–21.

letters of the alphabet. "Let the reader not be impeded in his reading," the text concludes (*Ne lector in legendo impediatur*). The author explains at the outset, incidentally, that he is making his treatise brief because of the difficulty of remembering the doctrine (*propter memorie debilitatem*). There are echoes of Ciceronian rhetoric in his statement in the Prologue that a writer can learn the art of dictamen through art, practice, and imitation, the most perfect artistry coming from an apt concurrence of all three. This brief paragraph out of the way, however, Ventura turns at once to the systematic handling of the five parts of a letter and their *notabilia*. The discussion of *salutationes,* in 44 rubrics that occupy twice as much space as all the other four parts combined, is based on the familiar principle of levels of addressees. Ventura declares, for instance, that there are six ways of writing the name of an addressee who is superior to the letter-writer, and four for an addressee of equal rank (fol. 64ᵛ).

There is a further echo of the *Rhetorica ad Herennium* in Ventura's statement that the introduction of a letter has two parts (*principium* and *insinuatio*). However, he does not develop the idea further, nor does he, in fact, mention Cicero here by name, although later he names Horace twice in connection with the vices listed in the second section of the manual. But when he comes to a listing of the "vices of composition" (fol. 68ᵛ) he quotes from "Tullius" (*ad Herennium* IX.xii.18), the frequently copied mnemonic example of excessive alliteration:

O Tite, tute, Tati, tibi tanta, tyranne, tulisti.

However, this example also occurs in many grammar texts. Ventura also names Horace's *Poetria* as a source of knowledge of vices. The "virtues" of composition, according to Ventura, are three things that lead to *distinctio,* namely *clausula, punctus,* and *cursus.* Each is given the equivalent of a long paragraph, the section on the *cursus* being the longest. The treatise ends with the discussion of orthography.

Obviously Ventura has some acquaintance with the *Rhetorica ad Herennium* and with Horace, either through direct study or some *florilegium.* Yet his whole concern is with the letter, and even when he cites Cicero he notes what the *moderni* have added to the lore of antiquity. He lists the usual grammatical vices (*solecismus, barbarismus*), for instance, but does not mention Donatus, Priscian, or even the term "grammar." In other words, Ventura is a thoroughly "modern" man with no particular awe of the ancients except where the obvious major sources lead him to name Cicero or Horace. He knows exactly what he is about, with no pretensions of professional mastery beyond what is needed for his task. The amount of dictaminal lore which he takes for granted is thus in itself a type of proof that the tradition is very strong in him.

No complete list of dictaminal works has yet been compiled, and so it is difficult to estimate how many other tracts like Ventura's remain to be studied. Since the production of such books was often linked to the teaching done in the *studio* of a city-state like Florence or Bologna, how-ever, some illuminating recent studies have shown how geographical investigations can uncover further materials.

Helene Wieruszowski's analysis of the *studium generale* in thirteenth-century Arezzo[101] might serve as a model for such efforts. The conflicts between lay and religious interests—seen already in the Bolognese rival-ries of Adalbertus and Hugo—are shown here as resolved in favor of ecclesiastical control over the *studium* through licensing. Miss Wieruszow-ski traces the complex relations between the Church, private schools, city government, and prominent professors imported at times from Bologna. A liberal arts course, including rhetoric, served as preparation for higher studies in law, medicine, and *ars notaria*. Among the more obscure grammarians and rhetoricians named are Orlandus or Rolandus, a Tebaldus of Orlando, and a certain Master John. More is known about four others: Bonfiglio d'Arezzo, who is credited with introducing the Sicilian *stilus altus* into the classes in rhetoric in 1258; Mino da Colle, his successor, who wrote on dictamen; Beltramo, who was eventually hired away by authorities in Siena to assist at a revived *studium;* and Bandino, who also went to Siena. All these men lived and taught in a city which during the century became increasingly what Miss Wieruszow-ski terms "a center of humanism." She notes that the poet Guittone (born ca. 1225) and the humanist Geri (born ca. 1260) both received their early education in Aretine schools, and of course Petrarch was born there in 1304. Toward the end of the thirteenth century she sees a growing use of the classics. She concludes:

Summing up, it can be said that the occupation with *dictamen* did not block the way to higher literary adventures. On the contrary, as the century drew to a close, some notaries and masters of grammar and *ars dictandi* even actively supported the 'classical' trend. They 'vulgarized' the ancient manu-als of rhetoric and even extracts from Cicero's orations (Fra Guidotto of

---

[101] Helene Wieruszowski, "Arezzo as a Center of Learning and Letters in the Thirteenth Century," *Traditio* 9 (1953), 321–91.

Bologna and Brunetto Latini); they attempted to return to the ancient manuals as a solid basis for *ars dictaminis* (the Bolognese professor Jacques de
Dinant); they drew on ancient examples for the illustration of rhetorical
colors (Mino da Colle).

Nevertheless it must be admitted that no major change took place in the
traditional dictaminal doctrine. The advent of the *stilus altus,* linked to
the Papal Curia, to legal studies, and to the models of skillful writers,
is adduced in her study only by a close analysis of the letters of Mino da
Colle. No major theoretical statement derives from Aretine activity. What
is interesting for our purposes, though, is the identification of *dictatores*
like Bonfiglio and Mino working in the surroundings of a municipal
*studium generale.* Many more such writers might well be identified
through close examination of other Italian educational centers. Bologna
itself contained at one time three of the most colorful *dictatores*—the
"triad" of Boncompagno, Guido Faba, and Bene of Florence.

The matter of the *stilus altus,* however, raises the question of dictaminal
style, or what the ancients called *elocutio.* There is an obvious Ciceronian
flavor to early manuals, and the *Rhetorica nova* (that is, the *Rhetorica ad
Herennium*) is often cited for the *colores* it describes; hence the term
*stilus Tullianus.* The manuals also mention *stilus Isidorianus* and *stilus
Gregorianus.* Cassiodorus, despite the popularity of the *Variae,* is perhaps too complex a model to attract much imitation by the *dictatores;*
in any case the writers usually content themselves with citing him as an
example of *dictamen prosaicum* in their preliminary distinctions, and do
not discuss his style.

Actually the dictaminal writers have very little to say about the precise uses of various kinds of style. The high incidence of models and
exemplary phrases in the manuals may help to account for this lack,
in that models are posited instead of theories. Proverbial materials, of
course, were expected to be pithy and brief, but even here examples far
outnumber precepts. There is certainly no well-developed dictaminal theory
of style for *narratio, petitio,* or *conclusio,* and the other two parts of
the letter are usually portrayed in so many examples that the writers
apparently see little need for stylistic discussion. Aside from a few
Ciceronian remarks about *humilis* in an *exordium,* for instance, little
preceptive is said. There would therefore seem to be little place in the
*ars dictaminis* for a complex theory of style.

Nevertheless, one of the most striking characteristics of the medieval *ars dictaminis* is the doctrine of the rhythmical prose system known as the *cursus*.

Rhythmical Latin prose was not a medieval invention. Cicero used it in his speeches and letters, referring in his *De oratore* (I.35) to *tantus cursus verborum*. The liturgy of the Western church naturally made use of such a striking medium to add dignity to ceremony and song; the prevalence of rhythmical hymn structure is further indication of such employment. *Rithmus* has a medieval literature of its own, and as we have already seen it even has a general theory of its own. This is perhaps so obvious that it needs restating, because the dictaminal absorption of that certain kind of *rithmus* known as the *cursus* gave it a special life of its own that proceeded quite independently of the general theory.[102]

A great deal of scholarly attention has been devoted to tracing the complex early history of the medieval *cursus*. But in terms of our study it is clear that the first major impulse toward regularizing the special style of the Roman Curia (*cursus Romanae curiae*) came from the same monastic school of Monte Cassino that nurtured Alberic's two pioneer theoretical works on the *ars dictaminis* itself. This impulse came in the person of John of Gaeta, onetime monk of Monte Cassino in Alberic's time, who was named Chancellor by Pope Urban II, and who held that office for thirty years before becoming pope himself (Gelasius II). As Poole says of him, "He set a memorable landmark in the history of the Chancery, not by altering its system but by renovating its style."[103] His biographer, Pandulph, records the nature of his commission as Chancellor:

> Then the Pope (Urban II), a well-lettered man and of ready speech, perceiving brother John to be both wise and prudent, ordained, promoted, and from careful deliberation appointed him his chancellor, so that through his eloquence which the Lord had granted him, John might under the guidance of the Holy Spirit by the grace of God reform the style of ancient grace and elegance in the apostolic see, which was now almost all lost, and might restore the Leonine rhythm (*Leoninum cursum*) with its lucid rapidity.[104]

Here, then, we have the phenomenon of a skilled stylist with an official appointment to restructure a widely used style; not only does he have the

---

[102] See above, in Chapter IV (Grammar) the discussion of the *ars rithmica*, pp. 157–61.

[103] Reginald Lane Poole, *Lectures on the History of the Papal Chancery, Down to the Time of Innocent III* (Cambridge, 1915), p. 75.

[104] Quoted in *ibid.*, p. 84.

support of the official head of the Latin Church, but John in his own turn becomes the highest authority. The papal *cursus,* then, enjoyed the strongest support from the very beginning, being broadcast in papal letters and other documents.

From the viewpoint of rhetorical history, though, it must be observed that the *cursus* developed independently of the *ars dictaminis;* it was attached regularly to the *artes* only long after it had reached its full form within the Curia itself. After all, one would expect a natural affinity to develop between a successful documentary style and a theory of letter-writing that had no special style of its own to advance. No doubt Alberic of Monte Cassino discussed the *cursus* with pupils like John of Gaeta—some scholars find evidence of the *cursus* in Alberic's own writings—but it is equally clear that the dictaminal movement itself does not in the beginning include the *cursus.* Adalbertus, Hugh, Bernard, and the anonymous author of the *Rationes dictandi* content themselves with general remarks about style, Cicero still being the prime exemplar. The method of transition from eleventh-century Curial usage to twelfth-century formulation of rules for the *cursus* is still not clear.

Albert of Morra (later Pope Gregory VIII) is often credited with having put into writing the rules already followed by the Curial writers. Unfortunately his *Forma dictandi* (c. 1180?) has not yet been edited, but, since we discover that Peter of Blois provides a quick survey of the same rules in England in the 1180's, it seems reasonable to infer that various formal statements of the rules were in circulation before Albert is supposed to have set them down. The school of Orléans is also found writing on the *cursus* at about the same time. Consequently we are unable to determine precisely who was the first dictaminal theoretician to graft the *cursus* onto the epistolary art. By the beginning of the thirteenth century, in any case, it is obvious that the marriage of the *cursus* and the *ars dictaminis* has been consummated, and indeed that the first quarrels have begun to occur. From 1200 onward a three-way difference of opinion arose between the Bolognists, the Orléanists, and the purists of the Curia. These differences, highly technical and always complex, did not obscure the essential agreement on the use of ordered *clausulae* to achieve certain desired effects.[105] Orléans, as one might expect from its humanistic aura,

---

[105] Given the prevalence of at least three variations of the *cursus,* it no longer seems likely—as was once supposed—that the papal *cursus* served as a proof against forgery of documents. Like any other style, it could be used by any adept compositor.

stood not only for greater freedom of usage in the *cursus* itself, but more frequently continued to draw analogies to metrics; it is Pons of Provence, for instance, who declares the *cursus* to be "the wedding of spondees with dactyls" (*matrimonium spondeorum cum dactilis*). Bene of Florence in fact accuses the Orléanists of employing *imaginarios dactilos et spondeos*. Apparently Albert of Morra and his associate Transmundus drew the same analogies, but later Curial authorities insisted on limiting the *cursus* to three primary forms—known as the *planus,* the *tardus,* and the *velox*—which they regarded as proper to the style. But the Bolognese ideas received wider circulation, especially after the publication of Guido Faba's *Summa de modo dictaminis* in the 1220's.[106]

Guido cut through the complexities of Curial Latinity in a typically pragmatic fashion. Basically he proposed ignoring the analogies to metrics and instead concentrated on the numbering of clause endings rather than the rhythm of whole clauses. In other words, he removed the subject from the realm of metrical quantity and substituted for it a system of syllable-sets. Shortly thereafter the basic rules are found versified even in Germany (in Ludolf of Hildesheim's *Summa*). Brief discussions of the *cursus* appear in almost every *ars dictaminis* after the middle of the thirteenth century, the very brevity of these notices being testimony to the acceptance of the concepts described.

A number of modern descriptions of the *cursus* have been attempted, the most revealing one being that of Paget Toynbee in his study of Dante's use of the *cursus* in his *De vulgari eloquentia*.[107] Toynbee's outline demonstrates the complexity of the matter, and may well serve here as a substitute for the lengthy textual citations from *Artes dictaminis* that would otherwise be necessary to make the same point:

> It must be borne in mind, to begin with, that the mediaeval *cursus* depends entirely upon accent, not quantity, and that there is no elision, the hiatus being tolerated. Three principal types of clausula are recognized, which are known respectively as *planus, tardus,* and *velox*. Of each of these, it may be observed, there are secondary forms, which were in common use, but for present purposes these may be disregarded.
>
> The *cursus planus* in its normal form (*pl*) consists of a paroxytone tri-syllable (or its equivalent, a monosyllable and a paroxytone dissyllable), preceded by a paroxytone dissyllable or polysyllable, the caesura falling after the

---

[106] See below, pp. 256–58.
[107] Paget Toynbee, "The Bearing of the *Cursus* on the Text of Dante's 'De vulgari eloquentia,'" *Proceedings of the British Academy* 10 (1923), 359–77. The following excerpt appears on pp. 360–62.

second syllable of the clausula; as (to take examples from the *De Vulgari Eloquentia* itself), (quod) clávem | vocábat (ii. 13, 30); (au)dácter | testámur (i. 9, 67); (na)túra | abhórret (i. 2, 9); ésse | opórtet (i. 16, 9); or, (vel) nóta, | vel mélos (ii. 8, 42); (regi)ónes | et úrbes (i. 6, 34); (asser)éndum | non pútet (i. 13, 47).

The *cursus tardus* in its normal form (*t*) consists of a proparoxytone tetrasyllable (or its equivalent), preceded by a paroxytone dissyllable or polysyllable, the caesura falling after the second syllable, as in the *planus;* as, vóces | incípiunt (i. 1, 24); (prod)ésse | tentábimus (i. 1, 12); (imit)ántes | accípimus (i. 1, 27); (repraesent)ántur | pulcérrimi (i. 2, 19); (variati)ónem | perpéndimus (i. 10, 78). The final tetrasyllable may be represented either by a paroxytone trisyllable followed by a monosyllable; as, ésse | credéndum est (i. 5, 28); (confusi)óne | percússi sunt (i. 7, 47); or by a proparoxytone trisyllable preceded by a monosyllable; as, íllud | quod quaérimus (i. 14, 47); (compil)ándo | ab áliis (i. 1, 15).

The *cursus velox* in its normal form (*v*) consists of a paroxytone tetrasyllable (or its equivalent) preceded by a proparoxytone trisyllable or polysyllable, the caesura falling after the third syllable of the clausula; as, próferunt | blandiéntes (i. 14, 17); última | eleménta (ii. 10, 8); (in)vénio | poetásse (ii. 2, 95); (avid)íssimi | speculántur (i. 2, 20). The final tetrasyllable may be represented either by a paroxytone trisyllable preceded by a monosyllable; as, (de) stántia | est agéndum (ii. 9, 6); (testi)mónio | se tuétur (i. 10, 12); or by two dissyllables; as, débeant | illud úti (ii. 1, 15); (proverbi)áliter | dici sólet (i. 7, 17).

Besides the above three simple types, what may be termed combined or compound clausulae, in which two or more of the recognized *cursus* formulae are used in combination, are of frequent occurrence; thus, bréviter pertractáre conémur (i. 2, 67), is a combination of the *velox*, bréviter pertractáre, with the *planus,* (pertract)áre conémur (*v + pl*); prími loquéntis sonáverit (i. 4, 27), is a combination of the *planus*, prími loquéntis, with the *tardus,* (loqu)éntis sonáverit (*pl + t*); húmeros Apenníni frondíferos (i. 14, 1), is a combination of the *velox*, húmeros Apenníni, with the *tardus,* (Apen)níni, frondíferos (*v + t*); (hu)mánae propáginis principális (i. 8, 6), is a combination of the *tardus*, (hu)mánae propáginis, with the *velox,* (pro)páginis principális (*t + v*); (in) quántum natúra permíttit (i. 1, 7), is a combination of the two *planus*, quántum natúra, and (na)túra permíttit (*pl + pl*).

In addition to two-membered clausulae of the foregoing types, compound clausulae consisting of three members are not infrequent; such as, (ut) ípsum perféctius edocére possímus (ii. 6, 8), which is a combination of the *tardus,* ípsum perféctius, with the *velox,* (per)féctius edocére, and of this again with the *planus,* (edoc)ére possímus (*t +v + pl*); or, (contra su)périus praelibáta vidétur insúrgere (i. 4, 48), which is a combination of the *velox,* (su)périus praelibáta, with the *planus,* (praelib)áta vidétur, and of this with the *tardus,* (vid)étur insúrgere (*v + pl + t*); or, (progressi)ónis província lucidáre expóstulat (ii. 7, 3), which is a combination of the *tardus,* (progressi)ónis província, with the *velox,* (pro)víncia lucidáre, and of this with the *tardus,* (lucid)áre expóstulat $(t + v + t)$; or, (potion)áre possímus dulcíssimum hydroméllum (i. 1, 16), which is a combination of the *planus* (potion)áre possímus, with the *tardus,* (poss)ímus dulcíssimum, and of this with the *velox,* (dulc)íssimum hydroméllum $(pl + t + v)$; and so on.

As we noted earlier, dictaminal writers do not really assign a place to the *cursus.* They do not make it clear whether they recommend it for one part, or all parts, of a letter. Yet the *cursus* appears as an appendix to a great number of the manuals. It could probably be argued that this placement represents an irresolution on the part of the *dictatores*—that on one hand they realize the need for theories of style, but at the same time they do not know what use to recommend for an imported system that is already well developed. In the typical manual the *cursus* is an undigested whole. The net effect in medieval practice was to stifle original thinking about *elocutio.* Medieval letter style thus suffered from the manipulation of language (and perhaps, at times, even meaning) in order to fit it into the mechanical requirements of a syllable-counting system. The paraphrases thus required could not always have been salutary. The history of the medieval *cursus,* then, stands as an example of what can happen when a block of ideas is grafted *in toto* onto an existing set of precepts.[108]

At this point it might be well to return to the *ars dictaminis* itself, and especially to the further Bolognese developments. Who were the dominant writers in the field?

The bizarre claims of Boncompagno (1165–1240)[109] and his temporary influence at the University of Bologna have sometimes led modern writers to attach more importance to him than he deserves. In the perspective of European development of the art, he is virtually without influence, and he is best viewed as a biographical curiosity who may help the modern reader to understand the strains of personal rivalries in medieval dictamen. One acute modern writer describes the personality

---

[108] De Ghellinck (*L'Essor,* p. 65) notes the dangers of the *cursus:* "C'est ainsi qu'un *Ars dictaminis* du XIII^e siècle frappe d'ostracisme non seulement le *Stylus* ou le *Cursus Gregorianus,* mais toute recherche du nombre et de la cadence. Il reproche aux *Dictaminum zelatores* leur manque de vrais principes littéraires, solides et stables, et blame le recours à des vanités de style, comme la multiplication des clausules. . . ."

[109] His influence is overestimated by Louis J. Paetow, *The Arts Course at Medieval Universities with Special Reference to Grammar and Rhetoric* (Champaign, Ill., 1910). C. S. Baldwin, *Medieval Rhetoric and Poetic* (New York, 1928), says of the *Boncompagnus* that it was so widely used "that Boncompagno's name, like Donatus, became a common noun . . ." (p. 212). For a biography, see Carl Sutter, *Aus Leben und Schriften des Magisters Buoncompagno* (Freiburg im Breisgau, 1894).

of Boncompagno as "scurrilous and eccentric," noting, however, that he has been studied more intensively than most of the other *dictatores*.[110] For one thing, Boncompagno revels in autobiographical detail as part of his continuous boasting. For another, he is quick to strike extravagant poses—in his *Palma* dismissing Cicero's rhetoric, for instance, as being beneath his attention and not worth reading (*Nunquam enim memini me Tullium legisse nec secundum alicuius doctrinam*).

Boncompagno himself names eleven works he has composed, all dealing in some way with letter-writing or with the preparation of documents. The best known of these are his *Rhetorica antiqua* (also called *Buoncompagnus*) (1215), which is more formulary than theoretical; his allegorically named *Cedrus, Palma,* and *Myrrha,* all dealing with testaments and closely allied to legal formularies; and finally his *Rhetorica novissima* (1235),[111] whose very title indicates his intention to provide the ultimate in rhetorical lore. But this last work reveals most of all the school-centered approach which even this self-professed successor of Cicero brought to bear on his subject. The *Rhetorica novissima* is divided into thirteen books, the first of which is on the origin of law, and the last four on various types of discourse, including those at the *contio* or "gatherings of the people" (*conventus populi*). But most of the treatise consists of ruminations on such matters as the parts of rhetoric, its instruments, and its function. Boncompagno defines a *rhetor* (III.1) as "herald of the art of rhetoric, for he does nothing else but transmit the precepts of the art." The office of the *rhetor,* then is to treat the rhetorical books and to set forth "letters" according to the annotations of learned doctors. The *dictator,* on the other hand, "reads and comments" on the speeches of orators.[112] This is a tightly constricted regimen for one am-

---

[110] Ernst Kantorowicz, "An 'Autobiography' of Guido Faba," *Medieval and Renaissance Studies* I (1941–43), 255. It might be noted also that Sutter (*Aus Leben*) finds it useful to include a chapter on Boncompagno's "Personalitkeit"; evidently flamboyance, as well as ability, is a road to fame.

[111] The *Rhetorica novissima* was edited by Augustus Gaudenzi in *Bibliotheca Iuridica Medii Aevi, Scripta Anecdota Glossatorum* (Bologna, 1892), II.249–97. Sutter (*Aus Leben,* pp. 105–27) includes an edition of the *Palma.* The *Cedrus* may be found in Rockinger (*Briefsteller,* pp. 121–27) who also provides a list of *capitula* for the *Boncompagnus* (pp. 128–74).

[112] Quid sit rhetor. Rhetor est preco artis rhetorice, quia nil aliud facit nisi quod artis precepta divulgat. Unde dicatur. Rhetor a rhetorica dicitur, a qua regulariter derivatur. De officio rhetoris. Officium rhetoris est transcurrere libros rhetoricos, et exponere litteras secundum glosas doctorum. De officio dictatoris. Dictator, prout hodie sumitur, est ille qui oratorum dicta legit et repetit, et repetit variat et componit. *Rhetorica novissima* III.1 (Gaudenzi, p. 275).

bitious enough to set himself up as the author of the "newest rhetoric," and betrays the essentially pedantic nature of Boncompagno's rhetoric. One is reminded, in fact, of the ancient complaint of Seneca the Elder that rhetoricians were but training for the schools.

Boncompagno attempted one major dictaminal reform, which failed utterly. First in the *Palma* and then in the *Rhetorica novissima,* he attempted to set up a system of three-part letters instead of five. But very few followed his lead. His reasons for the innovation are not made entirely clear, although he endeavors to distinguish between "principal" and "secondary" parts of a letter in an effort to relegate other parts to a subordinate position. In the *Palma* he names the three parts as *salutatio, narratio, petitio.* In the *Rhetorica novissima* he declares that the three integral parts are *exordium, narratio,* and *petitio.* Both of these listings prove to be mere quibbles, since in each case he tries to juggle the other parts in order to make them available in some "imperfect" way.

Intriguing though he may be as a spectacular figure, Boncompagno seems to have made no lasting impact either on his own university or on Europe at large. Paradoxically, his meteoric rise at the University of Bologna may have been an indirect cause of the rapid conquest made by the *ars notaria* at that institution following his death. He left no solid foundation, but it is probable that his academic enemies were in plentiful supply.

A brief word might be said about one of his rivals, Bene of Florence, author of an eight-part work called *Candelabrum* (c. 1220).[113] Bene is also reputed to have written an *Ars dictaminis,* still in manuscript. The *Candelabrum* is apparently the first treatise of Italian origin to take directly into account the French dictaminal approach, which emphasized the *ars grammatica.* In fact, Bene states in his Prologue that he will devote his sixth section to "the most elegant teachings of the French concerning the

---

[113] Bene's *Candelabrum* is still not available in a printed text. The first five books are summarized by Baldwin (*Medieval Rhetoric and Poetic,* pp. 216–23), who described it as "extremely systematic." But the best treatment can be found in Giuseppe Vecchi, *Il magistero delle "Artes" Latine a Bologna nel medioevo,* pubblicazioni della Facoltà di Magistero, Università di Bologna, 2 (Bologna, 1958). Vecchi notes that the manuscript used by Baldwin lacks Books 6–7-8, and then prints (pp. 18–19) the text of Bene's Prologue explaining the materials to be covered in the eight books. Vecchi credits Bene with a "rivoluzione di metodi." Lengthy excerpts from Books I and V of the *Candelabrum* are to be found in Vecchi, "Temi e momenti d'arte dettatoria nel candelabrum di Bene da Firenze," *Atti e Memorie della Deputazione di Storia Patria per le Province di Romagna* N.S. 10 (1958–59), 1–56.

doctrine of letter-writing, as we have heard from various doctors." [114]
Moreover, Bene quotes several times from the *Poetria nova* of Geoffrey
of Vinsauf, who apparently had taught briefly at Bologna just after the
turn of the century. It is the general tone of the *Candelabrum* that is
significant, however, for it goes beyond the typical Italian *ars dictaminis*
both by discussing *ars rhetorica* in general and by stressing such grammatical matters as amplificatory modes. Giuseppe Vecchi, who has
studied the manuscripts in some detail, points out that Bene nevertheless
has an anti-Orléanistic bias, certainly not unexpected in a writer influenced
by a Parisian figure like Geoffrey of Vinsauf. His grammatical interests
are not catholic to the point of welcoming the broad humanistic approach of Orléans. Bene's broader concerns therefore come to us through
the filter of a neo-Ciceronianism no doubt influenced in part by his con-
tact with Geoffrey or his writings.

But Guido Faba (or Fava) (c. 1190–c. 1240), the third member of the
"triad" of Bologna, was far and away the most influential. Ernst Kantorowicz describes him as "the truest exponent of Bolognese school-tradition
as it had gradually developed during the course of the preceding century, a master who, in his turn, conveniently transmitted this tradition
through his treatises and his way of teaching." [115] Guido was the author
of at least nine dictaminal works: *Arenge, Dictamina rhetorica, Epistole,
Exordia, Gemma purpurea, Parlamenta et epistole, Summa dictaminis,
Rota nova*, and a *Summa de vitiis et virtutibus*. Copies of these treatises
were circulated in profusion all over Europe.[116]

There is a remarkable homogeneity in these treatises despite the apparent diversity of their titles. At least one work—the *Rota nova*—may
well represent Guido's lectures at Bologna (i.e., an oral version of a
treatise meant to be seen in written form); Noel Denholm-Young has
indeed found the *Rota nova* (1225–26) to be in close agreement with

---

[114] Sextus, vero doctrinam Gallicorum elegantissimam de epistolari doctrina
aperit diligenter, ut sicut doctores diversos audivimus ita diversa diversis animis
largiamus. Vecchi, p. 19.

[115] Kantorowicz, "An 'Autobiography' of Guido Faba," *Medieval and Renaissance Studies* 1 (1941–43), 253–80. The statement appears on p. 253. Kantorowicz
includes (pp. 277–80) the text of the Prologue to Faba's *Rota nova*. This particular study might well be taken as a model of biographical reconstruction using an
author's own works to trace his career.

[116] A listing of Faba's published works is in Virgilio Pini, "La *Summa de vitiis
et virtutibus* di Guido Faba," *Quadrivium* 1 (1956), 42–43. Rockinger (*Briefsteller*,
pp. 185–96) prints a portion of the *Gemma purpurea* as *Doctrina ad inveniandas
incipiendas et formandas materias*. Faba's *Summa dictaminis* is edited by Augustus
Gaudenzi in *Il Propugnatore* 23 (N.S. 3) (1890), I, 287–338 and II, 345–93.

the treatise called *Summa dictaminis*.[117] In fact, Kantorowicz has shown by a close analysis of the *Rota nova* that Guido was deeply involved in Bolognese educational life. The *Summa de vitiis et virtutibus* is a collection—in both Latin and the Tuscan dialect—of proverbial material to be employed in the *exordium* (sometimes *proverbium*) of a letter; the *Arenge* serves the same purpose by listing sample argumentative or controversial statements that might be used in the same letter part. The *Dictamina*, as its title indicates, is a letter collection. The *Gemma purpurea* concentrates on the problems of inventing beginnings to letters. Guido seems to use three terms interchangeably—*exordium, proverbium, vel arenga*—when he notes in the *Gemma* that the wise letter-writer will "send ahead" one of these three to prepare the way for the narration of a letter. This matter of letter openings is of course a familiar preoccupation with dictaminal writers, so it is not surprising to find that Guido devotes four complete works to the subject.

Guido appears to have three quite different writing styles, a factor which may help to account for his evident popularity. His dictaminal doctrine is not unique, and indeed is highly conventional—but this fact no doubt made him even more acceptable to his readers. In his expository writings he is soberly clear, without the self-approving lust for novelty that condemned Boncompagno's writings to quick oblivion. In some of Guido's work (as in the prologue to the *Rota nova*), there is another, allegorical style reminiscent both of Boncompagno and of the Orléanistic masters of the same period. Kantorowicz has made an interesting study of the allegorical import of this prologue, demonstrating for instance that Guido's reference to working with hammer and anvil in a "smithy" really indicated that he had for some time studied in Bolognese law schools. This "smithy," Guido says, caused him to become lame, half-blind, and heavy-tongued—that is, he began to lose his rhetorical skill—and he decided to change his course of studies.

Guido's third style is that of his model letters, the expansive *stilus supremus* or *litterae sacrae* common to emperors and popes. Great men of course desired cosmic language. One of the great imponderables for the modern student of medieval dictaminal history is the relation between a *dictator's* theory and his models. Some students believe, for instance,

---

[117] Noel Denholm-Young, "The 'cursus' in England," in *Collected Papers on Medieval Subjects* (Oxford, 1946), p. 94. This key article first appeared in *Oxford Essays in Medieval History Presented to Herbert Edward Salter* (Oxford, 1934), pp. 68–103.

that the Orléanistic writers became popular not for their routine statements of theories but for the grace of their model letters. Guido might have been popular for the same reason. We can point to little that is innovative in his theory, but his wide acceptance must surely point to the influence of his *Dictamina, Epistole,* and the four books on letter beginnings. This is a matter not yet studied, however, and comprehensive examination must await the systematic collation of the numerous manuscripts scattered all over Europe.

Thomas of Capua (d. 1239), a prominent papal diplomat and contemporary of Guido Faba, demonstrates further the centrality of the dictaminal tradition. Thomas had a considerable European audience for his writing because of his Roman positions; first he was a notary under Pope Innocent III, then cardinal deacon by 1212, and cardinal priest of Santa Sabina. The full title of his major work indicates at once his sphere of influence: *Summa artis dictaminis sive de arte dictandi epistoles secundam stylum curiae.*[118] However, the "Curial style" is not explicitly described in his text, although in his Prologue Thomas castigates those who falsely claim to be *dictatores* but actually insult the *gloriosa Romana ecclesia* by their ignorance. The *Summa* concentrates half of its thirty sections on the *salutatio* and *exordium* (*Cap.* 5–22). As might be expected, the editor of the *Summa,* Emmy Heller, has identified a number of correspondences between the doctrines of Thomas, Guido Faba, and Boncompagno. The Capuan schools are later than those of Bologna, and it would be consistent with the whole tradition to find a great deal of doctrinal conformity among the various writers. In any case, the circulation of Thomas's *Summa* must have benefited greatly from his recognized association with the papacy.

The whole dictaminal tradition also pointed toward increasing uniformity of another kind, with the ultimate point reached in the curious *Practica sive usus dictaminis* (c. 1300?) of Lawrence of Aquilegia. The date of this work is not clear, most manuscripts being of the fourteenth century; Leopold Delisle on the other hand believes it was written at Paris at the end of the thirteenth century. Lawrence claims to have traveled to Naples and to Paris as well as Bologna. We have as yet no complete listing of the numerous manuscripts of the *Practica,* but it is

---

[118] Emmy Heller, ed., *Die Ars dictandi des Thomas von Capua,* Sitzungsberichte der Heidelberger Akademie der Wissenschaften, Philosophischhistorische Klasse, Jahrgang 1928–29: 4 Abhandlung (Heidelberg, 1929).

clear that they were circulated in Italy, France, England, and Germany.[119]

Lawrence is the author of several highly schematized dictaminal works, including a *Liber epythetorum,* which provides not only basic epithets of address for ten levels of society (from *Papa* down to *hereticos*), but alphabetical lists of 142 *verbi bona* and 167 *verbi mala* for use in letters.[120] His *Speculum dictaminis,* a letter collection, points out that "it is better to work from form rather than material" (*melius ex forma quam materia rei formande*).[121] There are several versions of his *Summa dictaminis,* which is dedicated to Philip the Fair (1296–1303) and was apparently written at Paris.[122] Some contain charts, and others are limited to a prose statement of basic theory; Lawrence's manuscripts are so widely scattered and so diversely copied, however, that these alternate versions may simply represent scribal mixtures rather than his own differing compositions. In either case it is perfectly consistent with dictaminal practice to find a *dictator* composing several forms or versions of the same basic manuscript (Guido Faba being a prime example).

Lawrence's *Practica sive usus dictaminis,* however, is clearly his own, and represents the final step in an automatizing tendency which had been an undercurrent in the *ars dictaminis* from its earliest days.[123] Simply put, the *Practica* attempts to make letter-writing a skill that is possible to any person capable of copying individual letters of the alphabet. No command of artistic principles or rhetorical theory is necessary, and indeed even a knowledge of the language is probably unnecessary. Lawrence's idea is to arrange horizontal charts of letter parts so that a "letter-writer" need only select one item from each section of the chart in order to fabricate a complete composition. The typical copy of the *Practica*

---

[119] The notice of Haskins is revealing: "Laurentius of Aquileia (or rather from Cividale in the neighborhood of Aquileia—cf. J. Loserth in *Neues Archiv.* xxii.300) was one of the most prominent of the traveling rhetoricians of the type of Pons of Provence. From his pompous addresses to students we learn that he visited Bologna, Naples, and Paris, while the models mention also Orléans and Toulouse. The student letters are rhetorical and commonplace and are generally adapted as well to another." *Studies in Medieval Culture,* p. 7n.

[120] For instance, Oxford Bodleian MS. Lyell 51 (formerly Admont MS. 596), fols. 153–160; this version attributed the work to "John": Incipit liber epythetorum compilatus a magistro iohanne de aquilegia in dictamine refulgente.

[121] Paris, Bibliotheque Nationale MS. Lat. 11384, fols. 23ᵛ–61ʳ.

[122] London, British Museum MS. Harley 3593, fols. 1–35.

[123] Rockinger (*Briefsteller,* pp. 956–66) prints a version of the *Practica* which he attributes to "John of Bondi." Perhaps "John" was a pupil of Lawrence, but the Rockinger text is adequate to provide a clear idea of his intentions. The manuscripts generally identify Lawrence as the author.

begins with a very short prologue, and then provides nothing else but a series of tabular charts arranged to give alternate phrasings for *salutationes, narrationes,* and other letter parts. For this reason, incidentally, some manuscripts contain the title *Universis tabellationes.*

The manuscript history of the *Practica* is extremely complex. Some manuscripts insert (by mistake or by design) a brief prologue which is actually the prologue of Richard de Pophis' *Summa secundum stilus curie,* a letter collection despite its title.[124] Jodocus (or Josse) de Haylprun apparently wrote or edited a paragraph version of the *Practica.*[125] Some other manuscripts include copies of the text without notation of title or author—a phenomenon not unusual in medieval manuscripts, of course— but since each of the *Practica*'s charts could be used as a self-sufficient entity, there are also examples of such things as the *narratio* charts appearing alone, or in abstracted form. We noted earlier that Rockinger has printed portions of a version of the *Practica* ascribed to "John of Bondi," who may have have been a pupil or associate of Lawrence. While the Rockinger text deals mainly with salutations, which naturally are of great importance to Lawrence, and omits the ending charts, it is sufficiently complete to show the general approach used by the author. All the complete versions of the *Practica* close, incidentally, with a chart of endings which begin with the term *Valete* ("Farewell"); although the salutations are rigidly ranked in a social hierarchy, the *Valete* series is generally in random order without any particular social distinctions.

Lawrence's basic procedure is to provide a horizontal table of alternate phrases or clauses. For instance, the first table of *narrationes* (to a Pope) as printed in Rockinger lists seven opening terms, then a single standard linking phrase, then three verb sets, a single demonstrative pronoun for a second link, and then three longer clause sets to finish the desired "sentence." The syntactical grab bag thus offered to the would-be letter writer is organized in a highly significant manner. The *Practica* consists of seven tables, each providing a method of composing a letter to a

---

[124] See Ernst Batzer, *Zur Kenntnis der Formularsammlung des Richard von Poß.* Heidelberger Abhandlungen zur mittlern und neueren Geschichte, 28 (Heidelberg, 1910).

[125] For example Oxford Bodleian Library MS. Lyell 51, which also contains the *Liber epythetorum,* includes (fols. 26–39ᵛ) a *Tractatus de modo et usu dictandi* attributed to Jodocus. It is a careless copy of the *Practica,* with some omissions, ending with the long *Valete* lists (i.e., ending phrases) typical of Lawrence's treatise. Could this be the same Jodocus de Hailbrunna, O.P. (d. 1457) who wrote a *Tractatus de predicatione?* See Harry Caplan, *Mediaeval artes praedicandi: A Handlist,* Cornell Studies in Classical Philology 24 (Ithaca, N.Y., 1934), No. 23.

different class of addressee. In other words, it is the addressee's level which determines the nature of the letter, not the subject matter or the level of the writer, or the intention of the writer. Lawrence's seven levels are:

I. Ad Pontificem
II. Ad cardinales, patriarchas, archiepiscopos, episcopos, abbates, patres, matres, avos, avunculos, amitas, matertas, novercas, et magnos prelatos
III. Ad imperatores, reges, principes, duces, comites, marchiones, potestates, milites, barones, castellanos, et alios quoscumque magnos laycos
IV. Ad minores quoscumque tam clericos quam laicos
V. Ad archdiacones, presbyteres, priores, magistres, monachos, et omnes alios huiusmodi
VI. Ad amicos, fratres, cognatos, germanos, mercatores, notarios
VII. Ad soldanos, haereticos, proditores, excommunicatores, falsos infidelos

By implication at least, each of these several levels requires some special mode of address. Forgotten is the traditional dictaminal doctrine that the level of both sender and addressee must be considered. Presumably each level demanded a certain style of address whether the message-sender was superior, inferior, or equal.

The *Practica sive usus dictaminis* of Lawrence of Aquilegia thus represents a rhetorical dead end unparalleled in the history of the arts of discourse. Given his postulates, there is no longer any need for invention of materials, for arrangement of parts, or for devising of language. Communication for him is simply a matter of completing a predetermined check list.

Yet it must be remembered that this is no isolated extremist living out his days in the seclusion of a monastic cell. Lawrence was apparently a successful traveling *dictator,* and the widespread survival of his *Practica* indicates that this "chartistic" approach did indeed find favor all over Western Europe. It apparently struck a responsive chord. The reason is not hard to see, and is bound up with an inherent, unresolved conflict over the medieval concepts of the nature of letter-writing. Is a letter a document bound by rules (*carta*), or is it a free statement by an individual (*oratio*)? [126] This conflict runs through the whole history of the *ars dictaminis,* as we have seen, with the "approved format" of Bologna

---

[126] The Englishman Thomas Sampson (fl. 1350–1400), for example, treats a letter as having thirteen parts, viewing it as a physical entity placed on a piece of paper. His *Modus dictandi* takes up each part in the order in which it occurs on the page, beginning with the opening words and ending with a signature, somewhat as a notary might view a formal document. See James J. Murphy, "Rhetoric in Fourteenth-Century Oxford," *Medium Aevum* 34 (1965), 1–20.

Lawrence of Aquilegia, *Practica sive usus dictaminis*. Oxford, Bodleian Library Ms. Lyell 13, fol. 256. (Courtesy of Bodleian Library.)

representing a compromise that skirted but did not resolve the issue. Lawrence of Aquilegia simply takes the chartistic view to its ultimate point.

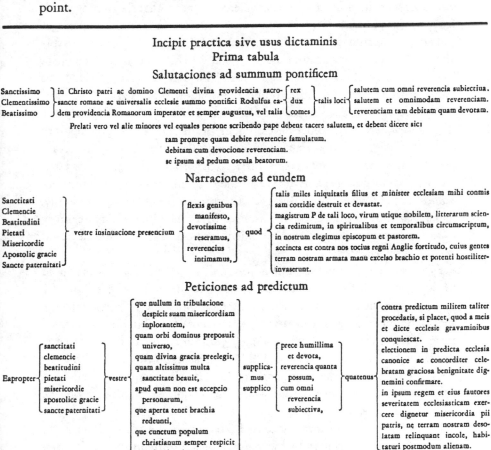

### Incipit practica sive usus dictaminis
### Prima tabula
### Salutaciones ad summum pontificem

Sanctissimo, Clementissimo, Beatissimo — in Christo patri ac domino Clementi divina providencia sacrosancte romane ac universalis ecclesie summo pontifici Rodulfus eadem providencia Romanorum imperator et semper augustus, vel talis — rex, dux, comes — talis loci — salutem cum omni reverencia subiectiua. salutem et omnimodam reverenciam. reverenciam tam debitam quam devotam.

Prelati vero vel alie minores vel equales persone scribendo pape debent tacere salutem, et debent dicere sici

tam prompte quam debite reverencie famulatum.
debitam cum devocione reverenciam.
se ipsum ad pedum oscula beatorum.

### Narraciones ad eundem

Sanctitati, Clemencie, Beatitudini, Pietati, Misericordie, Apostolic gracie, Sancte paternitati — vestre insinuacione presencium — flexis genibus manifesto, devotissime reseramus, reverencius intimamus, — quod — talis miles iniquitatis filius et minister ecclesiam mihi conmissam cottidie destruit et devastat. magistrum P de tali loco, virum utique nobilem, litterarum sciencia redimitum, in spiritualibus et temporalibus circumscriptum, in nostrum elegimus episcopum et pastorem. accincta est contra nos tocius regni Anglie fortitudo, cuius gentes terram nostram armata manu excelso brachio et potenti hostiliter invaserunt.

### Peticiones ad predictum

Eapropter — sanctitati, clemencie, beatitudini, pietati, misericordie, apostolice gracie, sancte paternitati — vestre — que nullum in tribulacione despicit suam misericordiam inplorantem, quam orbi dominus preposuit universo, quam divina gracia preelegit, quam altissimus multa sanctitate beauit, apud quam non est accepcio personarum, que aperta tenet brachia redeunti, que cunctum populum christianum semper respicit oculo pietatis, — supplicamus, supplico — prece humillima et devota, reverencia quanta possum, cum omni reverencia subiectiva, — quatenus — contra predictum militem taliter procedatis, si placet, quod a meis et dicte ecclesie gravaminibus conquiescat. electionem in predicta ecclesia canonice ac concorditer celebratam graciosa benignitate dignemini confirmare. in ipsum regem et eius fautores severitatem ecclesiasticam exercere dignetur misericordia pii patris, nę terram nostram desolatam relinquant incole, habitaturi postmodum alienam.

A printed text of a version of the *Practica* (see note 120).

With this in mind, it is perhaps easier to understand the rise of the *ars notaria* in Italy, and the corresponding decline of the influence of the *ars dictaminis*. The term "notary" (*notarius*) appears in ancient Rome to denote a certain type of professional secretary or even scribe, especially one who took down dictated material. Cicero's secretary, Tiro, for example, developed a system of shorthand for this purpose, although he did not have the title of *notarius*. The title was originally one attached to a function rather than to an official job or position. In the later Empire, however, the term *notarius* came to denote bureaucratic stenographers; the term was employed by both civil and ecclesiastical bureaucracies. As

Poole and others have shown, the papacy developed a number of official positions dealing with correspondence, record-keeping, and the like. For our purposes here it may be sufficient to note that beginning with Irnerius (1055–1130) there is a growing interest in notarial matters at Bologna. Unfortunately no coherent body of Irnerius's writings has survived, although some extant glosses may indicate his influence.[127] The next important notarial master was Rainerius of Perugia (fl. 1220). Rolandinus Passagerius (d. 1300) continued the domination of the art. The correspondence of these dates must be noted: Irnerius taught in Bologna while the *ars dictaminis* was under development; Rainerius was a contemporary of Boncompagno, Guido Faba, and Bene of Florence; Rolandinus composed a *Summa artis notariae* as early as 1256, and his career outlasted all the major *dictatores*. After 1250 there is mention of a faculty of *notaria* at the University of Bologna. The profession of notary, obviously, had reached a high level of importance. In France in the same century it was necessary for a government official to be a notary before he could become a secretary.[128]

Even before this, however, one adjunct of the *ars notaria* was produced in England in the form of a treatise on stenography by John of Tilbury (fl. 1174). His own *Ars notaria* (here, "Art of Notation")[129] describes the shorthand method (*velocitatem scribendi docere*) for taking down dictated material; it is a system of substituting *figurae* for words or phrases (e.g., the letter "C" represents *Centum*, "M" represents *Mille*, etc.). While he does not go beyond the shorthand method in his treatise to discuss the composition of documents, his whole discussion is predicated on the necessity of official transcriptions.

Basically, the *ars notaria* concerned itself with the physical forms of documents. The Prologue to the anonymous *Formularium tabellionum* (c. 1205) from Bologna indicates the primary subjects taken up:

---

[127] See Herman Kantorowicz, *Studies in the Glossators of the Roman Law: Newly Discovered Writings of the Twelfth Century* (Cambridge, 1938). Kantorowicz points out (p. 36) that the *Formularium tabellionum* long attributed to Irnerius was actually written by an anonymous notary of Bologna about 1205. See below, n. 130, for text of the Pseudo-Irnerius.

[128] See L. B. Dibben, "Secretaries in the Thirteenth and Fourteenth Centuries," *English Historical Review* 25 (1910), 430–44; and Geoffrey Barraclough, *Public Notaries and the Papal Curia: A Papal Calendar and a Study of a Formularium notariorum curie from the Early Years of the Fourteenth Century* (Rome, 1934).

[129] Valentine Rose, "*Ars notaria*: Tironischen Noten und Stenographie in 12. Jahrhundert," *Hermes* 8 (1874), 303–26. The text is on pp. 310–26.

Now this work we have composed in five books and compiled under certain titles. The first deals with the varied types of (legal) instruments according to their framers; second, with emphitities; third, with testaments; fourth, with donations, adoptions, emancipations, manumissions, conversions, and transactions; and fifth, with covenants, cautions, and other extraordinary contracts.[130]

The legal framework of the whole treatise, incidentally, is clear from the author's opening statement that it is a book of formularies dealing with both law and equity (*ius et equitatem*).

Rainerius of Perugia demonstrates more explicitly the close relation between the notarial art and the legal system. His *Ars notariae* (1226–33) [131] is divided into three parts, one dealing with contracts and covenants, another with legal judgments or decisions (*de iudiciis*), and the third with wills. His treatment consists of both exposition and examples, in a manner not unlike that of some of the dictaminal formularies. Moreover, he adds that the three subjects taken up in the book comprise the whole art of the notary. But the tone of the book is distinctly different from that of the dictaminal collections, for Rainerius speaks virtually as a lawyer. For example, he opens the second part of the *Ars notariae* with the observation that a legal judgment (i.e., a judge's decision) has the same effect as a statement of the law (*iudicium dictum est quasi iuris dictio*). He then discusses the effect of this precept on the framing of documents, with examples of phrasings to be used in various circumstances.

The notaries of Bologna ultimately organized themselves into a protective association (*societas notariorum civitatis Bononiae*) whose requirements for admission in 1304 included recommendations not only from eight notaries but from one judge and two lawyers as well.[132] The scholastic dominance of the field is clear enough from school records, and it is interesting to observe that Irnerius the legalist termed himself *magister artium* in the early twelfth century, but Rolandinus in the thirteenth century used the term *doctor artis notariae* and clearly preferred the professional designation which set him off from the nonspecialists at the university.

Certain failures of the *ars dictaminis* must have played a part in the

---

[130] [Pseudo-Irnerius], "Il *Formularium Tabellonium* di Irnerio," ed. G. B. Palmieri in *Appunti e documenti per la storia del glossatori* (Bologna, 1892), part I.

[131] Rainerius, *Ars notariae,* ed. Ludwig Wahrmund, Quellen zur Geschichte des Romisch-Kanonischen Prozesses im Mittelalter 3, Heft 2 (Innsbruck, 1917).

[132] *Ibid.,* p. 74.

rapid rise of the rival *ars notaria*. Italy itself provides prime examples of
the two opposite poles of dictaminal development—each in its way a dead
end—which demonstrate the ultimate sterility of the art. The *Practica*
of Lawrence of Aquilegia, after all, merely uses the spatial charting of
letter parts without need for human invention, and in that sense is almost
notarial; at the other extreme is the extravagant posturing of Boncompagno, whose unbridled invention leads him to absurd claims for his *ars
novissima*. What rational development for human society could be built
on either of these two foundations? Given the Bolognese respect for law,
and the considerable scholastic apparatus of commentary that soon sur-
rounded it, nothing as narrow as the *Practica* or as ephemeral as the
*Palma* could have had much lasting appeal. In 1910 Paetow pointed out
the "transient character" of the *ars dictaminis* at Bologna, noting in passing that its teachers never organized themselves into a coherent body of
masters;[133] we must observe, however, that this lack of organization was
not a cause of its decline, any more than the organization of the notaries
was a cause of their success. The reasons lie elsewhere.

Looking back over the development of the *ars dictaminis* from Alberic
of Monte Cassino (1087) to Lawrence of Aquilegia (1300), we can see
that the dictaminal movement was essentially an attempt to apply Ciceronian rhetoric to a specific compositional problem—that of writing
letters. After some false starts, the Bolognese *dictatores* popularized the
"approved format" of five formal letter parts. The first two parts—*salutatio* and *captatio benevolentiae*—always drew much more attention than
the rest of the letter, however, and as a matter of fact separate treatises
were sometimes composed merely to present multiple examples of salutations or other introductory materials. Although certain Ciceronian
*colores* were recommended by some authors, the stylistic doctrine most
characteristic of the *ars dictaminis* was the so-called *cursus* or rhythmical
prose style which depended upon clausular arrangement. Yet the art always faced the inherent dilemma of formalism versus invention; in the
long run the chartistic element lost ground to the notarial art which it
too closely resembled, and even the inventional element proved to be
too restricted. Italy itself thus furnishes a microcosmic history of the
whole development. Like any other cultural movement, of course, it
spilled across the Alps into France (and England), where it was assim-

---

[133] Paetow, *The Arts Course*, p. 80.

ilated by grammarians, and later into Germany where the formulary aspect was the most popular. New manuals continued to be written into the sixteenth century, but the basic doctrines continued to repeat what were essentially thirteenth-century Bolognese precepts. Two hundred years after Guido Faba, for instance, the Englishman Richard Kendale (fl. 1444)[134] is found writing an *ars dictaminis* based on the Bolognese concepts. Like some supernova whose light travels through space for millennia after the explosion that destroys the emitting star, the *ars dictaminis* flourished all over Europe for a long period after Italian writers had turned to other concerns. This turning away is a part of the story of the literary genius of the Quattrocento, however, and does not properly belong to this study. The fully formed *ars dictaminis* lived comfortably with the *rimatori* of what came to be called a Renaissance, but there was no major doctrinal development of the dictaminal art beyond that of Faba and Capua. Dante employed the *cursus,* presumably as result of his dictaminal studies, but as the career of Giovanni del Virgilio illustrates, the composition of manuals later became as much fashionable as useful. The almost imperceptible blending of dictamen, rhetoric, *contiones,* poetry, and other aspects of communication in Renaissance Italy is a matter for separate investigation.[135] The ultimate tidewater of dictaminal development was reached in Italy by 1300. All after that was replication.

A final remark might be made about the value of the medieval *ars dictaminis*. It began as a response to a need. Then it developed a life of its own. In the north—that is, in areas dominated by the dialectically oriented *studium generale* at Paris—it probably served to keep rhetorical interests alive during a period when Cicero's politically oriented rhetoric was simply not acceptable. On the other hand it may have contaminated or confused grammatical studies, in the sense that grammarians tended to accept the Bolognese package of dictaminal doctrine without serious study of the more fundamental relations between prose and poetry. In Germany it simply preempted study of such matters. In Italy it had no permanent effect, even the *cursus* having developed independently. The professional

---

[134] In fact, dictaminal treatises continued to be produced at least into the sixteenth century. Lidia Winniczuk, *Epistolografia* (Warsaw, 1952), covers the period 1487–1563, with a table of works for the years 1492–1555.

[135] See Jerrold Seigel, *Rhetoric and Philosophy in Renaissance Humanism: The Union of Eloquence and Wisdom, Petrarch to Valla* (Princeton, 1968).

notary soon demonstrated that his precision was a far better ally to the law than either the loose formalism or artistic invention of the dictaminal art.

Yet the *ars dictaminis* is important in the history of the arts of discourse as a rare example of applied rhetoric. Its treatises deserve further study, and the complex medieval relations between concepts of language and the social uses of language might well be illuminated for us by continued examination of this field.[136]

---

[136] An eloquent plea for further study is made by Jean Leclercq, "Le genre epistolaire au moyen âge," *Revue du moyen âge latin* 2 (1946), 63–70.

# Chapter VI

✤ ✤ ✤

# Ars praedicandi:
# The Art of Preaching

PREACHING is not a medieval—or even a Christian—invention. In the Gospel of Matthew (4:17) Jesus Christ first appears in his public life when he comes in from the desert "preaching and teaching." In other words, Christianity begins in his preaching. It is clear that the Gospel writer of the first century expected his readers to be familiar with the concept of "preaching." Indeed, the orality of the ancient Judaic liturgy was so pervasive that the regular Jewish worship service itself provided Christ with a regular and traditionally acceptable format for his speaking. It must be remembered that although Christ's religious message was revolutionary, his methods of communication were not. The preaching of Christ, then, occurs in a culture already long familiar with this particular rhetorical process.

Orthodox synagogue worship in Christ's time included three basic elements: prayer, Scriptural reading, and Scriptural discussion. All three were oral. Prayer, or a direct address to God, could be said aloud either by a delegate (priest, rabbi) of the congregation or by the whole assembled community speaking in concert. Extracts from Scripture itself could also be read aloud as prayer. Formal treatment of Scripture was the second major element in the liturgy. It involved oral reading of a text plus oral commentary, either in exposition of its meaning or in application of its message. While this took a variety of forms in Jewish practice—exegesis, comparison of texts, citing of parallels, and so forth—the basic pattern was invariably text–plus–commentary. Diverse views were accommodated by broadening the discussion to allow oral participation by the adult male members of the congregation. Outdoor speaking apparently followed a similar pattern. These practices were common many hundreds of years before the coming of Christ.

To the medieval mind, even Christ in his preaching was merely following a Creation-old pattern set by God the Father. Preaching was the second act of God following the creation of Man himself, and preaching formed for many ages the primary means of communication between God and man. In the words of the fourteenth-century writer Robert of Basevorn:[1]

> After creating man, God preached (if we extend the word "preaching"), saying to Adam (Gen. 2:17) *For in what day soever thou shalt eat of it, thou shalt die the death.* This was the first persuasion of which we read in Scripture. The preceding words, however, pertain more to a precept when it is said: *Of every tree in Paradise thou shalt eat;* or to a prophecy when it is said: *increase and multiply, etc.;* or, according to some, to establishment in power and possession. Afterward He preached frequently through angels who assumed bodies or, as some would have it, some other corporeal likeness which He Himself assumed not in union of substance, but only in moving as perhaps He spoke to Adam and many others. Then He preached frequently through Moses and some Prophets, and finally, with the approach to the end of the Old Testament, through John the Baptist, of whom is said (Matt. 3:1): *In those days came John the Baptist preaching in the desert of Judea, and saying, Do penance, for the kingdom of heaven is at hand.* And at last He Himself, taking on a human soul and body in the unity of substance came preaching the same theme which His precursor had preached before, as is seen in Matt. 4:17.

Humbert of Romans, the fifth master general of the Order of Preachers (Dominicans), who died in 1277, argues that human preaching is necessary to carry on the heavenly discourse which the saints in heaven have carried on ever since the creation of mankind:[2]

> To know how much preaching is necessary to the world, we should remember that the souls of the Saints in heaven lift their voices before the Lord in never-ending complaint of "those who dwell on earth" (Apoc. 6:11). This cry, according to the commentators, is directed against those unrepentant men who put off the fulness of joy of the elect. . . . But there is nothing that will hasten this hour of perfect reparation quicker than the voice of preachers; for they continue what Jesus their model began when He

---

[1] Robert of Basevorn, *The Form of Preaching,* trans. Leopold Krul, O.S.B., in James J. Murphy (ed.), *Three Medieval Rhetorical Arts* (Berkeley and Los Angeles, 1971), pp. 126–27.
[2] Humbert of Romans, *A Treatise on Preaching,* trans. The Dominican Students of the Province of St. Joseph (London, 1955), p. 4.

said: "Repent, for the kingdom of heaven is at hand" (Matt. 4:17). It is evident that it depends on the preachers to assure the elect the consummation of their heavenly joy.

The continuity of preaching since Creation is stressed by Humbert, quoting Psalm 68 from the Old Testament: "The Lord will give the word to them that preach good tidings with great power." Humbert said that even the Jews respected the value of preaching.

Indeed, the whole elaborate apparatus of Judaic liturgy demonstrates the enormous importance which the Jews attached to the Word. The Old Testament Prophets were essentially preachers, and the entire Judaic effort to preserve "the Testament"—the Book, the Writing, the Scripture—was based on an appreciation of the fact that Scripture was intended to be a written record of God's messages to mankind. Given their belief that God has been communicating with mankind since Creation through the Jewish race, it was only natural that the Jews studied carefully every word and every action reported in Scripture. The liturgy, or formal worship service, was designed to bring these studies to the whole community of believers.

The Jewish liturgy—the form of worship most familiar to Christ, Paul, Peter and the other Apostles—grew incrementally over many centuries.[3] But it had reached a stabilized form some two centuries before Christ. Originally short "lessons" (passages of Scripture) had been read at festivals and on special Sabbath days; later came a more formal procedure of weekly Sabbath readings from the Pentateuch, the first five books of Scripture. Ultimately this series of readings from the Pentateuch—the Law—was set up on a three-year cycle, so that by reading one of the 150 sections on each Sabbath, the whole could be covered in three years. An entire section or chapter was read without interruption before comment. Later, but at some time well before Christ, readings from the Prophets were introduced. Prayers and Psalms came before and after the readings and their discussion. The *Shema,* or iteration of beliefs coupled with a benediction, also had a part in the liturgy developed in pre-Christian times. At every stage of this liturgical development, Scriptural reading and Scriptural discussion had a prominent place in Jewish worship.

The great Temple of Jerusalem was the starting point for the national

---

[3] A convenient summary may be found in W. O. E. Oesterley, *The Jewish Background of the Christian Liturgy* (Oxford, 1925). For details of Judaic preaching in connection with the liturgy, see Siegmund Maybaum, *Judische Homiletik* (Berlin, 1890).

liturgy, but the worship service moved as well into the synagogue and—a critical factor for the spread of Christian liturgies—into all the synagogues established wherever Jewish communities sprang up in the Mediterranean world. For the devout Jew of Antioch or Corinth, unable to return to the Temple, his local synagogue was in a sense his own "Temple." After the destruction of the Temple by the Romans in A.D. 70, the local synagogues assumed even more importance.

But the religious community did not rely solely upon oral readings of the text of Scripture. In every case for which we have records, extending as far back as the time of Ezra (400 B.C.), the oral text was accompanied immediately by an oral exposition of its meaning and significance. In Nehemiah 8:8 we read: "And they read in the book, in the law of God, distinctly [or, "with an interpretation"]; and they gave the sense, so that they understood the meaning." In the worship service the reading-with-commentary was so integral a function that the service could not proceed at all without an audience; the *Mishnah,* a compilation of ancient oral traditions finally put in writing by Rabbi Juhah ha-nassi about A.D. 200, stipulates that neither reading nor exposition could proceed unless at least ten men were present.[4]

The same interpretive tradition flourished outside the formal worship service in respect to the Law as it related to actual human conduct. That is, the study of exact Scriptural text was one line of inquiry, while the abstraction of generic principles from it was quite another. Rabbi Ben-Sira (fl. 170 B.C.) tells of his Beth ha-Midrash, or "house of instruction" in which authorities lectured to their pupils about the Law (as opposed to text). Here again there was opportunity for oral citation of proofs for viewpoints, with the text of Scripture functioning as a type of what Aristotle would have called apodeictic proof. It will be recalled that when Christ was twelve years old he alarmed his parents by staying behind in Jerusalem to argue with learned authorities about the Law (Luke 2:41–50). They were amazed at the youth's command of the Scriptural text and his familiarity with the standard arguments of the day. Here, outside the liturgy, was an example of the continuing Jewish quest for a more complete understanding of God's Word.

When Jesus Christ entered upon his public life, then, he entered into a community which for centuries had been accustomed to the spoken text

---

[4] Oesterley, *The Jewish Background,* pp. 28–35 and 41–42.

of Scripture, accompanied always by oral explanation or interpretation. Moreover, it was a community accustomed to abstract discussion of generic principles based on that Scripture. It was, in short, a community accustomed to preaching.

Christ—and Christendom after him—continued in this corporate rhetorical tradition. There was every good reason for this. Scripture is remarkable in that it often contains directions for its own use, whether in the form of Yahweh's admonitions to the Jews or in the form of accounts of Prophets or others using the Book. It is thus frequently its own guide. Again, the sense of their special destiny made the Chosen People plumb the depths of the Book in search of revelations about the future, so that over the centuries they naturally developed sophisticated exegetical methodologies that had a high level of efficiency. These methodologies were for the sake of the community, not merely for the scholarly isolate (as in some Eastern religions); consequently Christ, as a member of this Jewish community, inherited an imposing array of rhetoro-grammatical tools that had been developed over time and shared with the whole community through the oral readings and discussions of the learned men among them. This purposeful corporate rhetoricality is not found in any other community of the ancient world.

This is an absolutely crucial distinction. Both Demosthenes and Cicero, for example, spoke to elite groups whose stratified societies were founded ultimately on slave labor. Neither Greek nor Roman civil society had a theocratic base, let alone a sense of divine destiny. Education in both societies was superimposed on the life style of its elite users (who were of course only a small portion of the total population); by contrast, the Jewish communal worship and Jewish private life merged so closely together that in a sense the whole ancient Judaic life was an integrated learning process. The means of learning and the means of expressing were inextricably interwoven through the pervasive Scriptural experience.

For this reason Christ's preaching practices reflect a profound communicative theory. However dimly this may have been perceived by medieval theorists, it was a fact destined to have enormous effect on Christian preaching. Before examining this factor, however, one more important event needs to be noted.

Christ also introduced a rhetorical element which had never before operated in human history—a direct command to his followers to spread his ideas through speech. This is stated clearly in the Synoptic Gospels, by

Matthew, Mark, and Luke. Mark 3:14-15 says: "And he appointed twelve that they might be with them and that he might send them forth to preach." Matthew 28:16-20 is even more explicit:

> And the eleven disciples went into Galilee, unto the mountain where Jesus had appointed them. And seeing him they adored: but some doubted. And Jesus coming, spoke to them, saying: All power is given to me in heaven and in earth. Going therefore, teach ye all nations; baptizing them in the name of the Father, and of the Son, and of the Holy Ghost. Teaching them to observe all things whatsoever I have commanded you: and behold, I am with you all days, even to the consummation of the world.

In other words, preaching is made a fundamental responsibility of the followers of Christ, in all places, and at all times, to the end of time. There was no precedent for this command. No ancient Greek or Roman was ever so presumptuous. Even the Jews had been asked merely to safeguard the Word, not to spread it to all mankind. The whole interpretive apparatus of Jewish scholarship was founded on the assumption that the Scripture was a finite, though mysterious, body of writings entrusted to Israel alone. The gulf between Jew and "Gentile" (i.e., non-Jew) was a practical result of this feeling.

Christ's command, on the other hand, pointed toward an infinite goal that envisioned enormous, continuing oratorical effort on a world-wide basis. There was to be no distinction among audiences, no perpetuation of the believer-outsider dichotomy. This of course placed an appalling responsibility on the Apostles and their successors. A keen appreciation of this responsibility is seen throughout the life of the Christian Church. Saint Paul constantly reminds the new Christians of their responsibility, as in Corinthians 14:9, where he points out "so likewise you, except you utter by the tongue plain speech, how shall it be known what is said?" Paul's own career demonstrates his full acceptance of the responsibility, for after his conversion he devoted his whole life to the arduous evangelistic travels spelled out in such human detail in the Acts of the Apostles and in his own four major Epistles to the new churches. Saint Augustine believed preaching to be so important for the salvation of its hearers that he said even hypocrites should preach if they have the talent: "thus they benefit many by preaching what they do not practice." [5] The castigation of

---

[5] Saint Augustine, *On Christian Doctrine,* trans. D. W. Robertson (New York, 1958), IV.xxvii, p. 165. Augustine also points out the value to the hearers as well: "Thus they may hear usefully those who do not act usefully." It would of course be even better if their lives matched their words, he says, but it is clear that for Augustine the preaching is more important than the preacher.

nonpreachers is common in medieval treatises. Guibert of Nogent, writing about 1084, declares that "just as it is damnable to set an example of vice, so it is almost equally worthy of damnation to refuse to aid sinners through preaching." [6] Humbert of Romans lists nine "guilts" and thirteen "frivolous reasons" to be found among those who refuse to preach. Robert of Basevorn declares flatly, "Preaching and teaching are necessary to the church." [7] Thomas Aquinas calls preachers "the mouth of Christ" and adds, "Preaching is the noblest of all ecclesiastical functions." [8] Acceptance of the preaching responsibility was thus immediate and continuous, even though no theory as such emerged in the early years.

Christian preaching had begun under a unique set of circumstances: Christ, its first preacher, preached within a rhetorically sophisticated community adept at Scriptural discussion; he himself as a member of the worshiping community shared a lifetime of communicative experience; then he deliberately commanded his followers to spread his doctrines through preaching; finally, his followers readily accepted the command and strove to carry it out.

The history of preaching theory—the *praecepta* that gave direction to these Christians wishing to preach—therefore has its first phase in the person of Christ. His own preaching, clearly based on a conscious appreciation of certain rhetorical objectives, shows certain patterns which became models for later theorists; in addition, the Synoptic Gospels report statements of Christ which can only be called preceptive; Paul follows him closely.

The second major phase of preaching theory occurs in the *De doctrina christiana* of Saint Augustine, which he completed in A.D. 426. After 426 until the thirteenth century there are only occasional and rather generalized contributions in books like Gregory the Great's *Cura pastoralis* (A.D. 591), the *De institutione clericorum* (A.D. 819) of Rabanus Maurus, the *Liber quo ordine sermo fieri debeat* (c. 1084), of Guibert of Nogent, and the *De arte praedicatoria* (1199?) of Alain de Lille.

The third phase begins in the first half of the thirteenth century with the comparatively sudden appearance of a fully developed theory of "thematic" preaching. More than three hundred treatises still survive from

---

[6] Joseph M. Miller, "Guibert de Nogent's *Liber quo ordine sermo fieri debeat*: A Translation of the Earliest Modern Speech Textbook," *Today's Speech* 17 (1969), p. 46.

[7] Basevorn, *The Form of Preaching*, p. 114.

[8] Quoted in Joachim Walsh, O.P., "St. Thomas on Preaching," *Dominicana* 5 (1921), 6–14.

this phase, which lasted into the Reformation. Early thirteenth-century writers like Thomas of Salisbury, Richard of Thetford, and Alexander of Ashby established a *modus* or *forma* for preaching based on divisions and amplifications. The *Forma praedicandi* (1322) of Robert of Basevorn is a typical manual which almost perfectly embodies the entire movement.

Christ set a model for Christian preachers in several ways. Most importantly, he confirmed and reinforced the Judaic practice of using Scripture as proof; he distinguished carefully between parables and "direct" discourse; he distinguished between evangelizing (announcement) and teaching (exposition of doctrine); and finally he made constant comparison of earthly and divine through the use of analogy and metaphor. Each of these features runs through Christian preaching even to the present, but they are especially prominent in the medieval period.

It will be recalled that Greek and Roman rhetoric purported to deal with what Aristotle described as nonapodeictic proofs—that is, means by which an audience could be led to believe an assertion without formal logical demonstration. For Aristotle, rhetoric deals with two psychological means—*ethos* and *pathos*—as well as the apparent reasonableness of the enthymeme in a sort of "logical" proof. Cicero and other Romans sought to make a case "plausible" (believable) mainly through probabilities. No ancient pagan rhetorician ever conceived of any single mode of proof as being conclusive or binding. (Even Aristotle's apodeictic proof depended upon a formal, continuous line of syllogistic reasoning in which every premise had to be true and every connection valid; in any case, as he points out in *Rhetoric* I.2, many men are not able to follow this method, and it is therefore not suitable for general communication.) The elaborate array of rhetorical "topics" (*topoi, loci*) developed between Aristotle and Quintilian, for instance, illustrates the relative insignificance of any single approach: every topic is for the speaker simply a suggestive line of inquiry leading to a suggestive line of thought to be planted in a hearer's mind. Therefore every topic is equal in value to every other one. Topics are distinguishable only by their varied suitability for this or that audience. But all share one major rhetorical fault: their maximum expectation is the creation of probability.[9]

---

[9] See, for instance, Cicero, *De inventione. De optimo genere oratorum. Topica,* trans. H. M. Hubbell (Cambridge, Mass., 1949), and Aristotle, *Topics,* trans. W. A. Pickard-Cambridge in *The Works of Aristotle,* ed. W. D. Ross (Oxford, 1949–56), Vol. I.

But note, on the other hand, the nature of Christian belief. Briefly, it is that a personal God, having created a universe from nothing, peopled it with men. The first men turned away from their Creator—"sinned"— and as a consequence were driven from a state of paradise and charged with the task of earning their divine salvation through adherence to God's commands. The Jews believed that their people were entrusted with the preservation of the historical record of God's direct commands, and that their nation was chosen by God to maintain this record until the promised coming of a Savior (Messiah), who would complete the return of mankind to God. "The Book"—or Testament—recounting the history of God's relation with men (and especially with the Jews) was therefore a sacred document. Its account of divine history was worthy of intense study so that men could determine God's wishes in the world. When Christ announced that he was the Savior so long expected, he therefore took the entire Testament as his support. His arrival was in itself further proof of the already proved.

Christ was therefore able to use the Testament as absolute, apodeictic proof. Other Jews were already accustomed to this, but his reinforcement transmitted the methodology to the newly conceived world-wide missionary effort which we have come to call Christianity. And of course his own statements and his own history, recounted by the Gospel writers, became themselves a "New" Testament ranking in "apodeicticity" with that known to the earlier Jews; thus Paul, Peter, and all other later preachers could quote him afterwards in absolute proof.

The distinction between "preaching" and "teaching" was also carried over from Jewish practice. In Matthew 4:17 Christ begins his public life by "preaching": "From that time Jesus began to preach, and to say, 'Repent, for the kingdom of heaven is at hand.'" The Greek word *to preach* comes from a word meaning *to proclaim,* that is, to announce as a herald would announce news. The Latin word *evangelium* thus means "bearer of news" or announcer of glad tidings.[10] (In this sense, John the Baptist would be regarded as the first Christian preacher in that he was the first to announce the arrival of Christ.) Jewish oral interpretation of the Scripture was of course primarily "teaching," addressed to a community

---

[10] Significantly, the modern English word "Gospel" comes from the West Saxon (i.e., Old English) term *God spellum*—literally, "good story." When Gregory the Great in the sixth century refers to the office of the preacher he says that the preacher "undertakes the office of herald." See below, p. 292.

already convinced of the truth of the Testament; nevertheless, the Jews recognized a different function for the Prophets and others who brought out major new ideas. In any case the synagogue discourse that moved from textual interpretation to moral exhortation clearly contained elements of both. Christ's usual practice, at least outside the synagogue, was to combine both functions depending upon circumstances. The Gospel writers are conscious of the distinction, however, especially in stressing the methodology of the parable.

While the apodeicticity of Scripture was clearly the most significant preceptive outcome of Christ's preaching, his distinction between parable and nonparable speaking is also very important. As the fourteenth-century writer Rypon of Durham expressed it, "In various parables and examples he instigated the people, both Jewish and Christian, to abstain from vices and pursue virtues. And this is what is said in Mark 4:2—'He taught them many things in parables.' " [11] The Jewish community had long distinguished between teaching (exposition of doctrine) and preaching (exhortation to action). Nevertheless, the discovery of meaning in the Testament was always with the implied purpose of determining human actions desired by God, so that it was not always easy to mark the precise line of demarcation between teaching and preaching. When Christ at the age of twelve debated with the learned doctors, the subject was obviously the interpretation of Scripture. When he began his public career he continued to use the synogogue for opportunities to address the congregation concerning Scripture (e.g., Luke 4:14-42). Undoubtedly these addresses in the synagogue were essentially expository. It might be surmised that the discourses followed the methods long familiar to Jewish exegesis: concordance of texts, multiple significations of terms, relation of text excerpts to other passages or to the whole Scripture history, and so forth. These methods naturally demanded intimate familiarity with the entire corpus of the Testament. Since synagogue practice allowed others present to comment upon the remarks, the ever-present challenge must also have acted as an effective spur to accuracy of citation.

But Christianity was founded outside the synagogue. The Testament had prophesied (Psalms 49:4 and 78:2-3) that the Savior would speak in parables. A parable may be defined as a method of speech in which a

---

[11] Cited in Gerald R. Owst, *Literature and Pulpit in Medieval England,* 2nd ed. (Oxford, 1961), p. 152.

moral or religious lesson is conveyed by an analogy to common experience. The three Synoptic Gospels report forty major parables from Christ's
public career. While these Gospels are of course summaries or abstracts—
hence the term Synoptic—they are fairly reliable for the general methods
Christ used even if they cannot be relied upon for exact verbal texts of
his discourses. Modern readers are familiar with the methods employed
in such famous parables as the Prodigal Son, the Unjust Steward, the
Good Samaritan, the Laborers in the Vineyard, the Lost Sheep, and the
Sower and the Seed. Each narrative is accompanied by a statement of the
moral lesson to be grasped in it. Christ's reason for the method, Matthew
tells us (13:10–16), was that it was not given to all men to know his message directly. This of course implies that some other men could receive
the message directly. The distinction is spelled out carefully in Mark
4:33–34: "And in many such parables he spoke the word to them, according as they were able to understand it; but without a parable he did not
speak to them. But privately he explained all things to his disciples."

This rhetorical judgment—basically a distinction between levels of
audience capability—is echoed throughout the history of Christian preaching. In its crudest form it divided humanity into the learned and the unlearned, with a special homiletic method for each. But its chief effect was
probably to remind preachers to be wary of differences between audiences.
Consequently it constitutes a rhetorical precept of great importance. In
fact, it provides the unifying theme for one of the earliest formal treatises
on preaching, the *Cura pastoralis* (A.D. 591) of Pope Gregory the Great,
and it merits attention from almost every later writer on preaching.

A third important feature of Christ's preaching is more difficult to assess. It is his insistence that the visible universe is a useful paradigm of
divine reality; that is, that human beings can learn something of God
through more complete understanding of things around them in the
world. This doctrine is closely related to his use of parables, which are
themselves intended to be worldly reminders of superworldly things.
Saint Paul readily summarized this idea—Christ did not himself state it
explicitly—when he made statements like his famous "All things are written for our instruction" (Romans 15:4). Jewish understanding of their
nation's mission in the world, of course, led them to understand their own
history as a tangible sign of God's intentions for humanity. Each event
in their history was therefore subject to study for possible signification.
The natural result in Scriptural scholarship was a tendency toward modes

of multiple interpretation.[12] Christ's parable of the Sower and the Seed (Mark 4:3–20), in which a significant religious meaning is found for every piece of data, is an excellent example of this tradition.

It must be emphasized here that insofar as Christ's actions and utterances became for Christians part of a "New" Testament equal in truth to the "Old" Testament, it was to be expected that Christ's sayings would have to be plumbed for their meanings just as Jewish readers had had to plumb Jeremiah, Solomon, or Job. It would have been surprising if every precept of Christ had been found fully elucidated in explicit terms within the New Testament itself. The task of the historian of preaching theory is to detect those underlying precepts which shaped the art, and to trace their preceptive influence. It seems abundantly clear that Christ shared the Jewish methodology of multiple interpretation, recommended it to his followers through his example, and expected it to be a major factor in the new Christian message system.

Saint Paul (A.D. 3–68) seems to have grasped all of this, and in his own reflections on the preaching mission of the new church went beyond Christ's explicit statements to enunciate what can only be called a theology of preaching.[13] He introduced several concepts that were to concern theorists throughout early Christian and medieval times: the relation of grace to preaching, the contrast between preaching and ordinary oratory, the question of who should preach, and even the relation between preaching and the worship service. Above all, he stressed the mandate of Christ.

Paul was by all odds one of the most spectacularly successful orators in history. He was born at Tarsus of a father who was a Roman citizen, and he had both a Jewish and Roman education. He tells of a striking conversion to Christ even while he was persecuting the new sect. In a period of 23 years, from A.D. 45 to his martyrdom at Rome in 68, he ranged throughout the known world from Spain to Asia preaching the new message. His common practice was to initiate his preaching in a city so that he could reach more people. If there was a synagogue he would

---

[12] The best single analysis of this development in respect to medieval preaching is probably that of Harry Caplan, "The Four Senses of Scriptural Interpretation and the Medieval Theory of Preaching," *Speculum* 4 (1929), 282–90. See also Henri Lubac, *Exégèse médiévale: Les quatres sens de l'écriture* (Paris, 1959); and Beryl Smalley, *The Study of the Bible in the Middle Ages* (Oxford, 1952).

[13] While Paul's career has drawn intensive study, there has been little systematic rhetorical analysis of his communicative process. Paul's rhetorical contribution is ignored by such standard works as Edwin C. Dargan, *A History of Preaching,* 2 vols. (New York, 1905; reprinted in 1 vol. 1954). But see Johann B. Schneyer, *Geschichte der katholischen Predigt* (Freiburg im Bresgau, 1969), pp. 30–37.

speak there; when the inevitable rupture came because of his new doctrines, he would take his followers away from the synagogue to found a new community (*ecclesia*) elsewhere in the city. Then he would move on, leaving someone else in charge, but writing frequently to the new community; his letters (the Epistles of the New Testament) were intended to be read aloud so that the community could share them. Where there was no synagogue, as in Athens, he would speak in some public place like the Areopagus.

He made striking use of Scripture as apodeictic proof. This method of course could only be effective with Jewish audiences, who already accepted the truth of the Testament. The Acts of the Apostles (18:28) explains this, "for with much vigor he convinced the Jews openly, showing by the scriptures that Jesus is the Christ." A revealing contrast in rhetorical method may be seen by comparing Paul's Areopagus speech (Acts 17:17–34) with one that he made in a synagogue (Acts 13:14–41). Both speeches are well organized into clearly demarcated sections. To the Athenians Paul addresses a reasoned argument to prove to them that their idols cannot truly be gods; he announces that Jesus Christ is God. To the Jews he cites David, Isaiah, and the Psalms, concluding with a warning that the prophecy of Hubaeus will fall upon them if they do not recognize the New Law. Except for the final section the Areopagus speech could as well have come from a pagan rhetor—but the synagogue speech uses the text of Scripture for proof in a way that no pagan could have found possible. Again, because Paul became a major part of the New Testament, this continuation of the Jewish methodology transmitted to all later Christian preachers the apodeicticity of Scripture.

This transmittal is especially important when one considers the potential influence of Paul's statements about the nature of preaching. His First Letter to the Corinthians contains within a few lines his most crucial pronouncements. He begins (I Cor. 1) with a reminder of Christ's mandate, and then identifies a number of key propositions which are perhaps best seen in these excerpts:

"For Christ sent me not to baptize, but to preach the Gospel; not in the wisdom of human speech, lest the cross of Christ be made void." (I Cor. 1:17)
what should be preached is "the message of the cross" (1:18) and not "the wisdom of the world." (1:20)
"and my speech and my preaching was not in the persuasive words of human wisdom, but in the showing of the Spirit and power." (2:4)
"for the kingdom of God is not in speech but in power." (4:20)

"So likewise you, except you utter by the tongue plain speech, how shall it be known what is said?" (14:9)
"But in the church I had rather speak five words with my understanding, that I may instruct others also, than ten thousand words in a strange tongue." (14:19)

The metarhetoric of Saint Paul—that is, his foundation for a theory of preaching—thus includes several new elements not found in pagan rhetoric. First is his keen appreciation of the responsibility for persuasion which Christ's mandate thrust upon the Church. He is also acutely conscious of God's possible intervention during the preaching event itself, in other words, of the possibility that the efficacy of a preaching discourse might depend not on the rhetorical skill of the speaker but on God's gift of grace to speaker and hearer. (Acts 20:32 in fact refers to grace as a gift that enables a hearer to comprehend the word of God transmitted through a human speaker.)[14] The possibility of grace also tends to derogate the human skill derived from rhetoric, since God's message is so powerful that its mere utterance will be persuasive. This is quite different from Plato's idea of truth being persuasive in itself, or the Stoic-Senecan view that a speaker should speak with utter simplicity to let the message transmit itself. It is also different from Aristotle's dictum that the truth will prevail if opponents have equal skill. What Paul means is that the message itself has divine power. One practical result of this principle was that for a dozen centuries the Church was almost exclusively concerned with *what* to preach—not *how*.

Another element new with Christianity is the concern for the spiritual welfare of the hearer rather than for the success of the speaker. Ancient rhetoric was entirely speaker-oriented. Concern for the audience was entirely in terms of analyzing ways to let the speaker have his way with his hearers. But Saint Paul visualizes the preacher as a Christ-knower who is charged with a duty to make all men come to know Christ. And this is to be done because Christ so commanded, for the sake of the unpersuaded hearer—"that I may instruct others also"—with the preacher as a mere instrument of transmission. The Christian orator is to work for the salvation of his hearers, not for his own speaking success.[15]

---

[14] Note the remark of Thomas Aquinas: ". . . the Holy Spirit makes use of the human tongue as an instrument, but it is He who perfects the work within us." *Summa theologica,* 2a 2ae, 177.1.
[15] This was to become a constant theme of writers on preaching. At the Second Council of Vaison (A.D. 529), for example, when the centuries-old preaching mo-

On the question of who should preach, Paul clearly believes that a divine "call" will identify the preacher. He tells of his own spectacular call by God while on the road to Damascus (Acts 9:1–19). In turn he urges certain others to preach, such as Timothy, whom he bade "preach the word" (II Tim. 2:4). But Paul says that women should not preach. And if preaching power is in some way the product of a gift from God, Paul would no doubt say, then a man's mere desire to preach would not in itself qualify him to do so. As a practical matter this principle tended to limit the preaching function to a small number of men ("bishops"), even in the earliest days of the Church. By the time ecclesiastical regulations became formalized in the fourth century—after the end of the persecutions —the principle of priestly preaching had long been cemented into church life.[16]

Finally, Paul's efforts to set up a communication network among the new Christian churches had the indirect result of strengthening the position of the spoken word in Christian worship. The Jewish liturgy of course called for Scripture readings. This practice was apparently followed in the new Christian communities as well, and Paul asked that his letters to the churches be read aloud so they could be shared with the

---

nopoly of the bishops was broken by allowing priests to preach, the reason given was that it was "for the edification of all the churches and the benefit of all the people not only in the cities but also in the rural areas." And even this extension of powers was allowed because of the importance of the preaching function: "If, because of illness, the priest is unable to preach, let the homilies of the holy fathers be read by the deacons." Cited by P. F. Mulhern, "The History of Homiletic Theory," in the New Catholic Encyclopedia, Vol. 12 (1967), p. 685.

[16] At the first "ecumenical" (i.e., "world-wide") Church council at Nicea in A.D. 325, the twenty canons promulgated by the church fathers dealt as often with administrative details as with religious doctrine. Some examples: clergy belong to a particular diocese administered by a bishop, and cannot move freely into another diocese without his consent; a bishop must be chosen by the other bishops in an eparchy (civil province); prayers shall be offered standing. Preaching is taken for granted as a special function of a bishop. Two centuries elapsed before the Second Council of Vaison broadened this interpretation to include priests, but the difference may have been merely a technical one. Obviously a bishop could not preach simultaneously everywhere in his diocese, and the responsibility was frequently delegated to others. Saint Augustine first began his preaching in the 380's as a "presbyter," that is, a special church officer designated as a preacher, and even as early as Paul's lifetime (according to Acts 2:15) there was a suggestion that a certain Hippolytus was a preacher without the title of bishop. The main point, however, is that preaching remained a clerical duty from the very earliest times. For Greek and English texts of the early councils, see Charles J. Hefele, A History of the Christian Councils from the Original Documents to the Close of the Council of Nicaea, A.D. 325 (Edinburgh, 1871).

community (Col. 4:16, I Thess. 5:27).[17] A more direct liturgical connection occurred in Troas, where Paul delivered a discourse before the "breaking of bread" (Acts 20:7 ff.). All the evidence indicates that the early churches had a regular (weekly) worship service which included readings with discourses, as well as prayers and the breaking of bread (the Eucharist). Paul's epistles, originally addressed to specific communities, were so universal in scope that they could be read profitably by other churches as well. In the very early days, when the faithful met in private houses, the informal atmosphere must surely have encouraged conversational discussion of the epistle after its oral reading. In any case it is clear from Paul's own words that he encouraged the spoken word.

It is clear, then, that later preachers could find much instruction in both the preaching practices and the metarhetorical statements of Christ and Paul. Both figures became enshrined apodeictically in what became the New Testament. Christ's mandate for preaching, his exemplary use of parables and multiple significations, Paul's theology of preaching and his influence on the liturgy—all these factors operated powerfully in the earliest centuries of the new church. We have very few details concerning the preaching of the first few centuries, though some sermon texts have survived. What is striking, though, is that when the Church emerged into public life after the end of the persecutions, each bishop's preaching was already so solidly established as a prime obligation that in respect to preaching the first Church councils (e.g., Nicaea, in 325) concerned themselves merely with the mechanics of episcopal administration.[18] Preaching was obviously important in the Christian church from its very beginning.

But the striking fact is that in the next twelve hundred years after Christ and Paul there is only one major preceptive treatise on preaching

---

[17] See Josef A. Jungmann, S.J., *The Early Liturgy to the Time of Gregory the Great,* trans. Francis A. Brunner, C.S.S.R. (London, 1960), esp. pp. 14, 42, 167. Following Jewish practice, the Scriptural reading was apparently a *lectio continuata,* or unbroken reading of a whole book. See also J. H. Srawley, *The Early History of the Liturgy* (Oxford, 1947), pp. 14–34.

[18] Even as late as A.D. 692 one finds a Council (Quinisext) stating that the prelate must preach to both clergy and people: "It behooves those who preside over the churches, every day but especially on the Lord's Day, to teach all the clergy and people words of piety and right religion, gathering out of Holy Scripture meditations and determinations of the truth, and not going beyond the limits now fixed, nor varying from the tradition of the God-bearing fathers." *The Seven Ecumenical Councils of the Undivided Church* in *The Select Library of Pre- and Post-Nicene Fathers,* 2nd Series, ed. Henry R. Percivel, Vol. XIV (London, 1900), p. 374.

—Saint Augustine's *De doctrina christiana* (396–426). Twelve hundred years is a very long time in the history of Western civilization. The entire development of Greek and Roman culture—roughly, Pindar to Quintilian—occupied only six and a half centuries. Why, in the face of a mandate from its founder, did Christianity for so long neglect to erect a theoretical foundation for an activity so clearly fundamental?

Naturally there are some reasons. The first several centuries of organization, hampered by spasmodic persecution, did not favor theory-building of any kind. When the persecutions ended, there was a revolt against pagan learning. By the time Saint Augustine's principles were formulated, the first barbarian invasions had begun to undermine Roman civilization. During the ensuing so-called Dark Ages, it might be argued, there was little time for the serious study necessary to establish a rhetoric of preaching.

But the plain fact was that during all those centuries preaching methodology was never an urgent matter for the Church. The urgent theoretical questions clearly did receive attention. Even Saint Paul's Epistles indicate the fierce controversies of the first century over such matters as the relation of Christians to Jews, the duty of love, the nature of sin, and a host of others. These questions demanded—and received—attention. Priestly celibacy, the divinity of Christ, the territorial jurisdiction of bishops, ownership of property by individual Christians—all these were debated by the early fourth century. The nature, form, or methodology of preaching was not debated. In the face of evidence that the Church did indeed debate its most pressing issues, it can only be concluded that preaching theory was not regarded as a key issue.

It was only on the specific question of the use of pagan learning—including rhetoric—that churchmen became involved at all in serious queries about preaching. And this controversy occurred only during the fourth and fifth centuries.

The debate about rhetoric in the fourth century shows, as well as anything could, the state of mind that led the Church as a whole to its long-held position on preaching theory. While that controversy properly belongs to the history of the ancient *ars rhetorica* of Cicero and Quintilian, and has been summarized above in Chapter Two in connection with the Age of Transition, it obviously has important implications for preaching.[19]

---

[19] See above, pp. 46–63.

To a modern observer it might well seem that the Christian Church needed only to take over the existing *ars rhetorica* to fulfill its mandated role of preaching. Rhetoric, after all, had been studied carefully since the time of Plato. A good deal of prudent advice for speakers was available within its five canons of invention, arrangement, style, memory, and delivery. However, there were serious difficulties involved. The stated objectives of rhetoric were either amoral or avowedly political; expediency seemed its hallmark; and the educational system built around it was studded with literary examples many Christians regarded as immoral. Moreover, it was not at all clear that the Church should in any case try to use secular wisdom of any kind. The Church, after all, was a new development in human history, and some argued that it should therefore develop in its own way. Contemporary examples of sophistry and Stoic logic-chopping provided fuel for this argument.

Saint Augustine's reply was contained in his *De doctrina christiana,* the first three books of which were completed in 396 and the fourth in 426. But other significant statements occur in his *De magistro* and *De cate-chizandis rudibus.* A metarhetoric of preaching is contained in these three works. That is, Augustine outlines the first principles upon which a rhetoric of preaching could be constructed.

It must be remembered that the fourth book of the *De doctrina christi-ana* is a defense of conventional Ciceronian rhetoric. Augustine recommends that Christians, especially preachers, study rhetoric to learn how to express their thoughts. Because he had grown up in a tradition steeped in Cicero and Quintilian and had devoted his pre-Christian career to teaching rhetoric, it is naturally the rhetoric of Cicero and the educational practices of the Roman schools which dominate Augustine's fourth book.

This is a well-known story which needs little repetition here. By his adamant insistence on the use of Roman education—that is, the rhetorical education of the Roman schools as described so ably by Quintilian— Augustine made it possible for later writers like Rabanus Maurus to weave his ideas directly into their manuals for the training of priests and preachers for the Church; thus his influence flowed into the medieval church. For instance, Augustine was able to point to passages in the Bible (both the Old and New Testaments) illustrating in detail the three styles espoused by Cicero and considered by intellectuals to be the hallmark of effective use of language; this helped make the Bible respectable for well-trained intellectuals, and was to have enormous effect upon the use of the Bible in literature in the middle ages and indeed even in the early Renaissance. This too is a well-known story.

There is really little new or innovative in this conventional view of rhetoric, its importance deriving primarily from its enormous influence upon the medieval habits of composition that follow the example of Augustine. In fact, Augustine assumes from the beginning that the reader of the *De doctrina* is familiar with Cicero's rhetorical theories; he merely refers the reader to Cicero. He says at one point that rhetoric should not be studied by older people unable to do the drill or imitative work which is so easy for the young; this idea is of course derived from Quintilian.

Augustine's metarhetoric, however, must be reconstructed from a variety of his works.[20] It is found by examining also Books One, Two, and Three of *De doctrina christiana* (which he wrote in the year 396); his short treatise called *Concerning the Teacher* (*De magistro,* 389); and a brief treatise he called *Instructing the Ignorant* (*De catechizandis rudibus,* 399). All three works involve him in a discussion of "sign," that is, "that which is used to signify something else." A proper understanding of how Augustine understands the term "sign" will lead the way in turn to our understanding of what can only be called his "metarhetoric."

Basically he believes that each man is an individual learner, placed in the universe by a God who has given him, as an individual, the means by which he may learn about the universe, and therefore about God, and therefore about the role in the universe which God intends him to play.

Thus for Augustine every *thing* in the universe is in itself a *sign* of something else which God intends an individual to understand. A rock, properly understood, can be viewed as a pointer toward the creative power of God which enables him to make a rock, or a mountain from rocks. Augustine would call that rock a "natural" sign; it exists without any agency of man intervening to make it a message-sender to the viewer. In Books One, Two, and Three of the *De doctrina,* Augustine goes beyond natural signs to discuss the ways in which human beings can by common agreement among themselves create what he calls "conventional signs."

---

[20] For a discussion of the concept of "metarhetoric," see James J. Murphy, "The Metarhetorics of Plato, Augustine, and McLuhan: A Pointing Essay," *Philosophy and Rhetoric* 4 (1971), 201–14. The other relevant works of Augustine are: *Concerning the Teacher* (*De magistro*), trans. George Leckie (New York, 1938); *The First Catechetical Instruction* (*De catechizandis rudibus*), trans. Joseph P. Christopher (Westminster, Md., 1946). Portions of the following discussion of Augustine's metarhetoric are taken from my article cited above.

A verbal language like Latin or Greek would be for Augustine such a conventional sign among Latins and Greeks, although of course for Jewish or Arabic people the Latinity of the Latin language would not be recognized as conventional enough to be a sign for those Jews or Arabs. In other words, to use Saint Augustine's own terms, "conventional signs are those which living creatures show to one another for the purpose of conveying, in so far as they are able, the motion of their spirits or something which they have sensed or understood." [21]

There are two more ideas of Augustine which must be considered in his doctrine of signs. The first has a theological ring. In his book *Concerning the Teacher* he points out that each man must balance the things he hears against what Augustine calls "interior truth," which is already resident in the person who hears the words of another. Augustine seems to be saying therefore that each man has a capacity to discriminate the true from the false, because of a natural talent he possesses. This has a Platonic tone. A second and even more profound concept, also from Augustine's *Concerning the Teacher,* is the proposition that "man is only 'prompted' by words in order that he may learn, and it is apparent that only a very small measure of what a speaker thinks is expressed in his words." This statement occurs in the last chapter (14) of the book, clearly in conclusion. The idea that words are mere "prompters," coupled with the earlier idea of an "interior truth," would seem to indicate a clear reliance upon an individual's powers as a private learner—as opposed to an exterior person's ability either to *instruct* the hearer or to *persuade* him merely by the force of the conventional signs he uses in communicating with him.

These ideas are of course expressed here in greatly simplified form, but they are important for an understanding of Augustine's view of even the ordinary Ciceronian rhetoric which he espouses in the fourth book of *De doctrina christiana.* If conventional signs like words are merely intended to prompt or evoke a learning response from a hearer, and are to be balanced by that hearer against an interior standard innately present in the individual, then it would follow that the use of any particular rhetorical device (a particular argument or rhetorical figure, for example) would have a peculiarly evocative intention for a follower of Augustine. That rhetorical device would merely be an evocative trigger, not a *cause* of action in the hearer. Modern students of medieval rhetoric and literature are constantly struck by the fact that medieval theorists do not

---

[21] *On Christian Doctrine,* trans. Robertson, II.ii, p. 34.

worry about what we would today call "composition," that is, a concern for the whole or unified nature of the speech or written document being prepared. It is a commonplace to note that medieval grammarians and rhetoricians concern themselves more with the bits and pieces of language than with what Cicero would have called invention or even arrangement. Yet this is not at all surprising if one understands the Augustinian view that a piece of conventional signage (what we call language) is merely intended to *remind* the hearer of an existing process, and to start it under way in the hearer's mind so that the hearer will himself carry his own mind along to a desired objective.[22]

In the *De doctrina,* for instance, Augustine constantly refers to the "law of love" as the final determinant of Scriptural interpretation. When in doubt, Saint Augustine says, one should keep in mind God's objective in making the Scriptures available to man, and one should judge dubious passages accordingly, by the so-called law of love. As he says in the book on teaching, "as teaching is superior to talking, in like degree speech is better than individual words. So of course doctrine is far superior to words."[23] The whole is better than the parts—or, to put it in newer terminology, the message is more important than the medium.

This whole congeries of ideas has enormous psychological and philosophical implications. It places a great stress upon individual judgment. It encourages private interpretation of messages received. It states flatly that rhetors do not persuade, but that hearers move themselves; that teachers do not teach, but instead that learners learn. Ultimately this is a denial of the preceptive theories implicit in Roman education; its corollary is increased reliance on *imitatio* as a learning process, encouraging individual activity by a student or reader.[24]

This analysis has so far proceeded without recourse to the usual terms used in explaining Augustine: *grace, beatitude, love,* and *sin.* Nevertheless these concepts underlie all that has been said here, and indeed are merely different ways of saying what has been said in nontheological terms. For Augustine, the inner man learns whatever it is the man can

---

[22] It will be recalled that Aristotle (*Rhetoric*) urges the orator to allow the audience member to feel that he is completing the speaker's thoughts for him.

[23] *Concerning the Teacher,* p. 22.

[24] See, for instance, *On Christian Doctrine* IV.iii, p. 121: "Therefore, since infants are not taught to speak except by learning the expressions of speakers, why can men not be made eloquent, not by teaching them rules of eloquence, but by having them read and hear the expressions of the eloquent and imitate them insofar as they are able to follow them?"

come to know in this universe, through the grace of God, aided by signs both natural and conventional. Man's ultimate happiness, or beatitude, lies in his own personal discovery that some things are to be used to secure other things; still others are to be enjoyed for their own sake. For Augustine only God is to be enjoyed for his own sake—therefore everything else in the universe is to be used to attain the end of union with God. Making a mistake about this determination, and trying to enjoy something like wealth or pleasure for its own sake, is what he calls sin, or being cut off from God.

Since all men learn whatever it is that God wishes them to learn in the universe through signs both natural and conventional, man's use of his own man-made conventional signs is of the utmost importance to Augustine. The proper use of conventional signs can prompt a fellow man to find his way to God, or can sidetrack him into error and disbelief and ultimately into sin, which is leading him away from God. Augustine therefore sees man's use of conventional signs—especially when arranged in the sophisticated patterns taught by a rhetor—as an enormous divine responsibility which God places upon every man. While rhetoric itself is neither virtuous nor vicious, Augustine would say, every use of it is either in virtue or in vice.[25]

Man is obliged to be as rhetorical as he can, in order to assist his neighbor in learning about the universe and God. Rhetoric brings signs to each man's neighbors. Thus the concluding sentence of *On Christian Doctrine* points out that the book has described "the kind of man he ought to be who seeks to labor in sound doctrine, which is Christian doctrine, not only for himself, but also for others."

With those "others" in mind, then, an examination of his little treatise on *Instructing the Ignorant* shows that the very act of religious instruction—what Augustine calls "catechizing"—is actually a sensitive use of signs, aided by rhetoric as a guide. The book, probably the earliest surviving treatise on pure exposition, reveals the innate humanism of its author.

Augustine's concern is to make a human match between the didactic

---

[25] This distinction was to become important in thirteenth-century efforts to analyze the moral aspect of rhetoric. See James J. Murphy, "The Scholastic Condemnation of Rhetoric in the Commentary of Giles of Rome on the *Rhetoric* of Aristotle," in *Arts libéraux et philosophie au moyen âge* (Montreal and Paris, 1969), 834–41.

intent of the catechizer—the speaker—and the learning capacity of the one he calls the "hearer." One example may illustrate this. In Chapter 15 Augustine points out that because the interaction of speaker and hearer is *reflex*—each human being is affecting the other during the rhetorical act[26]—then there is a level of communication at which *no* man can be called an "expert." That is, there is no possible rhetorical technique or skill that can be learned (or taught) that will equip one human heart to speak to another heart.

Therefore only Christian love (*caritas*) can supply this interconnection. This is in some ways a more sophisticated concept than that of Aristotle's *ethos,* because it involves the innate humanity of both speaker and listener. Moreover, since under Christ we owe *love* to all men, it is a natural corollary that our love places on us a duty to communicate to our fellow men. Since men differ in age, sex, wealth, knowledge, and a host of other factors, our communicative acts with them also vary, according to other mens' capacities. Rhetoric can help us learn the various modes or varieties of ways from which the loving expositor can choose the particular signs he will lay before the learner in order to "prompt" him. To coin a phrase, God controls the message and the rhetorician chooses the medium. When the medium fails, Augustine would say, it cannot be the fault of the message, but only the weakness of two imperfect human beings groping through a universe of multitudinous signs toward the signs that will *for them* reveal that message. The manifest love that passes between teacher and learner will help them to keep trying out different signs until the learner learns the message.

For Augustine, it is clear, his metarhetoric has theological and ethical meanings in addition to its purely technical uses in communication. The Christian communicator has a definite moral objective, he has an obligation to be as efficient as is humanly possible considering his personal talents (which implies study and practice), and he must lovingly seek the spiritual welfare of his hearer. Above all, he must understand God's purpose in providing a world full of signs.

A modern observer should consider carefully the profound implications of these concepts before assuming too blithely that the Christian Church might well have simply taken over the existing ancient rhetoric. For Augustine the root of Christian knowledge is in Scripture. Understand-

---

[26] Ut sermo, qui profertur, affectionis animi, a quo profertur.

ing Scripture requires the tools of both grammar and rhetoric, while transmitting knowledge to others requires a rhetoric based on love as well as evocative skill. The sign-using Christian, as Saint Paul had pointed out earlier, must be keenly aware of the role played by the grace of God. Roman rhetoric aimed to secure belief through probabilities, describing three civil typés of oratory (with heavy emphasis on forensic) and basing its whole complex operation on a philosophically skeptical view of human behavior. This simply could not be enough for the reflective Christian.

Saint Augustine argued with some success for the retention of ancient rhetoric, though he went far beyond his master Cicero in exploring the fundamental concept of sign. But no second Augustine appeared in the several centuries after him to pursue his line of inquiry.

Instead, the next famous writer on preaching—Pope Gregory the Great (c. A.D. 540–604)—concentrated again on the question of subject matter. Gregory had studied grammar, rhetoric, and dialectic before he became a monk. His most famous work, *Cura pastoralis* (*Pastoral Rule* or *Pastoral Care*) was published in 591, shortly after he was named Pope.[27] It became enormously popular almost at once, receiving a wide circulation in his lifetime; the Church councils of 813 and 836 ordered bishops to study it. King Alfred translated it into English in the early tenth century. Rabanus Maurus and other writers as late as the fourteenth century cited it.

Gregory's *Pastoral Care* is essentially a treatise on ecclesiastical administration, broadly conceived. That is, it is a treatment of a bishop's duties, with preaching naturally a major responsibility. The book has four parts. In the short opening section Gregory explains his purpose ("the care of souls") and stresses the importance of the preaching function; even in the Old Testament the preaching duty was made clear to the Jews; Isaiah, for instance, offered himself as preacher (Isa. 6:8) but Jeremiah at first declined the role and then was compelled to accept (Jer. 1:6). Part Two, which Gregory calls "Of the Life of the Pastor," includes a pungent reminder of the responsibility of the cleric:

> For it is true that whosoever enters on the priesthood undertakes the office of herald, so as to walk, himself crying aloud, before the coming of the judge who follows terribly. Wherefore, if the priest knows not how to preach, what voice of a loud cry shall the mute herald utter? For hence it is

---

[27] Saint Gregory, *Pastoral Rule* in *A Select Library of Nicene and Post-Nicene Fathers of the Christian Church,* 2nd Series, trans. under supervision of Henry Wace and Philip Schaff (New York, 1890–1900), Vol. XII (1895), 1–72.

that the Holy Spirit sat upon the first pastors under the appearances of tongues (Acts 2:3); because whomsoever He has filled, He himself at once makes eloquent.[28]

The life of the preacher is important as part of his appeal to his audience, and indeed Gregory recommends that for the sake of his message he should try to be loved: "For it is indeed difficult for a preacher who is not loved, however well he may preach, to be willingly listened to. He, then, that is over others ought to study to be loved, to the end that he be listened to." [29] He should also meditate daily "on the precepts of the Holy Writ," so that he will always be ready to preach. In a long and complex analogy he says that preaching is like the staves of the shittemwood put through gold rings to carry the Ark of the Covenant; these staves should always be in place. "For indeed to carry the ark by means of staves is through preaching to bring the holy church before the rude minds of unbelievers by means of good teachers." That the staves should always be in place means that pastors, already steeped in the lore of Scripture, should always be ready to preach, which means that pastors should never stop studying Scripture.[30] This passage is typical of Gregory's use of multiple analogy.

Two-thirds of the work is devoted to Part Three: "How the Ruler, While Living Well, Ought to Teach and Admonish Those That Are Put Under Him." The prologue to this section, often quoted by medieval writers, declares that while the message is unitary the hearers are diverse. Consequently the preacher must suit his discourse to the variety among his hearers. This is a truly rhetorical precept:

Since we have shown what manner of man the pastor ought to be, let us now set forth after what manner he should teach. For, as long before us Gregory Nazianzen of reverend memory has taught, one and the same exhortation does not suit all, inasmuch as neither are all bound together by similarity of character. . . . Therefore according to the quality of hearers ought the discourse of teachers be fashioned, so as to suit all and each in their several needs, and yet never deviate from the art of common edification. . . . Whence every teacher also, that he may edify all in the one virtue of charity, ought to touch the hearts of his hearers out of one doctrine, but not with one and the same exhortation.[31]

---

[28] Part Two, Cap. iv, p. 12.
[29] Part Two, Cap. vii, p. 20.
[30] *Ibid.*, pp. 23–24.
[31] Part Three, Prologue, p. 24. Alexander of Ashby transcribed it in his *On the Mode of Preaching* (c. 1200), and it found many users thereafter.

Later in Part Three (Cap. XXXVI) he adds, "These are the things that a Bishop of souls should observe in the diversity of his preaching, that he may solicitously oppose suitable medicines to the disease of his several hearers. . . . the speech is to be tempered with such art that the vices of the hearers being diverse, it may be found suitable to them severally and yet be not diverse from itself."

Gregory's appreciation of internal diversity within an audience is at first glance a hopeful sign. Most ancient rhetorical treatises treated audiences as homogeneous units, despite their frequent analyses of particular passions or attitudes that might sway individuals within the groups. Even Aristotle, despite the lengthy treatment of individual passions in the second book of *Rhetoric,* neglects to advise the orator how to cope with simultaneous diversity within a group of his hearers. The standardization of the "three types of oratory" (deliberative, judicial, forensic) in Roman rhetoric tended to make audience analysis depend upon the occasion of the speech rather than the nature of the hearers. This is a remarkable gap in ancient theory, because it is obvious that successful orators did indeed know how to make simultaneous appeals to masses of presumably differing individuals. The practical wisdom of the practitioners somehow never seemed to be written into the lore of the ancient theorists. Gregory seems to be breaking new ground.

But he very quickly demonstrates that he has no intention of providing a new rhetorical theory for preachers. Part Three, it develops, deals with subject matter, not rhetorical form. There are no further statements of principle. Instead, Gregory lists thirty-six pairs of opposed "characters" and then proceeds to write a brief sermonette that would be suitable to deliver to each pairing. There is no further discussion of the problem that any number of these diverse characters might be present at one time in an audience. The nature of the list requires a complete enumeration:

| | |
|---|---|
| Men | Women |
| The young | The old |
| The poor | The rich |
| The joyful | The sad |
| Subjects | Prelates |
| Servants | Masters |
| The wise | The dull |
| The impudent | The bashful |
| The forward | The faint-hearted |
| The impatient | The patient |
| The kindly disposed | The envious |

| | |
|---|---|
| The simple | The crafty |
| The whole | The sick |
| Those who fear scourges | Those who contemn them |
| The silent | The talkative |
| The slothful | The hasty |
| The meek | The passionate |
| The humble | The haughty |
| The obstinate | The fickle |
| Those who use food intemperately | Those who use it sparingly |
| Those who give away their own | Those who seize others' goods |
| Those who desire not, keep their own | Those who give their own, seize others' |
| Those at variance | Those at peace |
| The sowers of strife | The peacemakers |
| Those who do not understand Scripture | Those who do understand it |
| Those who decline to preach from humility | Those who seize on preaching |
| Those who succeed | Those who don't |
| The married | The single |
| Those with experience of sins of the flesh | Those without such experience |
| Those who lament sins of deed | Those who lament sins of thought |
| Those who do sins that they bewail | Those who bewail not but abstain from the sin |
| Those who praise unlawful things | Those who condemn them but do not guard against them |
| Those who sin by impulse | Those who sin deliberately |
| Those who commit small but frequent faults | Those who sometimes commit big faults |
| Those who do not begin good things | Those who do not finish them |
| Those who do bad things secretly and good things openly | Those who do good things secretly and bad things openly |

Some immediate observations may be made about this list. It is not systematic, since some items relate to personal habits, some to social position, some to states of knowledge, and others to sex or age. Nor do the items relate to each other in any discernible fashion. It must be concluded that Gregory intends it as a sample drawn from a potentially infinite set of human characters. But the most important observation is that this list is essentially a guide for detecting types of sins, based on the "character" of the potential sinner, rather than audience analysis for the sake of public exhortation. Thus it seems as suitable for a private confessional conference as it might be for the public sermon.[32] Each sample sermonette that follows is built around Gregory's exemplary arguments that might be addressed to the type of person involved; each argument is buttressed by Scriptural quotations and moral "significations." A good idea of the typical sermonette may be gained from the concluding section of Admonition II (Part III, Cap. x): "How the Kindly Disposed and the Envious Are to Be Admonished":

> The envious are to be told that, while they consume themselves with this inward plague, they destroy whatever good they seem to have within them. Whence it is written, *Soundness of heart is the life of the flesh, but envy the rottenness of the bones* (Prov. 14:30). For what is signified by the flesh but certain weak and tender actions, and what by the bones but brave ones? And for the most part it comes to pass that some, with innocence of heart, in some of their actions seem weak; but others, though performing stout deeds before human eyes, still pine away inwardly with the pestilence of envy towards what is good in others. Wherefore it is well said, *Soundness of heart is the life of the flesh;* because if innocence of mind is kept, even such things as are weak outwardly are in time strengthened. And rightly it is there added, *Envy is the rottenness of the bones;* because through the vice of spite what seems strong to human eyes perishes in the eyes of God. For the rotting of bones through envy means that certain even strong things utterly perish.

Gregory's method—essentially a constant comparison of divine and human life through various types of signification—must be learned by observing what he writes. He does not himself describe it, let alone recommend it as a rhetorical form for other preachers. It as as if Cicero instead of writing *De oratore* or *De inventione* had presented a great number of his own speech outlines in order to show other orators how to speak.

In short, Gregory's *Pastoral Care* is not a preceptive rhetorical treatise. It does not recommend ways to find and arrange ideas, nor how to put words to them before a living audience. Instead, Gregory stresses the preaching responsibility and then proceeds to summarize some moraliz-

---

[32] In orthodox Christian belief, the priest has the spiritual power to "absolve" sins—that is, to assist the sinner in securing God's forgiveness for sin—when the sinner confesses his faults to the priest. As a consequence a vast confessional literature was produced during the middle ages to aid the cleric in his duties as confessor. The priest who was both confessor and preacher, then, could look to a work like the *Pastoral Care* with a double purpose in mind; even so, Gregory treats only possible subject matter and not the actual modes of presentation.

ing approaches that might be made to thirty-six pairs of individual audience types. He treats sin as a "disease" to be removed with the help of the pastor, but the *Pastoral Care* remains a treatise on moral pathology rather than a guide to future rhetorical practice. He answers the question, *What to preach?* He does not answer the question, *How to preach?*

His approach is typical of the entire Church for the whole period up to the early thirteenth century. Despite the collapse of education during the barbarian invasions of Europe, despite the frequent avowals that study is necessary to the preacher,[33] despite the consistent acceptance of preaching responsibility in council after council, no second Augustine appeared to propose a rhetoric of preaching. Meanwhile great intellectual strides were made in other directions. In the fourth century Saint Jerome had supervised the translation of the Scripture into Latin—the so-called Vulgate Bible—to provide a standard text for the most important book in Christendom. Walafrid Strabo (c. 809–849) produced a widely accepted "gloss" or commentary on the Scripture—the *Glossa ordinaria*—which presented on each page the Biblical text and a commentary for the passages on that page.[34] Every Christian cleric of any education presented his own comments on the meaning of Scriptural passages, sometimes in sermons that have been preserved or in more formal treatises designed for private reading. Saint Augustine's treatise on the Gospel of Saint John, for instance, remained popular throughout the middle ages and enjoyed even more attention in the early Reformation. If the Bible was the most important book in human history, it was generally agreed, then it deserved the highest attention.

It must be remembered that the Christian liturgy consistently included both the reading of Scripture and some form of commentary upon that reading. A regular worship service was held at least once each Sunday in each community throughout the Christian world. A staggering total of discourses was involved, when one considers the thousands of churches active over many hundreds of years.[35] The entire oratorical output of pagan Greece and Rome was miniscule by comparison.

---

[33] Even John Chrysostom, who evidently preferred the organic type of homily to any highly structured mode of preaching, declared (*On the Priesthood*, Book III) that preachers need to acquire eloquence because they no longer have the power of working miracles that the Apostles possessed.

[34] For the Latin text, see Migne, *Patrologia Latina*, 113–114.

[35] The addition of vernacular sermons to the Latin also served to increase this total. Canon 17 of the Third Council of Tours (813), for example, called on bishops to provide for vernacular preaching "so that all could more easily understand what is said."

The preaching patterns emerging from this enormous activity would be the proper subject for a different kind of history, except for two factors. One factor is that the later medieval preaching theorists made their own analyses of earlier sermon modes in devising the preceptive treatises in the thirteenth to fifteenth centuries; this development is best studied by examining the medieval *artes praedicandi* themselves.

The second factor is the emergence of the so-called "homily" type of preaching. This development is extremely difficult to discuss in theoretical terms because the homily was based ultimately on nonform or antitheory. In the very earliest days of the Church the worship service was held in private homes, where Scriptural readings and discussion could take place informally in comparatively small quarters. A formal *oratio* would have been unsuitable for such gatherings. A clear description of such a scene is given by Justin Martyr about A.D. 150: a special reader (*lector*) reads aloud a lengthy section of either the Old or New Testament, "as long as time permits." Then Justin continues: "After the reader has finished his task, the one presiding gives an address, urgently admonishing his hearers to practice these beautiful teachings in their lives. Then all stand up together and recite prayers." [36] As congregations grew larger, and large public buildings were erected for exclusively liturgical purposes, some changes in liturgical form took place. The communal recitation of prayers, for instance, was replaced by the time of Pope Gelasius I (472–496) with a Latin statement uttered by the priest on behalf of the silent congregation; later this "collect" (summary on behalf of the congregation) was moved to another place in the service. But the reading and its attached discourse remained where it was, early in the service. [37] It might have been expected that the discourse would have grown more formal as church size increased and the liturgy became more complex. For instance the *ambo* or reading desk, which was a simple portable table in the earliest churches, developed into the *pulpitum,* which later became so elaborate that it was often built into a supporting pillar or the wall itself. (In medieval churches the pulpit often received the kind of parasacramental architectural elaboration that was lavished on altars or baptismal fonts.)

But the "homily" attempted to retain the closely personalized approach of the original conversational situation. Saint Augustine refers to "popular

---

[36] Quoted in Jungmann, *The Early Liturgy,* p. 42.
[37] *Ibid.,* p. 14.

discussions, which the Greeks call homilies." [38] The Latin term *homilia* as he uses it was not common before the fourth century, though Greek preachers like Origen (d. 253) had earlier popularized it in that language. (It is important to avoid confusion about this particular usage of the term, because modern broadening of the term has made "homiletics" come to mean the whole art of preaching.) In any case, the homily avoided the usual arrangement and style recommended by contemporary rhetoric, in favor of Scriptural closeness. Origen is especially famous for his use of figurative interpretations of Scripture following the Alexandrian tradition stemming ultimately from ancient Jewish scholarship. His careful delineation of multiple interpretations of a text, a practice which was to become a major amplifying tool of medieval preachers, depended upon a close oral examination of Scripture before his audiences. This method made the text, in effect, the organizer of the discourse. Following a text in this way also relieved the preacher of most memory and arrangement problems, so that his homily could become a sort of "spoken gloss" or "spoken commentary" on the Bible.

Perhaps the most striking example of fourth century homily practice may be seen in John Chrysostom's *On the Statues,* a series of 21 speeches delivered to the citizens of Antioch in A.D. 387.[39] During a riot some statues of the Emperor Theodosius had been destroyed—a treasonable offense— and Chrysostom preached to calm the people during the anxious period while they awaited news of the Emperor's reaction to the civic crime. His theme was calmness in the face of apparent disaster. But the homilies are remarkable for their purposeful lack of organization—any homily can begin or end at any section without damaging a theme—and for their careful avoidance of "rhetorical" language. In technical terms Chrysostom's simple yet highly effective discourses must have depended largely upon what Aristotle would have called the *ethos* of the speaker.

It is extremely difficult to discuss in theoretical terms a movement (one cannot call it a theory or a doctrine) seeking simplicity. The movement is apparently continuous with the whole history of the Church. The history of Christian preaching is filled with recurrent cycles of antipathy to

---

[38] Tractatus populares, quos Graeci homilias vocant. *De haeresibus* V. For a discussion of this concept, see A. Lecoy de la Marche, *La chaire française au moyen âge, spécialement au XIII^e siècle* (Paris, 1886), p. 6.

[39] Among the numerous translations, a most useful complete set is that of E. Budge, *The Homilies of S. John Chrysostom, Archbishop of Constantinople, On the Statues, or, To the People of Antioch* (Oxford, 1842). Budge's name does not appear on the title page.

rhetorical form—Paul, Chrysostom, Peter the Hermit, the early Franciscans, the Lollards, the Quakers, and so forth. Perhaps any history of the rhetoric of preaching must insist that, whatever the visible evidence for an interest in *praecepta* at a given period of time, there was probably always a sizable group of nontheorists and antitheorists, actually engaged in preaching, who as a matter of principle rejected the idea of systematic theory. By its very nature it is the kind of thinking that leaves few records. In the time of Saint Jerome and Saint Augustine the visible enemy of formalized preaching was the pagan Second Sophistic, and surely some of the Christian response was sheer overreaction to sophistic excesses. But all the evidence seems to point to the conclusion that a purposeful choice of nontheory was regarded by many churchmen, over many centuries, as a viable way to respond to Christ's preaching mandate. The so-called "homily" was the practical result of this decision, and therefore it merits our attention in attempting to trace the development of preaching theory itself.

For a variety of reasons, then, the Church did not produce during its first dozen centuries any coherent body of precepts that might be called a rhetoric of preaching. Augustine made the only major attempt, which was not to bear fruit for almost eight hundred years. Aside from Pope Gregory, there are only one or two other preaching theorists worth mentioning before A.D. 1200. In 819 the German writer Rabanus Maurus produced a manual for priests, *The Training of the Clergy* (*De institutione clericorum*), which made extensive use of both Augustine and Gregory in discussing preaching. As we have noted earlier (Chapter Two), the pragmatic selectivity of this book marked an important change in attitudes toward the old learning.[40] Rabanus devotes thirteen sections of his third book (Cap. 27–39) to preaching. Nevertheless, the discussion is essentially a patchwork of transcriptions from the fourth book of Augustine's *De doctrina christiana* aided by one long passage from Gregory's *Cura pastoralis*. There are in fact 78 quotations from Augustine; Gregory is used only to present suggestions for types of "admonitions" to be used in preaching. While the *De institutione clericorum* of Rabanus Maurus is important in the general history of medieval attitudes toward the arts of discourse, then, it does not in itself advance new ideas on preaching.

The young Benedictine monk who wrote the next treatise has left us an account of the circumstances in which he wrote it shortly before 1084.

---

[40] See above, pp. 82–87.

The writer Guibert (1053–1124), later to become abbot of Nogent himself, described his difficulties with Abbot Garnier:

> I proposed to undertake a moral commentary on the beginning of Genesis, that is, The Six Days of Creation. To the commentary I prefixed a treatise of moderate length showing how a sermon ought to be composed. I followed up this preface with a tropological exposition at length of the Six Days, with poor eloquence but such as I was capable of. When my abbot saw that I was commenting on the first chapter of the sacred history, he no longer took a favorable view of the matter and warned me, with great reproof, to put an end to these writings. I saw that such works only put thorns in his eyes, and by avoiding his presence and that of anyone who might report it to him, I pursued my task in secret.[41]

Abbot Garnier was apparently not objecting to the section on sermons, but rather to the young monk's undertaking a scholarly commentary on Genesis at so early an age. In any case Guibert notes that when Abbot Garnier retired (in 1084) he finished the book rapidly without further difficulty.

Guibert's *A Book About the Way a Sermon Ought to Be Given* (*Liber quo ordine sermo fieri debeat*) is therefore intended to be a prologue to the commentary on Genesis, rather than a separate work on preaching. It is important to remember this fact. The youth and lack of experience of the writer is another factor to keep in mind; a young monk could not have had much practical preaching experience, and indeed it is conceivable that Guibert had had none at all. Benedictines were not supposed to preach publicly.

In any case Guibert's *A Book About the Way a Sermon Ought to Be Given* is at best a very general discussion of preaching. It is more specific on the subject of Scriptural interpretation. Guibert spends the first part of the treatise on the sinfulness of men who either refuse to preach or preach for the wrong reasons. The exhortation of souls should only be about God, and anything else said should be said only because it relates to Him. If theft is most despised among men, how much greater a sacrilege it is for a man to steal from God for his own selfish benefit! Every Christian speaks for God, Guibert declares, even if he is not a bishop or abbot.

---

[41] Guibert's memoirs have been published as *Self and Society in Medieval France: The Memoirs of Abbot Guibert of Nogent*, ed. John F. Benton, revising trans. of C. C. Swinton Bland (New York, 1970). This passage occurs in Book One, pp. 90–91. Guibert's treatise has been translated as *A Book About the Way a Sermon Ought to Be Given* by Joseph Miller (see n. 6 above) from the Latin text in Migne, *PL* CLVI, cols. 11–21.

The second half of the work is a justification of multiple interpretations of Scripture, especially the tropological or moral sense. When a preacher addresses a mixed audience of the unlearned and the learned, Guibert says, he should take care that the unlearned hear simple, clear matter while the learned find in the same sermon some things they can understand at a more profound level. He uses the analogy of milk, which is by itself a food for infants but can also be used by older men who dip their bread in it. The Gospel writers added *sententiae* from the Old Testament to render their hearers more attentive, thus making new ideas sound familiar.[42] Those who inquire into the Scriptures should always keep this in mind. Guibert then turns to what "learned treatises" have developed:[43]

> There are four ways of interpreting Scripture; on them, as though on so many scrolls, each sacred page is rolled. The first is History, which speaks of actual events as they occurred; the second is Allegory, in which one thing stands for something else; the third is Tropology, or moral instruction, which treats of the ordering and arranging of one's life; and the last is Anagogy, or spiritual enlightenment, through which we who are about to treat of heavenly and lofty topics are led to a higher way of life. For example, the word "Jerusalem": historically it represents a specific city; in allegory it represents the holy Church; tropologically, or morally, it is the soul of every faithful man who longs for the vision of eternal peace; and anagogically it refers to the life of the heavenly citizens, who already see the God of Gods, revealed in all his glory in Sion. Granted that all four of these methods of interpretation are valid and can be used, either together or singly, yet the most appropriate and prudent for use in matters referring to the lives of men seems to be the moral approach.

Allegory is best used for strengthening faith, but since virtue and vice are the real concerns of living men the moral (tropological) approach is the most important. In fact, he continues, men profit more from learning about vice than from hearing virtue stressed: "When the nature of sin is clearly recognized, its opposite, the nature of virtue, will be known with equal clarity, as grain is clearly distinguished from chaff."

After some further reflections on the value of personal spiritual experience (which gives every man a special eloquence before his hearers), and some general remarks about the need for lively preaching, Guibert con-

---

[42] Apparently Guibert does not fully comprehend the use of Scripture as apodeictic proof.

[43] Guibert, *A Book,* trans., Miller, p. 49. For some reason Miller translates the Latin term *anagoge* as "ascetic," though its standard meaning is "anagogical"; I have altered his translation in this one instance to indicate the traditional term for that sense.

cludes by stating that his aim is to "seek out further riches from the various senses of Holy Scripture." The lengthy *Commentary on Genesis* then follows.

Brief as it is, Guibert's treatise marks an early medieval explanation of how the "four senses" of Scriptural interpretation should be used for the invention of preaching material. Obviously, Scripture continues to be the starting point. And moral instruction is to be preferred to mere exposition of doctrine. Insofar as tropology furnished a *topos* or *locus* for invention, this recommendation may be seen as an advance in preaching theory; nevertheless Guibert posited it primarily as a defense of his own extrapolative method in the *Commentary on Genesis*. He seems to see no inherent difference between oral discourse—as in preaching—and the written discourse he presents in his *Commentary*. The same method applies to both. Of course Guibert had not invented the concept of multiple interpretation, which has roots at least as far back as Judaic exegesis long before Christ. Gregory, Jerome, and Augustine had all commented on the practice; Origen and other preachers had made it popular in the early church. But Guibert's ready acceptance, coupled with what seems to be a necessary defense of his method, argues that at least in the late eleventh century the idea was well understood but still needed support. In any case Guibert's defense shows a clear role for it in preaching. His little treatise is otherwise unexceptional. Except for a couple of passing remarks on delivery he does not discuss any other aspect of preaching. Like Gregory he is more interested in vices and virtues, though stressing the negative more than Gregory had done. In sum it is probably only the date of the book that makes it of some interest to the historian. Guibert's *Book On the Way a Sermon Ought to Be Given* might as well have been titled *A Book On the Way to Interpret Scripture*. It contributes very little else to the theory of preaching.

The Cistercian monk Alain de Lille (Alanus de Insulis) has left us a more substantial work, *On the Preacher's Art* (*De arte praedicatoria*) (1199?).[44] Alain was a prominent figure in what has come to be called "the Renaissance of the Twelfth Century." His works include theological, logical, literary, and polemic treatises. His famous *Anti-Claudianus*, an allegorical poem of six thousand lines, was written as part of a literary

---

[44] Latin text in Migne, *PL* 210, cols. 111–198. The Preface and Caps. I, XXXVIII, XXXIX, and XLI have been translated by Joseph M. Miller in "A *Compendium on the Art of Preaching*, Preface and Selected Chapters," in *Readings in Medieval Rhetoric*, ed. Joseph M. Miller, Michael H. Prosser, Thomas W. Benson (Bloomington, Indiana, 1973), pp. 228–39. However, translations from the *De arte praedicatoria* in this chapter are my own.

controversy over levels of style.[45] Another work, *Complaint of Nature* (*De planctu naturae*) is based on the literary form popularized by Boethius' *Consolation of Philosophy*; his *Distinctiones* provides a Scriptural lexicon in alphabetical order. The *Wise Sayings* (*Parabolae*) are a set of verse *sententiae*. Alain was, in short, a writer of breadth and intelligence, utilizing both classical and ecclesiastical sources.

His *On the Preacher's Art* contains 48 *capitula* or sections. However, only the Preface and the first section contain substantial preceptive material about preaching. It is important to understand the nature of the whole work before making an assessment of these opening sections. The remaining 47 sections treat the subject matter to be presented to various kinds of auditors, or the themes to be used in handling certain virtues or vices. The second section, for instance, is titled "On Contempt for the World," which is followed by a section "On Contempt of Self" and then by ones "Against Gluttony" and "Against Luxury." Other subjects include such positive virtues as Obedience (XVI) and Perseverance (XVII). Toward the end (XXXVIII–XLVII) Alain makes some further general remarks about sermons addressed by prelates to nine special audiences: soldiers, advocates (*oratores*), doctors, other prelates, princes, those in cloisters, the married, the widowed, and virgins. His method, in each section after the first one, is to provide a sample sermonette similar to the sort provided by Gregory in his *Cura pastoralis*. Like Gregory, Alain seems more interested in the subdivisions of doctrine than he is in the modes of presentation. Like Gregory, he speaks in the third person: "If truly the preacher intends to invite the hearers to contempt of self . . ." (Cap. III). Sometimes he merely begins by listing some useful authorities, as in Cap. XXII (Peace), where he quotes John, Mark, and Matthew. The subject matter for each section is the doctrine to be transmitted. Of Peace, for instance, Alain says there are three kinds, each of which in turn has subdivisions; although he cites Seneca for a definition, his other supports are entirely Scriptural. Many of the sections quote other classical authors (Horace, Ovid, Virgil), but the overwhelming weight of quotation goes to Scripture; most narrative examples are from Scripture as well. Alain's *De arte praedicatoria* is clearly in the genre of Gregory's *Regula*.

Like Gregory, Alain views preaching as part of a combat with sin, stressing eradication of vice more than positive exhortation to virtue. Just

---

[45] A good survey of Alain's career may be found in M.-T. d'Alverny, *Alain de Lille, Textes inédits* (Paris, 1965). Also see Max Manitius, *Geschichte der lateinischen Literatur des Mittelalters*, III (1931), pp. 794–804.

as the materials of medicine vary according to the variety of illnesses, he says, so the preacher ought to apply a variety of admonitions as spiritual remedies. Indeed, Alain says (Cap. XXXIX), the preacher is engaged in a "dispute with vice." As a matter of fact, both Gregory and Alain write about preaching in the same way they write about confession and penitence for sins. In some of the manuscripts of the *De arte praedicatoria* there is an addition to the section on Contrition: "O happy medicine, by which the disease of sins is purged." This is exactly Alain's description of preaching.

The methodology of Alain's treatment is important. Writing at the end of the twelfth century, he already displays in stabilized form the twin habits of *divisio* and *auctoritas,* coupled with a habit of *correspondentia,* that were to become the hallmarks of later theory. His use of "authorities" is overwhelming. In one section of about 700 words on "verbosity and looseness of language" (Cap. XXVI) Alain includes fifteen direct quotations from nine *auctores,* Jerome (3), Gregory (2), Paul (2), Sixtus (2), Augustine, Matthew, Proverbs, Psalms, and an unidentified Jacobus, plus a general appeal to "Scripture." About a third of the section consists of quoted material. Sometimes he weaves a quotation into his own sentence, as in Cap. XXXVIII (Exhortation to Doctrine), when he refers to a preacher "you who are a vicar of Christ (ought) to imitate this work, who *set out to do and to teach.*" [46] (In the Latin Alain writes in the second person but uses a run-on with a Scriptural passage in the third person.)

The *divisio* is equally pervasive. Most of his divisions are into threes. There are three kinds of night of the soul (Cap. XLVIII), three kinds of vanity (Cap. II), three kinds of preaching (Cap. I), and so forth. A single example from his section on "The Sleepy Ones" (Cap. XLVIII) might well illustrate his use of correspondences as well as division and authority:

> Triplex is the night: the night of ignorance, the night of guilt, and the night of worldly tributation. Concerning the night of ignorance it is said, *The night wears on, the day draws near* (Rom. 13). Concerning the night of guilt it is said, *I wash my bed by single nights* (Psalm 6). Concerning the night of worldly tribulation it is said, *In the day the Lord extended his mercy, and by night his song* (Psalm 41). In the first go the foolish, in the second the impious, in the third the miserable.[47]

---

[46] Tu qui es vicarius Christi, imitari ipsius opus, qui *coepit facere et docere.* Col. 184.

[47] Triplex est nox, nox ignorantiae, nox culpae, nox tribulationis mundanae. De nocte ignorantiae dicitur, *Nox proecessit, Dies autem appropinquavit* (Rom. XIII).

On a larger scale this is his method for each section. There is constant back-reference (i.e., "correspondence") to the initial division made for each subject. "Authorities" are routinely introduced as support.

Keeping in mind the nature of the whole treatise, then, it is now possible to make a more accurate assessment of Alain's general remarks in the Preface and opening section. He defines preaching, clarifies its relation to Scripture, pronounces its subjects to be faith and morals, distinguishes it from other types of discourse, and remarks briefly on the proper use of "authorities." Brief as it is—the Preface and Cap. I together amount to no more than about 1400 Latin words—Alain presents here for the first time since Saint Augustine a considered attempt to establish a rhetoric of preaching.

It is important to remember that the entire treatise after Cap. I is intended to be a series of examples illustrating what he says in the opening sections. Cap. I, "On Preaching, What It Is and What Its Nature Ought to Be, etc." ends with these words: "In conclusion, note that one ought to profit by examples for showing what he intends, because exemplified doctrine is assimilated doctrine. For example: . . . [then follow the other 47 sections]." [48] In other words, the terse precepts of the Preface and Cap. I are to be understood by careful study of the 47 sample sermonettes. Any serious study of the *De arte praedicatoria* must therefore match the precepts of these opening sections against the practices of the other forty-seven.

Alain begins with a quotation from Genesis 28 (Jacob's ladder), and then declares that preaching is the highest of the seven steps to perfect manhood. The steps are: confession, prayer, the act of grace, study of Scripture, more serious study of Scripture should some doubt occur, exposition of Scripture, and preaching. Man reaches the seventh step "when he preaches openly those things which he has drawn out (*didicit*) from Scripture." But it is because very little has been said about this seventh step, Alain says, that he sets forth his treatise to draw together answers to a number of specific "questions" about preaching. The term "headings" might be a more appropriate translation in this case, since the organizing questions prove to be the traditional rhetorical topics for *inventio:* "Con-

---

De nocte culpae dicitur, *Lavabo per singulas noctes lectum meum* (Psal. vi). De nocte tribulationis mundanae dicitur: *In die mandavit Dominus misericordiam suam, et nocte canticum ejus* (Psal. xli). In prima ambulant fatui, in secunda impii, in tertia miseri. Col. 196.

[48] In fine vero, debet uti exemplis, ad probandum quod intendit, quia familiaris est doctrina exemplaris. Verbi gratia: . . . Col. 114.

cerning preaching, then, (we ask) what its nature ought to be, and of whom, and to whom it ought to be set forth, and from whom, and in what way, and when, and where." [49] Thus the Preface promises a highly organized exposition of the subject.

The *caput primum,* however, is not nearly so neat as this. Instead, Alain offers a definition of preaching—the first formal definition in the 1200-year history of the church—and then amplifies his definition (both positively and negatively) before commenting on the use of Scripture and other authorities. He also includes some now-familiar admonitions about the necessity of the preacher's humility and example. The function of preaching to promote faith and morals is included in the development of his definition.

Alain defines preaching as "manifest and public instruction in faith and morals, zealously serving the information of mankind, proceeding by the narrow path of reason and the fountain of authority." [50] Each key term in the definition is then explained. Preaching is "manifest" because it is set forth openly. It is "public" because it is delivered to many, not to one. This is how preaching differs from doctrine (the erudition of a science), from prophecy (revelation of the future), and from "concionation" (civil admonition). For preaching deals with instruction in faith and morals, just as there are two parts of theology: rational, which deals with divine science; and moral, which involves moral instruction. The two aspects of preaching are signified by angels ascending and descending (i.e., in Jacob's ladder in Alain's opening quotation), for the angels here are preachers—ascending when they preach of heavenly things, descending when for the sake of moral things they shape themselves to the inferior. Thus it follows that preaching is "zealously serving the information of mankind," which signified the final cause or utility of preaching. And because preaching ought to be submixed with reasons and corroborated by authorities, it is also said, "proceeding by the narrow path of reason and the fountain of authority."

(It might be noted here that Alain's method in respect to his own definition is the same one he uses elsewhere to amplify ideas in the 47 sample sermonettes. His method might properly be called "thematic," in that he posits a Scriptural quotation as a theme, introduces a proposition [the

---

[49] De praedicatione, vero, qualis esse debeat, et quorum, et quibus, proponenda sit, et de quo, et quomodo, et quando, et ubi. Col. 111.

[50] Praedicatio est, manifesta et publica instructio moram et fidei, informationi hominum deserviens, ex ratione semita, et auctoritatem fonte proveniens. Col. 111.

definition], divides it, and then amplifies the proposition with a reintroduction of the theme.)

Following this, Alain makes some general remarks about the necessity of preaching for the sake of the hearer, not for the welfare or greed of the preacher. He says that overly ornate language should be avoided. Twice he declares that theatrics should be avoided. Preachers should above all seek whatever is useful to enable the audience to hear the word of God. There are three types of preaching: by word, by writing, and by deed: Christ enjoined the first, Paul exemplified the second in his Epistles, and the third is seen in the expression that "every act of Christ is for our instruction." The form of preaching (*forma praedicandi*) should take its origin from theological authority, especially from the Gospels, Psalms, Epistles of Paul, and the Book of Solomon because these especially lead to moral instruction. Other books of Scripture are authorities if they should be necessary and are useful to a particular proposition.

The preacher ought to gain the good will of his hearers by his humility, then seek those things that in speaking will "bear fruit in their minds" while avoiding inane popular clamor and other faults.

One paragraph deals with the use of authorities. Authorities should be used to aid the exposition of the proposition. Instruction of the hearers is the entire purpose, so the preacher should not use confusing or difficult authorities, or ones that the hearers will despise, or that will lessen their attention. Nor ought they to detract from the proposition or be discordant with other parts. On occasion it is possible to include sayings of the Gentiles, as the Apostle Paul does in his Epistles when he introduces his authorities from the pagan philosophers.

A number of observations can be made about the *De arte praedicatoria* of Alain. The first and most important is his absolute acceptance of Scripture as apodeictically exemplary. Scripture becomes both matter and form. On the one hand Alain makes the Bible the beginning point from which theological "propositions" are drawn; then, in turn, the Bible provides verbatim quotations as "authorities" that both explain and prove the propositions. In other words, he continues the tradition seen first in Judaic preaching, then again in Paul, with later reinforcements by Augustine, Gregory, Alcuin, Guibert of Nogent, and a host of others.

A second point is Alain's habit of division as a mode of exposition. He never discusses the principle of division, but every section contains examples of its use. The typical division is into three. Another observation is that his readiness to make preceptive statements—for instance, his definition of preaching—argues a willingness to approach the hallowed subject from an intellectual point of view. This analytic spirit may be his most significant contribution. Not for almost 800 years had a major Christian writer attempted to posit a theoretical base for the activity the Church had long proclaimed to be one of its most critical tasks. As Alain himself points out, "little has been said about this." Whatever else might be said about the so-called Renaissance of the Twelfth Century, it is surely true that both analysis and commentary were encouraged by the new works appearing all over Western Europe. The translation of Aristotle's logical works, the renewed study of grammar, the new impetus to literature which followed that study, the ready interchanges of learned men through travel and correspondence—all these form the background of Alain's times. He himself played a prominent part. It should not be surprising, then, to find him turning the tools of his time onto the holy duty of the preachers. His personalist bent makes him write primarily about the preacher—not a book on the art of preaching in general, but a treatise *On the Preacher's Art*. This is perfectly consistent with the spirit of his times. The difference may seem slight to modern minds, but to detect it one needs only compare his book with some later examples of the depersonalized *ars praedicandi*.

But finally it should be noted that his *De arte praedicatoria* provides only an augury of change, not the change itself. It is interesting to observe what he does not say. He says nothing of how to organize a sermon —what ancient rhetoricians called *dispositio* or arrangement—nor does he make a judgment about *elocutio* or style. Aside from quite generalized advice not to alienate the hearers by extravagant delivery, he ignores this subject almost as completely as he ignores memory. For Alain the Scripture is the double source book for invention: the preacher's study of it produces ideas which are presented to the hearers, and he also finds in Scripture direct quotations which act as confirmation or proof of the ideas. His definition of preaching includes "reasons" (*rationes*) as supports for propositions, but he never discusses what he means by that term. Whenever he speaks for himself in his sermonettes (i.e., without "authorities") he commonly uses analogies or other comparisons rather than syllogistic forms.

By the year 1200, then, the Christian Church had produced only four writers who could by any stretch of the imagination be called theorists of preaching: Saint Augustine, Pope Gregory, Guibert de Nogent, and Alain de Lille. Nor was there by 1200 any visible general agreement that the ancient *ars rhetorica* could serve as a theory of preaching. This was not due to ignorance of that ancient art, of course—by the year 1200 the post-Ciceronian adaptation of rhetoric to the *ars dictaminis* was already eleven decades old, formal commentaries on Cicero's rhetoric were available even to Alain and his circle, and popular authors like Boethius had written extensively about rhetoric.[51] Clearly, as we have consistently seen, the nontheory approach to preaching had long been a deliberate ecclesiastical choice.

But within twenty years of 1200 a whole new rhetoric of preaching leaped into prominence, unleashing hundreds of theoretical manuals written all over Europe during the next three centuries. This standardized "form of preaching" (to use Alain's own term) included inventional and organizational precepts, statements of logical and psychological objectives, and a bewildering array of modes of support. Several hundred such preceptive manuals still survive in various European libraries. All this constituted what can only be called a homiletic revolution—a complete new rhetorical genre.

How did this come about so rapidly? The plain truth is that we do not yet know the complete answer. However, the growth pattern is quite obvious. The genre was well established by 1220. By the middle of the thirteenth century it was fully developed, complete with a technical vocabulary and a stabilized pattern of organization. Key authors in the period between 1200 and 1250 were Alexander of Ashby, Thomas Chabham, Richard of Thetford, Jean de la Rochelle, and William of Auvergne. Three of these five are English. After 1250 appeared other men like Arnold of Podio, John of Wales, and Walter of Paris. In the period 1300 to 1400 more than 30 authors have been identified, in addition to the scores of works whose writers remain anonymous. At least 20 more writers have been named from the fifteenth century.

The exact origins of this remarkable movement have never been fully investigated. It has long been the opinion of scholars that this new preaching mode originated in the medieval university, sometime during the first half of the thirteenth century. The earliest such sermon collection that has survived, for instance, is a set of 84 sermons preached at the University of Paris during the academic year 1230–31; these sermons display the use of theme, division, and other features described in the standard preceptive

---

[51] See, for instance, Mary Dickey, "Some Commentaries on *De inventione* and *Ad Herennium* of the Eleventh and Early Twelfth Centuries," *Medieval and Renaissance Studies* 6 (1968), 1–41.

manuals of the *ars praedicandi*.[52] Proof of ability to preach was a requirement for the attainment of the university degree in theology. The typical
*ars praedicandi* clearly assumes an educated audience for the preacher. For
such reasons the new thematic sermon mode is often called the "university
style" sermon.

Nevertheless, there is reason to believe that the basic elements of this
new approach were available outside the universities before they were
taken up and popularized by the academics. Indeed the sermon structure
and amplificatory devices of what came to be a separate genre were in
evidence even before 1200. The Cistercian Alain de Lille demonstrates the
habit of *divisio* in his *On the Preacher's Art*. The dominating use of
Scriptural quotation was of course familiar many centuries before Alain.
No doubt single examples could be found of every feature later coordi-
nated into the genre known as *ars praedicandi*.

What was lacking before 1200 was the analytic spirit that would have
enabled a rhetorical observer to distill a number of critical experiences
into a statement of theory. Alain begins to show the way just before 1200.
Significantly, he bases his precepts on experience—not on the doctrines of
ancient rhetoric—so that his book becomes truly "critical" in the sense of
making generic observations about existing and future practice. Even so,
Alain is still tied to the long ecclesiastical tradition which made *materia*
the prime concern. He is unable or unwilling to speak precisely about
"the form of preaching," even though he actually uses the term. What
happened after 1200 was that writers were increasingly interested in discussing the form (as distinct from the subject matter) of preaching.

Three early thirteenth-century writers demonstrate this new concern,
and may therefore provide us with a key to the development of the new
genre of the *ars praedicandi* which is reflected in those Paris sermons of
1230–31. The writers are: Alexander, prior of the Augustinian house at
Ashby in Northamptonshire, who wrote about 1200; Thomas Chabham

---

[52] The sermons are printed by M. M. Davy, *Les sermons universitaires parisiens
de 1230-31: Contribution à l'histoire de la prédication médiévale* (Paris, 1931).
The influence of ancient rhetoric is argued by Harry Caplan, "Classical Rhetoric
and the Medieval Theory of Preaching," *Classical Philology* 28 (1933), 73–96. On
the other hand, Th.-M. Charland, *Artes praedicandi* (Paris and Ottawa, 1936) sees
the "scholastic method" as the prime influence; this work is hereafter cited as
Charland. Dorothea Roth traces the development of the genre from the thirteenth-
century writer William of Auvergne, in her *Die mittelalterliche Predigttheorie und
das Manuale Curatorum des Johann Ulrich Surgant* (Basel and Stuttgart, 1956).
All these studies, however, are based on analysis of the perfected genre (i.e., later
treatises) rather than analysis of the evolutionary process by which the genre came
into being.

(or Thomas of Salisbury), who was a master by 1208 and taught at Paris during the next few years but spent most of his adult life associated with the cathedral at Salisbury; and Richard of Thetford, a shadowy figure about whom little is known except that he was said to be the author of a famous treatise on eight modes of amplification for sermons.

Alexander of Ashby is the author of a treatise, *On the Mode of Preaching* (*De modo praedicandi*), which survives in two manuscripts at Oxford and Cambridge.[53] Alexander was apparently prior of the house of Austin friars at Ashby between 1205 and 1215. However, his Prologue is addressed to the resident abbot and dedicated to the dead abbot who was presumably predecessor of the resident. Since Alexander became abbot himself sometime after 1205, *On the Mode of Preaching* was apparently written before that date. Further, it is known that Alexander's unnamed predecessor took office in 1197; the Prologue indicates that Alexander had already completed another book on "The Miracles of the Saints" which he had already given to this same abbot.[54] This of course had to take place after 1197. Assuming that the preaching treatise and its accompanying sample sermons took some time to prepare after he finished the earlier book, it seems safe to date *On the Mode of Preaching* at about the year 1200. This dating is important, marking as it does the first surviving evidence of a new trend in preaching theory.

Alexander begins his work with a passage reminiscent of Ciceronian rhetorical doctrine: "In every written work and speech what is needed first is the intention of the wise man that he should render his readers or hearers docile, well disposed, and attentive." [55] On this principle, he says, there is agreement among poets, philosophers, and all writers on the arts.

---

[53] Oxford Magdalen College MS. 168 (XIII Cent.), fols. 128ᵛ–130ʳ, and Cambridge University Library MS. Ii.I.24 (XIV Cent.), fols. 169–73 (formerly numbered 332–39). The Oxford manuscript lacks the Prologue and the exemplary sermons. A fragment is also said to be in Cambridge Univ. Lib. MS. Dd. VI.27, fols. 6–9. For the listing of these and other manuscripts of the genre, consult Harry Caplan, *Medieval Artes Praedicandi: A Handlist,* Cornell Studies in Classical Philology 24 (Ithaca, New York, 1934), hereafter cited as Caplan, and his *Supplement* (Ithaca, 1936). Alexander's work is No. 15 in Caplan. And for Ashby see Charland, pp. 23–24. The Oxford manuscript has a marginal ascription falsely naming "William Ruffo" as the author. For biographical data on Alexander, see J. C. Russell, *Dictionary of Writers of Thirteenth-Century England* (London, 1936), pp. 12–13.

[54] Quod vero in subsequenta opere moneo ut in sacro sermone aliqua sacrorum exempla plerumque ad simplicium edificacionem intenseras, forte adhuc tibi transmittam libellum de miraculis sanctorum quem iam ex parte metrice composui. Camb. Univ. MS. Ii.I.24, fol. 169ᵛᵇ.

[55] In omni scriptura et sermone primum satagit sapientis intencio ut lectores sive auditores [reddat] dociles, benivoles, et attentos.

Shortly thereafter he comes to the heart of his treatise: "The mode of preaching consists in the parts of a sermon, and in its delivery. There are four parts of a sermon, to wit: prologue, division, proof, and conclusion. The entire material of the sermon is proposition and authority." [56]

Alexander says the prologue renders the hearers docile, attentive, and well disposed. The division lays out the sermon plan, comprehended in two divisions, or three, or even more. But undue multiplication of members of the division will strain the patience of the hearers, though it may be suitable to the learned. In order to have many proofs, a separate proof should follow each division and subdivision, so that each member of the division is confirmed at once by authorities or reasons.

About proof Alexander says:

> There are three observations to be made about proof when preaching is addressed at the same time to both unlearned and learned men. The first is to be sparing of using authorities for the proof of words, and to avoid using so many proofs that the patience of the audience is affected. The second is sometimes to present a charming allegory and sometimes to tell a pleasant story (*exemplum*), so that the learned may savor the profundity of the allegory while the humble may profit from the lightness of the story. The third is that the preacher ought not to be less vehement in his commendation of virtue than he is in the reprehension of vices.[57]

Alexander then introduces two long quotations from Gregory's *Pastoral Care,* both dealing with the problem of preaching one doctrine to many diverse hearers. Both concern what Alexander calls the "triple labor of the preacher"—to teach doctrine, to exhort to good conduct, and to serve as a good example.

For the conclusion Alexander says there are three things to observe: that a brief recapitulation will aid the memory of the hearers, that exhortation to fear of punishment is useful, and so is exhortation to continued devotion to God. This concludes his treatment of the parts of a sermon.

About delivery he is extremely brief. Delivery should not be proud nor

---

[56] Modus vero consistit in partibus sermonis et pronunciacione. Quartorum autem est partes sermonis, scilicet prologus, divisio, confirmacio, conclusio. Propositio atque auctoritas que sit sermonis tocius materia. Oxford Magd. Coll. 168, fol. 129ʳ.

[57] In confirmacione tria sunt observanda qui simul simplicibus et eruditis praedicatur. Primum est paucis ad confirmactionem dictionarum inducere auditoritates ne si multe inducte fuerint impediatur docilitas. Secundus aliqua dulce exponere allegoriam et aliquod iocondere enarrare exemplum ut eruditos delecte allegorie profunditas et simplices edificer exempli levitas ut habeant itaque qui secum reportent. Tercium ut predicator non sit nimis vehemens in commendacione virtutum nec reprehensione viciorum. Oxford Magd. Coll. 168, fol. 129ʳ.

rough nor unctuous nor harsh, but modest and humble, agreeable, and consistent with the plan of the sermon and the nature of the subject matter.

Alexander ends the treatise with the statement that he is subjoining sample or exemplary sermons.[58] These sermons are interesting in that they do indeed exemplify the organizational plan laid out in the preceptive part of the treatise. In the fourteenth-century Cambridge copy the scribe has indicated in the margin of the longest sermon—"Sermon to the Learned and Unlearned Together"—the point at which each of Alexander's four parts begins. He notes, for instance, that Alexander divides things into two, and that each of the two divisions has three subdivisions. It is not clear how many sermons were in the original collection, since some intervening leaves are now missing from the manuscript. At least six sermons are included in the surviving manuscript, though closer study might reveal more precisely whether some of the longer pieces contain more than one sermon under a single rubricated title. Most begin with a direct quotation from Scripture, with various kinds of amplification used to develop the quotation throughout the sermon.

Alexander of Ashby therefore ranks as the first preceptive writer in a new approach to the form of preaching. Unlike Alain de Lille, he is concerned entirely with the "mode" of preaching rather than its material. He is apparently the first writer after Saint Augustine to do so. Brief as it is, his *On the Mode of Preaching* introduces a theory of organization coupled with ideas on division and proof that were to become standard within the next few decades.

Particularly important is his assumption that there is a standard form to be followed in preaching. This is a new element. Whereas Alain says that very little has been written about preaching, Alexander takes for granted that there is a stabilized and presumably well-accepted "mode" to be followed. The difference in attitude is enormous. Alexander's acceptance of the concept should be compared to that of the Italian *dictatores* a century earlier, who quickly adopted the "approved format" of the *ars dictaminis,* which then remained standard during the next three centuries.[59] If, as Aristotle says (*Topics* VIII), "the first step in any science is the most important one," then Alexander's flat statement about the

---

[58] The Cambridge copy of the treatise ends (fol. 170ᵛᵇ) as follows: De sermone sermonem fecimus. A modo sermonis exempla subiciemus. Then comes the rubric: *Sermones prioris de essebi.*

[59] See above, pp. 224–25. Also, cf. Anonymous of Bologna, *The Principles of Letter-Writing,* in James J. Murphy (ed.), *Three Medieval Rhetorical Arts* (Berkeley and Los Angeles, 1971), pp. 1–25.

"mode" of preaching can be seen as the opening of a new approach to the preparation of sermons.

In this light, his comments about division (*divisio*) are of the highest importance. Four-part speech plans were of course not new to the history of rhetoric; Aristotle among others had proposed introduction, statement, proof, and conclusion. Cicero and Roman rhetoricians generally had proposed a six-part or five-part speech plan under the heading of arrangement (*dispositio*), the second of the usual five canons of rhetorical study. All these Roman proposals included partition (*partitio*), a section of the speech following the introduction (*exordium*), in which the speaker told his audience which points he intended to cover. The standard classical works widely circulated in the twelfth century, Cicero's *De inventione* and the Pseudo–Ciceronian *Rhetorica ad Herennium,* both have this format. The late classical commentary of Victorinus, which also circulated in that century, makes a further distinction in discussing Cicero's use of the term "partition": "Partition is the ordering of the entire case according to its parts, while division is the setting out of the parts within the partition." [60] For Victorinus, in other words, division is actually a type of subpartition. Alexander makes the same distinction, except that he uses the terms division and subdivision. The debt to classical rhetoric seems obvious.

The connection between division and proof is also critically important. Alexander proposes that each "member" (*membrum*) set out as a divided part should be followed immediately by a proof. This is a radical departure from standard Ciceronian rhetorical doctrine, which makes proof a separate part of the speech plan. Alexander's format might result in a sermon outline as follows:

I. Introduction
II. Division (e.g., into three parts)
    Part A (e.g., into two subdivisions)
        Subdivision 1
            Proof from authority, etc.[61]
            Proof by reason, etc.
        Subdivision 2
            Proof by exemplum, etc.
            Proof by allegory, etc.

---

[60] *Q. Fabii Laurentii Victorini explanationum in rhetoricam M. Tullii Ciceronis libri duo,* I.22, in Ch. Halm, *Rhetores latini minores* (Leipzig, 1863), p. 208.

[61] While Alexander does not explicitly say so, he seems to assume that proofs will be both varied and mixed, and this outline indicates one possible method of mixing.

> Part B (e.g., into three subdivisions)
>     As above, etc.
> Part C (e.g., into two subdivisions)
>     As above, etc.
> III. Conclusion

In other words, the insertion of proofs one by one under the subdivisions would actually result in a three-part sermon with the subdivisions acting as a scaffolding from which all the proofs would depend. The net effect is a series of mini-sermons, each complete with its own proposition (the statement of subdivision) and its own proofs, yet relating to the original theme because all the divisions and subdivisions have been derived from it.

It is just possible that the rationale for this plan was derived indirectly from the Pseudo–Ciceronian *Rhetorica ad Herennium*. During his discussion of judicial causes in Book Two, the Pseudo–Cicero says that "the most complete and perfect argument, then, is that which is comprised of five parts: the Proposition, the Reason, the Proof of the Reason, the Embellishment, and the Resume," in other words, that each argument should be regarded as a mini-speech with its own self-contained plan of arrangement. He has earlier declared that this is primarily for the sake of memory: "By the following method, therefore, we can ourselves remember what we have said in each place, and the hearer can perceive and remember the distribution of the parts in the whole cause and also in each particular argument." [62] While Alexander's details are different, the concept is the same.

Canon Ashby, the Augustinian house in which Alexander lived, was in Northamptonshire only about 40 miles from Oxford. While the early records of the university show no mention of him, it is not inconceivable that he had had some connection with it. We do not know what his own library contained. In any case his opening remarks about the three purposes of an introduction point to an acquaintance with at least that part of the rhetorical lore contained in both Cicero and the Pseudo–Cicero. Pending a more complete study of surviving rhetorical commentaries of the eleventh and twelfth centuries, we cannot be sure what Alexander's contemporaries were saying about passages like the one cited above from the *Rhetorica ad Herennium*.

One final question remains. If, as Alexander proposes, the preacher is to present a Division, then what is it that is to be divided? Alexander

---

[62] *Ad Herennium* II.xvii.27.

does not tell us. He apparently assumes that his readers will know. But given the continuous tradition of the Christian church, and given the explicit statements of every major Christian writer on the subject—plus Alexander's own example in his model sermons—it seems highly probable that he expects the preacher to use the Scripture itself as the subject of division, as preachers had traditionally done. It is for this reason that he cautions the preacher to be sparing in his use of authorities to "prove" individual words; in this context he can only mean individual words from a quotation. In other words, Alexander assumes that a Scriptural passage will supply the material for the form of preaching.

Alexander of Ashby, then, presents a specified "mode" for preaching, which includes a standardized arrangement of parts, an emphasis on "division," and the nomination of certain major methods of "proof."

It seems unlikely that he personally invented this approach. Rather, it seems probable that he crystallizes for us a number of ideas already current in his time. We know nothing of his education, or his travels—rural Northamptonshire was certainly not an intellectual center in twelfth-century England—and he may indeed have studied elsewhere. But of all the surviving writings on preaching, Alexander's *On the Mode of Preaching* is the first to lay out the fundamental attitude and the particular rhetorical principles which only a few years later came to be widely known as the "modern" form of preaching—the *ars praedicandi.*

The prevalence of these ideas is further demonstrated by a contemporary of Alexander, also an Englishman—"Thomas of Salisbury," who is probably identical with Thomas Chabham (or Chobham).

The *Summa de arte praedicandi* of Thomas of Salisbury is even more important than Alexander's treatise in showing us how the new genre was developing in the early thirteenth century. Thomas explains the new nomenclature—terms such as *thema, antethema, divisio*—compares the preacher's tasks to those of the ancient orators as laid out in the Roman *ars rhetorica,* discusses the problems of persuasion and dissuasion, and treats a number of specific questions such as audience memory. The entire discussion is framed by constant comparisons between rhetoric, poetry, theology, and preaching. He points out that preaching is the duty of both "doctors" and "pastors." In other words, Thomas's *Summa* sets the *ars praedicandi* solidly within the intellectual framework of the late twelfth and early thirteenth centuries. For these reasons the work deserves careful attention by anyone interested in the evolution of medieval rhetorical principles.

Modern scholars have generally overlooked the work. Neither Caplan nor Charland included it in their master lists of manuscripts, and it was first mentioned by Gerald Owst in 1938. His citation, however, was embedded in a paragraph within a book review,[63] and apparently attracted no notice. This unfortunate lapse has meant that for more than three decades the numerous students of the *ars praedicandi* were not able to assess what may well prove to be the most significant single thirteenth-century treatise on the subject.

The dating and authorship of the work are therefore critical. The general tone of the treatise echoes the concerns of the late twelfth-century "Renaissance"—the relation between various arts, and the relation between ancient and modern learning. Quotations from Horace and the *Rhetorica ad Herennium* are mixed with Scriptural passages and citations from twelfth-century grammarians. (Significantly, perhaps, the thirteenth-century grammarians are not mentioned.) Thomas uses a definition from the *Verbum abbreviatum* (1187) of Peter Cantor, who taught in Paris until his death in 1197.

The work survives in a single thirteenth-century manuscript now in Corpus Christi College, Cambridge.[64] The manuscript lists the author as "Master Thomas of Salisbury." This is undoubtedly Thomas Chabham (or Chobham). Everything in the work is consistent with his views and his educational background. This identification is important because Chabham's career is well documented, and thus we are able to speak with some certainty about the probable date of composition of the *Summa de arte predicandi.*

Chabham is best known for his popular *Summa de poenitentia,* a general manual of pastoral care which he completed between 1219 and 1222. It survives in 84 manuscripts.[65] Chabham was educated at Paris, where

---

[63] Review of Charland's *Artes praedicandi,* published in *Speculum* 13 (1938), 352–54, citing Owst's earlier review of Caplan's *Handlist* in *Medium Aevum* 6 (1937), 155.

[64] Cambridge Corpus Christi College MS. 455, fols. 1–96. I am indebted to Mr. R. I. Page, Librarian of Corpus Christi College, for making the manuscript available. (It might be noted, incidentally, that the *Speculum* review cited above mistakenly lists the number as MS. 445.)

[65] For biographical details, see Palémon Glorieux, *Répertoire des maîtres en théologie de Paris au XIIIᵉ siècle* (Paris, 1933), pp. 275–76. For "Thomas of Salisbury," see Russell, *Writers of Thirteenth-Century England,* p. 169. Early modern cataloguers (e.g., Tanner) suggested that Thomas of Salisbury might be Thomas Chabham but hesitated to make a positive identification. Charland, p. 91, names Thomas of Salisbury as a fifteenth-century figure, possibly because he was not aware of the thirteenth-century manuscript at Cambridge. Chabham's biography has been summarized by Leonard Boyle, O.P., "A Study of Works Attributed to William of Pagula with Special Reference to the *Oculus Sacerdotis* and *Summa summarum,*" 2 vols., unpublished D.Phil. thesis (Oxford, 1956), I, 214–24.

he may have studied under Peter Cantor. He became subdeacon of Salisbury shortly after 1206. He was apparently teaching at Paris in 1213, when Pope Innocent III addressed a letter to "the deacon of Salisbury, teaching theology in Paris." He was in England at least briefly around 1222, the time of the Council of Oxford, though he may already have been there for some time before that date; a Master Thomas of Salisbury witnessed a charter of Hugh de Templo who had been a clerk by 1208, a canon in 1214, and was probably dead by 1226. The grammarian John of Garland, who was at Paris before 1220, speaks of a famous master named Thomas who came from Salisbury. Records indicate that Chabham was probably a subdeacon at Salisbury as late as 1238.

It seems likely, then, that his *Summa de arte predicandi* was written sometime during the first three decades of the century. His references to twelfth-century figures would seem to indicate a date earlier rather than later in his career. Despite his numerous references to grammar, for instance, there is no mention of Parisians like Alexander of Villedieu and Geoffrey of Vinsauf, who became famous shortly after 1210. Thomas may have turned to other subjects upon his return to England—he is known to have written at least seven other works besides *Summa de poenitentia*—and may not have kept in touch with academic circles in Paris. Or, more probably, he may have written the *Summa de arte predicandi* before 1210 or 1215. Perhaps the final answer to the question of exact dating must await a detailed comparison of all his books; nevertheless, it is clear that he wrote in the early years of the thirteenth century.

The *Summa de arte predicandi* is divided into two unequal parts. The first (fols. 1–74$^r$) deals with such general matters as the relation of preaching to theology, the perils to faith, questions asked about doctrine by the unlearned, the cardinal virtues and the theological virtues, and the seven fallacies of the devil. The second part (fols. 74$^v$–89$^v$) deals with what Thomas calls "those things necessary to be considered in artistic preaching." The rubricated headings indicate his topics:

Fols. 74$^{va}$  On Preaching
    75$^{rb}$  (On the Distinction between Rhetoric and Preaching)[66]
    76$^{ra}$  On Prohemia or Prologues
    77$^{vb}$  On Preaching and Invention and Its Parts
    79$^{va}$  On Narration
    80$^{ra}$  On the Art of Varying Narrations and Parabolas
    81$^{ra}$  On Artistic Narration by Means of Persons

---

[66] This rubric is missing because of a hole in the manuscript leaf, and is reconstructed from the opening lines of the section.

Major portions of these sixteen sections are organized around double comparisons between preaching and the six Roman "parts of an oration" —exordium, narration, partition, confirmation, refutation, and peroration —and a comparison between preaching and the five "parts of rhetoric": invention, arrangement, style, memory, and delivery.

In the first part of the *Summa* Thomas argues that just as physics provides the rationale of bodily things, so ethics and logic deal with the spiritual things. Ethics and logic are parts of philosophy. Theology, like philosophy, uses "significations" drawn from words. But of the four types of significations, the literal or historical sense belongs particularly to philosophy and theology; the other three—tropological, allegorical, and anagogical—belong to the study of sacred Scripture. The literal sense derives signification from a *thing* (*res*), whereas the other three derive them from a *locution* (*vocum*). Locutions involve verbal accounts of things in fables, arguments, or true accounts of events. Analogy and metaphor are two modes useful in educing significations through words; analogy is subsumed under grammar and dialectic, while metaphor falls under rhetoric. Thomas declares that it is the office of a theologian to take part in three kinds of activities: reading, disputing, and preaching;[67] the third, preaching, is common to both "doctors" and "pastors." Consequently it behooves the preacher, whether a pastor or a learned doctor, to study everything that can help him perform his office. While Thomas goes on to mention grammar several times, and to point to the value of such

---

[67] Theologie autem officium quantum ad scolasticam exercitationem in tribus consistent: in legendo, in disputendo, in predicando. . . . Cum igitur officium predicandi doctoribus et pastoribus sit commune, merito predicationis scientiam optinet privilegium. Fol. 1$^{rb}$. Compare this statement with that of Peter Cantor, *Verbum abbreviatum* (Migne, *PL* 205, col. 25): In tribus consistit exercitium sacrae scripturae: circa lectionem, disputationem et praedicationem. (By "reading" Peter of course means "teaching aloud.") Thomas Chabham (Oxford Oriel College MS. 17, fol. 110$^r$) refers to *Cantor. . . . Parisiensis bone memorie dixit*. Peter Cantor died in 1197. In other words, "Thomas of Salisbury" and "Thomas Chabham" both seem to have known, or known about, the Parisian teacher Peter Cantor.

grammatical transformations as *transumptio,* he virtually ignores dialectic and continually praises rhetoric as a source of knowledge for the preacher.

Preaching for Thomas has two aims: announcement and instruction. The materials to be discussed are faith and good morals, their contraries, and the virtues and vices. It is not surprising then to find him devoting the long remainder of the first part to such matters as the detestation of vices and the imitation of virtues. For example he includes a long section (fols. 27–34) on Saint Augustine's preaching on the Beatitudes, and another section on contempt for the body (fols. 73–74). The bulk of the first part is therefore in the older tradition of providing *materia* for the preacher.[68] Except for the opening argument about theology and the other arts, the first part could almost as easily have been written in the time of Gregory.

The second part of the *Summa de arte predicandi* is much more revealing. It shows a thoughtful awareness both of the older Ciceronian rhetorical tradition and of the newer genre, which is obviously already well established by this time. Thomas begins by promising to compare preaching with the orations of rhetoric and with the works (*orationes*) of the poets. He begins with the poets. Comic poets like Virgil, as Horace says, set forth their works in three parts: argument, movement, and happy ending. The argument consists of the entire material spoken, while the movement or action includes both the emotional responses and the actions of the persons involved. Argument can be seen in certain epistles of Paul and "in certain other books." The fables of poets provide action both of words and of people.

Thomas adds that poets also arrange their poems into three parts: proposition, invocation, and narration. In this preachers are like poets, for they first propose a theme (*thema*) from which they derive the text of the sermon. Then they pray for the help of God in reaching the hearers. Then they "expose" the theme in the form of narration. The practice of invocation is found in antiquity too, "as in certain ancient philosophers and in Plato's *Timaeus,*" and it is the custom of certain religious (in modern times) to ask divine aid. We are accustomed, he says, to invoke divine aid for important reasons in the university. So if even the pagan philosophers invoke the divine aid to make their hearers attentive and willing to learn, how much more so should we do so who have the divine

---

[68] For instance, fol. 18 deals with subjects to preach to men who are in a state of mortal sin; fol. 41 with detestation of vices and praise of virtues; and fol. 73 with contempt for the body.

word to transmit! We seek the salvation of both hearers and readers.
Thomas concludes the first section by pointing out that the invocation
will ensure that God's word, and not the preacher's arrogance, will come
forth; this is important because, as Augustine shows, God's message is a
joyful one—the "happy ending" of the comic poets, in other words.

Thomas then declares that orators divide their speeches in a different
way, so that it is easier to show the relation between rhetoric and preaching than it is to show it between poetry and preaching. "Rhetoric," he
states, "is the art of speaking for the sake of persuading." [69] Therefore
the whole intention of the preacher ought to be that he persuade men to
good conduct and dissuade them from bad conduct; thus the end of the
orator and the end of the preacher are the same. "Therefore the doctrine
of the orator is absolutely necessary to carry out the office of a preacher." [70]

This is the first explicit statement of the kind since Augustine. Neither
Alain de Lille nor Alexander of Ashby made such a statement, despite
Alexander's radically new attitude toward the form of preaching.

Thomas proves, moreover, that his is no passing remark, for he then
proceeds to demonstrate how the parts of a sermon compare with Roman
rhetorical doctrine. Even though the concepts of Cicero and the Pseudo-
Cicero are so similar that it is difficult in most cases to determine the
exact source of Thomas's ideas, nevertheless some of the definitions are
taken verbatim from the *Rhetorica ad Herennium*. There is nothing in
the *Summa* inconsistent with the notion that Thomas may have used
that book as his sole source.[71] His Parisian background would of course
indicate a probable familiarity with both the *ad Herennium* and the *De
inventione*.

Thomas's detailed comparison of the six parts of sermon and the five
parts of rhetoric is far too long to repeat here. But a short passage from
his discussion of introductions may provide a good example of his method.

---

[69] Rethorica enim est ars dicendi apposite ad persuadendum. Fol. 75$^{rb}$.
[70] Ideo valde neccessaria est doctrina oratoris ad officium predicatoris. Fol. 75$^{va}$.
[71] For instance, his definition of invention is taken almost verbatim from *ad
Herennium* I.ii.3. Thomas says (fol. 77$^{vr}$): Inventio excogitatio rerum verarum vel
verisimilium que id quidam dedere (sic) est probabile reddant. The *ad Herennium*
says: Inventio est excogitatio rerum verarum aut veri similium quae causam probabilem reddant. It is interesting to note that Thomas sometimes uses the term
"philosopher" (*philosophus*) when quoting from *ad Herennium*; at other times
he says "in the rhetoric" (*in rhetorica*) or makes no mention of source at all.
After the second quarter of the thirteenth century, when Aristotle had been
securely ensconced as an authority in medieval universities, the use of the term
"philosopher" almost always meant *the philosopher*—Aristotle. This may be another indication of an early date of composition for the *Summa*.

After warning the preacher that he can never assume that his audience will have good will in advance of his speaking, Thomas notes the distinction made *in rhetorica* (here, the *ad Herennium* I.iii.6) between the direct approach (*principium*) and the subtle approach (*insinuatio*).[72] He notes also that there are various traditional rhetorical names for introductions—terms such as "prologue," or "prohemium," or "exordium." Then he goes on to point out why the new "artistic" sermon theory uses different terms: the term "prohemium" is not used by preachers in either the customary or the artistic mode. Instead, Thomas says: "Some preachers call their prologue a 'protheme,' because it is for the *thema* an *antethema*, that is, certain ones, before they proceed with the main *thema*, lay out a sort of brief theme before the main one, thus helping to make the audience attentive, docile, and well disposed." [73] Here is not only part of the new vocabulary for the new genre, but a justification for the new nomenclature. Obviously the genre itself is well established.

The acute rhetorical sense of the author is demonstrated by a remark he makes in this same section. It is the kind of remark that seems likely to have come only from fairly serious study and discussion of the point involved. Thomas says that the direct approach is not suitable to the introductions of artistic sermons. His reason: the direct approach involves a statement about the nature of the discourse to follow, but this function, Thomas declares, properly belongs to the *divisio* of the sermon and not to its introduction. This kind of judgment reveals that after twelve centuries of nontheory, students of preaching in the early thirteenth century were at last discussing their task in analytic, preceptive terms.

Concerning the discovery of proofs, Thomas points out that "the sacred page has its own special topics (*loci*) beyond those of dialectic and rhetoric." [74] Scripture, with aid from theology, is therefore the basic source for the preacher. It provides him with both valid and probable proofs. (Again, these terms are taken from the *Rhetorica ad Herennium* and used in a systematic comparison between preaching and the "oration of rhetoric.")

---

[72] He illustrates the difference by a citation from the Acts of the Apostles.

[73] Vocant predicatores quidam prologum suum prothema, quia thema antethema, ut scilicet quidam autem prosequantur principale thema proponant quiddam breve themate et exponant ad capiendum benivolentiam et preparandam attentionem auditorum et docilitatem eorum. Fol. 76^{va}.

[74] Sacra pagina habet locos suos speciales praeter locos dialecticos et rethoricos. Fol. 77^{rb}. Elsewhere (fol. 76^{ra}) he mentions the "topic of law" (locus autem legis) as a way of finding in the Old Testament the means to praise the glory of God; he uses the example of Abraham in Mesopotamia.

Two sections of Thomas's *Summa* deserve special attention—the one on means of varying narrations, and the one on division. Thomas first refers to the mode of "significations" he has discussed at the beginning of the *Summa,* and then promises a discussion of variations through "persons." Actually he provides six modes through persons and one through "the properties of things." His six are: God with His angels; demons; the Church Militant; the Church Triumphant; the life of Christ; and "the synagogue of the devil." Thomas says that the preacher should investigate the properties of things so that he may show their significations to his audience.[75]

Division is necessary in a sermon so that the hearer may understand what is to follow. Besides, division is natural: Augustine and other authors divide their books into chapters and headings, and a sermon should do the same. All things are divided, into genus and species. The sins are divided into seven, just as this seven is further subdivided into subdivisions of two bodily sins and five spiritual sins. Thomas suggests the following means of division: first, dividing the theme into its words; second, into classes of things (e.g., genus and species); third, whole and all potential parts; fourth, substance and accident; fifth, accidents into their kinds; sixth, various significations of individual words in the theme. He adds some now-familiar advice that the preacher should not make so many divisions and subdivisions that the audience will be confused. Moreover, Thomas stresses, it would be a grave fault if the preacher should neglect to provide at least one Scriptural authority to prove each of the members of the division. (It will be recalled that Alexander of Ashby insists that every member should be followed at once by its proofs.) Thomas shows concern for the realities of audience response, as when he warns that a preacher should not be too detailed in giving citations for his authorities—it suffices to say "as in Augustine" or "as Gregory says," without naming author and book and chapter. Some care must also be exercised in determining whether the parts of a division should equal each other—the preacher should not, for instance, equate mortal sins with venial sins for the sake of a neat division.

One difficulty Thomas faces in organizing his *Summa* is that the ancient rhetorical lore is divided in two ways—into parts of a speech and parts of the art itself—which are different from what he himself regards as the proper parts of an artistic sermon. Consequently he sometimes discusses

---

[75] For a brief study of this approach, see Lynn Thorndike, "The Properties of Things of Nature Adapted to Sermons," *Medievalia et Humanistica* 12 (1958), 78-83.

subjects like the sermon's "theme" in three or four different places in his comparisons. He is not quite sure whether the "division" of the sermon belongs under the Roman part called "partition" or under the part called "confirmation" (because the division also involves a statement of what the audience is supposed to accept); Thomas returns to division under "memory," declaring that division is for the sake of the audience's memory and not the speaker's. He also says that a sweet style produces a pleasure in the hearers' ears which enables them to remember what they hear.

This difficulty of Thomas is ours also. Rather than pursue him through all the repetitive details of his comparisons, it might be better here to summarize Thomas of Salisbury's view of the "artistic sermon."

The artistic sermon has the following organizational plan:

1. Opening prayer for divine aid
2. Protheme (antetheme), or introduction of theme
3. Theme, or statement of a Scriptural quotation
4. Division, or statement of parts of the theme
5. Development (*prosecutio*) of the members named in the division
6. Conclusion (not an integral part of the sermon)

Here, two decades or more before the earliest statement heretofore known to modern scholars, is the complete theory of the "thematic" or "university-style" sermon which dominated the rhetoric of preaching well down into Reformation times.

We can of course say of Thomas of Salisbury what we said earlier of Alexander of Ashby, that is, that he did not invent the "modern" or "artistic" sermon. He evidently found it in existence already. But Thomas of Salisbury has given us a rare insight into the kind of thinking that led to the formation of the new genre. It was a natural outgrowth of the twelfth-century concern over the relation of the arts. The resulting mode of preaching, based as it was on a consideration of several arts but especially rhetoric, must have seemed quite satisfactory to all concerned. Theology continues as an aid to Scripture; dialectic and grammar have a place in the development of ideas (though not in their organization); physics is another source of development of ideas; Scripture remains dominant, with rhetoric the prime vehicle for bringing it to the minds and hearts of the people. Most important, the artistic mode was set up as a self-contained genre which contained all that was needed by the preacher.

The *Summa de arte predicandi* is therefore a reasoned statement not only about how a sermon should be preached, but why it should be preached in that particular way.

It is inconceivable that this unique fusion of subject matter and mechanism could have come from the thirteenth-century university. It was popular later in sermons *ad prelatos* or *ad eruditos,* of course, and must have been especially congenial to the academic mind. But the peculiar demands of the dialectical establishment, especially in the northern universities of Paris and Oxford, if left to itself would surely have produced a quite different approach to preaching; dialectic, after all, was universally recognized as an art of exchanges between persons, while preaching was always uninterrupted discourse. The rather abstract philosophic theorizing which was characteristic of midcentury academic theology (e.g., Thomas Aquinas) would have had little room for the psychological requirements of a preaching theory. But the most convincing argument against a university origin for the new genre is simply one of chronology. Both Alexander of Ashby and Thomas of Salisbury demonstrate that all the elements of the new genre were in circulation by the year 1200 and shortly thereafter. Their testimony leads to the inference that the basic theory of the *ars praedicandi* was known at least in the 1190's and perhaps in the 1180's or earlier. Whatever views one holds about the effective dates of university organization, the work of Alexander and especially of Thomas would seem to point instead to the intellectual milieu of the non-university schools of the twelfth century. Thomas and Alexander are in the humane tradition of Alexander Neckham and John of Salisbury, not the dialectical tradition of Aquinas.

With this background in mind, then, it is now possible to place in some perspective the other prominent homiletic writers of the early and middle thirteenth century: Richard of Thetford, William of Auvergne, Jean de la Rochelle, and the anonymous author of the treatise *Omnis tractatio,* once attributed to Saint Bonaventure.

By far the most important of these is Richard of Thetford (fl. 1245?), author of an extremely popular work on the *Art of Amplifying Sermons* (*Ars dilatandi sermones*), which marked out eight particular "modes of amplification." The work itself survives in 27 manuscripts; it influenced at least seven other anonymous treatises, and finds echoes in such major writers as Robert of Basevorn.[76] Richard's biography is obscure. One manuscript (Oxford Magdalen College MS. 168, fol. 129) contains a marginal notation alongside his *Ars* referring to him as "Richard of Thetford,

---

[76] For a list of manuscripts, see Caplan, No. 154, and Charland, pp. 77–80. See also Russell, *Writers of Thirteenth Century England,* pp. 122–23. Caplan, incidentally, prefers the term "dilatation" rather than "dilation"; I have followed the manuscript spelling of *dilatio.*

Canon." It has been suggested that he was a canon of the Order of the Holy Sepulchre, which had a house in Thetford; a chaplain by the name of Richard was presented to Thetford chapel in 1247–48 by Robert and Gilbert of Thetford, knights. His *Ars* was certainly written before 1268, when it first appears in a library catalogue.

An incomplete but adequate version of Richard's treatise on the eight modes of amplification has been published by Quaracchi as the third part of a work by Saint Bonaventure.[77] (The work has also been attributed to Albertus Magnus.) The Quaracchi text is adequate for general study, in that it contains all the eight standard modes even if it omits the Prologue to the tract and the lengthy general remarks which follow the eight modes in some manuscripts. In other words, the Quaracchi text provides the general reader with a good sense of Thetford's principles, and of course the printed text of the Pseudo-Bonaventure is far more easily available than the various manuscripts scattered in fifteen European libraries.

One important observation needs to be made at the outset. All of Richard's eight modes are for the amplification of "themes." He simply assumes that his readers will know what that means. In other words, Richard deals with that single task of amplification (or "prosecution," to use Thomas of Salisbury's term) which follows the division and subdivision of the theme in the new genre of the artistic sermon. Richard simply assumes the existence of the new genre.

His eight modes of dilation are as follows:

1. Placing a locution in place of a name, as in defining, describing, interpreting, or any other kind of exposition
2. Dividing
3. Reasoning, including syllogism, induction, example, and enthymeme
4. Using concordant authorities
5. Using roots of the known
6. Proposing metaphors and showing their aptness for instruction
7. Exposing the theme through diverse modes, that is, literal, allegorical, tropological or moral, and anagogical senses
8. Assigning cause and effect

---

[77] Published as Part Three of Bonaventura, *Ars Concionandi,* in *Doctoris seraphici S. Bonaventurae opera omnia* (Florence: Ad claras aquas [Quaracchi], 1901), IX, 16–21. Part One of the "Ars concionandi" is actually an anonymous treatise, *Omnis tractatio* (Caplan No. 114), dealing with modes of amplification. The so-called Part Two is merely a paragraph of transition. A translation of the entire three parts has been prepared for publication by Ernest Gallo of the University of Massachusetts. Another translation appears as Chapter 4 in Harry C. Hazel, "A Translation, with Commentary, of the Bonaventuran 'Ars Concionandi,'" unpublished Ph.D. thesis, Washington State University, 1972.

This tidy set of eight contains no item not previously found elsewhere. That is not the point. What is significant about the set is that it is indeed a set, a standardized list. Its conciseness must have made it useful. Certainly the prevalence of other medieval works dealing with *Octo modis* shows the popularity of the concept of "eightness."

Dialectical influence is seen particularly in two of these eight—dividing and reasoning—where Aristotle's *Topics,* Porphyry, and Boethius are cited in addition to the customary Scriptural references and the usual quotations from Augustine's *De doctrina christiana* and Gregory's *Cura pastoralis.* It is interesting to note, too, that example (*exemplum*) is included here as a type of formal argumentation. Richard concludes the section on reasoning, however, by warning that preaching is not a form of disputation; thus it does not lead from proposition to conclusion.[78]

Otherwise Richard's listings are remarkable only in that they demonstrate the continuing popularity of the "four senses of interpretation," the identification of metaphor as a separate form of support, and the relegation of reasoning to a place as merely one method among many. One could no doubt attempt to trace each of the eight items back to a particular discipline—for instance, tracking the roots of the known back to grammatical etymology. But by the middle of the thirteenth century the cross-fertilization of the arts of discourse had proceeded for so long that such a tracing exercise today would be merely pedantic. Richard's first mode, for instance, first appears in Aristotle's *Rhetoric* and *Topics,* then in Ciceronian rhetoric, later in the basic grammar of Donatus, and then— nearer in time to Richard of Thetford—in the works of medieval grammarians like Geoffrey of Vinsauf and John of Garland. The concept thus runs through the whole medieval *trivium* of grammar, dialectic, and rhetoric.

And why not? What we have already seen in Thomas of Salisbury's *Summa* is the gradual separation of the new genre from its ultimate sources. It did the medieval preacher very little good to be told (as Augustine tells him in many a quotation) that he ought to study all the arts of language. What the preacher really needed was a single special art. And this is what the *ars praedicandi* set out to give him.

The process is analogous to what occurred in Italy more than a century

---

[78] Ne praedicatio videatur esse disputatio, oportet, quod sic fiat, quasi non esset argumentatio, ut scilicet non praemittantur propositiones, et postea inferatur conclusio; sed magis dicatur sic: nam ita est, et hoc multiplici rationes. Quaracchi, p. 19.

earlier in the development of another independent art, the *ars dictaminis*. The first authors, like Alberic, were still close to their sources; once the genre was established, however, the *ars dictaminis* functioned independently and writers no longer bothered to justify their principles. Ultimately the genre fed upon itself, so that the "authorities" became other dictaminal writers rather than Cicero. Moreover, the fully developed genre accumulated an auxiliary apparatus which included specialized treatments of small segments of the total art; in the case of the *ars dictaminis* it was separate treatises dealing only with salutations, or only with proverbs, or the like.

Richard of Thetford's *Art of Amplifying Sermons* is just such a specialized treatment of a segment of the whole art, the step of amplification. Its relevance depends upon the existence of the larger genre of which it is a part.

The same judgment can be made about another thirteenth-century work, the tract beginning *Omnis tractatio,* which is published as the first part of the *Ars concionandi,* attributed by Quaracchi to Saint Bonaventure. It survives in ten manuscripts.[79] This work, apparently anonymous, is explicitly limited to means of amplification. It is not clear whether it has any direct relation to Thetford's treatise, though some of its concepts are similar. Its exact date is uncertain.

The author begins with Augustine's statement (from the opening of the *De doctrina christiana*) that discourse about Scripture includes "a way of discovering these things which are to be understood, and a way of teaching what we have learned." Most important for the purpose of the preacher are three things: divisions, distinctions, and dilations. Propriety is the desired quality in division, brevity in distinction, and usefulness in dilation. Just as Augustine said that "to teach is a necessity, to please is sweetness, to persuade is a victory," so division instructs through propriety, distinction pleases through brevity, and dilation persuades through utility.

This rather strained reasoning is typical of the approach used in the rest of the treatise. The author picks his way through hundreds of examples, mostly Scriptural, which illustrate various ways to divide, distinguish, and dilate. Perhaps 90 to 95 percent of the text is devoted to examples. In all cases, however, the author makes it clear that the primary

---

[79] Caplan No. 114; Caplan adds three additional manuscripts to the seven listed in Quaracchi. One of the additional ones, Oxford Balliol College MS. 179, fols. 321–25, lists its title as *Ars dividendi themata.*

rhetorical function of the preacher is to amplify a "theme." Sometimes he proposes different examples for sermons *ad cleros* as opposed to *ad populos*. In one case (Cap. 25) he refers to a certain triplex division as one "like the scholastic" (*quasi scholasticus*). But for the most part he offers a detailed, item-by-item set of themes such as he would develop them himself.

The rapidity with which such suggestions became cemented into "rules" is shown by the *Art of Preparing Sermons* (*Ars conficiendi sermones*) of the Franciscan Jean de la Rochelle (died 1245).[80] His treatise, which survives in three and possibly four manuscripts, discusses the problems arising when a preacher has to make choices among many ways of treating a theme. Jean's solution is to propose "rules" (*regulae*) to help him make the choices. This is a considerable step beyond the mere proferring of possibilities. Jean does not always succeed in making the rules fit the problems, but it is an interesting sign of increasing sophistication within the new genre. One rule, for instance, is that, when choosing between the senses of interpretation, maximum effect can be achieved with either the tropological or the anagogical. When one is confused over roots (the fifth mode of Thetford), the preacher should state that it is not possible to find a root. If a theme has many parts, he should arbitrarily choose four. In discussing persons, he should always arouse detestation for one and exhort his hearers to imitate another. He should always use a multiplicity of modes of amplification but should not make concordances too complex. He should always draw a moral. In making distinctions, Jean declares, always indicate the chief or principal one to be noted.

This is practical stuff. Obviously it depends again on the existence of a certain body of well-known rhetorical doctrine, and is designed not only for its own sake but also as a supplement to what is to be found elsewhere.

Somewhat the same thing can be said about the only other preaching manual that has come down to us from the first part of the thirteenth century. This is the short treatise *On the Art of Preaching* (*De arte predicandi*), attributed to William of Auvergne (Bishop of Paris, 1228–49) and edited by A. de Poorter from a Bruges manuscript.[81] William of

---

[80] Caplan No. 31; Charland, pp. 62–64. A paragraph from the Prologue is printed in Quaracchi, p. 15. I have used London British Museum MS. Arundel 275 (XV), fols. 83rb–86rb. The author is also known as Johannis de Rupella.

[81] A. de Poorter, "Un manuel de prédication médiévale," *Revue néoscolastique de philosophie* 25 (1923), 192–209.

Auvergne is known to have written three works that may be said to relate generally to preaching: *Rhetorica divina,* which actually deals with prayer (man's "speech to God" through prayer); *De faciebus mundi,* which deals with the false appearances of the world which lead to sin;[82] and a third, *De arte predicandi.* The editor, de Poorter, believes this to be the work found in his Bruges manuscript. The treatise in any case dates from the thirteenth century, and there is no strong reason to disbelieve the attribution to William of Auvergne.

*On the Art of Preaching* is a rather unsystematic collection of twenty sections, some only a brief paragraph in length. The Prologue begins with definitions answering the six familiar questions: *Quis, quibus, ubi, quando, quomodo, quid.* His answers are very general; for instance, his answer to the question "in what way?" (*quomodo*) is "according to the capacity of the hearers." [83] He says that preachers can generate an ample supply of material through distinctions, divisions, metaphors, and definitions (to which he later adds derivations, compositions, and etymologies). Even grammatical word changes, as in number or case, can be useful. About one-half of the work deals with praise of preaching, the other half with means of amplification. This tract too seems to depend on the existence of an accepted genre.

These then are the known authors of the first half of the thirteenth century: Alexander of Ashby, Thomas of Salisbury (Thomas Chabham), Richard of Thetford, the anonymous author of *Omnis tractatio,* Jean de la Rochelle, and William of Auvergne.

It is now possible to state some conclusions about the development of the new rhetorical genre we know as the *ars praedicandi.* Apparently the genre came into being just before 1200, to judge from Alexander and Thomas. The *ars praedicandi* specifies a special subject matter and then lays out a plan of arrangement for sermons, with "protheme" or "ante-theme" followed by a "prayer" and then statement of "theme" (Scriptural quotation) with "division" and "subdivision" of that quotation "amplified' through a variety of modes. Alexander and Thomas propose a final step, "conclusion," but, as we shall see, the later theorists generally

---

[82] For early printed editions of *De faciebus mundi,* see Caplan, No. 229; and also see David M. Murphy, "Rhetorical Sections from William of Auvergne's *Rhetorica Divina* Rendered into English," unpublished M.A. thesis, Cornell University, 1956.

[83] It is worth noting also that the list of 20 *capitula* in William's Prologue (de Poorter, p. 197) is not a table of contents, but merely a list of the opening words (*incipits*) for each section. A reader could get quite a false impression of the contents if he were not aware of this fact.

abandoned this idea; it is not mentioned by other early writers like William of Auvergne.

This was the first major new oratorical plan to be proposed in the Western world since about 125 B.C., when Hellenistic rhetoricians developed the sequence made familiar by Cicero and the Pseudo-Cicero.

The details of the *ars praedicandi* itself are summarized in scores of excellent modern studies.[84] So clear-cut is the plan, and so habitual the means of amplification, that despite the welter of medieval authors a modern observer has little difficulty in analyzing the theory. Sadly, however, very few treatises are available in modern editions or translations— fewer than ten, in fact; as a consequence most readers must rely heavily on the abstracts or summaries which are more readily available, or accept the judgment of others about the typicality of the few texts that are available.

At this point, then, it might be best to note briefly a dozen or so later tracts in the *ars praedicandi* mode, either in print or in manuscript, which are of special interest. Then, to provide opportunity for a clearer understanding of a "typical" *ars praedicandi,* a full abstract of Robert of Basevorn's *Form of Preaching (Forma praedicandi)* of 1322 will be presented to illustrate the fully developed genre. This particular treatise has been chosen for several reasons: it is indeed typical of the genre, having influenced a number of others, and—most important—it is available in both a complete Latin text and a recent English translation which allow for further study.

The treatises now accessible in print or typescript (in theses) cannot be said to provide any systematic coverage. Their dates range from late thirteenth century to the early fifteenth. Countries of origin seem to be England, France, Italy, Germany, and Spain. Despite their scattered sources and times, however, there is a remarkable homogeneity among them.

The earliest is a work, *The Form of Preaching (Forma praedicandi),*

---

[84] In addition to those already mentioned (Charland, Caplan, Davy, etc.), the reader might consult Etienne Gilson, "Michel Menot et la technique du sermon médiévale," in *Les idées et les lettres* (Paris, 1932), pp. 93–154; this article was originally printed in *Revue d'histoire franciscaine* 2 (1925), 301–50. Excellent short summaries occur in Charles Smyth, *The Art of Preaching: A Practical Survey of Preaching in the Church of England, 747–1939* (London, 1940); and in the Introduction to *Middle English Sermons,* ed. Woodburn O. Ross, Early English Text Society, No. 209 (London, 1940). For a more complete bibliography see James J. Murphy, *Medieval Rhetoric: A Select Bibliography* (University of Toronto Press, 1972), items P1–P70.

dating from the second half of the thirteenth century. It has been attributed tentatively to John of Wales, a Franciscan who studied at Oxford and later (c. 1270) taught at Paris; he died in 1302. A shortened version of it has been published by Woodburn O. Ross, who declares that the condensation (which occurs in six English manuscripts) is a faithful abstract of Part Two of the complete text (the treatise *In isto libello*).[85] The assimilation of the new genre is again demonstrated by the fact that John defines preaching entirely in terms of the accepted format—theme, division, amplification, and so forth. For example, he says that every member of every subdivision must have a proof by Scriptural authority. There is no mention of a conclusion or epilogue, the treatise ending with the treatment of concordances in subdivisions. Here, too, is another feature of the developed genre—the purposeful omission of a *conclusio* or *epilogus;* it is a feature repeated again and again in later works.

The most important work of the fourteenth century, after that of Basevorn (discussed below), was the lengthy treatise of Thomas Waleys, *On the Mode of Composing Sermons, With Principles to Follow (De modo componendi sermones cum documentis).*[86] Thomas was an English Dominican, master of theology at Oxford at least as late as 1349. His nine chapters deal with what he calls the "modern" methods of preaching— that is, the four key matters of "assumption" (identification) of the theme, "introducing the theme," "dividing the theme," and "amplifying the theme." One charming feature of Waleys' writing is its prolixity, for he writes in such personal detail that a great deal of humanity comes through the otherwise dry recital of principles. For example "Documentum twelve" (Cap. I, pp. 339-40) urges the new preacher to seek out some secret place to practice, away from the view of men, where he can practice voice and gesture without fear of ridicule. He should preach to trees and to stones before he preaches to men. The injunction is not new—Plutarch says it was the method of Demosthenes—but with Waleys it comes through with a flavor of personal experience that other treatises often lack. His discussion of delivery is more complete than most, and occurs at the outset as part of the twelve attributes of a good preacher; most of the other *artes praedicandi* treat delivery as an afterthought if at all. His view

---

[85] Woodburn O. Ross, "A Brief *Forma predicandi,*" *Modern Philology* 34 (1937), 337–44. See Caplan No. 62 (*In isto libello* [libro] *quattuor capitula continentur*), for which he identifies 12 manuscripts.

[86] Latin text published by Charland, pp. 328–403. For a translation see Dorothy Grosser, "Thomas Waleys' *De modo componendi sermones* Rendered into English," unpublished M.A. thesis, Cornell University, 1949.

is quite clear: "Let the preacher therefore take care, most importantly among these factors, to have a way of speaking that is intelligible and comprehensible, because the way of speaking itself will carry to the hearers no less than the thing said." [87]

Waleys mentions at one point that both the teaching of Aristotle and common experience support the notion of varying vocal delivery to suit the material used. And overlong sermons with "superfluity *ad nauseam*" not only tire the audience but lead them to reject the food for the soul just as the stomach rejects too sumptuous a diet. Even when quoting authorities like Gregory (from whom he takes the food metaphor) he adds his own personal touch, and in later sections (e.g., Cap. VIII) he often says "I believe this is better" (*credo tamen quod iste modus sit melior*) instead of appealing to abstract rules or "the modern mode" as other authors tend to do.

Yet he can be relentlessly systematic. His book is, after all, a summary of the modern mode as he understands it. Despite the traditional disclaimer in his Preface to archbishop Theobald that it would be impossible to summarize all the modern ways to prepare sermons, Waleys does indeed summarize the standard doctrine already familiar to us from other documents. Thus in Cap. IX he lists and exemplifies fifteen ways to show "connections" between theme and authorities, depending upon whether the connection is intrinsic, mediate, by exposition, by definition, by description, by causality, by specification, by modification, by confirmation, by totality or partiality, by suppletion, by one authority with another made intrinsic by the occasion, by contrariety, by exception, or extrinsic. "It is therefore clear," he concludes, "that there are many ways by which authorities are connected [to themes]."

Thomas Waleys' book is well worth the modern reader's study, for it shows the typical doctrine of the day handled by an intelligent writer. Beryl Smalley has shown us in some detail the innate humanism of the author.[88] The careful reader can learn a good deal about the mid-fourteenth century from his *On the Mode of Composing Sermons*.

Another fourteenth-century preaching manual, also by an Englishman,

---

[87] Studet igitur praedicator, inter coetera, praecipue habere modum dicendi intelligibilem et allectivum, quia modus ipse dicendi non minus proderit auditoribus quam res dicta. Cap. I, p. 333.

[88] Beryl Smalley, *English Friars and Antiquity in the Middle Ages* (Oxford, 1960), pp. 75–108.

is the *Art of Composing Sermons* (*Ars componendi sermones*) of the Benedictine Ranulph Higden.[89] Higden is best known for his *Polychronicon,* a Latin history of the world, which was translated into English by John Trevisa in 1387. He also wrote two or three other works, as yet unedited: a *Speculum curatorum,* a *Distinctiones theologicae,* and possibly a *Paedigogicon grammatices,* now lost. Higden was a monk of the Saint Werberg monastery in Chester. He died in 1364. Since he borrows heavily from Robert of Basevorn's *Forma praedicandi,* which was written in 1322, his own treatise must have come after that date. Authorship is conclusively determined, as two manuscript colophons point out, by the fact that the initial letters of the *Prefacio* and the 20 *capitula* spell out his name and place: *Ars ranulphi cestrensis*—"The Art of Ranulph of Chester." (His model, Robert of Basevorn, uses the same device to identify himself.)

The basic doctrine of Higden's *Art* is not exceptional. He devotes four chapters to the character and attributes of the preacher, three to choosing themes, one each to the prayer and to the protheme, one to concordances, four to division and subdivision, four to dilation, and two to audience preparation. Twelve chapters follow Basevorn closely, sometimes to the inclusion of verbatim passages from the *Forma praedicandi.*[90] The most original chapters are the first four dealing with the person of the preacher, and the last three of the dilation chapters; that is, they are original with Higden in the sense that they do not necessarily come from Basevorn, though they are otherwise unexceptional. It is interesting to note again the presence of "rules" to be followed. In Cap. XIX Higden lays down a number of rules for dilation; for instance, an exposition of Scripture must not contradict the literal sense, nor contradict an article of faith nor go against truth. There are also complex rules to resolve the problem of deciding how to amplify a theme when the Gospel for the day differs in emphasis

---

[89] Caplan No. 156; Charland, p. 76. To the three manuscripts listed by Caplan and Charland can be added two more: London British Museum MS. Harley 866, fols. 8-17; and Oxford Bodley MS. Auct. F.3.5, fols. 9-25. An edition of Higden is being prepared for publication by Sister Margaret Jennings. It might be noted that Higden's *Ars* influenced the later tract of the Englishman Thomas Penketh (d. 1487); see Charland, p. 90. For the *Polychronicon,* see John Taylor, *The Universal Chronicle of Ranulf Higden* (Oxford, 1966).

[90] The corresponding *capitula* are as follows (Higden's listed first, Basevorn's second): 5/15, 7/16, 8/19-21, 9/22, 10/23, 11/25, 12/24, 13/31, 14/32-33, 15/33, 16/39, 17/40. During a good part of the composition of his book, Higden must have had a copy of Basevorn before him.

from liturgical feast set for that day. Throughout the *Ars,* in fact, Ranulph is much concerned with types of themes for various feast days and other occasions.[91]

Sometimes the title of an *ars praedicandi* will promise something different. Medieval titles of course tend to be quite generic, and often were simply added to a work by a later scribe or cataloguer for convenience in identification. We have already noted the prevalence of simple titles like *Ars dictaminis* or *Ars praedicandi.* So prevalent are the generic titles, in fact, that to ensure proper identification medieval cataloguers frequently list the opening few words of a work (its *incipit*), plus the first word on the second folio of the manuscript.

Hence a reader's eye might well be caught by the title which Jean de Chalons (fl. 1372) attached to his work on preaching: *A Brief and Clear Treatise on Composing Sermons Following the Syllogistic Form.* It survives in eight manuscripts.[92] Jean was apparently abbot of the Cistercian house at Pontigny in France. At first glance Jean seems to be advocating a new organizational plan for the sermon, though what he is actually doing is subdividing the normal thematic framework into a quasi-logical pattern. His 14-point sermon plan is too complex to describe fully here, but the following outline may show what he has in mind:

A. Theme
1. Statement of theme
2. Admission of postulate in theme
3. Assumption of theme by stating its application
4. Formation of major term in the proposition
5. Proof of major term by probability
6. Dilation of major term [in some manuscripts: by correspondence]
7. Subscription of minor term
8. Dilation or prolongation of material
9. Digression concerning morals

[91] The comment of Owst is interesting: "In his work Higden suggested texts for every occasion, for visitations, elections, synods, processions, and funerals. To interest the medieval audience, illustrations and *exempla,* such as are found in the *Polychronicon* itself, might be used. With its selection of texts, its notes on sermon divisions, and its warnings against inordinate length, the *Ars componendi sermones* was a useful guide to the medieval preacher." *Preaching in Medieval England: An Introduction to Sermon Manuscripts of the Period, c. 1350–1450* (Cambridge, England, 1926; reprinted New York, 1965), p. 4.

[92] Caplan No. 52; Charland, p. 53. I have used four manuscripts: Rome Vatican Library Ottob. 396 (XV), fols. 14r–29v; and three from Paris Bibliothèque Nationale: MS. 3464 (A.D. 1458), fols. 95–118v; MS. 14580 (XV), fols. 152–160; and MS. 15173 (A.D. 1390), fols. 12–24v. I am also preparing a critical edition of the treatise. Professor Ernest Gallo has also announced his plan to edit the work.

    10. Proposition concerning postulate, if pertinent
    11. Scriptural authority introduced as concordance or circumlocution
    12. Conclusion of theme
B. Division
    13. Division of the theme when it is useful for prosecution (i.e., amplification)
C. Conclusion
    14. Presentation of the whole as befits a conclusion

Actually, this proves to be a handy way for Jean to arrange his own observations on preaching, and does not turn out to be a systematic proposal for making each sermon into a vast syllogism. He says that "Preaching is nothing else but the organized and beneficial spreading of the word of God." [93] It differs therefore from the discourses of physics and logic, which do not deal with the divine word. The 14 points turn out to be more ingenious than practical. Like most medieval writers on the subject, Jean ends up spending most of his time on means of amplification. In this connection he cites Book Four of the *Rhetorica ad Herennium* as well as "Gaufrid"—presumably, Geoffrey of Vinsauf. In his very first sentence he declares that he will write about "the syllogistic form to which all other forms may be reduced." But he is unable to carry out this intriguing approach. Nevertheless Jean de Chalons' *Brief and Clear Treatise* marks the attempt of at least one theorist to go beyond the usual mechanics of the art into a more profound investigation of its underlying basis. His ultimate inability to create a logic of preaching may therefore tell us something about the true nature of the rhetorical situation facing the preacher.

A great many of the treatises, unlike Jean's, attempt nothing more than a sober summary of the basic concepts. The anonymous *Modus sermocinandi* (fourteenth century) states flatly that there are three integral parts of a sermon: assumption of theme, division of theme, and prosecution or exposition of the divisions.[94] Then each of the three items is handled summarily. A very short passage (six lines) on delivery refers the reader to Augustine for more information. The English Dominican, John of Gwidernia (date unknown), has left in a fourteenth-century manuscript a brief treatise which he calls *Remarks On the Mode of Preaching* (*Nota-*

---

[93] Predicacio non est aliud que verbi divini convenientis et salubris distributio. Ex ista descriptione sequitur primo que collaciones que sint in aliis scientis, sicut in physica vel logica, non sint propre predicatione quia non sunt conveniens et salubris verbis dei distributiones.

[94] Caplan No. 71; Charland, p. 101. Charland lists a third manuscript (at Arezzo) in addition to the two named by Caplan. I have used Rome Vatican Library MS. Lat. 829 (27) (XIV), fols. 143$^r$-145$^r$.

*bilia de modo predicandi*).[95] The term "notabilia" is often used by medieval writers who wish to range freely over a subject without being bound to offer a complete or systematic treatment of it. Yet John of Gwidernia speeds through the typical injunctions about three main parts of a sermon —theme, division, and prosecution—with few significant digressions.

Occasionally the preface of a tract will indicate some apparent divergence from standard doctrine of the genre, only to have the work itself demonstrate that the preface is little more than a rearranging or rephrasing of the ordinary. Such is an untitled, anonymous piece in a fifteenth-century manuscript now at Munich. It begins: "There are seven integral parts of a sermon." [96] Again, like Jean de Chalons, the unknown author is simply redividing the standard organizational plan to fit the number seven. His parts are: salutation to the people, proposing of the theme, plea for divine aid, introduction for the theme, division of theme, division of the divisions (*divisarum divisio*), prosecution of the divisions, and conclusion. Perhaps the only novel thing about it is that he proposes ten different ways to phrase a conclusion.

The *artes praedicandi* of two Spanish authors have been printed, though in journal articles that may be somewhat difficult for most readers to obtain. They are Martin of Córdoba from the fifteenth century and Franciscus Eximenis from the fourteenth.[97]

Harry Caplan has pointed out that two preaching manuals were among the earliest works printed in Germany, both apparently before 1500. One, the so-called "Aquinas-Tract" citing Thomas Aquinas, has been translated by Caplan as *A Brief Religious Tract on the Art and True*

---

[95] Caplan No. 78; Charland, p. 61. The tract ends: Explicit tractatus introductarius de modo praedicandi editus a fratre Johanne de Gwuidernia de provincia anglie, ordinis praedicatorum. This colophon again demonstrates the interchangeability of "titles" for these treatises; as in most medieval works the so-called title is likely to be a generic description of the type of tract rather than a specific designation to identify a particular work.

[96] Caplan No. 167; Charland, p. 105. It survives in only one manuscript (Munich Bayerische Staatsbibliothek 15606 (XV), fols. 97–103ᵛ). It might be compared to another treatise also surviving in only one manuscript: London British Museum MS. Arundel 275 (XIV), 86ᵛ–89ᵛ. The British Museum manuscript names eight "sequences" to be considered in preparing "collations" or brief sermons (*collatio est sermo brevis*): definition of a theme, acceptance of a theme, adducing authorities, dilation, integration, terminations, ordinance, and concordance. But neither of these two tracts does anything else but give different names to the same sermon parts.

[97] (Caplan No. 192; Charland, p. 70) Martin of Córdoba, *Ars praedicandi*, ed. Fernando Rubio, S.A., *La cuidad de dios* 172 (1959), 327–48; and (Caplan No. 73; Charland pp. 35–36) Marti de Barcelona, "L'*Ars praedicandi* de Francisco Eixemenis," *Analecta sacra terraconensia* 12 (1936), 301–40.

*Method of Preaching.*[98] The Aquinas-Tract manages to make the sermon into four parts by adding protheme to theme, division, and subdivision. The author's nine ways to amplify a sermon, while different in some details from the eight of Richard of Thetford, obviously stem from the same tradition. When he says toward the end that "the method of preaching is threefold," he is doing little else but shuffling around the same sermon parts in slightly different order. The treatise is avowedly eclectic, and the unknown Dominican author cites Gregory, Alain, Cicero, and Augustine in his general opening section in praise of preaching. The descriptions of the "modern" preaching methods themselves could easily have come from any number of standard contemporary sources. Apparently there is no basis for the author's claim that he follows Thomas Aquinas, for there is no record of a preaching manual among the works of that prolific and well-studied saint. It would hardly seem likely that so obvious a work would have escaped the attention of medieval admirers of The Most Holy Doctor.

The other late tract treated by Caplan, the *Short and Very Useful Tract On the Art of Preaching* attributed to "Henry of Hesse," also makes protheme the fourth part of the sermon in what he calls the "modern" method.[99] Nevertheless, he adds that a sermon has only two essential parts: theme and division. A major portion of the treatise is devoted to means of using the four senses of interpretation.

Simon Alcock (d. 1459) devises methods of division matching the terms in his verse prologue. The work is *On the Mode of Dividing a Theme for Dilating Sermon Material.*[100] The verse prologue begins *Ad quare propter . . . ,* so Alcock proceeds to set out a paragraph headed *Ad,* then another headed *quare,* another *propter,* and so on. Alcock was English, but the dictional approach was certainly not limited to that nation: the Italian Thomas of Todi (fl. c. 1380) states in his *Art of Sermonizing (Ars sermocinandi)*[101] that the first method for developing a theme is to choose a word from a given text and then state whether its first letter is also the initial letter of any virtue, duty, name, etc.

---

[98] Harry Caplan, "A Late Medieval Tractate on Preaching," in *Studies in Rhetoric and Public Speaking in Honor of James Albert Winans,* ed. A. M. Drummond (New York, 1962), pp. 61–90.

[99] Harry Caplan, " 'Henry of Hesse' *On the Art of Preaching,*" *PMLA* 48 (1933), 340–61.

[100] Ed. Mary F. Boynton in "Simon Alcock on Expanding the Sermon," *Harvard Theological Review* 33 (1941), 201–16.

[101] Ed. by June Babcock in "Thomas of Todi, *Ars sermocinandi ac etiam faciendi collationes,*" unpublished M.A. thesis, Cornell University, 1941.

Thomas of Todi is better noted, however, for his systematic distinction between "proof" and "amplification," and for the fact that he is virtually the only author of an *ars praedicandi* to propose the use of *rithmus* in preaching. He lists five types of proof (*probatio*): recourse to authority, use of figures and metaphorical symbolism, reasons and causes, examples, and testimony of history. For expansion of a theme (*prolixitas et multiplicatio*) he lists seven modes: accumulation of authorities, detailed subdivisions, analysis of figures, analysis for the purpose of praise or blame, complicated rhythms, refutation, and examples. Since the two lists are not mutually exclusive, and since these various items tend to be used interchangeably by most authors, the separation of the two categories may not be particularly significant.

Thomas gives five rules for the formation of rhythms in preaching. The first principle is that rhythm is to be formed for "the pleasure of the ears of the hearers." The other four, as might be expected, are complex directions for management of single-syllable and multi-syllable members. One of his examples is from a poem. Then he defines and exemplifies twelve kinds of rhythms, from two-word members through ten-word lines, with three of them being variations of the first nine types. But he concludes the section by pointing out that the modes of rhythm are "innumerable," allowing for much variation, thus implying that his twelve types are intended merely to be samples rather than an exhaustive taxonomy. It is not immediately clear whether his ultimate sources are in the generic *ars rithmica,* with its grammatical background, or in the popular *cursus* of the contemporary *ars dictaminis;* many formal hymns were of course rhythmical, and he may have seen parallels between the vocalisms of the preacher and the vocalizing by church choirs of his day.[102]

There are literally hundreds of other manuscripts of the *ars praedicandi* still lodged in European libraries.[103] No doubt further study will unearth

---

[102] For a consideration of the medieval *ars rithmica,* see above, pp. 157–161.

[103] This brief survey has not attempted to discuss all the authors identified by Caplan and Charland. Many intriguing questions await further research. Did Jodocus Weiler de Haylprunn (Caplan No. 23) also write a treatise on the *ars dictaminis* now in Oxford MS. Lyell 51 (formerly Admont MS. 596)? If so, his was a rare combination of writing talents not often found among authors of preaching manuals. In Stuttgart Wurt. Landesbibliothek MS. H. B. I. Ascet 118 (c. A.D. 1400), fols. 252ᵛ–256, there is a treatise—not listed in either Charland or Caplan—which attempts to set forth a common doctrine for *arenga,* collations, and sermons. The anonymous author says that Aristotle recommends a common approach. How many other such unlisted treatises still rest in European libraries? (Or in American libraries, for that matter; the Benedictine Saint Vincent College, Latrobe, Pennsylvania, has as its MS. 1 a copy of a treatise by Jacobus Fusignano [Caplan No. 115] which is not listed in either Caplan or Charland).

a variety of interesting observations about preaching. Yet it must be admitted that the highly standardized genre produced, generally, the same basic precepts over the several centuries of its popularity. Theme, division, prosecution—these concepts recur again and again, producing a remarkable homogeneity even when some refinements like protheme or conclusion are added. The standard means of amplification remain just that—typical and standard. Almost every writer, for instance, is sure to include both the four senses of interpretation and the use of *exempla*.

Not every medieval writer on preaching pursued the systematic precepts of the genre, of course. One prominent exception was Humbert of Romans (d. 1277), fifth master general of the Dominicans, whose *Treatise on Preaching*[104] is directed more to the conduct of preachers than to the form of preaching. It would be misleading to say that his book is merely a general discussion of the values and motives of preaching, for it is a good deal more than that. Humbert dispenses a wealth of practical advice. In forty-four sections, divided into seven chapters, he takes up the qualities of good preachers, their problems, the duties of listeners, the effects of preaching, and a variety of other matters like things to avoid when a preacher is traveling. Humbert points out that Christ said Mass only once, at the Last Supper, never celebrated the divine office, never heard confession—but preached many times.[105] While Humbert ranges widely over many aspects of his subject, often dividing each topic into many subpoints, he never takes up the technical matters associated with the genre. Instead, the book is a vast collection of small, personalized observations. For instance, Humbert opposes oversubtlety and endless prolixity:

> It is true, however, that there are preachers who have abundant matter, but they are afraid to omit the least detail, useful or not, dragging out their sermons indefinitely. They are like the host who serves his guests generously with beef, excluding all other dishes; serving for the second the hide; for the third, the hoofs, and so on. That certainly is not the technique of a good cook or host; on the contrary he removes the less suitable parts, carefully preparing and serving the best.[106]

But he does stress the necessity for careful study: ". . . granted the grace of speaking well is a special gift of God, nevertheless it demands from the

---

[104] For an early printed edition, see Caplan No. 224 and Charland, p. 47. It has been translated by the Dominican Students of the Province of Saint Joseph as *A Treatise on Preaching* (Westminster, Md., 1951); it must be noted that this translation was made—without acknowledgment—from a French translation of the original Latin. Excerpts here will, however, be from that English translation.

[105] *Ibid.*, p. 86.

[106] *Ibid.*, pp. 33–34. He also notes that a preacher should use moderation, "for everything found in a grocery store cannot be used by a host."

preacher full application to the study of whatever is needed for the proper execution of his office." [107] He does not however go further into the question of what to study.

One final observation must be made before turning to that most typical of the *ars praedicandi,* the *Form of Preaching* by Robert of Basevorn. That observation is that the theoretical manual we know as the *ars praedicandi* gradually came to gather around itself a whole range of ancillary or auxiliary treatises which, together with the *ars* itself, might properly be called a "rhetorical system." It will be recalled that the *ars metrica* is associated with satellite tracts on the tropes and figures, just as the *ars dictaminis* accrued numerous collections of model letters (*dictamina*) designed to be used in conjunction with the theoretical manual. Both these phenomena might also be termed rhetorical systems—systematic collations of related treatises designed for a particular communicative function. So too, in the preaching field, except that the homiletic apparatus was much more complex than the other two. The intricate relations between the segments of this apparatus have never been fully investigated.

The rhetorical system afforded the medieval preacher had five elements:

1. The Scripture itself (with its glosses), furnishing both proposition and apodeictic proof;
2. Collections of *exempla* and other bits of information about man, animals, or the world;[108]
3. Concordances, alphabetical lists, topic charts, and other bibliographical aids designed to help find material;[109]

---

[107] *Ibid.,* p. 31. This is typical of the array of *sententiae* which stud the book. Humbert never develops any one point beyond the equivalent of a paragraph, though he may line up three or four such paragraphs about one subtopic. The book might almost be called "Random Reflections on Preaching."

[108] The most famous medieval collection of *exempla* was that of Jacques de Vitry. See *The Exempla or Illustrative Stories from the Sermones Vulgares of Jacques de Vitry,* ed. Thomas F. Crane, Publications of the Folk-Lore Society, 26 (London, 1890). Also J.-Th. Welter, *L'Exemplum dans la littérature religieuse et didactique du moyen âge* (Paris, 1927). The best single treatment in English is still Joseph A. Mosher, *The Exemplum in the Early Religious and Didactic Literature of England* (New York, 1911). Also, *Liber exemplorum ad usum praedicantium,* ed. A. G. Little, British Society of Franciscan Studies, 1 (Aberdeen, 1908). The reader should be warned, however, that studies of medieval *exempla* usually concentrate on trying to trace the sources of the stories, and seldom treat the rhetorical aspects of their actual use.

[109] See, for instance, Homer G. Pfander, "The Mediaeval Friars and Some Alphabetical Reference Books for Sermons," *Medium Aevum* 3 (1934), 19–29. There are numerous *florilegia,* or excerpt collections; Oxford Merton College 248, for instance, contains sets of *Themata* for various Sundays, and handy quotations. The massive *Summa praedicantium* of John Bromyard (Caplan No. 219) is a famous example. "The Mode of the Compendium" is a familiar description of some collections, as in London British Museum MS. Arundel 243 (XV), fols. 388ᵛ–391 (Caplan No. 2),

4. Collections of sermons, including sermon outlines and sermons for specified occasions;[110]

5. The *ars* itself, corresponding to the type of preceptive rhetorical treatise written by Aristotle or Cicero.

Taken together, then, this considerable apparatus provided the preacher with ample means for accomplishing his mandated task. Yet it is an interdependent system, each part gaining usefulness from the others, and the modern student of medieval preaching can appreciate the value of each element only when he realizes that purposeful interdependence.

Perhaps it is now possible to conclude this brief survey of the development of the medieval *ars praedicandi*, not with a further recapitulation of what has already been summarized many times in the preceding pages, but with a full abstract of one of the most typical of those preceptive manuals.[111] We know virtually nothing about Robert of Basevorn, except that he was familiar with both Paris and Oxford, and that he wrote in 1322. He dedicates his *Form of Preaching* to a Cistercian abbot of Basingwerk in Flint, though his editor, Charland, believes that Basevorn himself was not a religious man. Basevorn gives us his name clearly enough, pointing out that the initial letters of his fifty chapters spell it out. (Ranulph Higden, as we have seen, used this same device to identify his own preaching manual a few years later.)

A careful reader can find in Basevorn virtually every element we have

in which the anonymous author says, "It is easier to go to a collection than to get it [material] for one's self." He includes items from Seneca, Bede, Jerome, Ambrose, and Augustine in addition to his favorite, Gregory.

[110] This vast field is largely unexplored. There have been many histories of preaching, and frequent studies of individual preachers, but very little has been done to explicate the numerous sermon collections surviving from the middle ages. Unlike the situation in the *ars dictaminis*, where a model-letter collection (*dictaminum*) is usually attached to a preceptive treatise, the medieval sermon collections do not generally appear to be connected to a preceptive *ars praedicandi*. One reason may be that the model letters were often intended for almost verbatim transliteration (by changing names or places) while the "model" sermon may have been intended instead as merely a guide to an originally composed sermon based on it. Certainly the audience situations in the two fields were vastly different. Whatever the reasons, more research is needed before we can state with confidence the exact relation of model sermons to the preceptive *ars praedicandi*. Father Jean Leclercq, O.S.B. outlined the problem in a perceptive essay, "Le magistere du prédicateur au XIII siècle," *Archives d'histoire doctrinale et littéraire du moyen âge* 15 (1946), 105–47. A useful catalogue of known Latin sermons is being published by Johann Baptist Schneyer, *Repertorium der lateinischen Sermones des Mittelalters für die Zeit von 1150-1350* (Freiburg im Bresgau, 1969 to present); the *Reportorium* lists sermon manuscrips alphabetically by author: A-D (1969); E-H (1970); I-J (1971); K-L (1972).

[111] Robert of Basevorn, *The Form of Preaching*, trans. Leopold Krul, O.S.B., in James J. Murphy, ed., *Three Medieval Rhetorical Arts* (Berkeley and Los Angeles, 1971), pp. 114–215. The Latin text is in Charland, pp. 233–323.

seen in the development of the *ars praedicandi*. If one remembers that up to the year 1200 the Christian Church had not developed a rhetoric of preaching, and then notes the completely assimilated theory in the *Form of Preaching* in 1322, one can gain a greater appreciation of the contributions made by early writers like Alexander of Ashby, Thomas of Salisbury, and (no doubt) others unknown to us. By Basevorn's time the future of the genre was assured. The *ars praedicandi* survived as a rhetorical genre through occasional attacks by Lollards and orthodox reformers, and persisted even into Reformation times; the history of its decline lies outside the limits of this study. It was supplanted as a major theoretical force only after the revival of Ciceronianism in what is usually called the European Renaissance.[112]

Robert of Basevorn, then, can well serve as a prime example of developments after 1200 when the Christian church created a new rhetoric of preaching in the genre we know as the *ars praedicandi*.

## THE *FORMA PRAEDICANDI* (1322) OF ROBERT OF BASEVORN

Notwithstanding, the Lord stood with me, and strengthened me, that by me the preaching should be fully known (II Tim. 4:17).

Prologue. Just as some men attempt to reason without knowing logic, so some men attempt to preach without knowing the form of preaching, which is the system and method of preaching on every subject, as logic is the system of syllogizing in every field of knowledge. Since teaching and preaching are necessary to the Church, that science presents the form of preaching artistically. The four causes of this work are as follows: the final cause is designated when it is said: *The Lord stood with me and strengthened me,* for He is my end; the efficient cause is designated when we say: *by me;* although He who is also the end may be the efficient cause affecting the whole, the material cause is designated when it is said: *preaching,* because the form of preaching is here considered as well as the matter; fourthly, the formal cause is designated implicitly when it is said: *should be fully known,* for a thing is formally transmitted and taught when a continuation carries through in an orderly way what the beginning of the work promises or proffers for investigation, and

---

[112] This too is an unwritten history. The survival of the allegorical mode, for instance, is well documented, and is readily seen in such English literary productions as Bunyan's *Pilgrim's Progress*. John Donne's sermons, like those of many of his contemporaries, still have medieval echoes. For some discussion of these survivals, together with the forces of change at work, see J. W. Blench, *Preaching in England in the Late Fifteenth and Sixteenth Centuries: A Study of English Sermons, 1450–c. 1600* (Oxford, 1964).

what the end brings to a conclusion: thus one should have an organized method of procedure. This work includes fifty chapters.

1. Preaching is the persuasion of the multitude, within a moderate length of time, to worthy conduct. For when some determine questions, such determination is not preaching, because it is not persuasion by intent, but rather an investigation of the truth. Nor is a political orator a preacher, for worthy conduct is not his primary aim, but the aid of the state. In like manner, if someone with one small reason persuades many of something which pertains to the merits of eternal life, that is not properly preaching, for I could then write on this paper forty sermons, a thing that is hardly possible. Therefore preaching requires time neither too short nor too long. It is difficult to say how long, but it is commonly held now that preaching should last no more than the space of a Solemn Mass with music, nor less than a Low Mass without music.

2. Who can preach. The Pope, bishops, cardinals, and preachers by office. Religious, constituted preachers by privileges given them, are preachers by commission.

3. Preachers by ordinary institution are held to preach by necessity of salvation, through themselves or through others if that is fitting; if they do not do this they are guilty of a mortal sin. Preachers by commission can preach if they wish, but do not commit a mortal sin if they neglect to do so. And this is why the Church has ordained that stipends be given to ordinary preachers, through tithes and the like, because of necessity they are burdened with sowing spiritual thoughts in their subjects. From pure debt, temporal rewards are due them.

4. The two kinds of preachers may overlap. Three things are necessary for one exercising the act of preaching: the first is purity of life, the second is competent knowledge (at least explicit knowledge of the articles of Faith, the Ten Commandments, and the distinction between sin and non-sin), and the third is authority given by the Church. No lay person or religious, unless permitted by the Bishop or Pope, and no woman, no matter how learned or saintly, ought to preach. Thus parish priests cannot preach without permission, nor is it enough that they be licensed by the rectors.

5. The preacher should see to it above all that he have a good purpose for his sermon, such as the praise of God, or His saints, or the edification of his neighbor, or some object deserving eternal life. He should not seek fame unless by that fame he shows himself learned or wise so that people will listen to him preach the word of God. Seekers after gain should not be preachers: (1) because they frequently have wives or concubines, and do like things, which are opposed to the purity demanded of the preacher; (2) because they are generally uneducated, which is opposed to the knowledge required of the preacher; and (3) because they are not accepted but universally rejected; and

finally (4) because they do not have the proper end in view. Whoever permits them to preach sins mortally.

6. We must now come closer to our task, which is to show the required form of preaching. There are as many different kinds of preaching as there are capable preachers; since we cannot present all of them, we shall present a commonly used modern method. God preached many times through others— Moses, the Prophets, etc.—so that those men are proud and vainglorious who disdain to preach using themes of other men; if novelty is to be sought, then everyone's books should be burnt at his death lest things well said in them should be said again. This is absurd. It would be quite praiseworthy to try and imitate the methods of any of the five great preachers: Christ, Paul, Augustine, Gregory, and Bernard.

7. Among the modern methods those more commonly used are the French and the English, emanating from the two famous universities. They have their origin in the aforementioned doctors, and yet follow no particular one. They use in part the method of one or the other and in part their own and also many devices which, as it seems to me, appertain more to curiosity than to edification—for example, vowel concordances. But this practice is characteristic more of the English method. They say that a preacher should please his hearers so that they will listen. Indeed, so great is man's vanity, especially that of the English, that they only consider the elegant and do not commend anything else. When they preach to lay people, these preachers sometimes give their theme in Latin, because it is difficult for the ignorant to do this. Because I can be deceived in my judgment, and in order to satisfy the requests of others, I will explain each of the five approved and honored methods.

8. It is not easy to understand all the methods which Christ used in preaching, for He included all praiseworthy methods in His own as the origin of good. Sometimes he preached clearly; other times he Preached profoundly and obscurely. His methods were many: (1) by means of promises, as in the Sermon on the Mount; (2) by threats, a method suitable for the stubborn; (3) by example, a method now used extensively in Paris and in many other places; (4) by reason; (5) obscurely, for it is frequently said of his hearers that they did not understand the Word; and (6) clearly.

9. Paul used reason together with authority. Moving themes may be found readily in Paul's Epistles and sayings, because in a sense he includes the entire Gospel, the Law, and the Prophets.

10. Augustine more than the other Fathers read Paul. It is sometimes his custom to explain one whole Gospel or some great passage from Scripture, and do so diffusely; sometimes it is his habit to take one theme and follow it up extensively. But often he rests his case on reasons. This is why he says that where authority is lacking, we must rest on reason, without which even authority is not authority. The first method should be good for those with poor memories, for the thread of some great Gospel is more easily followed than

that of a subtle argument. The second method is of greater use, since it is more novel.

11. Gregory has a praiseworthy method, one that operates through figures of the Old Testament, tangible examples, and entreaties. He devotes his whole discourse to a Gospel or something pertaining to Faith. Frequently he multiplies authorities for the same matter and frequently divides one noun into many significations. The latter two devices are allowed only within reason in common sermons to lay people, nor are they used much. He also adds to his discourse edifying stories.

12. The method of Saint Bernard is without method, exceeding the style and capability of almost all men of genius. He more than all the rest stresses Scripture in all his sayings, so that scarcely one statement is his own which does not depend upon an authority in the Bible or on a multitude of authorities. His procedure is always devout, always artful. He takes a certain theme or something in place of it and begins it artfully, divides it into two, three, or many members, confirms it and ends it, using every rhetorical color so that the whole work shines with a double glow, earthly and heavenly; and this, it seems to me, invites to devotion those who understand more feelingly, and helps more in the novel methods which we are now discussing. No one has so effectively joined the two at the same time.

13. It is therefore reprehensible to say that preaching ought not to shine with false verbal embellishments, for in very many sermons of Saint Bernard the whole is almost always rich in colors. The same is true in the sermons of other saints, as is clear to one who knows rhetoric and examines these sermons. Further, Pope Leo says: this is the virtue of eloquence, that there is nothing foreign to it that cannot be extolled. Who will hesitate to say that wisdom and eloquence together move us more than either does by itself? Thus we must insist upon eloquence and yet not depart from wisdom, which is the better of the two. If both cannot be achieved, then neither can wisdom be achieved. It remains then that it is better to have eloquence than to lack every good. For of what use would an opinion be in which there was neither eloquence nor wisdom? Therefore let those who are not productive through wisdom strive to be eloquent. It is without doubt very blameworthy that one should preferably strive after eloquence when he can have wisdom by the striving, as Saint Augustine teaches in *De doctrina christiana,* where he wants a preacher to strive to teach, please, and move. About those who try only to please so that they neither teach nor move, he says that their eloquence is the more damnable the finer eloquence it is. Therefore they are better when joined, and are a sweet mixture of good things.

14. There are twenty-two ornaments employed in the most carefully contrived sermons:

(1) Invention of the Theme
(2) Winning Over of Audience

(3) Prayer
(4) Introduction
(5) Division
(6) Statement of Parts
(7) Proof of Parts
(8) Amplification
(9) Digression, or "Transition"
(10) Correspondence
(11) Agreement of Correspondence
(12) Circuitous Development
(13) Convolution
(14) Unification
(15) Conclusion
(16) Coloration
(17) Modulation of Voice
(18) Appropriate Gesture
(19) Humor
(20) Allusion
(21) Firm Impression
(22) Weighing of Subject Matter

The first fifteen of these are inserted into their proper places once, or at any rate into a few places; the remainder, and generally Allusion and Firm Impression, can be placed almost anywhere. The element that follows after these, Humor, ought to be used in a few places and very sparingly. All these, when concurring, embellish a sermon elegantly, and so can be called the ornaments of a sermon.

15. For a good Invention of the Theme, the following are required:
(1) that it concur with the feast
(2) that it beget full understanding
(3) that it be on a Bible text which is not changed or corrupted
(4) that it contain not more than three statements or a statement convertible to three
(5) that sufficient concordances can be found on these three ideas, even if only verbal
(6) that the theme itself can serve in place of the antetheme or protheme

[16–23. Discussion of the six criteria for selecting themes.]

24. The second ornament is Winning Over the Audience. The preacher ought to attract the minds of the listeners in such a way as to render them willing to hear and retain. This can be done in many ways:
(1) by placing at the beginning something subtle and interesting, as some authentic marvel which can be fittingly drawn in for the purpose of the theme

(2) by using an unknown cause of some saying (e.g., by explaining why the eye does not have a definite color: it would perceive only that one color)

(3) by frightening them with some terrifying tale or example (a tale from Jacques de Vitry)

(4) by showing by example or story that the devil always tries to hinder the word of God and the hearing of it

(5) by showing that the word of God is a great sign of predestination of good for listeners

(6) by telling the audience that he preaches only to convert them (not to beg from them)

25. In the beginning it is also customary to offer a prayer, and that is well, because as Plato says in the *Timaeus*: Divine help should be implored in the smallest things. Since even the smallest things cannot occur without its influence, how much more should it be implored in the greatest? Saint Augustine in *De doctrina christiana* urges that the preacher should be first a man of prayer before a talker. To me it seems good to propose the theme, and to immediately make a prayer about it. I have not seen it mentioned in any genuine author that such a prayer ought to be said before the theme. Yet I have frequently seen it done. It is proper in either place, since both theme and prayer belong at the beginning. It should also be noted here that the prayer which is at the end of the antetheme ought always to depend upon what has preceded, so that it contains something which pertains to the prayer and at the same time contains a word of the theme even vocally, and especially that word on which depends the persuasion to prayer; this is the method of the Oxonians.

26. A theme may be taken from any authentic book of the Scriptures; they are in error who say that themes should be taken only from the Gospels, the Psalms, the Epistles of Saint Paul, and the Books of Solomon. It must be understood that all the books in the Bible are authentic except the third and fourth books of Esdras, a psalm of David found in some Bibles, the Book of the Pastor, and the letter to the Laodiceans.

27. Some preachers take their themes only from the Gospel or Epistle of the feast on which they preach; this is commendable, but it can be done as above. [Charland and the translator omit examples of themes which appear in this and the next three chapters.]

28. Examples of themes which can be adduced for the more famous saints.

29. It is also always useful to have prepared a few sermons which can provide for every saint and for the dedication of a Church because it frequently happens that the church or place where the preacher happens to be preaching solemnizes a saint or the dedication, of which he had not even a thought. [Examples of such themes.]

30. It is now appropriate to specify what themes can be taken for incidental

material, as on visitations, at elections, in synods, in processions, in disaster, on solemnities, . . . to religious, . . . at a council, . . . to the sick, . . . to merchants, . . . .

31. And now according to the order set out in Chapter XIV, we shall consider the ornaments of the theme, of which the first is Introduction and which in the whole is the fourth ornament. It must be known that after the prayer the same theme must be resumed . . . and the book and chapter must be quoted. This ought to be done on principle in the antetheme, and, following the modern method, nothing must be quoted regarding the chapters. The theme must be quoted again in full, especially on account of some who by accident, as frequently happens, were not present for the antetheme. In the third place [i.e., third place in the sermon] comes the Introduction, which can be formed in three ways:

    (1) by authority
    (2) by argument
    (3) by both together

Authority is a method used more commonly in the antetheme than afterwards; no other introduction must be made in the antetheme for fear of prolixity; indeed the antetheme can exist without it, so that Introduction is not postulated as an ornament of the antetheme. An authority forming an Introduction can come from:

    (1) something original
    (2) a philosopher
    (3) a poet
    (4) someone with authority
    (5) not from the Bible

The second method is through argument, and it is appropriate to form the Introduction in as many ways as there are kinds of argument:

    (1) by induction
    (2) by example
    (3) by syllogism
    (4) by enthemyme

Induction accounts for particular details to support the theme. Example may be used in three different ways:

    (1) examples in nature
    (2) examples in arts
    (3) examples in history

In using a syllogism, the major premise ought to be proved immediately if it is not self-evident. Then the minor premise must be given with its proof; if the proofs be too extended, after the proofs of the major and the minor the premises must be stated again, and the theme immediately concluded by saying that it has already been proved. Enthemymes are of two kinds:

(1) "compelling" (described in Aristotle's *Prior Analytics*)

(2) "probable" (described in Boethius's *Topics*)

The Oxonians use all seven of these methods. The Parisians use an eighth method, a better one, in that no matter what kind of argument they use for the Introduction, all parts are confirmed with the authority of Holy Writ. Anyone may use all of these methods of forming an Introduction in themes that are comprised of two statements or more. But when a theme is comprised of only one explicit statement, it is not convenient to use all these methods indiscriminately.

32. I think a more elegant mode of forming an Introduction of such a theme occurs if a theme is first introduced by an authority, so that from the authority three members which correspond to the feast and the theme can be immediately drawn. [Then follows a lengthy example based on the theme: *understand*. In the city of God, the manner in which man, the angels, and God understand things is revealed as a correspondence to the excellences of Peter's understanding.]

33. Division is the fifth ornament. Though not expressed, the force of a word should be expressed first; that is, the divisions of a word should put the same idea into different words without repeating the same word which was originally divided. If it should happen that it is not possible to find an authority to fit the force of the word, it is acceptable to add adjectives or other determinants so that the authority will fit. The division of the second word should not be placed before the division of the first. The division ought to occur in one of three ways:

(1) according to the thing done

(2) according to the order of construction

(3) according to the order of delivery

It is very artistic if by a single division, Division is according to the order of construction and at the same time according to the order of material.

34. The sixth ornament, Statement of Parts, ought to show the distinction of parts in one of three ways:

(1) by showing parts of a virtual whole

(2) by showing parts of a universal whole

(3) by some other way

The statement can be made by means of different parts of speech, except that pronouns, conjunctions, and interjections cannot ordinarily administer to this purpose. Statement of Parts can be made especially with a substantive:

(1) through its accidents

a. comparison

b. case

(2) by means of adjectives without comparison

35. The seventh ornament, Proof of Parts, follows immediately after the

preceding. This is done in various ways. The Parisians supply an authority
for each part which is divisible into three; some, however, divide the first
authority of verification into three, the second into two, and merely explain
the third. Other methods aim at producing verbal correspondences between
the divisions of the authorities and the divisions of the theme or its parts. It
is obvious that consummate artistry resides in these methods:

(1) It verifies the division of the first member by a verbal and real
authority.

(2) The further division is taken from something real.

(3) The proposition is verified by a corresponding verbal authority
either by means of allusion or direct expression.

36. [A long example of the Parisian method.] Whoever understands this
method, understands the more famous methods used at Paris in respect to
antethemes. He understands that there is a short Introduction with an example for the same; how that example is verified by Scripture; how both the
verification and the example are concluded by one authority which agrees with
both; how every theme agrees with the three aforementioned things; how
the theme is divided; how all parts are stated with sensible examples and
verified with agreeing authorities; how the last authority agrees with the first,
that is, the authority of the Introduction; how one proceeds from the authority
to the prayer.

37. Further exemplification of Parisian method.

38. Some preachers, especially in England, do not follow this method of
developing the parts, but multiply the statement in such a way that they add
to the division of the theme a double statement of the parts without authorities, and afterwards a third statement of the parts and an expression of the
words of the theme, and then immediately add to this third statement of
parts a brief verification of the parts. Some add to this mode, after verification
by Biblical authority, verification by an original authority, and this is elegant
if it agrees with and explains the authority to which it is added. In using this
method it is important to repeat the explicit statement before giving its verification, since some of the hearers may have forgotten the statement which was
made earlier.

39. The eighth ornament, Amplification, has eight main species or methods:

(1) by discussing a noun by giving its definition or its opposite

(2) by division

(3) by reasoning or argumentation

a. by resolution of contraries

b. by enthymeme, asking the hearer to draw a conclusion

c. by examples

(4) by concordances
   a. when authorities with different meanings come together in one statement
   b. when authorities come together in meaning but not in expression
   c. when one authority speaks fully and another speaks more fully
(5) through those things which agree in essence but differ in accidents
(6) by devising metaphors through the properties of things
(7) by expounding the theme in various ways
   a. historically, when the literal fact is understood
   b. allegorically, when one part is understood by another
   c. morally, when one deed that must be done is understood through another
   d. anagogically, when by some deed on earth is understood another that must be done in heaven or in the Church triumphant
(8) by causes and effects

40. Because the method of the Oxonians is more commonly used, we must illustrate it more specifically. This method consists of adding a division, called Subdivision, immediately after the verification of parts of the theme once the theme has been divided and the parts stated. [Then follows a long example on the term *just*.] This method is very artistic. Preachers using this method should make sure that when they divide themes they make a general description of the first division; thus in the subdivision descend as it were from genus to species or from some whole to its parts.

41. The ninth ornament is Digression, which is equivalent to Transition. It occurs when one proceeds artistically from one part to another. One who looks at the *Rhetoric* of Cicero (*De inv.* I.l1.97) can see that this is improperly called digression. If digression is considered as something incidental, it does not belong in a sermon. But the digression which we are discussing here consists of a certain skillful connecting of two principal statements, by verbal and real concordance.

42. The tenth ornament is Correspondence, or the express agreement of parts among themselves, as, for instance, when the first principal part is divided into *a b c*, the second into *d e f*, and the third into *g h i*. Then, according to this ornament, there must be agreement among *a d g*, *b e h*, and *c f i*.

43. The eleventh ornament, Agreement of Correspondence, is the completion of the former ornament. It is a clause or statement expressing the substance of the connection made between the parts of the principal statements.

44. The twelfth ornament is called Circuitous Development. It is nothing else beyond Correspondence than an artificial linking of the first part of the last principal statement with the second part of the first principal statement, namely *g* to *b*, and again the linking of the second part of the last principal

statement, namely *h*, to the third part of the first principal set [*a b c*], namely
*c*. This ornament is in the image of a circle where the end and the beginning
are the same. Some doubt the usefulness of this ornament. I know that it is
more decorative than useful, because it dulls the mind of the listener by making
an unsolvable labyrinth.

45. The thirteenth ornament is called Convolution, in which any part of
a statement corresponds to every part of every other statement. It is called
Convolution because there is not the determined application of one part to
one part, but of all parts to all parts. One cannot easily use this ornament.
[No example is cited.]

46. The fourteenth ornament is Unification, which is a period or *clausula*
which contains in a unit what has been said separately in the development.
It is useful following Convolution or Circuitous Development. If possible,
some authority should be employed which verbally contains all the statements
treated in the sermon.

47. Finally, there must be a Conclusion. This is a prayer ending the sermon
and directing the mind to God as towards an end. Just as nature, if bent from
its natural path by violence, always returns to its original state, so the sermon
must end as it began. The more the end is like the beginning, so much the
more elegantly does it end.

48. There are some other modes of preaching besides those I have mentioned, and it would be well to mention them briefly. [A description then follows of various methods used in dividing themes.]

49. There remain still two more methods. The first, suitable in any vulgar
idiom to the ordinary people, is partly Parisian and partly Gregorian; it consists in choosing three materials suited to the listeners, and then developing
the theme in each three parts as follows:

(1) by some proof from nature or arts
(2) by some proof from Scripture
(3) by some authoritative narrative

It seems superfluous to me and incorrect to handle more than three figures
in one sermon, and likewise to adduce more than three narratives. It should
be noted that stories may be taken not only from the Bible but from other
authors like Augustine, Gregory, Helinandus, Valerius, Seneca, or Macrobius.

50. The second method should be used only before the most intelligent
people. The method is such that in the whole sermon not one authority is
brought forth, unless it be the theme at the beginning. It should be used by
only the most intelligent preachers, for its art conceals its very artfulness.

We have dispatched all fifteen ornaments which directly apply to the form
or execution of the sermon. There remain seven more which are extrinsic, but
which serve for beauty:

(1) Coloration
 a. in the number of terminations of the statements
 b. in cadence, which occurs in pauses or at the end of clauses
 c. in rhetorical colors, which can occur anywhere; it is sufficient to use those which appear in the last book of Cicero's *Rhetorica Secunda*

(2) Voice Modulation, as Augustine teaches in *De doctrina christiana.*

(3) Appropriate Gesture, as Hugh [of St. Victor] teaches in his *De institutione novitiorum.*

(4) Opportune Humor, according to Cicero, occurs when we add something jocular which will give pleasure when the audience is bored. This must be used especially when they begin to sleep.

(5) Allusion, when Scripture is touched upon but not adduced, but not in the same way it is written.

(6) Firm Impression, when allusion occurs in many places, or continually.

(7) Reflecting on the Subject Matter, which is the consideration of who, to whom, what, and how much is to be spoken.

To these fifty chapters I will add one of silence.

# Epilogue:
# Rediscovery and
# Implications

In September, 1416, three Italian travelers visited a monastery at St. Gall in Switzerland. The travelers were Bartolomeo de Montepulciano, Cincio Romano, and a one-time apostolic secretary named Poggio Bracciolini (who sometimes termed himself "Poggio Florentinus"). All three had been attending the Council of Constance, which had begun in 1414 and was fated to drag on for two more years until April 22, 1418, in its attempt to end the schism in the Church. Poggio had come to the Council as secretary to Pope John XXIII, but when John XXIII was forced to resign (March, 1415), Poggio stayed on to await developments, that is, further employment. In this period of enforced leisure, Poggio went to the baths at Baden in the spring of 1416, but his main interests were humanistic.[1] That autumn he and his two fellow Italians took advantage of a recess in the Council to travel to St. Gall in the hope of finding some literary treasure there in the possession of the German monks.

They do not leave a record of their reception by Abbot Heinrich von Gundelfingen, but Cincio was later to write that "there were in the monastery an abbot and monks divorced from any knowledge of letters." [2] Judging from what was to be found there, Cincio's judgment seems quite sound.

There at St. Gall, not in a library but in a dungeon which Poggio de-

---

[1] Poggio was an assiduous seeker of manuscripts. See Ernest Walser, *Poggius Florentinus: Leben und Werke* (Leipzig, 1914). A far more interesting, if sometimes romantic, account of Poggio's life may be found in William Shepherd, *The Life of Poggio Bracciolini* (Liverpool: 1st ed., 1802; 2nd ed., 1837). Shepherd's treatment is still extremely useful, for it portrays well the excitement surrounding the humanists' efforts to recover the ancient classics.

[2] Erant in monastrio illo Abbas, Monachique ab omni litterarum cognitione alieni. Quoted in Walser, *Leben*, p. 52.

clared to be not even fit for a condemned man, he found something that apparently no interested scholar had seen for nearly six centuries—a complete copy of the *Institutio oratoria* of Quintilian.[3]

Lupus of Ferriers, a ninth-century scholar, may well have been the last scholar to have had the complete text available to him before Poggio's discovery. The so-called *textus mulilatus,* with numerous important gaps, was the version in circulation during the intervening six centuries. Gasparino Barzizza, Petrarch, and other Italian humanists so admired Quintilian that they even attempted to fill in the missing sections themselves in an effort at reconstruction. There was a widespread enthusiasm for recovery of ancient texts. Plutarch's essay on education had been translated into Latin by Guarino Veronese just before Poggio's discovery, kindling even more interest among the humanists. Poggio himself had ranged as far as Paris hunting for manuscripts.

So enthusiastic was Poggio over his discovery that he sat down at once and transcribed the *capitula* or headings of the manuscript to send to his friend Guarino back in Italy. Then, as he tells us, he personally transcribed the manuscript in his own hand. The task took 54 days.[4] Even while he copied, another humanist, Leonardo Aretino, wrote him a fervid letter of appreciation for the discovery. Leonardo's letter may well serve as an example of the importance the men of his time attached to the Quintilian text:

> In my opinion the republic of letters has reason to rejoice, not only on account of the acquisition of works which you have already recovered, but also on account of the hope which I see you entertain of the recovery of others. It will be your glory to restore to the present age, by your labour and diligence, the writings of excellent authors, which have hitherto escaped the researches of the learned. The accomplishment of your undertaking will confer an obligation, not on us alone, but on the successors to our studies. The memory of your services will never be obliterated. It will be recorded

---

[3] The basic account of this and other such discoveries is in Remigio Sabbadini, *Storia e Critica di Testi Latini* (Catania, 1914): Quintilian, pp. 379–407; Cicero, pp. 9–194 (rhetorical works, pp. 101–45). Sabbadini also published a summary, *Le scoperte dei Codice Latini e Greci ne' Secoli XIV e XV* (Florence, 1967). The Latin text of Poggio's letter announcing the discovery is in *Poggii epistolae,* ed. T. de Tonellis. 3 vols. (Turin, 1963), I, Epistola V (pp. 25–29). Poggio writes: Erant enim non in Bibliotheca libri illi, ut eorum dignitas postulabat, sed in teterrimo quodam, et obscuro carcere, fundo scilicet unius turris, quo ne capitalis quidem rei damnati retruderentur.

[4] A description of surviving Quintilian manuscripts, including the St. Gall exemplar and its copies, is in *M. Fabii Quintiliani Institutionis Oratoriae Libri Duodecim,* rec. M(ichael) Winterbottom, 2 vols. (Oxford, 1970), I, v–xv.

to distant ages, that these works, the loss of which had been for so long a period a subject of lamentation to the friends of literature, have been recovered by your industry. As Camillus, on account of his having rebuilt the city of Rome, was stiled its second founder, so you may justly be denominated the second author of all those pieces which are restored to the world by your meritorious exertions. I therefore most earnestly exhort you not to relax in your endeavors to prosecute this laudable design. Let not the expense which you are likely to incur discourage you from proceeding. I will take care to provide the necessary funds. I have the pleasure of informing you, that from this discovery of yours, we have already derived more advantage than you seem to be aware of; for by your exertions we are at length in possession of a perfect copy of Quintilian. I have inspected the titles of the books. We have now the entire treatise, of which, before this happy discovery, we had only one half, and that in a very mutilated state. Oh, what a valuable acquisition! What an unexpected pleasure! Shall I then behold Quintilian whole and entire, who, even in his imperfect state, was so rich a source of delight? I entreat you, my dear Poggio, send me the manuscript as soon as possible, that I may see it before I die.[5]

The impact of Quintilian's rediscovery has been well documented.[6] Leonardo Aretino's letter, even allowing for its hyperbole, shows clearly the immense interest of the time in the subjects of education, rhetoric, and literature. Lorenzo Valla says that he himself knew Quintilian almost by heart. Vittorino da Feltre so admired and imitated Quintilian that he was known as *Quintilianus redivivus*—"Quintilian living again." Quintilian's educational program influenced Erasmus, Juan Vives, Luther, Melancthon, and a host of others. By the time the iconoclastic Peter Ramus launched his attacks on the rhetoro-literary establishment in the following century, Quintilian was solidly linked with Cicero and Aristotle as one of a trilogy of ancient masters. All this is properly a part of the yet unwritten history of "Renaissance" rhetoric.[7]

It is easy to see why Poggio's discovery aroused such interest. Quintilian's *Institutio* proposes a coherent program of literary and rhetorical training, with a strong moral base, aimed at the formation of a literate and responsible citizenry. Medieval rhetoric, with its fragmentation into

---

[5] Shepherd, *Life of Poggio* (2nd ed.), pp. 95–96.

[6] See F. H. Colson, *M. Fabii Quintiliani institutionis oratoriae, liber I* (Cambridge, 1924), pp. ix–xx: "Knowledge and Use of Quintilian After 1416." For a discussion of the *textus mutilatus* circulated during the middle ages, see above, Chapter Three, pp. 124–25.

[7] For England, however, see Wilbur S. Howell, *Logic and Rhetoric in England, 1500–1700* (Princeton, 1956), and Donald Lemen Clark, *Rhetoric and Poetry in the Renaissance* (New York, 1922). There is as yet no reliable general history of rhetoric in Western Europe during this period.

specialized genres, did not provide for the humanists the kind of synthesizing approach for which they yearned. The available rhetoric of Cicero—the *De inventione* and *Rhetorica ad Herennium*—fastened entirely on technique without an explicit rationale for the use of rhetoric. Cicero and the Pseudo-Cicero, after all, had written for an audience already familiar with the expected public role of rhetoric; it is not surprising therefore that their books dwell on the pragmatic. Aristotle's *Rhetorica* was virtually unknown, and its scholastic commentaries (such as that of Giles of Rome) must have seemed arid and condemnatory to those humanists who knew them. But Poggio made it possible, for the first time since the final collapse of the Roman schools in the fifth century, for a reader to view rhetoric as part of an integrated social system built around a respect for civic life.

Poggio's discovery of Quintilian's *Institutio,* then, reintroduced into Western Europe with comparative suddenness a balanced view of rhetoric and its purpose. Moreover, it came at a time when the intellectual climate of humanistic Italy was highly favorable, and it came as an attractive alternative to medieval patterns.[8]

Five years after the find at St. Gall there was a second major discovery, this time in the Italian city of Lodi. Bishop Gerardo Landriani found a manuscript in the cathedral of Lodi containing five Ciceronian rhetorical works: *De inventione, Rhetorica ad Herennium, Brutus, Orator,* and, for the first time in centuries, a complete text of Cicero's *De oratore.*[9] Landriani could not read the abbreviated handwriting of manuscript, so he sent it to Barzizza in Milan. The flurry of letters between them shows again, as in the case of Quintilian, the intense interest aroused by the discovery. Barzizza had a copy made for Landriani, and within a short time other humanists like Guarino Veronese were making their own copies.

Cicero's *De oratore* is of course radically different from his youthful *De*

---

[8] An interesting survey of four Italian humanists concerned with the relation between eloquence and philosophy may be found in Jerrold Seigel, *Rhetoric and Philosophy in Renaissance Humanism: The Union of Eloquence and Wisdom, Petrarch to Valla* (Princeton, 1968). Also see Seigel, "The Teaching of Argyropulos and the Rhetoric of the First Humanists," in *Action and Conviction in Early Modern Europe: Essays in Memory of E. H. Harbison,* ed. Theodore K. Rabb and Jerrold Seigel (Princeton, 1969), pp. 237–60.

[9] Sabbadini, *Storia e Critica,* pp. 103 ff. For a description of surviving manuscripts, see *M. Tulli Ciceronis scripta quae manserunt omnia,* Fasc. 3: *De oratore,* ed. Kazimierz F. Kumaniecki (Leipzig, 1969), pp. v–xxiv; a summary of the Lodi discovery and its editorial aftermath is included on pp. viii–xiii.

*inventione*. The *De oratore* is in dialogue form, features many varying viewpoints on the subjects it treats, and is reflective rather than nakedly didactic like *De inventione*; beyond these differences in form, however, it is a humane, far-ranging discussion of civic duty, literature, the active life, human character, philosophy, and a number of other subjects which had been under discussion among fifteenth-century humanists. Cicero was already a revered figure, the *magister eloquentiae,* respected for his orations and letters as well as the rhetorical works attributed to him. A mutilated text of *De oratore* had been available to Petrarch and others in the preceding century, and the work itself was admired even in its faulty state. But the discovery of the complete text was a dazzling addition to the fame of the Master of Eloquence. Moreover, like Quintilian's *Institutio,* the *De oratore* opened the way for profound study of rhetoric and its relation to society.

Ultimately both books played a major role in the so-called "Renaissance" of Western Europe. Both have a part in the movement called "Ciceronianism."

The account of these developments lies outside the scope of this study. But what is significant is that within only five years, 1416 to 1421, Italian humanists located complete texts of two major classical rhetorical works whose application to contemporary life helped to institute major changes in Western society. Whether or not one believes fully in the concept of a European "Renaissance," it seems evident that there are major differences in attitude between, say, Guido Faba and Erasmus, or between Geoffrey of Vinsauf and Sir Philip Sydney, or between Robert of Basevorn and François Fenelon. These figures are separated not only by time but by approach. A full appreciation of their differences naturally demands careful study of a multitude of factors; unfortunately this particular study has not yet been carried out at the level of detail which the subject requires, so that we do not yet have the materials assembled which enable us to compare "medieval" and "postmedieval" approaches to the theory of communication.

Nevertheless it does seem clear that the rediscovery of Quintilian and of Cicero's *De oratore* forms part of something different from the medieval preceptive traditions. Of the two, Quintilian is by far the more important in that the *Institutio oratoria* helped reshape education as well as support literary studies, while stressing the moral aspect of civic activity. September, 1416, then, is a highly significant date in the history of rhetoric; insofar as any single point in time can be said to be a turning point, that date can be seen as the beginning of a new European outlook on rhetoric. It was of course only the harbinger of the new, not the end of the old. Dictaminal manuals continued to be written for another century; there was no major break in preaching theory until the seventeenth century, with François Fenelon. The medieval *ars metrica* was the first to be supplanted, though it had actually foundered in the fourteenth century and had had little popularity after its short-lived vogue in the thirteenth. In a sense none of the three major medieval rhetorical genres has ever completely disappeared, for letter-writing manuals still roll off our presses, thematic sermons are still divided and subdivided in our churches, and grammar textbooks still advise writers how to use certain of the ancient tropes and figures to "develop" their paragraphs.

It remains to be seen how "different" sixteenth-century rhetoric was from thirteenth-century rhetoric. One purpose of this study is to lay out some features of medieval theories of communication to facilitate the answering of just such questions as this.

But, above all, it must be remembered that medieval rhetoric—a thousand years of reflection on the process of human communication—is worth our serious study for its own sake. Every medieval writer was living in what was for him "modern times." Each treatise was written for a particular reason. It is easy to deride a dictaminal buffoon like Boncompagno, with his wild pretensions of outdoing Cicero, but all over Europe hundreds of earnest writers did their best to lay out their subject matter for the use of their fellow men. This vast human activity deserves our attention, both because it can reveal the spirit of a millenium of Western Europe and because these theorists may also be able to teach us in our own times something about the rhetorical process itself.

It would be presumptuous to attempt to summarize here the contents of the preceding chapters. Such a summary is needed, but much more study —especially of unpublished manuscripts—must come before we can safely pronounce a final judgment on these medieval rhetorical genres.

Two general observations can be made, however. The first is that medieval theorists did indeed make pragmatic adaptations of ancient materials to shape special genres for their own purposes. As we have seen, Rabanus Maurus was the first to enunciate the principle of pragmatic adaptation; then in turn came the *ars dictaminis,* the *ars praedicandi,* and the *ars metrica.* There seems to be a general pattern to the development of each genre, in six steps: identification of ultimate source (i.e., Cicero or Donatus), then initial adaptation without abandonment of the source, then establishment of a genre with only acknowledgment but little use of the source, then absolute departure from the source, then interbreeding among treatises in the same genre, followed finally by more repetition and decay. The *ars dictaminis* most fully displays these six steps, the *ars metrica* only the first four. There are of course geographical and conceptual variations within each genre, for instance, Orleanistic versus Lombardic in the *ars dictaminis,* or eight-mode versus multiple-mode amplification in the *ars praedicandi.* But the genres do cohere within themselves, retaining common purpose and outlook. Each is a whole rhetorical system.

A second and even more important observation is that despite the existence of four streams of medieval preceptive treatises—the classical Ciceronian and the three medieval genres—all the writers share one dominant concern for order. All the treatises are *preceptive,* designed to give specific advice (*praecepta*) to future writers and speakers. The medieval writers are thus clearly in the Greco-Roman preceptive tradition which begins with Aristotle's *Rhetoric* and continues through Cicero, Horace, Quintilian, Donatus, and Saint Augustine. Both grammatical and rhetorical influences play a part in these medieval developments, with dialectic in a minor role. Cicero is the specific source named most often (Aristotle's *Rhetoric* being virtually unknown), but the writers show little compunction about mixing grammatical and rhetorical materials to accomplish their ends. Underlying every medieval rhetorical treatise, whatever its genre, is the assumption that the communication process can be analyzed, its principles abstracted, and methods of procedure written down to be used by others. This is the essence of rhetoric. This commonality makes it possible for the modern observer to understand the basic agreement among the various genres despite the apparently bewildering array of writers, books, and subjects. The *dictator,* the grammar master, and the preaching theorist of the middle ages all would agree with the dictum of Cicero (*De oratore* III.v.23) that "Eloquence is one . . . regardless of the regions of discourse it is diverted into."

This may well be the most significant conclusion to be drawn from this entire study.

# Appendix
## Figures of Diction and of Thought from Rhetorica ad Herennium, Book IV

*(handwritten margin note: a distinction made here for 1st time; better discussed by Quintilian. Doesn't use "tropes" which Quintilian will.)*

### FIGURES OF DICTION

1. Epanaphora (*repetitio*) occurs when one and the same word forms *(handwritten: XXII. 19)* successive beginnings for phrases expressing like and different ideas. This figure has much charm and also impressiveness and vigor in a high degree; therefore it ought to be used for both embellishment and amplification. *(handwritten: To you... To you...   it was... it was.)*

2. Antistrophe (*conversio*) occurs when we repeat, not the first word in successive phrases, but the last. *(handwritten: after this dis appeared; ... that disappeared, rn)*

3. Interlacement (*complexio*) is the union of both figures, the combined use of Antistrophe and Epanaphora; we repeat both the first word and the last word in a series of phrases. *(handwritten: who are? the sour / who are ... the sour)*

4. Transplacement (*traductio*) makes it possible for the same word to be frequently reintroduced, not only without offense to good taste, but even so as to render the style more elegant. To this kind of figure also belongs that which occurs when the same word is used first in one function and then in another. *(handwritten: dear vs dear)*

5. Antithesis (*contentio*) occurs when the style is built on contraries. *(handwritten: XV)*

6. Apostrophe (*exclamatio*) is the figure which expresses grief or indignation by means of an address to some man or city or place or object.

SOURCE: This Appendix is comprised of definitions reprinted, by permission of the publisher and Loeb Classical Library, from pp. 275-405 of Cicero, *Ad C. Herennium Libri IV*, translated by Harry Caplan, Cambridge, Mass.: Harvard University Press, 1954. All rights reserved.

*(handwritten footnote: * 1-4 have repetition not dictated by verbal poverty, but from rep that is elegant to ear + hard to explain.)*

If we use Apostrophe in the proper place, sparingly, and when the importance of the subject seems to demand it, we shall instill in our listener as much indignation as we desire. (Caplan: Quintilian, 9.3.97, assigns *exclamatio* to figures of thought.) *unless simulated + artfully composed*

7. Interrogation (*interrogatio*) reinforces the argument that has just been delivered, after the case against the opponents has been summed up; but not all interrogation is impressive or elegant.

8. Reasoning by Question and Answer (*ratiocinatio*) occurs when we ask ourselves the reason for every statement we make, and seek the meaning of each successive affirmation. This figure is exceedingly well adapted to a conversational style, and both by its stylistic grace and the anticipation of the reasons, holds the hearer's attention. (Caplan: Quintilian, 9.3.98, assigns it to figures of thought.) This figure is to be distinguished from *ratiocinatio,* the type of Issue which employs Reasoning from Analogy.

9. A Maxim (*sententia*) is a saying drawn from life, which shows concisely either what happens or ought to happen in life. Maxims may be either Simple or Double, and be presented either with or without reasons. We should insert maxims only rarely, that we may be looked upon as pleading the case, not preaching morals. When so interspersed, they will add much distinction. Furthermore, the hearer, when he perceives that an indisputable principle drawn from practical life is being applied to a cause, he must give it his tacit approval. *Brevity has charm*

*xviii*

10. Reasoning by Contraries (*contrarium*) is the figure which, of two opposite statements, uses one so as neatly and directly to prove the other, as follows: "Now how should you expect one who has ever been hostile to his own interests to be friendly to another's?" (Caplan: Quintilian regards this as more a kind of argument than a figure of speech, and notes the similarity to Aristotle's *a fortiori* commonplace.) *Be brief + unbroken + carefully rounded off for sake of ear*

11. Colon or Clause (*membrum*) is the name given to a sentence member, brief and complete, which does not express the entire thought, but is in turn supplemented by another colon. (Caplan: The doctrine of Colon, Comma, Period is Peripatetic in origin; Quintilian excluded Comma and Colon from the list of figures.) *On the one hand you like H*

12. Comma or Phrase (*articulus*) occurs when single words are set apart by pauses in staccato speech. *By more vigor*

13. A Period (*continuatio*) is a close-packed and uninterrupted group of words embracing a complete thought. We shall best use it in three places: (1) Maxim, (2) Contrast, or (3) Conclusion.

14. Isocolon (*conpar*) is the figure comprised of cola which consist of a virtually equal number of syllables. (Caplan: Isocolon, Antithesis, and the next three figures—Homoeoptoton, Homoeoteleuton, and Paronomasia— are the so-called "Figures of Gorgias.")

15. Homoeoptoton (*similiter cadens*) occurs when in the same period two or more words appear in the same case, and with like terminations.

16. Homoeoteleuton (*similiter desinens*) occurs when the word endings are similar, although the words are indeclinable.

17. Paronomasia (*adnominatio*) is the figure in which, by means of a modification of sound, or change of letters, a close resemblance to a verb or noun is produced, so that similar words express dissimilar things. This is done in three ways:
    (1) through slight change or lengthening or transposition
        (a) by thinning or contracting the same letter
        (b) by the reverse
        (c) by lengthening the same letter
        (d) by shortening the same letter
        (e) by adding letters
        (f) by omitting letters
        (g) by transposing letters
        (h) by changing letters
    (2) through greater changes
    (3) through a change of case in one of the nouns
(Caplan: The author knows only four parts of speech, so that "noun" would include "adjective.")

These last three figures are to be used very sparingly when we speak in an actual cause, because their invention seems impossible without labor and pains.

18. Hypophora (*subiectio*) occurs when we inquire of our adversary or ask ourselves what the adversaries can say in their favor, or what can be said against us. (Caplan: Quintilian, 9.3.98, assigns this to figures of thought.)

*xxv*

19. Climax (*gradatio*) is the figure in which the speaker passes to the following word only after advancing by steps to the preceding one. (Caplan: This figure joins with Epanaphora, Antistrophe, Interlacement, and Transplacement or Antanaklasis (*traductio*) to form a complete theory of Repetition.)

20. Definition (*definitio*) in brief and clear-cut fashion grasps the characteristic qualities of a thing. (*N.B.: Definitio* is also the subtype of "Legal Issue," i.11.19 of the *Rhetorica ad Herennium*.)

*xxvi*

21. Transition (*transitio*) is the name given to the figure which briefly recalls what has been said, and likewise briefly sets forth what is to follow next. (Caplan: This figure combines the functions of *enumeratio* and *propositio* used by the author in the Division and Conclusion.)

22. Correction (*correctio*) retracts what has been said and replaces it with what seems more suitable. -- *but adds to grace by calling attn to phrase*

23. Paralipsis (*occultatio*) occurs when we say that we are passing by, or do not know, or refuse to say that which precisely now we are saying. (Caplan: Sometimes *praeteritio*. Quintilian, 9.3.98, puts this in figures of thought.)   *strike from record   -- suspicion created*

24. Disjunction (*disjunctum*) is used when each of two or more clauses ends with a special verb. (Caplan: Quintilian, 9.3.64, says that devices like this and the two following are so common that they cannot lay claim to that art which figures involve.)   *elegance*

25. Conjunction (*conjunctio*) occurs when both the previous and the succeeding phrases are held together by placing the verb between them.   *brevity*   *from single type*

26. Adjunction (*adiunctio*) occurs when the verb holding the sentence together is not placed in the middle, but at the beginning or end.

27. Reduplication (*conduplicatio*) is the repetition of one or more words for the purpose of Amplification in Appeal to Pity. The reiteration of the same word makes a deep impression upon the hearer.   *like multiple stabs*

28. Synonymy or Interpretation (*interpretatio*) is the figure which does not duplicate the same word by repeating it, but replaces the word that has been used by another with the same meaning. The hearer cannot but be impressed when the force of the first expression is renewed by the explanatory synonym. (Caplan: Quintilian, 9.3.98, denies that this is a figure.)

29. Reciprocal Change (*commutatio*) occurs when two discrepant thoughts are so expressed by transposition that the latter follows from the former although contradictory to it, as follows: "You must eat to live, not live to eat."

30. Surrender (*permissio*) is used when we indicate in speaking that we yield and submit the whole matter to another's will. It is especially useful for evoking pity.

31. Indecision (*dubitatio*) occurs when the speaker seems to ask which of two or more words he had better use. *ought to say*

32. Elimination (*expeditio*) occurs when we have enumerated the several ways by which something could have been brought about, and all are then discarded except the one on which we are insisting. (Caplan: Cicero, Quintilian, and Aristotle all regard this as a form of argument, not a figure. It is known in modern argumentation as the Method of Residues.) *support for conjectural argument*

33. Asyndeton (*dissolutum*) is a presentation in separate parts, conjunctions being suppressed. *animation + great force*                 *XXX*

34. Aposiopesis (*praecisio*) occurs when something is said and then the rest of what the speaker had begun to say is left unfinished. (Also: *interruptio.*) *No, I don't dare tell .. suspicion, unexpressed, is more telling than detailed explanation*

35. Conclusion (*conclusio*) deduces, by means of a brief argument, the necessary consequences of what has been said or done before. (Caplan: Quintilian, 9.3.98, denies that this is a figure.)

There remain also ten Figures of Diction, which I have intentionally not scattered at random, but have separated from those above, because they all belong to one class. They indeed all have this in common, that the language departs from the ordinary meaning of the words, and is, with a certain grace, applied in another sense.      *XXXI.42*

(Caplan: These ten figures of diction are *tropi*, a term which the author here does not employ. Quintilian, 8.6.1, defines a trope as "an artistic change of word or phrase from its proper signification to another." It is to be noted that tropes are not here separated from figures of diction.)

36. Onomatopoeia (*nominatio*) is a figure which suggests to us that we should ourselves designate with a suitable word, whether for the sake of imitation or for expressiveness, a thing which either lacks a name or has an inappropriate name. *hiss     hullabaloo*

37. Antonomasia or Pronominatio (*pronominatio*) designates by a kind of adventitious epithet a thing that cannot be called by its proper name.

38. Metonymy (*denominatio*) is a figure which draws from an object closely akin or associated an expression suggesting this object meant, but not called by its own name.

    (1) by substituting the name of the greater for that of the lesser
    (2) by substituting the name of the thing invented for the inventor
    (3) by substituting the instrument for the possessor
    (4) by substituting the cause for the effect
    (5) by substituting the effect for the cause
    (6) by substituting the container for the content
    (7) by substituting the content for the container

39. Periphrasis (*circumitio*) is a manner of speech used to express a simple idea by means of a circumlocution.

40. Hyperbaton (*transgressio*) upsets the word order by means of either
    (1) Anastrophe (*perversio*), or reversal of natural order, or
    (2) Transposition (*transiectio*) changes the word order to gain more favorable rhythm.

41. Hyperbole (*superlatio*) is a manner of speech exaggerating the truth, whether for the sake of magnifying or minifying something. This is used either independently or by comparison.

42. Synecdoche (*intellectio*) occurs when the whole is known from a small part or a part from the whole.
    (1) The whole may be understood from the part, or part from the whole.
    (2) Singular may be understood from plural, and plural from singular.

43. Catechresis (*abusio*) is the inexact use of a like and kindred word in place of a more precise and proper one.

44. Metaphor (*translatio*) occurs when a word applying to one thing is transferred to another, because the similarity seems to justify this transference. It is used
    (1) for vividness
    (2) for brevity —

(3) to avoid obscenity *— euphanism (marrage for sex)*
(4) for magnifying *— glut cruety*
(5) for minifying *—*
(6) for embellishing

45. Allegory (*permutatio*) is a manner of speech denoting one thing by the letter of the words, but another by their meaning. It assumes three aspects:

(1) Comparison, when a number of metaphors originating in a similarity in the mode of expression are set together.

(2) Argument, when a similitude is drawn from a person or place or object in order to magnify or minify.

(3) Contrast, when one mockingly calls a thing that which is its contrary.

## FIGURES OF THOUGHT

1. Distribution (*distributio*) occurs when certain specified roles are assigned among a number of things or persons.

2. Frankness of Speech (*licentia*) occurs when, talking before those to whom we owe reverence or fear, we yet exercise our right to speak out, because we seem justified in reprehending them, or persons dear to them, for some fault. (Caplan: Quintilian, 9.2.27, denies that this is a figure.)

3. Understatement (*diminutio*) occurs when we say that by nature, fortune, or diligence, we or our clients possess some exceptional advantage, and in order to avoid the impression of arrogant display, we moderate or soften the statement of it.

4. Vivid Description (*descriptio*) is the name for the figure which contains a clear, lucid, and impressive exposition of the consequences of an act.

5. Division (*divisio*) separates the alternatives of a question and resolves each by means of a reason subjoined. There is this difference between the present kind of Division and that other which forms the third part of a discourse (in Book One): the former division operates through the Enumeration or Exposition of the topics to be discussed throughout the whole discourse, whereas here the division at once unfolds itself, and by briefly adding the reasons for the two or more parts, embellishes the style.

6. Accumulation (*frequentatio*) occurs when the points scattered throughout the whole cause are collected in one place so as to make the speech more impressive or sharp or accusatory.

7. Refining (*expolitio*) consists in dwelling on the same topic and yet seeming to say something ever new. It is accomplished in two ways:
  (1) by repeating the same idea
      (a) in equivalent words
      (b) in different styles of delivery as we change words
      (c) by the treatment
          (i) in dialogue form
          (ii) in arousal form
  (2) by descanting upon the theme
      (a) by simple pronouncement
      (b) by reason
      (c) by a second expression in new form
      (d) by comparison
      (e) by contrary
      (f) by example
      (g) by conclusion

8. Dwelling on the Point (*commoratio*) occurs when one remains rather long upon, and often returns to, the strongest topic on which the whole cause rests. There is no appropriate example of this figure, because this topic is not isolated from the whole cause like some limb, but like blood is spread through the whole body of discourse.

9. Antithesis (*contentio*) occurs when contraries meet. The Antithesis which is a Figure of Diction presents a rapid opposition of words, while in the Figure of Thought the opposing thoughts will meet in a comparison.

10. Comparison (*similitudo*) is a manner of speech that carries over an element of likeness from one thing to a different thing. It has four forms of presentation, each of which has a separate aim:
  (1) Contrast, whose purpose is embellishment
  (2) Negation, whose purpose is proof
  (3) Abridgment, whose purpose is clarity
  (4) Detailed Parallel, whose purpose is vividness

11. Exemplification (*exemplum*) is the citing of something done or said in the past, along with the definite naming of the doer or author. (Caplan: Examples are drawn from history.)

12. Simile (*imago*) is the comparison of one figure (*forma*) with another, implying a certain resemblance between them. It is used for either praise or censure.

13. Portrayal (*effictio*) consists in representing and depicting in words clearly enough for recognition the bodily form of some person.

14. Character Delineation (*notatio*) consists in describing a person's character by the definite signs which, like distinctive marks, are attributes of that character. (Caplan: Quintilian, 9.3.99, excludes this from the figures.) [Following this brief definition, the author supplies the longest single example of the book, portraying the character of a bragging beggar, iv.50.63–64.]

15. Dialogue (*sermocinatio*) consists in assigning to some person language which as set forth conforms with his character. (Caplan: Quintilian, 9.2.29, joins this figure and Personification as one.)

16. Personification (*conformatio*) consists in representing an absent person as present, or in making a mute thing or one lacking form articulate, and attributing to it a definite form and a language or a certain behavior appropriate to its character. (Caplan: This figure sometimes became a *progymnasma,* or composition exercise.)

17. Emphasis (*significatio*) is the figure which leaves more to be suspected than has actually been asserted. It is produced through:
   (1) Hyperbole
   (2) Ambiguity
   (3) Logical Consequence
   (4) Aposiopesis
   (5) Analogy

18. Conciseness (*brevitas*) is the expressing of an idea by the very minimum of essential words. (Caplan: Quintilian does not admit it as a figure, 9.3.99, but does treat it as a form of Asyndeton in 9.3.50.)

19. Ocular Demonstration (*demonstratio*) occurs when an event is so described in words that the business seems to be enacted and the subject to pass vividly before our eyes.

If you exercise yourself in these figures, Herennius, your speaking will possess impressiveness, distinction, and charm. As a result you will speak like a true orator, and the product of your invention will not be bare and inelegant, nor will it be expressed in commonplace language.

Remember always that you must combine both study and exercise to master the art.

If we follow these principles above, our Invention will be keen and prompt, our Arrangement clear and orderly, our Delivery impressive and graceful, our Memory sure and lasting, our Style brilliant and charming. In the art of rhetoric, then, there is no more.

# Index

This Index lists all proper names of ancient and medieval authors cited in the preceding pages, together with titles of works cited. It includes a number of key technical terms, but does not index all references to individual tropes and figures; the Appendix (pp. 365–374) provides the standard definitions of 64 figures as found in the Pseudo-Ciceronian *Rhetorica ad Herennium*. The Index does not include modern authors or secondary sources. Latin technical terms (e.g. *dictator*) are not capitalized; Latin titles of individual works, however, have the first word capitalized. Page references for individual works are listed only under the entry for the author (where known), with a separate cross-referencing entry for the title itself; for anonymous works, however, the page reference is listed under the entry for the title of the work.